# Bonjour!

TEACHER'S EDITION

## FRENCH FOR MASTERY

Jean-Paul Valette
Rebecca M. Valette

Illustrations by Mel Dietmeier

D.C. HEATH AND COMPANY
Lexington, Massachusetts / Toronto, Ontario

# The Teacher's Edition

The Teacher's Edition for BONJOUR! is an enlarged version of the Student Text. At the front of the book is a teacher's manual, which consists of four parts: a description of the characteristics and organization of the BONJOUR! program; suggestions about how to use the various components of the program; hints on how to supplement the basic materials; and a Reference Guide containing useful classroom expressions and a detailed listing of the contents of the program.

In the textbook itself, an overprint of small, blue type provides teachers with several kinds of information:

- Unit summaries of the main grammatical, vocabulary, and cultural objectives
- Supplementary questions on the *Presentation texts*
- Supplementary grammatical information
- Supplementary cultural information
- Supplementary vocabulary
- Suggestions for expanding and modifying exercises
- Suggested realia to enliven the presentation of culture
- Suggested optional activities
- Responses to all *Observations* questions
- Material designated as optional
- Correlation of the text to the components

**Notes:**

1. It is important to emphasize that the term "optional" does not mean that the material should be left out. It simply designates material that can be adapted or omitted according to the specific objectives of the class, and/or that can be considered supplementary for better students or for students with a particular interest in the topic.
2. The key **Str. A, B, C,** or **D** is used to cross-reference the *Observations* to the *Structure* section(s) to which they correspond.
3. The key to the overprint symbols and codes is found on page T54.
4. References in the overprint to the Unités or to specific pages in the Unités may be either to BONJOUR! (pp. 1–219) or to EN AVANT! (pp. 180–398).

---

International Standard Book Number: 0-669-11978-4

1 2 3 4 5 6 7 8 9 0

# Contents

# Part One
## Description of BONJOUR!

## 1. General Characteristics of the Program

BONJOUR! / EN AVANT! is a two-volume edition of FRENCH FOR MASTERY, *Salut, les amis!* The text for BONJOUR! consists of *Prélude* and Units 1–4 of *Salut, les amis!* The text for EN AVANT! consists of a new opening unit (*Interlude*) that systematically reviews the material presented in BONJOUR!, Unit 4 from BONJOUR!, and Units 5–8 of *Salut, les amis!* This division of *Salut, les amis!* allows for greater flexibility when using the program at the middle school or junior high school level or with slower learners.

The BONJOUR! program comprises four components: the Student Text, the Teacher's Edition, the Workbook, and the Cassette Program (including the Tapescript). The last two components are optional. The Activity Masters, the Testing Program, the Overhead Transparencies, and the Teacher's Resource Binder of *Salut, les amis!* as well as FRENCH FOR MASTERY *SOFTWARE* are also adaptable for use with this program.

### 1.1 Objectives and Philosophy

The basic objectives of BONJOUR! are:

• to help each student attain proficiency in the four skills of listening, speaking, reading, and writing within a minimum period of time and in a way that makes language-learning seem effortless; and

• to present the language within the context of the contemporary French-speaking world and its culture.

In pursuing this goal, the authors have adopted a pragmatic approach and purposely have avoided relying on any one linguistic theory of language-learning. Their guiding principle has been that the material in itself should elicit a high level of student participation in the learning process. To this end, they have evaluated a variety of pedagogical techniques and have selected those that have produced the best results inside and outside the classroom situation. This interweaving and integration of techniques is at the heart of BONJOUR! Teachers can adapt the program to their own teaching styles and to the needs of their own students.

### 1.2 Key Features

**1.2.1 Broad cultural focus.** In BONJOUR!, the cultural material is integrated into the learning process so that students attain an awareness of French culture as they read, study structures, and do the activities. In addition, there are segments of the program designed specifically to emphasize French culture:

- the *Note culturelle* of each lesson
- the two, full-color, illustrated sections in the text entitled *Section Magazine*
- the *Récréation culturelle* sections of the Workbook
- the photographs and realia presented throughout the text

From the beginning of the program, the students are exposed to the geographic, ethnic, and cultural variety of the French-speaking world, from Louisiana to the Ivory Coast, from Tahiti to Tunisia. For many students, this awareness will open a new dimension in their studies and stimulate their interest in learning French.

**1.2.2 Accent on youth.** An effective way of involving students in the learning of a foreign language is to make communication in the new language relevant to their own lives and subculture. The majority of the activities in this program have youth-related themes: hobbies, travel, schoolwork, dating, choice of career, relationships with parents, and attitudes toward love, friendship, money, success, and failure.

**1.2.3 Adaptability of the program.** BONJOUR! can be used in a variety of teaching situations:

- large or small classes
- slow or fast tracks
- audio-lingual or more traditional
  classes

The program is also adaptable to small-group teaching and lends itself to individualized and self-paced instruction. Part Two of this manual will suggest the various approaches available to the teacher in the presentation of the material.

**1.2.4 Several approaches to grammar.** Because there is no one way of teaching a foreign language, BONJOUR! incorporates several classroom-proven approaches to the presentation of French structures:

- *Guided discovery approach.* The new structures in each lesson are presented in key sentences in the *Presentation text* that begins each lesson. The *Conversation/ Observations* section that follows presents a limited number of short questions that pertain to the new structures. The questions are phrased in such a way that the students formulate their own generalizations about the new material.
- *Descriptive approach.* In the *Structure* sections the new material is explained in English and, where appropriate, presented graphically with examples and related exercises. These sections also serve as a grammar reference manual.
- *Modified contrastive approach.* When appropriate, new structures are compared and contrasted with previously learned French structures or with English equivalents. Areas of potential interference between French and English are mentioned explicitly: see, for example, Unit 3, Lesson 3, where in discussing the formation of the possessive, the difference in word order in French and in English is shown.
- *Analytic-synthetic approach.* More complex points of grammar are introduced across two or more lessons in minimal learning steps. Finally the entire pattern is summarized.

**1.2.5 Variety in the learning material.** Variety in presentation as well as in the content of the material is an essential element in fostering and maintaining student interest. Throughout BONJOUR! this feature has been given particular attention. For instance, instead of relying exclusively on dialogs, the lessons are also built around narratives, questionnaires, a datebook, or a scene from a play. Similarly, the exercises encompass a wide variety of formats, such as role-playing activities, *Questions personnelles,* open-ended sentences requiring a personal completion, and *Un jeu,* in which students match words to create sentences.

**1.2.6 Focus on communication.** To elicit the students' active participation in the learning process, all exercises of BONJOUR!, including those of the Cassette Program and the Workbook, are set in situational contexts. The situations may be practical, such as planning a trip or purchasing items in a store. Sometimes the situations are imaginative; the students may be asked to play the role of a reporter or an exchange student. The purpose of these contextual exercises is to induce the students to use French in communication and self-expression rather than as a rote response to artificial drill stimuli.

**1.2.7 Flexibility and efficiency in developing language skills.** The language is presented and practiced through all four language skills. However, because of the variety of teaching materials included in BONJOUR!, the teacher may wish to focus on only one or two skills. For instance, if speaking is to be highlighted, the teacher can stress the communication activities of the program: *Questions personnelles,* role-playing activities, the *Conversation* activity following each *Presentation,* and the oral *Entre nous* sections of the Student Text as well as the *Speaking* and *Conversation* activities of the Cassette Program. The teacher could also use the *Récréation culturelle* sections in the Workbook to promote conversation.

Each skill is developed in its several aspects. For instance, for reading, many types of materials are presented: *Presentation texts, Entre nous* segments, and *Sections Magazines.* A similar scope of development characterizes the listening activities of the Cassette Program, which involve active listening to recorded material from the Student Text, selective listening for grammatical signals such as verb tenses, gender, or number, and general listening comprehension of unfamiliar passages.

**1.2.8 Logical organization.** The learning pace is carefully programmed through a concise, measured grammatical progression. The presentation of the simpler and more frequently used structures precedes that of the more complex and less common ones. Each lesson in BONJOUR! concentrates on two to four aspects of grammar, and the amount of new vocabulary is carefully controlled. The introductory *Presentation text* of the lesson incorporates the new material into the context of previously mastered patterns and structures. Any unknown words are glossed in the margin or presented in the vocabulary section immediately following the *Presentation text.*

**1.2.9 Systematic reentry of grammar and vocabulary.** All vocabulary introduced in the *Vocabulaire pratique,* in the *Vocabulaire spécialisé,* and in the *Expressions pour la conversation* is active, as are all the *Structures;* that is, the students should have control of this vocabulary in communicative situations. Lists of these words and expressions by unit appear in the Activity Masters. Passive vocabulary, for recognition only, is glossed when it appears and is also included in the French-English end vocabulary.

As the program progresses, the structures and vocabulary items are reentered in the exercises and reading materials. Suggestions for reviewing the structures and vocabulary are made in the overprint if the mastery of these elements is a requisite for learning the new material of the lesson.

All basic aspects of grammar and active vocabulary are incorporated in the *Tests de contrôle* that are found at the end of the Workbook. The teacher may use these tests informally for review if desired.

EN AVANT! opens with a systematic review, in new contexts, of all the important material presented in BONJOUR! For additional flexibility, Unit 4 of BONJOUR! is repeated in EN AVANT! Because of this articulation between the two books, second-year students who have not completed BONJOUR! or who have used materials other than FRENCH FOR MASTERY can confidently begin the school year with EN AVANT!

**1.2.10 Emphasis on French.** BONJOUR! has been written in such a way that French may be used almost exclusively. The *Prélude* section provides basic vocabulary and structure in context so that students can use French from the very first day. French names (pp. iv–v) and classroom expressions (see Part Four of this Teacher's Edition or the Activity Masters) should be introduced at the beginning of the course.

**1.2.11 Naturalness of the language.** Language presented to beginning students must be simple, yet it must also be natural and idiomatic. The apparent conflict between simplicity and authenticity is resolved in BONJOUR! by the addition of *Expressions pour la conversation* in the *Entre nous* sections that end each lesson. In these sections, the students learn authentic, common expressions through dialog practice. Expressions introduced in this way (e.g., **Eh bien!, Zut alors!, Tiens!, Dis donc!**) are then reentered in the *Presentation texts* of subsequent lessons.

## 2. Organization of BONJOUR!

The following pages describe the BONJOUR! program; the EN AVANT! program has a similar organization with some slight modifications, as indicated in the Teacher's Edition of that text. Included here as well is a description of the Activity Masters, the Testing Program, the Overhead Transparencies, and the Teacher's Resource Binder of FRENCH FOR MASTERY, *Salut, les amis!*, and of FRENCH FOR MASTERY SOFTWARE. Although these components were designed originally to supplement *Salut, les amis!*, they can be used successfully with BONJOUR! and EN AVANT! *Prélude* and Units 1–4 of the components correspond to the material in BONJOUR! Units 4–8 of the components correspond to the material in EN AVANT!

## 2.1 The Student Text

The Student Text contains a preliminary unit (*Prélude*), four basic units, and two illustrated cultural sections (*Section Magazine*). The book concludes with appendices, a complete French-English Vocabulary, and an active English-French Vocabulary.

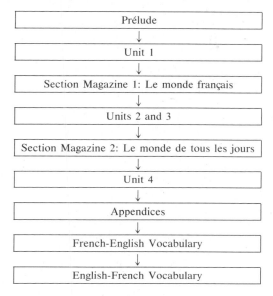

### 2.1.1 Organization of a unit.
Each unit is built around a particular theme (such as hobbies, other leisure-time activities, shopping, and friendships) and has a main grammatical focus (such as object pronouns or adjectives). The unit is divided into five basic lessons that present the new structures and vocabulary of the unit.

### 2.1.2 Organization of a basic lesson.
Each basic lesson consists of three parts: the presentation material, the instruction material, and the recombination material. The diagram shows the construction of a typical lesson.

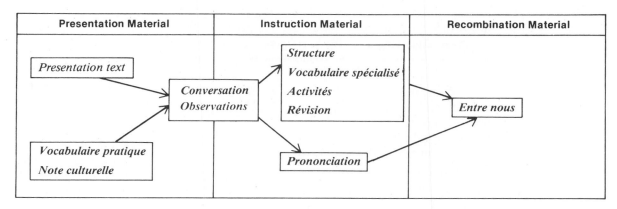

- *The Presentation Material.* The function of the *Presentation text* is to introduce, in context, samples of the basic structures and vocabulary taught in the lesson. The context may assume a variety of formats:

  — A dialog (**Le vélomoteur de Sylvie** – Lesson 2.2)

  — A conversation with the reader or a playlet (**En vacances** – Lesson 1.5)

  — A narrative (**Marie-Noëlle** – Lesson 3.2)

  — A series of humorous cartoons (**Vive les grandes vacances!** – Lesson 3.4)

The *Presentation text* is built on previous learned material plus the new structures and vocabulary of the lesson. Words that the students do not know are glossed or appear in the *Vocabulaire pratique/spécialisé* that immediately follows the *Presentation.*

The *Note culturelle* is a short reading passage about an aspect of French culture. It is derived from a reference in the *Presentation text.* For example, in Lesson 4.2, after a dialog with two girls looking at clothes, the *Note culturelle* describes French fashion and how teenagers dress.

The *Conversation/Observations* section links the *Presentation text* and the instruction material. Through the carefully sequenced *Observations* questions, the students are able to generalize about the new grammatical material of the lesson.

- *The Instruction Material.* In the **Structure** section, new grammar is explained in a simple, clear, and schematic manner. Immediately after the grammar explanations, the rules are applied in situational exercises.

The exercises assume a variety of formats:

  — Situational activities, which require transformation skills

  — *Questions personnelles,* which are yes/no and open-ended questions about the student's life. These incorporate the new grammatical structures of the lesson while reviewing previously learned structures.

  — Open-ended sentences, which students complete with personal information

  — Given situations from which students draw conclusions

  — *Un jeu,* a recombination drill game in which the students are asked to derive as many logical sentences as they can from a given set of elements containing the new grammatical structures

All of these activities can be done either orally or in writing. Activities particularly suited to writing are indicated in the overprint throughout.

The vocabulary items in the *Vocabulaire spécialisé* are grouped thematically (sports, family, clothing) for ease in assimilation. Where feasible, the items are presented in a pictorial or sentence context.

The *Prononciation* sections, which are recorded in the Cassette Program, introduce new sounds, intonation patterns, and spelling. As the course progresses, specific elements are reentered for practice or further explanation. For easy reference and to prepare students to use French-language dictionaries, the sounds are transcribed in the International Phonetic Alphabet.

- *The Recombination Material.* The *Entre nous* sections reinforce the new material of the lesson.

These sections contain *Mini-dialogues* and *L'art du dialogue* that help the students to further develop conversation skills through dramatization and directed dialog.

Each *Entre nous* section contains a subsection, *Expressions pour la conversation,* that provides the students with conversational fillers useful in developing natural communication skills.

**2.1.3 *Section Magazine.*** Two separate, full-color sections in the text, the *Sections Magazines* focus on the contemporary French-speaking world and specifically include material on young people and their interests. The students assimilate culture through exposure to illustrations, photographs, and varied readings in an exciting magazine format.

| CONTENTS | |
| --- | --- |
| *Section Magazine 1* | **Le monde français** |
| *Section Magazine 2* | **Le monde de tous les jours** |

Since the *Sections Magazines* are entirely in French, they serve as an aid in developing reading skills. The various illustrations, photographs, and realia also provide points of departure for conversation. The cultural projects at the end of each *Section Magazine* suggest further areas of study. In addition, the Activity Masters contain Reading Activities based on the *Section Magazine* material.

**2.1.4 End matter.** The end matter contains the following elements:

- Appendices
    - Appendix 1 — Sound-Spelling Correspondences
    - Appendix 2 — Numbers
    - Appendix 3 — Verbs
- French-English Vocabulary

This vocabulary lists all words in the text, except obvious passive cognates. Each word and expression considered "active" is followed by a reference number that provides the unit and lesson number where the word or expression first appeared actively in the text.

- English-French Vocabulary

This vocabulary lists only the active words and expressions: those from the *Vocabulaire pratique, Vocabulaire spécialisé, Expressions pour la conversation,* and *Structure* sections. Each entry in this vocabulary has a unit and lesson number referring the reader to the first active usage in the text.

## 2.2 The Workbook

The Workbook, adapted from the Workbook of FRENCH FOR MASTERY, *Salut, les amis!,* supplements the Student Text. In addition to providing written exercises to accompany the basic instructional material of the Student Text, each unit of the Workbook contains an illustrated cultural section entitled *Récréation culturelle* and a games section entitled *Le coin des jeux.* (The games section is reprinted from the FRENCH FOR MASTERY, *Salut, les amis!* Activity Masters.) The **Tests de côntrole** are also included in the Workbook.

**2.2.1 Written exercises.** For each basic lesson of the Student Text, the Workbook contains two to four pages of written exercises in situational contexts. Each lesson begins on a right-hand page so that students can tear out specific pages to hand in if the teacher so requests.

To avoid monotony and to stimulate the students' interest, all basic exercises are set in situational or game contexts. Most exercises require thoughtful rather than mechanical answers. Where appropriate, the activities are based on visual cues.

The answer key at the back of the Workbook enables students to correct their own work. The teacher may prefer to remove the key and provide the answers to the appropriate exercises only after students have completed them.

**2.2.2 *Récréation culturelle.*** Each Workbook unit includes a section called **Récréation culturelle.** This section contains realia with related activities. The realia reinforce the cultural themes developed in the unit.

**2.2.3 *Tests de contrôle. Tests de contrôle*** are included in the Workbook. These tests consist of a series of situational review exercises. The students take these tests on their own and check their responses against the answer key at the back of the Workbook. The answer key contains an *Interpretation* section to help students evaluate their results and to refer them back to sections of the unit for further study if they get a prescribed number of wrong answers on any given point of structure. The **Tests de contrôle** sections were intentionally designed to be relatively simple in order to give students a feeling of achievement. These sections prepare them for the corresponding *Unit Tests* in the Testing Program.

### 2.3 The Cassette Program

**2.3.1 General description.** The Cassette Program is designed to supplement the Student Text, providing additional practice in the development of audio-lingual skills. The Cassette Program for each lesson runs approximately 25 minutes. All the activities in the Cassette Program, together with the correct oral and written responses, are printed in the Tapescript, a separate booklet included with each set of cassettes.

**2.3.2 Types of Tape activities.** The tape for each lesson contains a variety of activities. These are introduced in English so that all students may work independently with the Cassette Program. The activities include the following categories:

• *Listening.* The students listen to an unpaused, dramatized reading of the *Presentation text.*

• *Listening and Repeating.* (1) The speaker models words and sentences from the **Prononciation** sections of the Student Text. The students repeat these in the pauses provided. (2) The speaker models words from selected vocabulary, verb, and grammar charts of the Student Text. When the chart contains both words and sentences in which the words are used, the students repeat the words and listen to the sentences.

- *Listening for Signals.* The students hear a series of sentences and are asked to discriminate among sounds that signal grammatical information, such as singular or plural, masculine or feminine. Students mark their responses on the grids provided in the Activity Masters. When needed, or when a new activity format occurs, models are supplied. At the end the speaker gives the correct answers.

- *Listening Comprehension with Visual Cues.* The students see illustrations and hear several statements pertaining to them. They may be asked to match the statements with the illustrations, to indicate whether the statements are true based on the information in the visual, or to complete the illustrations based on the clues given in the sentences. For example, the students see detailed portraits, hear a corresponding number of descriptions, and decide which descriptions go with which persons. The students also indicate whether they understand specific words or expressions heard on the tape. This type of exercise is used chiefly to practice numbers and other specialized vocabulary.

- *Speaking.* (1) Directed activities: The students participate in situation drills similar, but not identical, to the activities in the Student Text. These provide variety in oral practice while helping to develop listening comprehension skills. In these activities each cue is followed by a pause for the student response. Then the speaker on the tape gives a confirmation of the appropriate response. (2) Open-ended activities: The speaker asks the students personal questions that incorporate the structures and vocabulary introduced in the lesson. Because the students give original answers, no corrective response is given on the tape.

- *Dictation.* The students listen to short sentences and write down what they hear. Write-on lines are provided in the Activity Masters.

- *French Songs.* Each unit features a traditional French song, a portion of which is heard at the beginning and end of each lesson and at intervals throughout. At the end of the unit, the entire song is sung in French. The music and lyrics for student participation are included in the Activity Masters.

## 2.4 The Activity Masters for FRENCH FOR MASTERY, *Salut, les amis!*

The Activity Masters are a set of duplicating masters that include the following teaching aids:

- Cassette Program Material
  - Tape Activity Sheets containing the answer grids and visual cues for the *Listening for Signals* and *Listening Comprehension* activities; write-on lines for the *Dictation* activities; the music and lyrics of the unit songs

- Non-Cassette Program Material
  - Games for enjoyment and a change of pace (reprinted from the Workbook)
  - Reading Activities to accompany the *Sections Magazines*
  - Active Vocabulary Sheets by unit for reference and review
  - Useful Expressions (reprinted from the Teacher's Edition)

The Activity Masters are also available as copymasters in the Teacher's Resource Binder for FRENCH FOR MASTERY, *Salut, les amis!*

## 2.5 The Testing Program for FRENCH FOR MASTERY, *Salut, les amis!*

The Testing Program offers three types of testing materials: *Lesson Quizzes, Unit Tests,* and *Achievement Tests.* The tests are printed on duplicating masters and the listening portions are recorded on cassettes. The tests are also available as copymasters in the Teacher's Resource Binder for FRENCH FOR MASTERY, *Salut, les amis!* The Answer Key to the Testing Program is found in the accompanying Test Guide.

**2.5.1 Lesson Quizzes.** The *Lesson Quiz,* designed to be administered in about 20 minutes, permits a quick and frequent evaluation of the students' mastery of the structures and vocabulary of a lesson. The test items are based on tape, visual, or printed-word cues, to allow for all possible learning styles. A Student Progress Chart (on a duplicating master) allows the teacher to keep track of each student's progress.

**2.5.2 Unit Tests.** The *Unit Test,* designed to be administered in about 45 minutes, focuses on the content of the unit and also evaluates communication skills. The test items, more varied than in the *Lesson Quizzes,* emphasize the elements of language.

**2.5.3 Achievement Tests.** The Testing Program provides two *Achievement Tests* (to follow Unit 4 of BONJOUR! or EN AVANT! and Unit 8 of EN AVANT!), each designed to be administered over two 45-minute class periods. Broader in scope than the *Unit Tests,* the *Achievement Tests* go beyond the elements of language and focus on the listening, reading, and writing skills.

## 2.6 The Overhead Transparencies for FRENCH FOR MASTERY, *Salut, les amis!*

The BONJOUR! / EN AVANT! program includes a boxed set of 39 Overhead Transparencies. Each transparency comes with a master for making additional one-color transparencies. In this way, each teacher can have a set.

The transparencies correspond to specific vocabulary or visual items in the Student Text and are keyed to it with identifying titles and page numbers. (The page numbers for BONJOUR! / EN AVANT! are the same as for *Salut, les amis!*

The Overhead Transparencies have been designed to teach and reinforce vocabulary; to practice essential verb forms; to introduce the students to the geography of the French-speaking world; to serve as a basis for oral compositions; and to help the teacher avoid the use of English in the classroom.

## 2.7 The Teacher's Resource Binder for FRENCH FOR MASTERY, *Salut, les amis!*

The Teacher's Resource Binder is a 3-ring binder of teaching aids. Included is the complete Testing Program as copymasters, the Test Guide, the Tapescript, and the Activity Masters as copymasters. A chart correlating these components to the lessons is printed on each of the unit dividers. Also included is a section on teaching strategies.

## 2.8 FRENCH FOR MASTERY *SOFTWARE*

FRENCH FOR MASTERY *SOFTWARE* is a computer program that provides varied and extensive practice using the vocabulary of *Salut, les amis*! The program, on three double-sided disks, is self-contained and easy to use, allowing students to improve their vocabulary control without teacher supervision. The manual that accompanies the program gives suggestions for individual and group use, as well as ideas for integrating the software into the language program.

# Part Two
## Using BONJOUR!

## 3. Suggested Techniques

A basic characteristic of the BONJOUR! program is its flexibility. The classroom teacher can easily adapt the textbook and its related components to the needs and learning styles of the students. Each unit of BONJOUR! contains more activities than can be completed by the average class. The teacher should therefore select those that are most appropriate for specific classes and specific individuals. The purpose of this section is to help the teacher make these choices by showing how each of the components may be used. The suggestions are not exhaustive, but they form a base upon which the teacher may wish to build.

### 3.1 Using French in the Classroom

With the communicative tools and approach provided in BONJOUR!, students can use French in classroom interaction from the very beginning.

• The *Prélude,* the first six lessons of the text, provides basic French vocabulary that students are anxious to learn and that they need for basic communication: names, greetings, numbers, and information on telling time, giving the date, and talking about the weather.

• The teacher can copy the Classroom Expressions, found in this manual, and distribute the list to the class for communicating everyday classroom needs. This list is also in the Activity Masters, and teachers who have this component may run it off for easy distribution.

• The interrogative forms for yes/no questions and information questions are presented in Unit 1.

### 3.2 The First Day of Class

The goal of the first day of class should be to stimulate interest in French language and culture as well as to show that learning French is a profitable and not overwhelming task. The following suggestions can be used in whole or in part to plan the first day's lesson.

• Show the breadth and diversity of the French-speaking world. The map on pp. vi–vii is a good starting point.

• Explain that France played a role in the development of our country. (Check encyclopedias and American history textbooks for information about French people who influenced American history.)

- Explain that close to our country and even *within* our country there are large concentrations of French-speaking people—the province of Quebec in Canada, parts of Louisiana, and the northern New England states. (See *Note culturelle* on p. 43.)
- Show French influence in the names of American cities. (See *Section Magazine 1* p. 84.)
- Show the linguistic relationship between French and English. (*Section Magazine 1* pp. 80–89 includes a large number of French/English cognates.) Students will feel that they already know some French.
- Explain that knowing French can be an asset when looking for a job. (See *Section Magazine 1* pp. 86–87.)

## 3.3 Suggestions for Teaching the Basic Lessons

**3.3.1 Using the Presentation text.** The *Presentation* is not intended for memorization, but rather for initial exposure to the basic structures of the lesson and as a point of departure for other activities. This material is available as an unpaused, dramatized recording in the Cassette Program. The *Presentation text* can be used in the following ways:

- The students listen to an unpaused version either on the tape provided in the Cassette Program or as read by the teacher.

  — *With books open following the text.* In this way students see if they can understand the spoken word well enough to follow it in their texts. Students also hear the correct pronunciation as they are seeing the words.

  — *With the books closed before having seen the text.* The teacher could pause or stop the tape at various intervals to ask questions. For a shorter presentation, the teacher could wait until the students have heard the entire text before stopping the tape or the reading.

- The teacher presents the *Vocabulaire pratique* or corresponding *Vocabulaire spécialisé* before the students hear the *Presentation* so that they will know the new vocabulary. Or, with faster groups, the teacher asks if the students can guess the new words from their contexts.

- The students perform various activities based on the *Presentation texts.*

  — The students act out conversational *Presentation texts* by taking various parts.

  — The students dramatize the text as the tape is being played.

  — The students guess from illustrations what is going to happen and explain it in French as well as they can. They then listen to the tape and see what actually happens.

  — The students use the illustrations to make up different stories.

  — The students bring in visuals—posters, maps, original drawings—explain them and how they are related to the *Presentation,* and hang them on the bulletin board.

  — Students prepare their own skits based on the situations of the *Presentations.*

— At the end of the lesson, the students reread, summarize, or enact the *Presentation* so that they can see how much they have learned.

**3.3.2 Using the *Note culturelle*.** The purpose of the *Note culturelle* is twofold: to awaken students to the culture of the French-speaking world, and to stimulate and reinforce the students' reading comprehension.

• If the cultural note relates to a topic that the teacher wishes to emphasize, the students may listen to the recording, learn the new vocabulary, read the note aloud, and summarize the information in French. A study of France would not be complete, for example, without a discussion of French cuisine. The cultural note of Unit 4, Lesson 4 provides a point of departure for such a discussion.

• The teacher and students could bring in photos or other materials relating to the topic of the cultural note. For example, the teacher might want to make a bulletin board display of young French people and their pastimes. The *Note culturelle* on **La Maison des Jeunes** in Unit 2, Lesson 5, would be a natural tie-in to such a display.

• Other notes may be used primarily for reading practice, for listening comprehension, or assigned as homework.

• When assigned as homework, the teacher may also ask the students to prepare true/false items or comprehension quizzes for other members of the class.

**3.3.3 Using the *Conversation*/*Observations*.** The questions of the *Conversation* allow the students to use some of the new structures of the lesson: they also serve as a springboard to the *Observations* segment, which in turn leads to the *Structure* sections.

In going over the *Observations* sections with the students, the teacher may ask them to open their textbooks to the appropriate page. In many lessons it is also possible, and sometimes preferable, to show the *Conversation* sentences on the chalkboard, on a chart, or on an overhead transparency. In this way, the teacher can more readily point to specific features of the sentences, drawing the students' attention to those points under discussion. If the sentences are reproduced on larger visuals, color of boxing may replace the boldface used in the text.

**3.3.4 Teaching structure.** In the *Structure* sections, each grammar point is presented with succinct explanations in English, with examples in French and, where appropriate, with illustrations. These descriptions, however, are intended to serve as reference sections, because in most classes the teacher will first introduce the grammar of the lesson orally. This oral introduction to the grammar may be done in one of the following ways:

• The teacher may introduce the structure in the context of the *Presentation text.*

• The teacher may prefer to begin with the *Conversation/Observations,* the inductive teaching tool that is already prepared for them.

• To increase student motivation, the teacher may begin by explaining why the students need to know the structure. For example, in Unit 3, Lesson 1, the teacher may explain to the student that someone may ask what she or he is going to do tomorrow. To answer in French, the student needs to know the construction **aller + infinitive.**

• For some students, it helps to present certain structures with props. For example, in order to teach **avoir** in Unit 2, Lesson 2, teachers might have items on their desks or in their pockets and ask the students questions about these items.

• When students learn a new structure, the teacher should have them practice with the *Listening for Signals* activities in the Cassette Program until they can hear differences, in gender and in number, for example. Some students may need to play these tape activities repeatedly until they can recognize the new forms easily.

### 3.3.5 Using the *Activités*.

After the teacher presents the structure orally, the student must internalize it. It is at this point that differences in learning rate and learning mode become most apparent. In order to accommodate these differences, BONJOUR! provides many kinds of learning activities—more than any one teacher would be likely to use in a year. These cover a wide range, from simple to more challenging. They are also in a variety of formats so that students who need extra practice in a given structure will not be repeating the same kinds of activities. These learning activities are in the text, with variations suggested in the overprint of the Teacher's Edition, as well as in the Workbook and Cassette Program.

Students learn new structures by practicing them in role-playing or situational exercises and by using the language for personal expression. In BONJOUR!, students are never given a series of unrelated sentences to transform; they always practice new structures in a situational context.

### Types of Activities

*Simple situational activities*. The first activity after the oral presentation of a structure is usually a simple situational activity requiring a transformation. Students of all levels should do this first activity.

• The teacher could give the situation and cues while the students give responses with their books closed. It is better if the teacher gives the cue before mentioning the student's name so that everyone will pay attention.

• Students could break into pairs or small groups and cue each other for responses.

*Questions personnelles* and *open-ended sentences*. These are either yes/no questions, information questions, or open-ended sentences that require students to use French for personal expression.

• The teacher may ask these of several students individually in order to receive a variety of responses. Again, the question should be asked before calling on a student to answer it.

• Teachers should foster communication by encouraging students to listen to each other. When teachers ask questions, they should not repeat the students' responses but should check to see that other students are listening. For example: Teacher: **"Jean-Michel, à quelle heure dînez-vous?"** After Jean-Michel answers, the teacher calls on another student. Teacher: **"Anne, à quelle heure dîne Jean-Michel?"** If Anne cannot answer, the teacher tells her to ask Jean-Michel. In this type of activity, the students learn to listen to each other as they practice different personal pronouns, verb forms, structures, and vocabulary.

• The *Questions personnelles* also lend themselves to working in pairs. One student might ask another student a question and write the response. They could then switch roles.

• The teacher may prefer to assign these personal activities as written homework since the responses will be different. The teacher would then correct the papers individually and have the students rewrite the sentences that have errors.

• For an in-class writing activity, one student could give a response, which the other class members would write.

*Un jeu.* This activity requires a knowledge of the structure and basic vocabulary of the lesson. It is also challenging and fun for the students. In it they must use the words given in the three or four columns of the activity to create logical, grammatically correct sentences.

• As an oral activity, each student could be called upon to create a sentence. Other students could judge it for logic and correctness.

• As a special challenge, students may compete to see who can write the greatest number of logical, correct sentences within a given time frame, such as five or ten minutes.

**3.3.6 Teaching vocabulary.** One teacher may present vocabulary as it occurs in the *Presentation text* and the *Structure* sections. Another teacher may prefer to use the visuals of the unit to teach the words without reference to English. Still another teacher may rely more heavily on the groupings in the *Vocabulaire pratique, Vocabulaire spécialisé, Structure,* and *Expressions pour la conversation*. These sections comprise all of the active vocabulary and use art, thematic grouping, and words in context to aid in vocabulary acquisition.

The vocabulary is reentered in activities and readings so that student progression through the text will reinforce its assimilation.

• Vocabulary learning is another area in which students could participate by the creation of collages. The *Vocabulaire spécialisé* on **Pays et nationalités** in Unit 2, Lesson 4 provides a wide range of possibilities for photos.

• There are numerous games that the teacher may play with the students in class to teach, build, and review vocabulary. For some possibilities, the teacher should see the game section in Part Three of this Teacher's Edition.

• The teacher may ask the students to write compositions or to prepare skits using new words. For example, when the class is studying clothing (*Vocabulaire spécialisé* in Unit 4, Lesson 3), two students could play the roles of shoppers telling a sales clerk, played by a third student, what they wish to buy.

• Visuals in the text are a source of variety in practicing vocabulary. The teacher could pick a line drawing or a photo from an earlier unit and have the students describe it. Or one student could describe a portion of the illustration as other students try to guess what the object is. The drawing of four people at the dinner table in Unit 2, Lesson 2 (p. 107), provides rich opportunities for vocabulary practice on weather, transportation, and clothing. Students could also use this type of drawing to practice adverbs or adjectives.

• For the convenience of teachers in preparing additional materials, the active vocabulary is listed by unit in the Activity Masters.

**3.3.7 Teaching pronunciation.** Each lesson of the Student Text concludes with a *Prononciation* section that focuses on particular sounds, linkings, or intonation. However, it is very important that students understand that they cannot separate pronunciation from the rest of their study of French any more than they can separate structure or vocabulary. Students must hear and be encouraged to communicate in correct French whenever possible, hearing and imitating not only the sounds but the intonation patterns of French speakers.

The *Prélude* of the text is important in the teaching of pronunciation, not only because it represents the students' first exposure to the study of French, but also because it introduces the students to small but significant slices of the French language. As the teacher (or the tape) models the greetings, introductions, and sentences, the students must be encouraged to imitate as accurately as possible. At the outset of instruction the teacher should also insist on correct rhythm and stress patterns.

In the *Prononciation* sections, the sounds to be practiced are given in phonetic transcription. The teacher need not teach the International Phonetic Alphabet nor bring the students' attention to the complete alphabet in Appendix 1 unless the class expresses a real interest. Even then it is unwise to present the entire alphabet at once; it is better to teach a few symbols, using words the students know as examples.

Occasionally the *Prononciation* sections compare French sounds to related English sounds. You may wish to explain to students that French vowels and consonants are generally sharper and more tense than their English counterparts. All the *Prononciation* sections are recorded in the Cassette Program so that the students may practice specific sounds by themselves.

**3.3.8 Using the *Entre nous*.** The *Entre nous* section, at the end of each lesson, emphasizes the conversation skill. Teachers may use these sections as they occur or wait until the end of the unit and use them as part of a review.

• If the teacher uses these at the end of the unit, the class can be divided into five groups, giving each group an *Entre nous* activity to develop. Each group could then share its results with the rest of the class.

• Students may write new dialogs based on suggestions given in *L'art du dialogue* sections. For example, *L'art du dialogue* in Lesson 3 of Unit 3 suggests that students act out a new dialog by reversing the roles. The students would then be practicing family vocabulary and making other appropriate changes, as they gained confidence in pronunciation and sentence formation.

• The *Entre nous* sections may be used as practice for the faster learners while the teacher helps other students with problems they have in the unit.

### 3.4 Using the *Section Magazine*

The purpose of the *Sections Magazines* is, first and foremost, to interest and engage the students and encourage them to explore French culture and civilization. These sections also furnish additional reading practice and provide the basis for discussions and mini-speeches in French. They should be considered optional and supplementary to the units.

• At all stages of instruction, the *Sections Magazines* can be used to reinforce oral communication skills. In the beginning, simple questions can be asked about the passage and/or the illustrations, using vocabulary that the students already know. Towards the middle of the year, students can give mini-talks in which they describe one of the illustrations or ask the class simple questions about it.

• The teacher may assign a selection from a *Section Magazine* as homework. The students then prepare four statements that may be true or false, such as **"Le vélomoteur n'est pas pratique."** This obviously false statement is based on the reading **Vive le vélomoteur!** in *Section Magazine 2.* In class, students form small groups and together prepare a list of the best true/false items. At a given signal, each group passes its list to the next group, which answers the questions. The first group to answer all ten items is the winner.

• Some teachers prefer to intersperse parts of the magazine sections with the normal classroom instruction and select a segment a week for a lesson in culture and reading practice. Because of the structure and vocabulary progression, however, these mini-treatments should not be undertaken before these sections occur in the text.

• Projects for student involvement are found in each *Section Magazine.* The teacher may assign these or have the students think up projects of their own. Students may also enjoy expanding the ideas of particular articles. For **Les secrets du visage,** in *Section Magazine 2,* the students could bring in photos of their favorite personalities and analyze them according to the perspective of the article.

• Reading Activities based on the two *Sections Magazines* are provided in the Activity Masters. These serve as a valuable supplement. The activities include questions on content, personal questions, exercises such as multiple choice, matching, fill-ins, sentence building, and sentence completion, and projects such as polls.

• The teacher and students may bring in posters, photographs, or other materials related to the *Section Magazine* being studied. In addition to the more obvious materials, such as photographs of places or of French-speaking youth, students could also bring in realia. For example, after reading **Parlez-vous français?** in *Section Magazine 1*, students could expand the topic by bringing in place names from newspapers, labels from products, or foods from recipe books.

• The teacher may use the magazine sections as departure points for compositions in which students write their own magazine articles. Students could create their own photo album and write about their family and friends in the style of **L'album de photos de Brigitte** *(Section Magazine 2.)*

• The students will find that the photographs, realia, and art inspire discussion. They may discuss what is in a given piece, tell a story about it, or create a conversation among the people pictured. Students may also enjoy providing captions for various pictures. The more the students work with the visual material, the more they will internalize the cultural content.

## 3.5 Using the Workbook

Teachers will want to use this component in ways that best suit the needs of their particular classes.

**3.5.1 Using the written exercises.** The Workbook contains numerous situational activities based on points of structure or vocabulary. Each Workbook activity is keyed to the text so teachers will know at what point they can assign a particular activity. Each lesson begins on a right-hand page so that teachers may request that students tear out specific lessons to hand in.

• The teacher may assign these activities as written homework for all students, only for students who need extra drill on specific items, or for students seeking extra credit.

• Part of the class can do the Workbook activities individually, while the teacher helps other students with concepts that were causing them difficulty.

• The teacher may assign all activities upon completion of a unit as a review.

• The students can use the Workbook for self-help by checking their answers with the answer key at the back. Those teachers who don't want their students to have access to the answers can tear out the answer key before distributing the Workbook.

**3.5.2 Using the *Récréation culturelle*.** An original feature of the Workbook is the *Récréation culturelle* section included in each unit. This section provides a change of pace between units. It contains games and realia that introduce students to authentic samples of the French language. The realia can provide a point of departure for oral communication activities. The various games may be done outside of class for homework, or in class as written activities in pairs or small groups.

**3.5.3 Using the *Tests de contrôle*.** *Tests de contrôle* are found at the back of the Workbook. They provide a written review of the basic structures and vocabulary of each unit. The *Tests de contrôle* should precede any other Unit Test.

• The teacher may use these tests informally for review.

• The students may take these tests on their own and check their answers in the answer key of the Workbook. The answer key for these tests contains an *Interpretation* segment. This refers students to the structure, vocabulary section, or cultural note of their texts corresponding to areas with which they are having difficulties.

## 3.6 Using the Cassette Program

The Cassette Program introduces the student to spoken French through the voices of a number of French speakers, thus supplementing and complementing the model provided by the teacher. The tape activities are recorded at natural conversational speed to foster authentic listening comprehension. Students should be warned that they may not understand everything the first time they hear the tape. In some cases the teacher may wish to present a passage or exercise before playing the tape. At other times the teacher may stop the tape to have students repeat a sentence or phrase they have just heard. The more opportunity the students have to listen to the tape, the more readily they will grow to understand spoken French.

• *Listening to the Presentation text.* The teacher may wish to play the *Presentation text* as an introduction to the unit. The students can listen with their books closed, or follow along with their books open, to get a general idea of what the text is about.

- *Listening for Signals*. These exercises are designed to test the students' ability to distinguish among sounds that signal grammatical information: noun markers, verb forms, and the like.
- *Speaking*. The speaking exercises are similar to the situational textbook exercises. Since the students cannot read the cues, they are forced to listen carefully. Two types of activities form the basis of this section:
  — directed activities, in which there is only one correct response; and
  — open-ended activities, such as the simple personal questions that appear later on in the program.
- *Dictation*. Students hear short sentences read three times. The first time they listen; the second time each sentence is broken up into short phrases, which the students write down; the third time they check what they have written.
- *Listening Comprehension with Visual Cues*. This activity is based on an illustration in the Activity Masters. Students are actively involved, since the listening process is accompanied by "pencil work": they are asked to trace a path, to locate certain items by marking them with an *X*, to draw a picture, etc. Listening reinforced with a written activity causes the students to pay closer attention to what is being said, and the exercise becomes more meaningful to them.
- *Listening and Repeating*. Students hear a recorded version of the **Prononciation** sections, the **Vocabulaire spécialisé,** and the verb charts, and practice imitating the new sounds.
- *French Songs*. Each unit concludes with a song in French, the melody of which will have been heard at intervals throughout. Students can sing along with the tape, reading from the music and lyrics in the Activity Masters. Songs feature simple lyrics, often with a familiar melody. For extra credit, musical students can learn and perform the songs for the class; whole-class performances can become part of a larger festival.

## 3.7 Using the Testing Program for FRENCH FOR MASTERY, *Salut, les amis!*

The Testing Program, which includes five *Lesson Quizzes* and a *Unit Test* for each unit, and two *Achievement Tests*, may be used with both BONJOUR! and EN AVANT! The accompanying Test Guide also provides ideas for developing speaking tests and written composition tests.

**3.7.1 Using the Lesson Quizzes.** The five *Lesson Quizzes* that accompany each unit are desiged to be administered upon completion of each lesson. The *Quiz* items present a variety of formats, including fill-ins, short answers, multiple choice, statement completion, and full answers. The students should be able to complete each *Lesson Quiz* in about 20 minutes.

For slower learners, the teacher may wish to administer the *Lesson Quiz* as a series of short quizzes given upon completion of the individual sections of the lesson.

**3.7.2 Using the Unit Tests.** The *Unit Tests* are designed to be administered upon completion of each unit. The students should be able to complete each *Test* in about 45 minutes. All the material of the unit is evaluated in discrete-point exercises.

For slower learners, the teacher may wish to administer each *Unit Test* over a two-day period. The listening portion could be given on the first day and the written portion on the second day.

**3.7.3 Using the Achievement Tests.** The *Achievement Tests* are designed to be administered upon completion of the corresponding units (*Achievement Test 1: Prélude,* Units 1–4, BONJOUR!; *Achievement Test 2:* Units 5–8, EN AVANT!). The students should be able to complete each *Test* in two 45-minute class periods. The teacher may choose to administer the listening portion on the first day and the written portion on the second day.

For slower learners, the teacher may wish to include only selected items from each part of the *Test,* adjusting the scoring as necessary.

## 3.8 Using the Overhead Transparencies for FRENCH FOR MASTERY, *Salut, les amis!*

**3.8.1 When to use them.** The Overhead Transparencies have been selected with particular attention to flexibility and multiple use. The transparencies may be used for (1) review (structures and vocabulary); (2) testing (especially vocabulary); (3) reentry and variety (previously learned vocabulary, and familiar transparencies in new contexts); (4) guided self-expression (conversation and composition); and (5) cultural awareness (maps).

**3.8.2 How to use them.** There are several basic techniques for using the Overhead Transparencies. These are:

• *Transparency plus pointer.* The teacher projects the transparency and uses a pencil, a ruler, or a pointer to point to various images.

• *Transparency plus marker.* The teacher may write on the transparency with a water-soluble transparency marker and then easily wipe off these additions with a damp cloth or paper towel. Colored markers may be used to distinguish and reinforce various linguistic features.

• *Transparency plus overlay.* An overlay is a second transparency used to add visual material to an initial transparency. Besides the overlays provided in the box of visuals, teachers may use blank sheets of acetate to develop their own.

• *Transparency plus mask.* If the teacher wishes to project only a portion of the visual, a sheet of paper may be laid on the transparency as a mask.

• *Transparency plus moving elements.* It is possible to project both a still image (the original transparency) and a mobile image. Adding movable hands to a clockface is perhaps the most obvious example.

## 3.9 Using FRENCH FOR MASTERY *SOFTWARE*

FRENCH FOR MASTERY *SOFTWARE* provides supplementary practice with the active vocabulary of FRENCH FOR MASTERY, *Salut, les amis!* The program is organized by unit. Within a given unit, the students may be asked to practice a specific vocabulary topic or may select a set of contextualized activities that randomly mix the vocabulary items of the unit.

To provide variety, the program utilizes fifteen different types of activities that can be categorized as follows:

— receptive or recognition activities, where students indicate their responses in a multiple choice format, and

— productive or writing activities, where students must type in the appropriate responses (using correct accents).
Within each category, the activities are sequenced in order of increasing difficulty.

In working through the activities, the students receive immediate feedback. Once they have entered an answer, they are immediately informed whether the response is correct. If they have answered incorrectly, they are given a second chance. If the second try is wrong, they are shown the correct response. At the end of an activity, the students are shown what percent of items were answered correctly, as well as perk screens.

**3.9.1 How to Use FRENCH FOR MASTERY SOFTWARE.** FRENCH FOR MASTERY SOFT-WARE is a flexible learning tool that can be incorporated into the lesson plan as a workbook, an exercise, or a class activity. Some of the ways the program can be integrated are:

• Whole classes may be assigned a unit review once the material has been presented in class. Students may work individually or in groups during class time while others are involved in teacher-guided activities.

• Specific parts of a unit might be assigned to individual students based on their needs.

• Students may be assigned computer drill before the material is practiced in class in order to be better prepared for classroom activities requiring a knowledge of vocabulary.

• Segments of the program can be selected to reinforce a particular group of vocabulary items.

• Students of varied linguistic backgrounds may be brought to a similar level of proficiency through the selective assignment of drill activities.

• More advanced students may move ahead independently while the teacher is working with the rest of the class.

# 4. Lesson Plans

Drawing up lesson plans helps the teacher to visualize how a unit is going to be presented. By emphasizing certain aspects of the program and playing down others, the teacher can change the focus of a unit to meet the students' needs. Provided here are sample lesson plans that show how BONJOUR! can be used successfully, whether a class meets five times a week or three times a week. A list of suggestions for adapting the material to slower and faster learners follows the lesson plans (pages T28–T30).

## 4.1 Sample Lesson Plans

The following pages show sample lesson plans for Unit 3, Lesson 1 for
- a class meeting 5 days a week for 45 minutes
- a class meeting 3 days a week for 45 minutes

The plan for each day covers five types of classroom activities: (1) review, (2) correction, (3) presentation, (4) oral activities, and (5) written activities and/or assignments. Additional information regarding these classroom activities follows the charts (pages T27–T28). Suggestions for teaching the various elements of the lesson and for using the various components of the program can be found in Part Two of this manual.

### Notes:

1. The lesson plan for the class that meets five days a week usually allows the teacher approximately ten minutes each day for additional activities. These can include selections from the *Sections Magazines,* games based on the structures and on the vocabulary, vocabulary quizzes, dictations, or cultural activities. The lesson plan for the class that meets three days a week provides material for a full class period. This plan will have to be followed closely in order to complete the program in one year. To allow time for additional activities, some features of the lesson—and of the program—can be shortened or omitted. For the teacher's convenience, the structures and activities that can be omitted are labeled ''optional'' in the overprint of the Teacher's Edition.
2. Since the lessons vary in length, the units will not all take the same number of days to complete.
3. The Cassette Program may be used effectively both in schools with labs and in schools without.
4. The *Unit Test* may be administered over a two-day period by giving the listening portion on one day and the written portion on the other.

### 4.1.1 Lesson Plans for Unit 3, Lesson 1, for a class meeting five days a week

**Day 1**  1. Go over Unit Test 2.  (10 minutes)
2. Have students look at the pictures and try to guess what's going on in the *Presentation text* for Unit 3, Lesson 1. Then play the tape and go over the *Vocabulaire practique.*  (15 minutes)
3. Present *Structure* A: **Le verbe *aller*** and go through *Activités* 1 and 2 orally.  (10 minutes)
4. Assignment: Have students study **aller** and write the answers to *Activité* 1 and Workbook activity A1.

**Day 2**  1. Review the *Presentation text* and ***Vocabulaire pratique*** and ask the comprehension questions in the overprint.   (10 minutes)
2. Present the ***Note culturelle.*** (Bring in pictures of the Centre Pompidou.) (10 minutes)
3. Review **aller** and correct assignment.   (5 minutes)
4. Present the ***Vocabulaire spécialisé*** and go through ***Activité*** 3 orally. (15 minutes)
5. Assignment: Study the vocabulary and bring in pictures cut out from magazines for two of the places. Write the answers to ***Activité*** 3.

**Day 3**  1. Begin class with a review of the vocabulary by having each student show his or her pictures. Correct written assignment.   (10 minutes)
2. Present ***Structure*** B: ***à*** + **l'article défini.**   (10 minutes)
3. Go through ***Activités*** 4, 5, and 6 orally.   (15 minutes)
4. Assignment: Write the answers to Workbook activities B1, B2, and B3.

**Day 4**  1. Begin class with a brief review of the vocabulary and ***Structure*** B by asking students questions: **Où allez-vous après la classe? Allez-vous... (au stade,** etc.)? **Où est-ce que Paul va?**   (5 minutes)
2. Correct Workbook assignment.   (10 minutes)
3. Return to ***Conversation.*** Ask questions of half the students. Have each of these students ask the same question of a student who has not had a turn. Ask for volunteers to answer the questions in ***Observations.*** (10 minutes)
4. Present ***Structure*** C: ***aller*** + **l'infinitif** and go through ***Activités*** 7 and 8 orally.   (15 minutes)
5. Assignment: Write the answers to Workbook activities C1 and C2.

**Day 5**  1. Review ***aller*** + **l'infinitif** and correct assignment.   (10 minutes)
2. Review the forms of **avoir** and **être.** In groups of four, have students create sentences using the elements in ***Activité de révision.***   (10 minutes)
3. Present the ***Prononciation*** section.   (5 minutes)
4. Go over the **Expressions pour la conversation** and the **Mini-dialogue** in the ***Entre nous.*** Have two or three sets of volunteers act out the original and the new dialogue.   (15 minutes)
5. Assignment: Write out ten sentences using the elements of **Un jeu.**

**Day 6**  1. Ask questions to review the structures and vocabulary: **Où allez-vous samedi? Aujourd'hui, est-ce que vous allez... (nager)?**   (5 minutes)
2. Correct **Un jeu** by having each student read a sentence from his or her assignment.   (5 minutes)
3. Use the Cassette Program activities for Lesson 1.   (25 minutes)
4. Assignment: Prepare for *Lesson Quiz.*

**Day 7**  1. *Lesson Quiz.*   (20 minutes)
2. Begin Unit 3, Lesson 2.

### 4.1.2 Lesson Plans for Unit 3, Lesson 1 for a class meeting three days a week

**Day 1**
1. Go over Unit Test 2. (10 minutes)
2. Have students look at the pictures and try to guess what's going on in the *Presentation text* for Unit 3, Lesson 1. Then play the tape and go over the ***Vocabulaire pratique.*** (10 minutes)
3. Present the ***Note culturelle.*** (Bring in pictures of the Centre Pompidou.) (10 minutes)
4. Present **Structure** A: **Le verbe *aller*** and go through *Activités* 1 and 2 orally. (10 minutes)
5. Assignment: Have students study **aller** and write the answers to *Activité* 1 and Workbook activity A1.

**Day 2**
1. Review the *Presentation text* and ***Vocabulaire pratique,*** and ask the comprehension questions in the overprint. (10 minutes)
2. Review **aller** and correct assignment. (5 minutes)
3. Present the ***Vocabulaire spécialisé*** and go through *Activité* 3 orally. (10 minutes)
4. Present **Structure** B: ***à* + l'article défini** and go through *Activités* 4, 5, and 6 orally. (20 minutes)
5. Assignment: Write out Workbook activities B1, B2, and B3.

**Day 3**
1. Begin class with a brief review of the vocabulary and **Structure** B by asking students questions: **Où allez-vous après la classe? Allez-vous... (au stade,** etc.)? **Où est-ce que Paul va?** (5 minutes)
2. Correct Workbook assignment. (10 minutes)
3. Return to ***Conversation.*** Ask questions of half the students. Have each of these students ask the same questions of a student who has not had a turn. Ask for volunteers to answer the questions in ***Observations.*** (10 minutes)
4. Present **Structure** C: ***aller* + l'infinitif,** and go through *Activités* 7 and 8 orally. (15 minutes)
5. Assignment: Write the answers to Workbook activities C1 and C2.

**Day 4**
1. Ask questions to review the structures and vocabulary: **Où allez-vous samedi? Aujourd'hui, est-ce que vous allez... (nager)?** (5 minutes)
2. Correct Workbook assignment. (10 minutes)
3. Review the forms of **avoir** and **être.** In groups of four, have students create sentences using the elements in ***Activité de révision.*** (10 minutes)
4. Present the ***Prononciation*** section. (5 minutes)
5. Go over the **Expressions pour la conversation** and the **Mini-dialogue** in the ***Entre nous.*** Have two or three sets of volunteers act out the original and the new dialogue. (15 minutes)
6. Assignment: Write out ten sentences using the elements of **Un jeu.**

**Day 5**
1. Go back to the *Presentation text* and have students point out the structures they have learned. (10 minutes)
2. Correct **Un jeu** by having each student read a sentence from his or her assignment. (5 minutes)

3. Use the Cassette Program activities for Lesson 1. (25 minutes)
4. Assignment: Prepare for *Lesson Quiz.*

**Day 6** 1. *Lesson Quiz.* (20 minutes)
2. Begin Unit 3, Lesson 2.

## 4.2 Notes and Suggestions Regarding the Five Classroom Activities

- *Review* (5–8 minutes)
  - — Can be used at the beginning of class or following *Correction.*
  - — Can include items from previous day's homework or classwork.
  - — Should anticipate new material or review items whenever possible.
  - — Should review or correct mistakes the teacher found while correcting previous day's tests or homework papers.
  - — Could include conversational items, such as discussions of school or class events, weekends, weather, etc.
  - — Should be in French as often as possible as this sets the tone for the rest of the class.
- *Correction* (5–10 minutes)
  - — Should be in French whenever possible. Teach the alphabet, grammatical terms, accents, and punctuation early.
  - — Could be first activity in teaching sequence.
  - — Quizzes can occasionally be corrected immediately in class. This is especially good for teacher-prepared dictées and vocabulary quizzes.
  - — Questions should be encouraged, concepts reviewed, and misunderstandings straightened out as this is really a teaching time.
  - — Mistakes commonly made should be pointed out and any necessary reteaching should take place.
- *Presentation* (10–15 minutes)
  - — New material can be presented first, or immediately following *Review.*
  - — Tapes may be used when appropriate.
  - — Comments and explanations should be in English only initially; on later days the material should be reexplained in French whenever possible.
  - — The *Presentation text* at the beginning of each lesson should be referred back to and used as a model, since the various structure elements of a lesson are presented there.
- *Oral Activities* (10 minutes)
  - — Presenting activities orally that will later be written reinforces what has been taught and minimizes the problem of students who might not understand the homework.
  - — Dramatic presentation of dialogs and conversations, as well as creative material, can be used.

— *Entre nous Mini-dialogues,* which are optional material, could be omitted and other material, such as the *Presentation text* of a lesson, substituted.

— Other optional or enrichment material can be added here: **Section Magazine** or **Récréation culturelle.**

• *Written Activities and/or Assignments* (5–10 minutes)

— Not all of every activity needs to be written out by every student. Faster learners might do only half, such as the even-numbered items.

— Some activities can be done in class, some outside of class as homework assignments. With a slower or beginning group, start each activity to be done for homework in class, so they know what to do.

— Testing might be best at the beginning of class on some occasions.

— Tests and Quizzes should be corrected immediately whenever possible, or at least by the next class meeting. They should be reviewed by the total group together, corrections made, questions asked. This makes testing a teaching time as well.

— Offer retakes on tests to those who want to prove they can do better.

— Individual vocabulary notebooks or flashcards are a good way to help review vocabulary.

— Corrected compositions or themes might also be recopied into a special notebook.

— A vocabulary quiz might be given in one of several ways:
  –labeling illustrations, such as a house, the body, or clothes
  –writing English meanings to given French words
  –writing French equivalents to given English words
  –spelling the French word correctly when it is said, then giving the English equivalent
  –matching two lists of French and English terms
  –writing a short sentence to show the meaning of a given French word

— Workbook Activities may be introduced along with each item of structure. They are keyed in the Teacher's Edition.

— Print and hand out a syllabus of all written assignments for the lesson or the unit. Absent youngsters will know what to do next; there will be no confusion as to exact assignment; also helps to keep class progressing at good pace.

### 4.3 Adapting the Material to Slower or Younger Learners

— Maximum repetition of material is needed, with as much student participation as possible.

— Review time should include the same or similar items for several days in a row.

— Teacher should stick to basic material from the text rather than introduce outside or extra material to enable students to master the essential concepts.

— Constant review is necessary.

— Required memorization and recitation over a period of several days by each class member helps all students to retain material: days, numbers, months, verbs, pronouns, etc.

— Flags, stickers, stars, seals, stamps, happy faces, and expressions such as "très bien," etc. really help when put on papers and tests.

— Have students make vocabulary notebooks or flashcards.

— Rewriting words/sentences correctly several times helps to avoid further mistakes.

— Sufficient variety in material and class activities helps to make drill less arduous.

— Do group work, board work, and have students check each other's work.

— Have students perform. They learn best when they say and do and are actively involved.

— Pictures, drawings, flashcards, charades, and objects help to make the material stick in their minds.

— Assign students to teach the rest of the class one word or phrase or verb from a vocabulary list; for example, several students each teach a different part of the body and drill the others until they know it.

— Invent games and use familiar ones to help drill and repeat work.

## 4.4 Adapting the Material to Faster Learners

— French should be used as much as possible in class. Use the alphabet, grammar terms, etc.

— Students should write original compositions, résumés, or dialogs at least once a week. Perhaps a special notebook could be kept of these things.

— Students should not be required to write out every word of every drill. If they understand what is going on they should be allowed to do only half of an exercise, such as the odd- or even-numbered items.

— Assign additional reading material: readers, newspapers, etc.

— Use the optional or enrichment material.

— Good students can function as group leaders for a particular task.

— Assign students as tutors for other students.

— Discuss "other things" of importance to students in French: the weekend, the concert, the dance, the school lunch.

— Students should be encouraged to perform (perhaps write) scenes and skits and presentations for other classes, live or on videotape.

— Students can write letters in French to absent class members, etc.

— Students can take mini-sabbaticals (which exempt them from a night's assignment) to French events: movies, restaurant, art display, etc. with the idea they will report back to the class.

— If they have a chance to travel to another French-speaking country, students could be exempted from routine work but be expected to bring back a full report, realia, journal, personal stories, and photos to share with the class. The general outline should be worked out with the students before leaving.

— Students might want to work on an independent study project. Design a contract together stating what you want and what the students think can be covered, including various types of activities, oral work, and written assignments. This can also be used for a student who wants to move ahead rapidly in the program and is capable of such independence.

# Part Three
## How to Supplement BONJOUR!

## 5. Supplementary Material and Activities

Foreign language methodologists stress the importance of using realia and supplementary cultural activities for a number of reasons:

- They enliven the atmosphere of the class.
- They provide that needed change of pace.
- They allow for a more natural exchange between student and teacher.
- They permit the less linguistically oriented students to express themselves in other areas such as music, art, or cooking.
- They present students with a practical application of the skills learned in the classroom.
- They provide an interdisciplinary link to students' other studies.

### 5.1 Realia: Where to Find It and How to Use It

Realia, that is, authentic items relating to the contemporary French-speaking world, provide additional exposure to culture, a change of pace, and departure points for conversational activities. Students see how learning French will help them understand everyday items of interest to them. This section lists some sources of these materials and suggests how the teacher might use them. The listing is not exhaustive, but seeks to provide variety. Depending on the teacher's geographical area, some of these materials may be easier or more difficult to obtain. In addition, every teacher will have a personal preference as to what materials he or she will want to use or will feel most comfortable with.

**5.1.1  The written language.** Many of the following French-language magazines and newspapers may be purchased at shops that sell foreign language periodicals. Others are available by single copy or by subscription from the distributor.

| Name | Country | Approx. Cost | Type | Useful contents | Distributor | Frequency |
|------|---------|--------------|------|-----------------|-------------|-----------|
| L'actualité | Canada | $1.50 per copy/ $18.00 per year | current events | ads, articles on travel, health, pastimes, current events | L'actualité, Suite 1100 1001 blvd  Maisonneuve ouest Montréal, P.Q. H3A 3E1 | monthly |
| Elle | France | $2.50/$105 | women's fashions | ads, trends, interior decorating, advice column, recipes, health, budget, horoscope | * | weekly |
| L'Express | France | $2.25/$94 | current events | entertainment, opinion polls, ads | * | weekly |
| Le Figaro | France | $1.00/$398 | newspaper | current events, sports, entertainment, ads, weather | * | daily |

| Title | U.S. | Price | Type | Content | Distributor | Frequency |
|---|---|---|---|---|---|---|
| Le Journal Français d'Amérique | U.S. | $.85/$18 | newspaper | current events, sports | Journal Français d'Amérique 1051 Divisadero St. San Francisco, CA 94115 | biweekly |
| Jours de France | France | $2.20/$100 | fashion | ads, horoscope, cartoons | * | weekly |
| Le Monde | France | $1.00/$390 | newspaper | games, hobbies, entertainment, weather, current events | * | daily |
| Ok âge tendre | France | $1.25/$56 | youth | youth culture, teen fashions, ads | * | weekly |
| Une semaine de Paris — Pariscope | France | $2.20/$100 | entertainment listings | movies, dance, music, theater, sports events | * | weekly |
| Paris-Match | France | $2.25/$80 | current events | stories, sports, opinion polls, ads, TV programs | Paris-Match P.O. Box 8500 S. 4075 Philadelphia, PA 19178 | weekly |
| Phosphore | France | $4.00/$36 | youth | lycée, careers, contemporary French life, "fiches" on varied topics | Bayard Presse 5, rue Bayard 75393 Paris cedex 08 France | monthly |
| Pilote | France | $1.75/$77 | humor | comics, ads, cartoons | * | weekly |
| La Presse | Canada (Montréal) | $.50/$250 | newspaper | current events, entertainment ads | La Presse Ltée 7, rue Saint-Jacques Montréal, P.Q. H2Y 1K9 | daily |
| Salut | France | $2.00/$40 | youth | youth culture, ads | * | biweekly |
| Sélections de Reader's Digest | Canada or France | $2.75/$18 | general | jokes, ads, stories, articles | Reader's Digest OEM Pleasantville, NY 10570 (specify Canadian or Parisian edition) | monthly |
| Le Soleil | Canada (Québec) | $.50/$250 | newspaper | current events, entertainment | Le Soleil 390 St.-Vallier est Québec, P.Q. G1K 7J6 | daily |
| Télé 7 jours | France | $1.25/$61 | TV guide | TV program, articles, ads | * | weekly |
| TV | Canada | $.75/$35 | TV guide | French version of TV Guide, with French résumés of all English and French programs; ads and articles | TV HEBDO, Inc. 1001 blvd Maisonneuve est Bureau 1100 Montréal, P.Q. H2L 4P9 | weekly |

* These periodicals can be purchased from any of the following distributors:

Larousse & Co., Inc.
572 Fifth Avenue
New York, NY 10036

French and European Publications, Inc.
610 Fifth Avenue
New York, NY 10020

French and European Publications, Inc.
652 South Olive Street
Los Angeles, CA 90014

European Publishers Representatives, Inc.
11-03 46th Avenue
Long Island City, NY 11101

**5.1.2 The spoken language.** There are a number of radio stations in the United States that broadcast in French at some point during the day. Also, near the Canadian border it may be possible to receive some television programs in French. Channel 10 in New York City and Channel 6 in San Francisco televise a few hours a week in French. The teacher and students should check the newspapers for stations and times of French programs. The following is only a sampling of some of the radio stations with French broadcasts on their schedule.

| City | State | Radio station call letters |
|------|-------|---------------------------|
| Columbus | OH | WRFD |
| Ephrata | WA | KULE |
| Hartford | CT | WCCC-FM; WRTC-FM |
| Holyoke | MA | WREB |
| Honolulu | HI | KNDI |
| Levelland | TX | KLVT |
| Lewiston | ME | WCOU; WCOU-FM; WLAM |
| Moultrie | GA | WMGA |
| New Orleans | LA | WWNO-FM |
| Reidsville | NC | WFRC |
| San Francisco | CA | KQED-FM |
| Winnetka | IL | WNTH-FM |

**5.1.3 Other sources.**

*Brochures and posters:* The sources for these are numerous; they are available both by mail and in the local community.

- Tourist offices.

— FRANCE
    French Government Tourist Office
    610 Fifth Avenue, Room 222
    New York, New York 10020

    Commissariat Général du Tourisme
    127, av. des Champs-Élysées
    75008 Paris, France

    Mission interministérielle pour le tourisme
    17, rue de l'Ingénieur Robert Keller
    75740 Paris, France

— Canada

Tourisme Canada
235 Queen Street
Ottawa, Ontario, Canada K1A OH6

Ministère de l'Industrie, du Commerce et du Tourisme
Direction Générale du Tourisme
710 Place d'Youville
Québec, P.Q., Canada G1R 4Y4

— Martinique and Guadeloupe

Caribbean Tourism Association
20 East 46th Street
New York, New York 10017

— Tahiti

Tahiti Tourist Board
1 Penn Plaza, Suite 2206
New York, New York 10119

— Haiti

Haiti Government Tourist Office
1270 Avenue of the Americas, Suite 508
New York, New York 10020

• ACTFL Materials Center
P.O. Box 408
Hastings-on-Hudson, New York 10706

• Embassies and consulates of French-speaking countries.
The teacher or student may request information in French or in English on the country, its educational system, or any other aspect of life in that country.

One can also write for information and posters to the Services Culturels of the French consulates in Washington, New York, Chicago, San Francisco, Los Angeles, Houston, New Orleans, and Boston.

• American offices of transportation companies.
Students can write the United States offices of airline or shipping companies of French-speaking countries requesting descriptive material in French or English, bilingual menus, bilingual brochures, or other realia. A local travel agency can furnish up-to-date addresses of companies such as Air France, Air Canada, Air Afrique, and Swissair.

• Friends and relatives.
Students, friends, or parents who are traveling to a French-speaking country can be asked to bring back useful and interesting items, such as menus, city maps, train and bus schedules, TV and movie guides, programs of plays and concerts, records, games, tickets, candy wrappers, or anything else that might be of interest to the class.

• Food and Wines from France, Inc.
Information Center for Food and Wine
24 East 21st Street
New York, New York 10010
Supplies posters on wine and cheese.

T35

• Students themselves can collect objects that have French words or that come from French-speaking countries: food labels and packaging, stamps, games such as Mille Bornes.

*Books:* Students may use travel books to plan itineraries for imaginary trips. Books from the school library and encyclopedias provide photos of French-speaking countries, monuments, and works of art.

*Pen pals:* Students may enjoy corresponding with French-speaking students. To obtain pen pals, the teacher can write to the American Association of Teachers of French.

Bureau de Correspondance Scolaire
AATF
57 East Armory Avenue
Champaign, IL 61820

It might be possible to make an arrangement with a class in a French-speaking country whereby that class could send French realia and the English-speaking class could send English realia in exchange.

**5.1.4 How to use the material.** The teacher may want to use realia to enrich classroom activities and to help students make the transition from the classroom to the everyday French-speaking world.

• *Preparing realia for the students.* It is important for the teacher to prepare the realia for the students before exposing them to it. If it is too difficult or if there are too many unknown words and structures, the students may become discouraged. Teachers should be selective in the realia that they bring to class. In the beginning, the realia should have visuals that reinforce vocabulary and structures that the students have already learned. The teacher should edit the realia before showing it to the students. It would also be helpful to underline words or structures that students already know and prepare a brief glossary of items that they don't know. Students should not translate but try to understand what is being said from the context.

Radio and television programs are often difficult to understand. The teacher should tell students to concentrate on what they are able to understand. For example, news items may be easy for students to understand if they have heard some of the names on English broadcasts.

• *Useful materials.* Newspapers and magazines not only include feature articles but a number of items that focus on the world of today and that are easy to understand. TV guides, movie schedules, weather reports, ads for restaurants, food, or clothes provide useful teaching tools and are easy for students to understand. They can be used for:

— identification of vocabulary and structures already learned

— vocabulary building (new words, especially concrete nouns)

— culture expansion

— points of departure for conversation

Examples of types of realia to teach specific points are:

— wedding or birth announcements to illustrate French names

— weather reports to illustrate weather expressions and vocabulary

— ads about clothing sales or fashion magazines to illustrate clothing

— labels from the supermarket or grocery store ads to illustrate food

Many French periodicals contain ads for U.S. products and carry publicity (and even articles) patterned on U.S. models. This may give the impression that the French-speaking world tends to copy the American model. While "Americanization" is a very real phenomenon, you should make sure that your students understand that the French speakers have their own traditions and values. (Observant students will notice that some U.S. products are marketed with different types of ads in French, reflecting the French rather than the American value system.)

## 5.2 Games: Their Preparation and Use

Games are useful learning tools that are accessible to every teacher and that provide variety for the class. Used at the beginning of the class, games capture the students' attention. In the middle of the period, games may serve as a transition from one activity to the next. At the end of the class, they fill in the few minutes between the final activity on the lesson plan and the bell. The teacher can play these games with the entire class. Games also lend themselves to pair and small-group activity.

The main purpose of games is to further the linguistic aim of the lesson; they should not become the exclusive focus of the class. As a teaching aid, each unit of the Workbook features a games section, *Le coin des jeux,* based on the material in the Student Text. (The games section is reprinted in the Activity Masters.)

Described below are sample games that the teacher can use or adapt.

**5.2.1 Commercial games.** There are many commercial games that are sold by companies handling foreign-language realia. Some games that are popular in English in the United States have French counterparts: French Scrabble, Scrabble pour Juniors, and Monopoly. Mille Bornes is a popular bilingual game in which players compete in a cross-country trip by car. Victoire! is a lotto game in French that can be played by beginners. In Word Master Mind, players try to duplicate each other's secret words.

**5.2.2 Games created by the teacher.** Many games that the students are familiar with in English may be played in French. Teacher-created games have a distinct advantage over commercial games; they can be "custom made" to fit the needs of a particular class or of a particular lesson.

A. Oral games

LE JEU DU PENDU, similar to HANGMAN

The teacher may suggest this game as a way to review the vocabulary of a given unit prior to the unit test. One student thinks of a word from a *Vocabulaire spécialisé* from one of the five lessons in the unit. This student then writes on the chalkboard a series of blanks corresponding to the number of letters in the word and draws a noose. When someone from the class guesses a letter that appears in the word, the student at the board enters that letter in all the spaces where it occurs in the word. When someone guesses a letter that is not in the word, the student leading the game adds a part of the body to the person in the noose. The object, of course, is to guess the word before being hanged. As the final activity, no matter who wins, a student should spell the complete word and supply the gender or identify the word as an adjective or verb, etc.

## DEVINEZ LE MOT!

The teacher thinks of a familiar word and announces the number of letters it contains; for example, **lit**—"**trois lettres.**" Students in the class volunteer possible three-letter words, and the teacher writes these possibilities on the board indicating how many letters in that word are the same as those in the key word.

|  | 0 | 1 | 2 | 3 |
|---|---|---|---|---|
| *qui* (une lettre) |  | *qui* |  |  |
| *son* (zéro lettre) | *son* |  |  |  |
| *les* (une lettre) |  | *les* |  |  |
| *ton* (une lettre) |  | *ton* |  |  |
| *dit* (deux lettres) |  |  | *dit* |  |

It is a good idea to ask the student to put the word in a sentence for clarity: "**Qu'est-ce qu'il *dit?***" vs. "***Dis* donc!**" The student who guesses the correct word goes to the board to lead the next round. The student should write the secret word on a piece of paper and share it with the teacher, who will then be able to help in confirming guesses if needed.

## DEVINEZ L'OBJET

In this game, one student thinks of an object, and the others take turns asking questions about it to find out what it is.

## LA CHAÎNE

One student says a word: **tennis,** for example. The next student must give a word that begins with the last letter of that word, such as **sympathique.** The next student continues with a word beginning with the last letter of the preceding word. In this case, the third student might say **excellent.** This game may also be played in teams, in which each player has a turn coming up with an appropriate word in five seconds. If not, the team forfeits a point.

## SIMON DIT

First the teacher goes through the motions of the game saying, for example, "**Simon dit: les mains sur la tête**" while touching his or her head. When the students understand, the teacher may lead the game without modeling the movements. Students learn to understand unfamiliar statements readily if they are asked to respond physically rather than orally.

## ADIEU!

This game is similar to "Ghost" in English. Playing in groups of five or six, each student has a turn in saying a letter that contributes to the spelling of a French word. If in so doing, the student completes a word, he or she gets an **A**, the next time a **D**, and so on until they are out by having completed the word **Adieu**. The last person remaining in the game is the winner. If a student says a letter that the next person does not believe contributes toward the building of a word, the student who said it may be challenged. If the challenged student does not have a French word in mind, he or she receives a letter toward being eliminated from the game. However, if the challenged student does know a French word with that sequence of letters, the student who challenged receives one of the letters of **Adieu.**

## B. Written games

### JOYEUX NOËL ET BONNE ANNÉE

The teacher writes a phrase on the board. The students have a limited amount of time to see how many words they can form using the letters contained in the phrase. In the case of **Joyeux Noël et Bonne Année** some of the words the students might find are **je, eux, non, bon, an, aux, bel,** or **beau.** The title of a lesson or of a unit frequently makes a good phrase for this kind of activity.

### JE L'AI!

After distributing sheets of paper divided into 16 squares, the teacher gives a category, such as food, clothing, or school life. The students then fill in the spaces with French words belonging to the category. One at a time, the teacher calls out words that belong in the category, and if the students have the words, they cross them off their sheets. The first one to get four in a row horizontally, vertically, or diagonally calls "**Je l'ai!**" and wins the game.

### FIND THE WORDS

The teacher may create these puzzles as a test on unit vocabulary or as a break in the students' routine. The following sample uses some of the vocabulary from Unit 3. The teacher prepares the letter blocks with words hidden horizontally, vertically, or diagonally.

| | | | | | | | | | | | |
|---|---|---|---|---|---|---|---|---|---|---|---|
| A | L | L | E | R | A | E | N | O | S | | PLAGE |
| M | R | P | M | O | D | M | L | L | E | | CAMPAGNE |
| A | D | P | L | A | G | E | G | T | A | | VILLE |
| C | E | I | T | B | R | A | M | G | N | | PISCINE |
| P | F | S | E | R | V | C | H | N | V | | STADE |
| I | T | C | Z | C | X | I | H | E | I | | MAISON |
| M | A | I | S | O | N | T | L | E | B | | MARCHER |
| C | D | N | L | J | V | B | G | L | R | | ALLER |
| E | R | E | S | T | E | R | F | H | E | | RESTER |
| C | A | M | P | A | G | N | E | I | J | | |

# CROSSWORD PUZZLES

Easy to prepare, crossword puzzles provide another method of checking vocabulary. The following puzzle, **Objets courants,** is based on the *Vocabulaire spécialisé* of Unit 2, Lesson 2.

The crossword grid contains the following filled-in answers:

- Across: SAC, VELOMOTEUR, RADIO
- Down: LIVRE, CAMERA, VELO

### Horizontalement

**2.**

**5.**

**6.**

### Verticalement

**1.**

**3.**

**4.**

## LA POÉSIE SURRÉALISTE

Using a paper cutter, the teacher cuts typing paper lengthwise into 11-inch strips, one for each student. The teacher gives a specific instruction and each student writes a word or phrase beginning at the far left side of the strip of paper. They then fold back what they have written and pass their piece of paper to the next student. Then all students write a second word or phrase according to instructions, fold that back, and pass the paper on. This procedure continues until the sentences are completed. Students may read their sentences aloud or put them on the bulletin board.

Some sample instructions that the teacher may give are:

a. Write a possessive adjective, masculine singular.

b. Write a masculine singular adjective that precedes a noun.

c. Write a masculine singular noun.

d. Write a verb in the present tense, third-person singular (**il** form). Choose a verb that takes a direct object.

e. Write an expression of quantity.

f. Write a feminine plural noun.

g. Write a feminine plural adjective that follows a noun.

Possible sentences:

**Mon grand sac mange beaucoup de dames furieuses.**

**Notre joli fromage choisit peu de trompettes rouges.**

## THÈMES ET CATÉGORIES

The teacher divides the class into several teams and assigns each team a section of the chalkboard. The first person of each team goes to the board and the teacher announces a category. The students at the board write as many words as they can think of in that category in ten seconds. After they return to their seats, a second student from each team goes to the board. The teacher announces a new category and the members of this group write as many words as they can think of in ten seconds. When every member of the team has been to the board, the class checks all the teams' entries and counts them. The team with the most correct words is the winner. If desired, the class can subtract the number of wrong words from the correct ones in calculating the team score. The teacher may use the themes of the *Vocabulaires spécialisés* as categories.

## 5.3 Poems and Songs

Poems and songs are a lively way to practice pronunciation, reinforce grammar, and teach French culture. It is helpful to present some background information on each poem or song before the students read or sing it. Songs with which the students are familiar and that emphasize repetition, such as **Alouette** and **Frère Jacques,** are best at the start. The unit songs recorded on the Tape Program (with music and lyrics printed in the Activity Masters) can serve to introduce songs into the classroom. Songs are a helpful and pleasant diversion, especially around the holiday season.

## 5.4 Cultural Activities

The opportunities for exposing students to French culture are numerous both in and outside the classroom.

**5.4.1 Inside the classroom.** For in-class activities, students could prepare an authentic French party with French pastries or prepare an authentic French meal.

During Foreign Language Week celebrations, a class may organize and run a French café. The teacher can, of course, arrange for pen pals in a French-speaking country.

**5.4.2 Outside the classroom.** Cultural field trips are also a good way to provide an introduction to French culture. In order for these outside activities to be successful, to have an impact on the students, and to make them see and experience the relevance of French, they need to be carefully planned. Students could be given special assignments such as outside reading, research, etc. and could report to the class before the trip. Or, the assignment could be given to everyone for homework. Some possible ideas for trips are:

- *Going to a French restaurant.* The teacher could call the restaurant a few days before the trip and get copies of the menu for the students. Ideally a trip such as this would immediately follow a unit on food.
- *Visiting the French wing of an art museum.* Students will learn something of art and French history.
- *Going to French movies and plays.* Except in the case of dubbed or sub-titled movies, or plays translated into English, the teacher will have to thoroughly prepare the students for what they will be seeing.
- *Taking a vacation trip to a French-speaking country.* For those people living in the Northeast, such a trip may be very affordable. Long weekends in Montreal and Quebec will expose students to a neighboring French-speaking population.

# Part Four
## Reference Guide for BONJOUR!

This part of the teacher's manual contains reference materials for easy accessibility.

## 6. Useful Expressions

The teacher who wishes to conduct the class entirely in French may use the following vocabulary supplements.

### 6.1 Classroom Expressions

These classroom expressions may be duplicated and distributed to the students.

### 6.1.1 Vocabulaire

**Sur le pupitre**

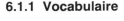   

un stylo      un crayon      un cahier      une feuille de papier      un sac

une gomme      une règle      un livre      un objet *object*      une chose *thing*

**Dans la classe**

un morceau de craie      un pupitre      un tableau noir      un écran      une chaise      une mini-cassette

un projecteur      un tableau d'affichage      une affiche      un magnétophone      un haut-parleur      une carte      un taille-crayon

## 6.1.2 Les matières

| | |
|---|---|
| l'anglais | *English* |
| les maths (mathématiques) | *math* |
|   l'algèbre | *algebra* |
|   la géométrie | *geometry* |
| les sciences | *science* |
|   la biologie | *biology* |
|   la chimie | *chemistry* |
|   la physique | *physics* |
| les sciences sociales | *social science* |
|   la géographie | *geography* |
|   l'histoire | *history* |
| l'allemand | *German* |
| l'espagnol | *Spanish* |
| le français | *French* |
| l'italien | *Italian* |
| le latin | *Latin* |
| le dessin | *art* |
| la musique | *music* |
| les travaux manuels | *shop* |
| la gymnastique | *gym* |
| le sport | *sports* |
| la cuisine | *cooking* |
| la couture | *sewing* |

## 6.1.3 Expressions pour la classe

| | |
|---|---|
| Écoutez (bien). | *Listen (carefully).* |
| Écoutez la bande. | *Listen to the tape.* |
| Répétez. (Ne répétez pas.) | *Repeat. (Don't repeat.)* |
| Parlez plus fort. | *Speak up. Speak louder.* |
| Écoutez la question. | *Listen to the question.* |
| Répondez. (Ne répondez pas.) | *Answer. (Don't answer.)* |
| Venez ici (devant la classe). | *Come here (in front of the class).* |
| Prenez le rôle de . . . | *Take the part of . . .* |
| Jouez le rôle de . . . | *Play the part of . . .* |
| Commencez. | *Begin.* |
| Merci. | *Thank you.* |
| Asseyez-vous. | *Sit down.* |
| Prenez votre livre (votre cahier). | *Take out your books (your notebooks).* |
| Ouvrez votre livre (votre cahier) à la page . . . | *Open your books (your notebooks) to page . . .* |
| Fermez votre livre (votre cahier). | *Close your books (your notebooks).* |
| Prenez un stylo (un crayon). | *Take out a pen (a pencil).* |

| | |
|---|---|
| **Prenez du papier.** | *Take out some paper.* |
| **Lisez (à haute voix).** | *Read (aloud).* |
| **Continuez.** | *Continue.* |
| **Écrivez. (N'écrivez pas.)** | *Write (Don't write.)* |
| **Levez-vous.** | *Get up.* |
| **Allez au tableau.** | *Go to the board.* |
| **Effacez.** | *Erase.* |
| **Regardez le tableau.** | *Look at the board.* |
| **Regardez-moi.** | *Look at me.* |
| **Faites attention.** | *Pay attention.* |
| **Silence.** | *Silence.* |
| **Taisez-vous.** | *Quiet.* |
| **Attention à la prononciation (l'orthographe).** | *Careful with the pronunciation (spelling).* |
| **Dites . . .** | *Say . . .* |
| **Tous ensemble.** | *All together.* |
| **Tout le monde.** | *Everyone.* |
| **Encore une fois.** | *Once more.* |
| **C'est bien.** | *That's good.* |
| **C'est très bien.** | *That's very good.* |
| **Ce n'est pas ça.** | *That's not it.* |
| **Essayez encore une fois.** | *Try once more.* |
| **Pour demain . . .** | *For tomorrow . . .* |
| **Pour la prochaine fois . . .** | *For the next time . . .* |
| **Préparez . . .** | *Prepare . . .* |
| **Faites l'exercice (les exercices) . . .** | *Do the exercise (the exercises) . . .* |
| **Je ne sais pas.** | *I don't know.* |
| **Je ne comprends pas.** | *I don't understand.* |
| **Répétez, s'il vous plaît.** | *Please repeat.* |
| **Que veut dire . . .?** | *What does . . . mean?* |
| **Comment dit-on . . .?** | *How do you say . . .?* |

# 7. Detailed Listing of the Contents

This section lists the contents of BONJOUR! in chart form. The teacher will find these charts useful in preparing course objectives, lesson plans, study guides, and tests. As the course progresses, the teacher may use the charts to recall where specific structures, vocabulary, sounds, or cultural topics were introduced. Lists have been established under the following headings: Structure, Vocabulary, Pronunciation, and Culture.

## 7.1 Structure

These charts list the grammar sections of the Student Text and cross-reference the related exercises in the Text, Workbook, and Tapescript.

| Structures | Text Exercises | Workbook Exercises | Tapescript Exercises |
|---|---|---|---|
| Unit 1   Parlez-vous français? | | | |
| 1.1   A. Les verbes en -er | | | |
| B. Le pronom sujet je | 1 | | 2 |
| C. L'élision | 2, 3 | C1 | |
| D. La négation avec ne . . . pas | 4, 5, 6 | D1, D2 | 3, 4, 5 |
| 1.2   A. Les pronoms sujets: il, elle, ils, elles | 1, 2, 3 4, 5, 6 | A1, A2, A3 | 2, 3, 4, 5 |
| B. Questions à réponse affirmative ou négative | 7, 8 | B1, B2 | 6, 7, 8 |
| 1.3   A. Les pronoms sujets: je, tu, nous, vous | 1, 2, 3 | A1, A2, A3 | 2, 3, 4, 5 |
| B. Questions d'information | 4, 5 | B1, B2, B3 | 7, 8, 9 |
| 1.4   A. Tu ou vous? | 1, 2 | A1 | 2 |
| B. Le présent des verbes réguliers en -er | 3, 4, 5 | B1 | 3, 4, 5, 6 |
| C. La construction: verbe + infinitif | 6, 7, 8 | C1, C2, C3 | 7, 8 |
| 1.5   A. Le verbe être | 1, 2 | A1, A2 | 3, 4, 6 |
| B. Qui? | 3 | B1 | |
| C. Expressions interrogatives avec qui | 4 | C1 | |
| D. L'interrogation avec inversion | 5, 6, 7 | D1 | 7, 8 |
| Unit 2   Salut, les amis! | | | |
| 2.1   A. Noms masculins, noms féminins; l'article indéfini: un/une | 1, 2 | A1, A2 | 3, 5 |
| B. L'article défini: le/la | 3, 4 | B1 | 6 |
| C. L'accord des adjectifs | 5, 6 | C1, C2 | 7, 8, 9, 10 |
| 2.2   A. Le genre des noms: les objets | 1, 2, 3, 4 | A1, A2, A3 | 3, 4 |
| B. Le verbe avoir | 5, 6 | B1 | 5 |
| C. L'article indéfini dans les phrases négatives | 7, 8, 9 | C1 | 6, 7 |

| | Structures | Text Exercises | Workbook Exercises | Tapescript Exercises |
|---|---|---|---|---|
| 2.3 | A. La place des adjectifs | 1, 2, 3 | A1, A2 | 2, 4, 5 |
| | B. *Il est* ou *c'est?* | 4, 5, 6 | B1, B2, B3 | 6, 7, 8 |
| 2.4 | A. L'article défini avec les noms géographiques | 1, 2 | A1 | |
| | B. Le pluriel: les noms et les articles | 3, 4, 5, 6 | B1 | 3, 4, 5 |
| | C. Le pluriel: les adjectifs | 7, 8 | C1 | 6, 7, 8 |
| | D. L'expression *il y a* | 9 | D1, D2 | 9 |
| | E. Récapitulation: la forme des adjectifs | 10 | E1 | |
| 2.5 | A. Les expressions impersonnelles avec *c'est* | 1, 2 | A1 | 2, 3 |
| | B. Les pronoms accentués | 3, 4, 5, 6 | B1, B2, B3, B4 | 4, 5, 6, 7 |
| **Unit 3** | **Loisirs et vacances** | | | |
| 3.1 | A. Le verbe *aller* | 1, 2 | A1 | 2, 3 |
| | B. *À* + l'article défini | 4, 5, 6 | B1, B2, B3 | 5, 6 |
| | C. *Aller* + l'infinitif | 7, 8 | C1, C2 | 7, 8, 9 |
| | Révision: *avoir* et *être* | AR | | |
| 3.2 | A. *Chez* | 1, 2, 3 | A1, A2 | 2, 3, 4 |
| | B. La possession avec *de* | 4, 5, 6 | B1 | 5, 6 |
| | C. *De* + l'article défini | 7, 8 | C1, C2 | 7, 8 |
| | D. *Jouer à* et *jouer de* | 9 | D1 | 9 |
| 3.3 | A. Les adjectifs possessifs: *mon, ma, mes; ton, ta, tes* | 1, 2, 3, 4 | A1, A2 | 4, 5 |
| | B. L'âge | 5 | B1 | 6 |
| | C. La construction: nom + *de* + nom | 6 | C1 | 7, 8 |
| 3.4 | A. L'adjectif possessif: *son, sa, ses* | 1, 2, 3 | A1 | 3, 4, 5 |
| | B. L'adjectif possessif: *leur, leurs* | 4 | B1, B2 | 6, 7 |
| | C. Les nombres ordinaux | 5 | C1 | 8 |
| 3.5 | A. Les adjectifs possessifs: *notre, nos; votre, vos* | 1 | A1 | 5 |
| | B. Récapitulation: les adjectifs possessifs | 2, 3 | B1, B2 | 2, 3, 4 |
| | C. *Être à* | 4, 5 | C1 | 6 |
| **Unit 4** | **En ville** | | | |
| 4.1 | A. Les verbes réguliers en *-ir* | 1, 2, 3 | A1, A2 | 2, 3 |
| | B. L'expression interrogative *qu'est-ce que* | 4 | B1 | 4 |
| | Révision: les nombres | AR | | |
| | C. Les nombres de 60 à 100 | 5, 6, 7 | C1, C2 | 5, 6 |
| | D. Les expressions interrogatives *combien* et *combien de* | 8, 9 | | 7 |
| 4.2 | A. *Acheter* | 2 | A1 | 2 |
| | B. Les nombres de 100 à 1.000.000 | 3 | | 8, 9 |
| | C. L'adjectif interrogatif *quel?* | 4, 5 | C1 | |
| | D. L'adjectif démonstratif *ce* | 6, 7, 8 | D1, D2 | 5, 6, 7 |

| | Structures | Text Exercises | Workbook Exercises | Tapescript Exercises |
|---|---|---|---|---|
| 4.3 | A. Les adjectifs *vieux, nouveau* et *beau* | 2, 3 | A1 | 4 |
| | B. La comparaison avec les adjectifs | 4, 5, 6 | B1, B2 | 5, 6, 7 |
| 4.4 | A. Expressions avec *avoir* | 1, 2 | A1, A2 | 2, 3, 4 |
| | B. Les expressions *avoir envie de, avoir besoin de* | 3, 4, 5 | B1 | 5, 7 |
| | C. Le superlatif | 6, 7 | C1, C2 | 6 |
| 4.5 | A. Les verbes réguliers en *-re* | 1 | A1 | 2, 3 |
| | B. Le pronom *on* | 2, 3, 4 | B1, B2 | 4, 5, 6, 8 |
| | C. Les prépositions avec les noms de pays | 5 | C1 | 9 |

## 7.2 Vocabulary

This chart summarizes the contents of the *Vocabulaire spécialisé* sections.

| Vocabulary Topic | Lesson | Page(s) |
|---|---|---|
| Les nombres | | |
|   Les achats et les nombres de 0 à 10 | P.3 | 16 |
|   Les nombres de 11 à 60 | P.3 | 20 |
| | Appendix 2 | 401 |
| L'heure, la date et le temps | | |
|   L'heure | P.4 | 24 |
|   L'heure et les minutes | P.4 | 26 |
|   La date | P.5 | 30 |
|   Le temps et les saisons | P.6 | 36 |
|   Quand? | 4.2 | 196 |

## 7.3 Pronunciation

The following list shows where specific phonemes (sounds), phonetic features, and sound-spelling correspondences are presented. Some consonants that show only slight phonetic differences between French and English have not been given individual attention and practice. See also the Sound-spelling Correspondences chart, Appendix 1.

| Phonemes | Page(s) |
|---|---|
| Oral vowels | |
| /a/ | 49 |
| /i/ | 49 |
| /u/ | 70 |
| /y/ | 70 |
| /o/ | 167 |
| /ɔ/ | 113 |
| /e/ | 77 |
| /ɛ/ | 77, 197 |
| /ə/ | 197 |
| /ø/ | 155 |
| /œ/ | 161 |
| Nasal vowels | |
| /ɑ̃/ | 106, 122 |
| /ɔ̃/ | 63 |
| /ɛ̃/ | 99, 122 |
| /œ̃/ | 122 |
| Semi-vowels | |
| /w/ | 128 |
| /j/ | 211 |
| Consonants | |
| /r/ | 56 |
| /ʒ/ | 139 |
| /ʃ/ | 146 |
| /k/ | 189 |

| Special Features | Page(s) |
|---|---|
| Les lettres muettes | 6 |
| L'alphabet | 12 |
| Les signes orthographiques | 12 |
| Les nombres de 1 à 10 | 18 |
| La liaison | 24 |
| Rythme et accent | 32 |
| L'intonation | 38 |
| Voyelles nasales | 218 |

## 7.4 Culture

This chart lists the cultural topic of each *Note culturelle* and of each *Section Magazine* reading selection. A specific cultural reading may be listed more than once if its topic fits different categories.

| Topic | Section Magazine | Note culturelle |
|---|---|---|
| Le monde francophone | | |
| Les Canadiens français | | 43 |
| Qui parle français en Afrique? | | 59 |
| Qui parle français en Europe? | | 65 |
| Qui parle français dans le monde? | | 73 |
| Bon voyage! | 80 | |
| Oui, ils parlent français! | 87 | |
| La carte du temps | 88 | |

| Topic | Section Magazine | Note culturelle |
|---|---|---|
| **La France: le pays** | | |
| Bonjour, la France! | | 35 |
| En France | 82 | |
| Nice | | 3 |
| Annecy | | 8 |
| Tours | | 15 |
| Dijon | | 22 |
| La Martinique | | 51 |
| La Guadeloupe | | 115 |
| **Aspects de la vie** | | |
| Salutations et présentations | | |
| Bonjour! | | 5 |
| Bonjour, Monsieur! Bonjour, Madame! Bonjour, Mademoiselle! | | 5 |
| Niveaux de langue | | 9 |
| Bonjour, Christine! | 85 | |
| Les noms | | |
| Les noms français | | 10 |
| Boîte aux lettres | 86 | |
| Claude et Dominique | | 92 |
| Les noms à la mode | 172 | |
| La langue | | |
| Niveaux de langue | | 9 |
| Je parle français. | 84 | |
| Parlez-vous français? | 84 | |
| Une surprise-partie | | 92 |
| L'américanisation | | 141 |
| Paris-Match | | 15 |
| L'argent français | | 17 |
| Le système métrique | | 36 |
| Professions | | |
| Boîte aux lettres | 86 | |
| La cuisine | | |
| Le Coca-Cola | | 15 |
| Le café | | 22 |
| Le téléphone | | 279 |
| Les animaux | | |
| Ils parlent français! | 89 | |
| Nos meilleurs amis | 178 | |
| Les fêtes | | |
| Les fêtes françaises | | 29 |
| Mardi Gras | | 115 |

## 8. Overprint Symbols and Codes

The following symbols and codes are used in the overprint to cue the use of the various components of the BONJOUR! program.

 material recorded on the Cassette Program

WB    additional exercises in the Workbook

SCRIPT
 additional activities in the Cassette Program with text in the Tapescript

MASTERS    answer sheets for written activities in the Cassette Program and additional activities in the Activity Masters

visual material on the Overhead Transparencies

QUIZ    indicates a *Lesson Quiz* in the Testing Program

TEST    indicates a *Unit Test* in the Testing Program

ACHIEVEMENT
TEST    indicates an *Achievement Test* in the Testing Program

 This symbol is used to signal ***Activités*** suitable for writing.

# 9. Correlation of BONJOUR! Components

## PRÉLUDE

| | Workbook | Tapescript | Cassette Program | Activity Masters | Overhead Trans-parencies | Testing Duplicating/Copy Masters and Cassettes | Test Guide — Recording Script | Test Guide — Answer Key |
|---|---|---|---|---|---|---|---|---|
| Les. 1 | Acts. 1, 2, 3, 4 | p. 1 Acts. 1–7 | Cassette 1 Side 1 | p. 1 Acts. 5, 6 | nos. 1, 2, 3 (maps) | p. 1 Lesson Quiz 1 Cassette 1, Side 1 | p. 9 Lesson Quiz 1 Part 1 | p. 30 Lesson Quiz 1 |
| Les. 2 | Acts. 1, 2, 3 | p. 1 Acts. 1–6 | Cassette 1 Side 1 | p. 2 Acts. 3, 5, 6 | no. 4 | p. 2 Lesson Quiz 2 Cassette 1, Side 1 | p. 9 Lesson Quiz 2 Part 1 | p. 30 Lesson Quiz 2 |
| Les. 3 | Acts. 1, 2, 3, 4 | pp. 1–2 Acts. 1–6 | Cassette 1 Side 2 | p. 3 Acts. 3, 6 | | p. 3 Lesson Quiz 3 Cassette 1, Side 1 | p. 9 Lesson Quiz 3 Part 1 | p. 30 Lesson Quiz 3 |
| Les. 4 | Acts. 1, 2, 3 | p. 2 Acts. 1–6 | Cassette 1 Side 2 | pp. 4–5 Acts. 2, 4, 5, 6 | nos. 5, 6, 7, 8 | p. 4 Lesson Quiz 4 Cassette 1, Side 1 | p. 9 Lesson Quiz 4 Part 1 | p.30 Lesson Quiz 4 |
| Les. 5 | Acts. 1, 2, 3 | pp. 2–3 Acts. 1–7 | Cassette 2 Side 1 | p. 6 Acts. 3, 4, 5 | | p. 5 Lesson Quiz 5 Cassette 1, Side 1 | p. 10 Lesson Quiz 5 Part 1 | p. 30 Lesson Quiz 5 |
| Les. 6 | Acts. 1, 2, 3 | p. 3 Acts. 1–5 | Cassette 2 Side 2 | p. 7 Acts. 3, 4 | no. 9 | p. 6 Lesson Quiz 6 Cassette 1, Side 1 | p. 10 Lesson Quiz 6 Part 1 | pp. 30–31 Lesson Quiz 6 |
| End of Unit | Récréation culturelle  Le coin des jeux  Tests de contrôle | | Cassette 2 Side 2 Song Les Champs-Élysées | p. 52 Song Les Champs-Élysées  pp. 62–64 Games 1–4  p. 100 Active Vocabulary Sheet | | pp. 7–11 Unit Test PRÉLUDE Cassette 3, Side 1 | p. 21 Unit Test PRÉLUDE Tests 1–3 | p. 39 Unit Test PRÉLUDE |

# UNIT 1

| | Workbook | Tapescript | Cassette Program | Activity Masters | Overhead Trans-parencies | Testing Duplicating/Copy Masters and Cassettes | Test Guide — Recording Script | Test Guide — Answer Key |
|---|---|---|---|---|---|---|---|---|
| Les. 1 | C1, D1, D2 | pp. 3–4 Acts. 1–8 | Cassette 3 Side 1 | p. 8 Acts. 4, 7 | nos. 10, 11, 13, 34 | pp. 12–13 *Lesson Quiz 1* Cassette 1, Side 1 | p. 10 *Lesson Quiz 1* Part 1 | p. 31 *Lesson Quiz 1* |
| Les. 2 | A1, A2, A3, B1, B2 | pp. 4–5 Acts. 1–10 | Cassette 3 Side 2 | p. 9 Acts. 3, 6, 9 | nos. 12, 13 | p. 14 *Lesson Quiz 2* Cassette 1, Side 1 | p. 10 *Lesson Quiz 2* Part 1 | p. 31 *Lesson Quiz 2* |
| Les. 3 | A1, A2, A3, B1, B2, B3 | pp. 5–6 Acts. 1–11 | Cassette 4 Side 1 | p. 10 Acts. 3, 10 | | pp. 15–16 *Lesson Quiz 3* Cassette 1, Side 1 | p. 11 *Lesson Quiz 3* Part 1 | p. 31 *Lesson Quiz 3* |
| Les. 4 | A1, B1, C1, C2, C3 | pp. 6–7 Acts. 1–10 | Cassette 4 Side 2 | p. 11 Acts. 2, 9 | nos. 12, 13 | pp. 17–18 *Lesson Quiz 4* Cassette 1, Side 1 | p. 11 *Lesson Quiz 4* Part 1 | p.31 *Lesson Quiz 4* |
| Les. 5 | A1, A2, B1, C1, D1 | pp. 7–8 Acts. 1–10 | Cassette 5 Side 1 | p. 12 Acts. 3, 6, 7, 9 | | p. 19 *Lesson Quiz 5* Cassette 1, Side 1 | p. 11 *Lesson Quiz 5* Part 1 | p. 31 *Lesson Quiz 5* |
| End of Unit | Récréation culturelle  Le coin des jeux  Tests de contrôle | | Cassette 5 Side 1 *Song Alouette* | p. 53 *Song Alouette*  pp. 65–66 Games 1–4  p. 101 Active Vocabulary Sheet | | pp. 20–23 *Unit Test 1* Cassette 3, Side 1 | p. 22 *Unit Test 1* Tests 1–3 | pp. 39–40 *Unit Test 1* |
| Sec. Mag. 1 | | | | pp. 85–88 Reading Activities | | | | |

# UNIT 2

| | Workbook | Tapescript | Cassette Program | Activity Masters | Overhead Transparencies | Testing Duplicating/Copy Masters and Cassettes | Test Guide — Recording Script | Test Guide — Answer Key |
|---|---|---|---|---|---|---|---|---|
| Les. 1 | A1, A2, B1, C1, C2, Auto-portrait | pp. 8–9 Acts. 1–12 | Cassette 5 Side 2 | pp. 13–14 Acts. 3, 8, 9, 11 | | pp. 24–25 Lesson Quiz 1 Cassette 1, Side 2 | p. 11 Lesson Quiz 1 Part 1 | pp. 31–32 Lesson Quiz 1 |
| Les. 2 | A1, A2, A3, V1, B1, C1, Vos possessions | pp. 9–10 Acts. 1–9 | Cassette 6 Side 1 | p. 15 Acts. 3, 4, 8 | nos. 14, 15, 16 | pp. 26–27 Lesson Quiz 2 Cassette 1, Side 2 | p. 12 Lesson Quiz 2 Part 1 | p. 32 Lesson Quiz 2 |
| Les. 3 | A1, A2, B1, B2, B3, La voiture familiale | p. 10 Acts. 1–10 | Cassette 6 Side 2 | p. 16 Acts. 8, 9 | no. 17 | pp. 28–29 Lesson Quiz 3 Cassette 1, Side 2 | p. 12 Lesson Quiz 3 Part 1 | p. 32 Lesson Quiz 3 |
| Les. 4 | A1, B1, C1, D1, D2, E1, Votre chambre | p. 11 Acts. 1–11 | Cassette 7 Side 1 | p. 17 Acts. 4, 9, 10 | | pp. 30–31 Lesson Quiz 4 Cassette 1, Side 2 | p. 12 Lesson Quiz 4 Part 1 | p. 32 Lesson Quiz 4 |
| Les. 5 | A1, B1, B2, B3, B4, Occupations | pp. 11–12 Acts. 1–9 | Cassette 7 Side 2 | p. 18 Acts. 5, 8 | | p. 32 Lesson Quiz 5 Cassette 1, Side 2 | p. 12 Lesson Quiz 5 Part 1 | p. 32 Lesson Quiz 5 |
| End of Unit | Récréation culturelle Le coin des jeux Tests de contrôle | | Cassette 7 Side 2 Song Il y a un rat | p. 54 Song Il y a un rat pp. 67–68 Games 1–4 p. 102 Active Vocabulary Sheet | | pp. 33–37 Unit Test 2 Cassette 3, Side 1 | pp. 22–23 Unit Test 2 Tests 1–2 | p. 40 Unit Test 2 |

# UNIT 3

| | Workbook | Tapescript | Cassette Program | Activity Masters | Overhead Trans-parencies | Testing Duplicating/Copy Masters and Cassettes | Recording Script | Answer Key |
|---|---|---|---|---|---|---|---|---|
| | | | | | | | Test Guide | |
| Les. 1 | A1, B1, B2, B3, C1, C2 | pp. 12–13 Acts. 1–11 | Cassette 8 Side 1 | p. 19 Acts. 3, 5, 7, 10 | nos. 18, 19 | p. 38 Lesson Quiz 1 Cassette 1, Side 2 | p. 13 Lesson Quiz 1 Part 1 | pp. 32–33 Lesson Quiz 1 |
| Les. 2 | A1, A2, B1, C1, C2, D1, Et vous? | pp. 13–14 Acts. 1–11 | Cassette 8 Side 2 | p. 20 Acts. 3, 5, 7, 10 | nos. 20, 21, 35 | pp. 39–40 Lesson Quiz 2 Cassette 1, Side 1 | p. 13 Lesson Quiz 2 Part 1 | p. 33 Lesson Quiz 2 |
| Les. 3 | A1, A2, B1, C1, Famille | pp. 14–15 Acts. 1–10 | Cassette 9 Side 1 | p. 21 Acts. 3, 9 | no. 22 | pp. 41–42 Lesson Quiz 3 Cassette 1, Side 2 | p. 13 Lesson Quiz 3 Part 1 | p. 33 Lesson Quiz 3 |
| Les. 4 | A1, B1, B2, C1, La famille de mes amis | pp. 15–16 Acts. 1–10 | Cassette 9 Side 2 | p. 22 Acts. 4, 6, 8, 9 | no. 23 | pp. 43–44 Lesson Quiz 4 Cassette 1, Side 2 | p. 13 Lesson Quiz 4 Part 1 | p. 33 Lesson Quiz 4 |
| Les. 5 | A1, B1, B2, C1, Objets | pp. 16–17 Acts. 1–8 | Cassette 10 Side 1 | p. 23 Acts. 3, 4, 6, 7 | | p. 45 Lesson Quiz 5 Cassette 1, Side 2 | p. 14 Lesson Quiz 5 Part 1 | p. 33 Lesson Quiz 5 |
| End of Unit | Récréation culturelle<br><br>Le coin des jeux<br><br>Tests de contrôle | | Cassette 10 Side 1 Song Bonhomme, bonhomme | p. 55 Song Bonhomme, bonhomme pp. 69–70 Games 1–3 p. 103 Active Vocabulary Sheet | | pp. 46–49 Unit Test 3 Cassette 3, Side 2 | p. 23 Unit Test 3 Tests 1–2 | pp. 40–41 Unit Test 3 |
| Sec. Mag. 2 | | | | pp. 89–92 Reading Activities | | | | |

# UNIT 4

| | Workbook | Tapescript | Cassette Program | Activity Masters | Overhead Transparencies | Testing Duplicating/Copy Masters and Cassettes | Test Guide — Recording Script | Test Guide — Answer Key |
|---|---|---|---|---|---|---|---|---|
| Les. 1 | A1, A2, B1, C1, C2 | p. 17-18 Acts. 1-9 | Cassette 10 Side 2 | p. 24 Acts. 5, 6, 8 | | pp. 50-51 *Lesson Quiz 1* Cassette 2, Side 1 | p. 14 *Lesson Quiz 1* Part 1 | p. 34 *Lesson Quiz 1* |
| Les. 2 | V1, A1, C1, D1, D2, Projets | p. 18 Acts. 1-11 | Cassette 11 Side 1 | p. 25 Acts. 4, 6, 8, 9, 10 | nos. 7, 24 | pp. 52-53 *Lesson Quiz 2* Cassette 2, Side 1 | p. 14 *Lesson Quiz 2* Part 1 | p. 34 *Lesson Quiz 2* |
| Les. 3 | V1, A1, B1, B2 | pp. 18-19 Acts. 1-9 | Cassette 11 Side 2 | pp. 26-27 Acts. 3, 6, 7, 8 | no. 25 | p. 54 *Lesson Quiz 3* Cassette 2, Side 1 | p. 14 *Lesson Quiz 3* Part 1 | p. 34 *Lesson Quiz 3* |
| Les. 4 | A1, A2, B1, C1, C2 | pp. 19-20 Acts. 1-9 | Cassette 12 Side 1 | p. 28 Acts. 3, 5, 8 | | pp. 55-56 *Lesson Quiz 4* Cassette 2, Side 1 | p. 15 *Lesson Quiz 4* Part 1 | p.34 *Lesson Quiz 4* |
| Les. 5 | A1, B1, B2, V1, C1, Les jeunes américains | pp. 20-21 Acts. 1-11 | Cassette 12 Side 2 | p. 29 Acts. 8, 10 | no. 26 | p. 57 *Lesson Quiz 5* Cassette 2, Side 1 | p. 15 *Lesson Quiz 5* Part 1 | p. 34 *Lesson Quiz 5* |
| End of Unit | Récréation culturelle  Le coin des jeux  Tests de contrôle | | Cassette 12 Side 2 *Songs* Le coucou; Frère Jacques; Orléans, Beaugency | pp. 56-57 *Songs* Le coucou; Frère Jacques; Orléans, Beaugency pp. 71-73 Games 1-4 p. 104 Active Vocabulary Sheet | | pp. 58-61 *Unit Test 4* Cassette 3, Side 2 | pp. 23-24 *Unit Test 4* Tests 1-2 | pp. 41-42 *Unit Test 4* |
| | | | | | | pp. 62-70 *Achievement Test 1* Cassette 4, Side 2 | pp. 27-28 *Achievement Test 1* Tests 1-5 | pp. 45-46 *Achievement Test 1* |

# Bonjour!

## FRENCH FOR MASTERY

Jean-Paul Valette
Rebecca M. Valette

Illustrations by Mel Dietmeier

**D.C. HEATH AND COMPANY**
Lexington, Massachusetts / Toronto, Ontario

## TEACHER CONSULTANTS

Charlotte Casgrain, Greenwich H.S., Greenwich, Connecticut
Karen Fritsche, Lincoln-Sudbury Regional H.S., Sudbury, Massachusetts
Natalie Goldschmidt, South Eugene H.S., Eugene, Oregon
Debra Griffin, Monnig Middle School, Fort Worth, Texas

## ACKNOWLEDGMENTS

In preparation for this edition of FRENCH FOR MASTERY, a survey was taken of teachers using the first edition. The many questionnaires returned were very encouraging in their positive evaluation of the program and very helpful in that they provided a direction for the planning of the second edition. The authors would like to thank those who participated. We also wish to thank the following teachers, who have used FRENCH FOR MASTERY, for their special assistance in the project: Jane Carlin, Anne Craven, Pat McCann, Lillian Scherban, and Maria Valis.

The authors would like to thank François Vergne for helping them assemble the realia that appear in the text.

**EXECUTIVE EDITOR**
Roger D. Coulombe

**PROJECT EDITOR**
Lawrence Lipson

**PRODUCT SPECIALIST**
Teresa Carrera-Hanley

**D.C. HEATH CONSULTANTS**
Denise St. Jean
Alison King
Karen Ralston

**DESIGN AND PRODUCTION**
Josephine McGrath and Claudia E. Simon, *Book Designers*
Maureen LaRiccia, *Production Coordinator*

Chers amis:

Before you begin your study of French, it might be worthwhile to review the many good reasons for learning this language — or for that matter any other modern language.

In today's world, French is a widely used language spoken daily by about 150 million people and understood by many millions more. French speakers represent a wide variety of ethnic and cultural backgrounds. They live not only in France and other parts of Europe, but also in North America, in Africa . . . in fact on all continents. French is the official language or one of the official languages in more than 30 countries around the world. Knowing French can help you communicate with a large and diverse segment of the modern world.

French is also the language used by great philosophers, writers, and artists whose ideas have helped shape our own ways of thinking and feeling. The knowledge of French may help you better understand these ideas and, therefore, the world in which we live.

Another important reason to study French, or any other language, is that language is a very important part of culture. In learning a language you not only learn how other people express themselves but also how they live and what they think. This insight into another culture is important in a world where people of different backgrounds live in close contact. Your experience in learning French will also help you understand your own language and your own culture. It is often by comparing ourselves with others — by investigating how we differ and how we are similar — that we begin to learn who we really are.

Last but not least, French is an important world language used in business and in the professions. A knowledge of another language is important not only to translators and foreign language teachers but also to the many people — secretaries, sales representatives, accountants, lawyers — who work in companies that do business with French-speaking countries and to many employees in our government's foreign service.

As you can see, knowing French is not an end in itself, but a step toward several worthwhile objectives: communication with others, increased knowledge of the world in which we live, better understanding of ourselves . . . and maybe an extra advantage when you are looking for a job!

Now let's start . . .

En avant et bon courage!

*Jean-Paul Valette*    *Rebecca M. Valette*

# Bonjour! Je m'appelle . . .

| | | | |
|---|---|---|---|
| | Geoffroy | Marc | Raphaël |
| | Georges | Matthieu | Raymond |
| | Gilbert | Michel | Richard |
| | Grégoire | Nicolas | Robert |
| | Guillaume | Olivier | Roger |
| | Henri | Patrick | Samuel |
| | Hugues | Paul | Simon |
| Alain | Jacques | Philippe | Thomas |
| Albert | Jean | Pierre | Vincent |
| André | Jean-Claude | Raoul | Yves |
| Antoine | Jean-François | | |
| Bernard | Jean-Louis | | |
| Charles | Jean-Paul | | |
| Christian | Jean-Philippe | | |
| Christophe | Jean-Pierre | | |
| Claude | Jérôme | | |
| Daniel | Joël | | |
| David | Joseph | | |
| Denis | Laurent | | |
| Édouard | Léon | | |
| Étienne | Louis | | |
| François | Luc | | |

# Je m'appelle . . .

| | | | |
|---|---|---|---|
| | Claire | Marianne | Marie-Thérèse |
| | Denise | Marie | Marthe |
| | Diane | Marie-Anne | Michèle |
| | Dominique | Marie-Hélène | Monique |
| | Éléonore | Marie-Louise | Nathalie |
| | Élisabeth | | Nicole |
| | Émilie | | Patricia |
| Agnès | Ève | | Pauline |
| Alice | Françoise | | Rachel |
| Andrée | Geneviève | | Renée |
| Anne | Hélène | | Rose |
| Anne-Marie | Irène | | Sophie |
| Annette | Isabelle | | Suzanne |
| Barbara | Janine | | Sylvie |
| Béatrice | Jeanne | | Thérèse |
| Brigitte | Joséphine | | Virginie |
| Caroline | Judith | | Viviane |
| Catherine | Laure | | |
| Cécile | Lise | | |
| Chantal | Louise | | |
| Charlotte | Lucie | | |
| Christine | Marguerite | | |

Yves?
Guy?
Jean?
Henri?
Jacques?
Sébastien?
Jean-Paul?
Lucien?
Guillaume?
Philippe?
Charles?
Armand?
Gérard?
Pierre?
Jean-Pierre?
Eugène?
André?
Georges?
François?
Michel?
Paul?
Marc?
Luc?

# Bonjour, le monde français!

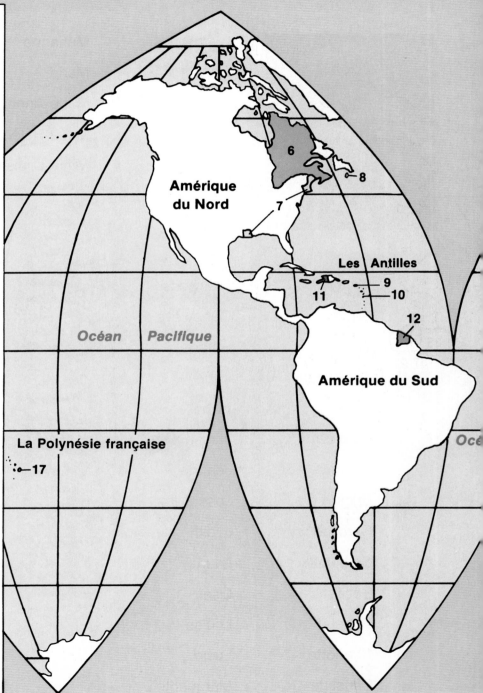

**Europe**
1. (la) France
2. Monaco
3. (la) Belgique
4. (la) Suisse
5. (le) Luxembourg

**Amérique du Nord**
6. (le) Canada:
   (le) Québec
7. (les) États-Unis:
   (la) Louisiane
   (la) Nouvelle-Angleterre
8. Saint-Pierre-et-Miquelon

**Amérique centrale,
Amérique du Sud**
9. (la) Guadeloupe
10. (la) Martinique
11. Haïti
12. (la) Guyane française

**Asie et Océanie**
13. (le) Cambodge
14. (le) Laos
15. (le) Viêt-nam
16. (la) Nouvelle-Calédonie
17. (la) Polynésie française:
    Tahiti

**Afrique**
18. (l') Algérie
19. (le) Bénin
20. (le) Burundi
21. (le) Cameroun
22. (la) Côte-d'Ivoire
23. (le) Gabon
24. (la) Guinée
25. (la) Haute-Volta / (le) Burkina
    Faso
26. Madagascar
27. (le) Mali
28. (le) Maroc
29. (la) Mauritanie
30. (le) Niger
31. (la) République centrafricaine
32. (la) République populaire du
    Congo
33. (la) République rwandaise
34. (la) Réunion
35. (le) Sénégal
36. (le) Tchad
37. (le) Togo
38. (la) Tunisie
39. (le) Zaïre

Amérique
du Nord

Les Antilles

Océan    Pacifique

Amérique du Sud

La Polynésie française

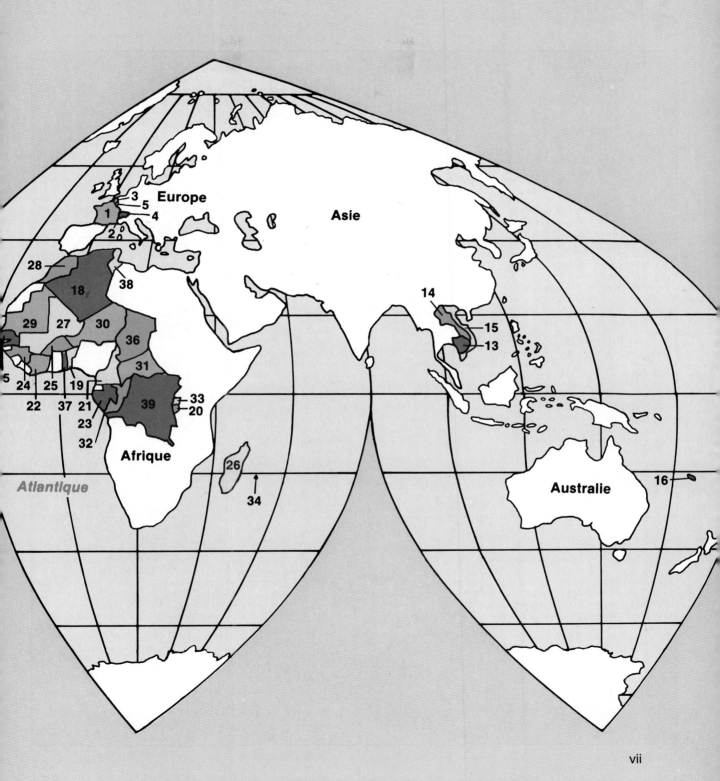

Europe

Asie

Australie

Afrique

Atlantique

3
5
1
4
2

28
18
38

29
27
30
36
31

5
24
25
19
22
37
21
23
32

39

33
20

26
34

14
15
13

16

# Bonjour, la France!

3

MER DU NORD

ANGLETERRE

HOLLANDE

ALLEMAGNE

BELGIQUE

La Manche

Lille

LUXEMBOURG

Le Havre

Seine

Meuse

Brest

Paris ★

Nancy

Strasbourg

VOSGES

Colmar

Loire

Nantes

Tours

Dijon

Saône

JURA

SUISSE

OCÉAN ATLANTIQUE

FRANCE

Vichy

Annecy

Lyon

Aix-les-Bains

ITALIE

Clermont-Ferrand

Grenoble

Bordeaux

Garonne

MASSIF CENTRAL

Valence

ALPES

Rhône

MONACO

Toulouse

Avignon

Aix-en-Provence

Nice

Cannes

Marseille

Toulon

PYRÉNÉES

ESPAGNE

MER MÉDITERRANÉE

CORSE

Ajaccio

# Contents

## Unité 2   Salut, les amis!

# Bonjour!

OBJECTIVES

The purpose of this preliminary unit is to introduce the students to the French language and French sounds through the presentation of a few stock phrases and other items that young people are generally eager to learn and will remember easily.

1. Greetings
2. Introductions
3. Numbers from 0 to 60
4. Time of day
5. Dates: days of the week and months of the year
6. Weather and the seasons

No formal grammar is presented in this unit. If you wish to begin your teaching of French with formal grammar, you may choose to start with Unité 1, which focuses on verbs. Then you may come back to these preliminary lessons as you progress through the book. The points at which you may present or review these materials are indicated in the overprint.

You may also wish to introduce the Classroom Expressions given in the teacher's manual (Part Four) and in the Activity Masters.

Note: References in the overprint to the Unités or to specific pages in the Unités may be either to BONJOUR! (pp. 1–219) or to EN AVANT! (pp. 180–398).

# PRÉLUDE
# Bonjour, les Français!

# Leçon 1  Bonjour!

Act. 1

SCRIPT
Act. 2

**À Nice . . . le premier jour de classe**
— Bonjour, Paul!
— Bonjour, Anne!

— Salut, Marc!
— Salut, Suzanne!

— Au revoir, Jacques!
— Au revoir, Monique!

— Qui est-ce?
— C'est Janine.

— Voici Philippe.
— Bonjour!

— Voilà Nathalie.
— Salut!

**Paul**

**Anne**

**Marc**

**Suzanne**

**Janine**

**Philippe**

**Jacques**

**Monique**

**Nathalie**

Act. 3

— Voici Monsieur Laval.
— Voici Madame Simonet.
— Voici Mademoiselle Rochette.

— Bonjour, Monsieur!
— Bonjour, Madame!
— Bonjour, Mademoiselle!

— Au revoir, Monsieur!
— Au revoir, Madame!
— Au revoir, Mademoiselle!

Monsieur Laval

Madame Simonet

Mademoiselle Rochette

**Hello!**

**In Nice . . . the first day of school**
Hello, Paul!
Hello, Anne!

Hi, Marc!
Hi, Suzanne!

Good-by, Jacques.
Good-by, Monique.

Who's that?
It's Janine.

Here's Philippe.
Hello!

There's Nathalie.
Hi!

Here's Mr. Laval.
Here's Mrs. Simonet.
Here's Miss Rochette.

Good morning, (Sir).
Good morning, (Ma'am).
Good morning, (Miss).

Good-by, (Sir).
Good-by, (Ma'am).
Good-by, (Miss).

## NOTE CULTURELLE   OPTIONAL

**Nice**   You may refer the students to the map of France on p. viii.
Nice, a popular resort on the French Riviera (**la Côte d'Azur**),
is one of the oldest cities in France. (It was founded by the
Greeks about 400 B.C.) Today Nice is a prosperous and
modern city. Every year its famous Mardi Gras celebrations
(**le Carnaval de Nice**) attract thousands of visitors.
Nice was named by the Greeks in honor of Nike, the goddess of victory.

Nice

Act. 4

You may point out that **bonjour** literally means *good day* and is used to say *hello* during the day. In the evening, the French say **bonsoir**.

## Vocabulaire spécialisé   Salutations *(Greetings)*

| | | |
|---|---|---|
| **Bonjour!** | *Hello!* | **Bonjour,** Jacques! |
| | *Good morning! Good afternoon!* | |
| **Salut!** | *Hi!* | **Salut,** Nathalie! |
| **Au revoir!** | *Good-by!* | **Au revoir,** Marc! |
| **Voici** . . . | *This is . . . Here's . . . Here comes . . .* | **Voici** Suzanne. |
| **Voilà** . . . | *That is . . . There's . . .* | **Voilà** Monsieur Laval. |
| **Qui est-ce?** | *Who's that? Who is it?* | **Qui est-ce?** |
| **C'est** . . . | *That's . . . It's . . .* | **C'est** Paul. |
| **Monsieur** | *Mr.* | **Voici Monsieur** Dumas. |
| **Madame** | *Mrs.* | **Voilà Madame** Pascal. |
| **Mademoiselle** | *Miss* | **Voilà Mademoiselle** Rochette. |

There is no French equivalent for the title "Ms."

You may point out that **voici** and **voilà** also correspond to *here are/come* and *there are.* **Voici Jacques et Nicole. Voilà Daniel et Suzanne.**

*Marie-Laure Ducamp*

*Dîner*

*Vendredi 17 Novembre*

*Réponse avant le 10 novembre*
*45-47, Rue Pauline Borghèse*
*92200 Neuilly*

. . . *écises*

FRANÇOIS F. VERGNE

258.12.49

85 RUE LA BOËTIE, 75008 PARIS

monsieur et madame georges malassis
25, av. gabriel péri - 94170 le perreux
tél. 872.69.59

**Note:** **Monsieur, Madame,** and **Mademoiselle** are often abbreviated **M., Mme,** and **Mlle** in writing.

WB
1

SCRIPT

Act. 5

MASTERS
p. 1

**4** Prélude

## NOTES CULTURELLES

**1. Bonjour!** In many situations the Americans and the French behave and react in very similar ways. However, in certain situations their behavior is different. Every morning, for instance, French children greet their parents not only by saying **bonjour**, but also by kissing them. Whenever French people meet, they shake hands, even if they meet more than once during the day. Teenagers, especially boys, also shake hands. Girls often greet one another with a kiss on each cheek.

**2. Bonjour, Monsieur! Bonjour, Madame! Bonjour, Mademoiselle!** On the whole, the relationships between adults and teenagers are much more formal in France than in the United States. It is, for instance, perfectly proper for American students to greet their teacher with "Good morning" or "Hi." French students, however, do not greet their teachers with a simple **Bonjour** and would not think of using the informal **Salut.** To a teacher it is customary to say **Bonjour, Monsieur** (or **Bonjour, Madame** or **Bonjour, Mademoiselle**).

You may have noted that the French do not use the last name when greeting a person. They say **Bonjour, Madame,** whereas English-speaking people would say "Hello, Mrs. Jones" or "Hello, Mrs. Smith."

The Panthéon, located in the Quartier Latin in Paris, is the burial place of Voltaire, Rousseau, Hugo, Zola, and La Fayette.

# Prononciation

Act. 7

**Les lettres muettes** *(The silent letters)*

Many letters in written French are not pronounced. These are called *silent letters*.

The **e** at the end of a word is silent.[1]

    Moniqu~e~    Ann~e~

The **s** at the end of a word is silent.

    Deni~s~    Jacque~s~    Other examples: Loui~s~, Charle~s~, Françoi~s~

The letter **h** is not pronounced.    However, as in English, the letters **ph** represent the sound /f/: Philippe. The letters **ch** represent the sound /ʃ/: Michel.

    T~h~omas    Nat~h~alie    Other examples: T~h~érèse, Élisabet~h~, Judit~h~

Usually a consonant at the end of a word is not pronounced. Exceptions: **c, f, l,** and sometimes **r** (the consonants of **careful**).    If necessary, review the difference between vowels and consonants.
    *vowels:* a, e, i, o, u, y
    *consonants:* all other letters

| SILENT | PRONOUNCED |
|---|---|
| Bernar~d~ | Mar<u>c</u>,  Lu<u>c</u> |
| Rober~t~ | Madam~e~ Resti<u>f</u>,  Mad~e~moisell~e~ Lebeu<u>f</u> |
| Vincen~t~ | Miche<u>l</u>,  Danie<u>l</u> |
| Roge~r~ | Bonjou<u>r</u>, Victo<u>r</u>! |

**Note:** French is a relatively easy language to learn because it contains many words which are similar to English words. French, however, is *not* pronounced like English, and every letter is *not* pronounced as it is written. The **Prononciation** sections of your book will help you learn the French sound system. However, the best way to acquire a good French pronunciation is to listen to your teacher, listen to the tapes, and, whenever possible, listen to French people and French records.

## *ACTIVITÉ 1*   Bonjour! Au revoir!

It is the first day of school. The following French boys and girls meet and say "hello." After classes they say "good-by." Play the roles of these students, using the words in parentheses.    You may want to model the names for the students.

➡ (bonjour)
    Paul / Louis    Paul: **Bonjour, Louis!**    Only the underlined final consonants are pronounced.
                Louis: **Bonjour, Paul!**

(bonjour)
1. Annie / Philippe
2. Isabelle / Monique
3. Louise / Denise
4. Jacques / Nicolas
5. Louis / Denis

(salut)
6. Nathalie / Thomas
7. Janine / Charles
8. Georges / Anne
9. Yves / Élisabeth
10. Mar<u>c</u> / Sylvie

(au revoir)
11. Lu<u>c</u> / Miche<u>l</u>
12. Paul / Victo<u>r</u>
13. Chanta<u>l</u> / Catherine
14. Louis / Louise
15. Denis / Denise

    [1]The slant line (/) is used to remind you that a letter is not pronounced.

## ACTIVITÉ 2 Présentations *(Introductions)*

Annie is a new student, and Pierre is introducing his friends to her. Annie says "hello" to each one. Play the roles of Pierre and Annie according to the model.

→ Thomas     Pierre: **Voici Thomas.**
                    Annie: **Bonjour, Thomas!**

*You should model the names. The final consonant of each name is silent.*

1. Albert            3. Charles          5. Robert         7. Denis
2. Bernard         4. Édouard        6. Roger          8. Vincent

VARIATION:   Pierre: **Voilà Thomas.**
                  Annie: **Salut, Thomas!**

## ACTIVITÉ 3 Les professeurs    OPTIONAL

Annie now asks Pierre who the teachers are. She greets them. Play the roles according to the model.

WB 2, 3

SCRIPT
Act. 6

MASTERS
p. 1

→ Madame Dumas     Annie: **Qui est-ce?**
                         Pierre: **C'est Madame Dumas.**
                         Annie: **Bonjour, Madame!**

*These family names are common not only in France, but also in French-speaking Canada and Louisiana. Be sure your students do not pronounce the final consonants. Remind them that they should not use last names when greeting these people.*

1. Madame Camus         4. Madame Michaud       7. Madame Brunet
2. Mademoiselle Ledoux    5. Monsieur Denis          8. Monsieur Lucas
3. Monsieur Simonet       6. Mademoiselle Dupont

VARIATION:   Say good-by to each one.
                 **Au revoir, Madame!**

# Entre nous

## Expressions pour la conversation

The French often use the following expressions:

     **Je sais.**         *I know.*
     **Je ne sais pas.**    *I don't know.*

## Mini-dialogues    OPTIONAL

Look at the first picture and the sample dialog; then create new dialogs based on the pictures below.

NATHALIE: Qui est-ce?
PHILIPPE: Je ne sais pas.
NATHALIE: Ah, je sais ... C'est Brigitte.

**Brigitte**

**Bernard**

**Monique**

**Monsieur Simon**

**Madame Pascal**

**Mademoiselle Thomas**

# Leçon 2

## Une coïncidence

Act. 1

### À Annecy ... à la Maison des Jeunes

—Ça va, Jean-Paul?
—Ça va. Et toi?
—Ça va bien.

—Je m'appelle Hélène. Et toi?
—Je m'appelle Marie-Noëlle.

—Comment t'appelles-tu?
—Je m'appelle Jean-Michel.
—Moi aussi. Jean-Michel Vallée.
—Moi, je m'appelle Jean-Michel Valette.
—Quelle coïncidence!

Teenagers playing **le baby-foot**.

## NOTE CULTURELLE    OPTIONAL

**Annecy**    You may have the students locate Annecy on the map of France on p. viii.

Annecy, one of the most beautiful cities in France, is situated in the Alps on the shores of the **Lac d'Annecy.** Like many other French cities and towns, it has a modern youth center (**Maison des Jeunes**), which offers a wide variety of cultural and sports activities.

Avoid giving word-for-word translations of expressions such as **je m'appelle**. However, you may want to point out quickly that different languages have different ways of expressing the same idea. E.g. **Je m'appelle** literally means *I call myself* and not *My name is.*

Act. 2

4

# Vocabulaire spécialisé   **Présentations** *(Introductions)*

| | |
|---|---|
| **Je m'appelle . . .** | *My name is . . .* |
| **Comment t'appelles-tu?** | *What's your name?* |
| **Ça va?** | *How are you? How's everything?* |
| **Ça va.** | *Fine. I'm OK. Everything's all right.* |
| **Et toi?** | *And you?* |
| **Moi aussi.** | *Me too.* |

You may want to point out that literally **Ça va?** means *Are things going (all right)?*

**Ça va . . .**  bien  très bien

mal  très mal  comme ci, comme ça

---

**A coincidence**

**In Annecy . . . at the Youth Center**
How's everything, Jean-Paul?
Fine. And you?
Everything's fine (going well).

My name is Hélène. And yours?
My name is Marie-Noëlle.

What's your name?
My name is Jean-Michel.
Mine too. Jean-Michel Vallée.
My name is Jean-Michel Valette.
What a coincidence!

## NOTE CULTURELLE   OPTIONAL

### Niveaux de langue *(Levels of language)*

French teenagers are much more formal with adults than with their friends. This level of formality (or familiarity) is reflected in the way they speak. French students, for instance, use **Ça va?** when talking to their friends. When talking to their teachers, they would say **Comment allez-vous?** which is the more formal way of asking *How are you?* As you will learn later on, the French have two ways of addressing people: a *formal* form and a *familiar* form.

Although the names are fictitious, the following streets and avenues are real places. You may ask the students to point out the various cities on a map of France.

ADRESSES

| NOM | RUE | VILLE |
|---|---|---|
| Jean-Pierre ALBERONI | boulevard Pasteur | Nice |
| Marie-Thérèse BAYARD | cours de la Libération | Bordeaux |
| Sylvie CAMUS | avenue du Président Kennedy | Lille |
| Anne-Marie DULAC | rue de la République | Nancy |
| François LEBAS | place de la Victoire | Vichy |
| Nathalie MALLET | boulevard Carnot | Cannes |
| Jean-Paul MARTINOT | avenue de Genève | Annecy |
| Marie-Noëlle SIMONET | rue Pascal | Clermont-Ferrand |
| Véronique TOMASINI | boulevard de la Liberté | Marseille |
| Jean-Michel VILLETTE | avenue du Maine | Paris |

WB
3

SCRIPT
Act. 3

MASTERS
p. 2

The following surnames are very common in France. You may ask the students if they know anyone with these names. You may also ask them to check a phone directory for these names: Aubry, Auclair, Beauchamp, Beaudet, Beaudoin, Beaulieu, Bernier, Bertrand, Blanc, Blanchard, Blanchet, Boudreau, Bouvier, Chevalier, Desmarais, Duchesne, Dumas, Dupont, Dupré Dupuis, Duval, Gautier, Hamel, Joli, Joly, Lebeau, Leblanc, Leclair, Leclerc, Lejeune, Letendre, Marchand, Mercier, Meunier, Moreau, Pasquier, Prévost, Renaud, Rousseau, Tessier, Tixier

# NOTE CULTURELLE  OPTIONAL
## Les noms français *(French names)*

Many French names have English equivalents:

| **Jean** | *John* | **Jacques** | *James* | **Guillaume** | *William* | **François** | *Frank* |
|---|---|---|---|---|---|---|---|
| **Hélène** | *Helen* | **Suzanne** | *Susan* | **Monique** | *Monica* | **Marie** | *Mary* |

SUGGESTED REALIA:
1. Map of a French city
2. French phone directory
3. Guide Michelin with city maps

It is not uncommon for French people to have two first names, usually beginning with **Jean** (for boys) or **Marie** (for girls). These names are hyphenated.

| **Jean-Pierre** | **Jean-Marc** | **Jean-Paul** | **Jean-Michel** | **Jean-Philippe** |
|---|---|---|---|---|
| **Marie-Hélène** | **Marie-Laure** | **Marie-Claire** | **Marie-France** | **Marie-Louise** |

Nicknames or shortened names are generally not used in France, except for young children.

| **Jojo** (for **Georges**) | **Pierrot** (for **Pierre**) | **Dédé** (for **André**) |
|---|---|---|
| **Mimi** (for **Michèle**) | **Gigi** (for **Ginette**) | **Kiki** (for **Christine**) |

You may assign French names to your students. If the American name doesn't have a French equivalent, you may use an approximation. For instance, Nancy may become Nathalie. See pp. iv–v for the list of names.

## ACTIVITÉ 1  Je m'appelle . . .

Introduce yourself and ask the student next to you to do the same.

→ **Je m'appelle Nancy Martin.**
  **Comment t'appelles-tu?**

## ACTIVITÉ 2  À la Maison des Jeunes *(At the Youth Center)* OPTIONAL

The following young people are introducing themselves. Play the roles of
each pair according to the model.

→ Paul / Sylvie    Paul: **Je m'appelle Paul. Et toi?**
                     Sylvie: **Je m'appelle Sylvie.**
                     Paul: **Ça va?**
                     Sylvie: **Ça va bien.**

The purpose of this exercise is to provide pronunciation practice. Be sure to model each name.

1. Jean / Marie
2. Thomas / Anne
3. Michel / Suzanne
4. Hélène / Philippe
5. Denis / Monique

6. François / Marie-Louise
7. Jean-Michel / Anne-Marie
8. Jean-Claude / Marie-Solange
9. Jean-Philippe / Marie-France
10. Jean-Louis / Mélanie

## ACTIVITÉ 3  Ça va?  OPTIONAL

Sometimes we feel good, sometimes we don't. What would you say to a
French friend who asked you **Ça va?** in each of the situations described
below? Use an appropriate expression from the **Vocabulaire spécialisé.**

→ You have the flu.    **Ça va comme ci, comme ça.**

1. You received an A in French.
2. Your grandparents sent you a check.
3. Your best friend invited you to a party.
4. You lost your wallet.
5. You bent a wheel on your bicycle.
6. You won a prize in a photo contest.
7. You received a B on an English paper.
8. It is your birthday.

WB
1, 2

# Prononciation

## L'alphabet et les signes orthographiques *(spelling marks)*

Act. 4

### 1. L'alphabet

Repeat after the teacher:

The alphabet is presented here to introduce the French sound system. By having the students repeat the letter, you may be able to identify those who have trouble hearing and repeating new sounds. These students may need extra practice with the tapes.

| | | | | | | | |
|---|---|---|---|---|---|---|---|
| A | a | H | hache | O | o | V | vé |
| B | bé | I | i | P | pé | W | double vé |
| C | cé | J | ji | Q | ku | X | ixe |
| D | dé | K | ka | R | erre | Y | i grec |
| E | e | L | elle | S | esse | Z | zède |
| F | effe | M | emme | T | té | | |
| G | gé | N | enne | U | u | | |

Appendix 1 contains a reference list of Sound-spelling Correspondences.

### 2. Les signes orthographiques

Four spelling marks may appear on vowels:

| | | |
|---|---|---|
| ( ´ ) | l'accent aigu *(acute accent)* | René |
| ( ` ) | l'accent grave *(grave accent)* | Voilà Michèle. |
| ( ^ ) | l'accent circonflexe *(circumflex accent)* | Jérôme, dîner |
| ( ¨ ) | le tréma *(diaeresis)* | Noël, naïf |

Spelling marks, with the exception of the cedilla, are often omitted on capital letters. In this text, accents are used on capital letters to simplify the learning of spelling and pronunciation. Accents will, however, be missing from much of the realia. Explain that accents are often dropped in journalistic usage, especially on capital letters.

One spelling mark may appear under the letter **c**:

SCRIPT
Act. 5

MASTERS
p. 2

| | | |
|---|---|---|
| ( ¸ ) | la cédille *(cedilla)* | Ça va, François? |

**Note:** These marks are part of the spelling of words. They cannot be left out.

---

***ACTIVITÉ 4*** **Au bureau des réservations** *(At the reservation desk)*

Imagine that you are an employee at the reservation desk of **Air France**, the French national airline. As you confirm the reservations of the following passengers, spell their last names in French.

→ Monsieur Marin     **Monsieur Marin. M.A.R.I.N.**     VARIATION: Have students spell their own names.

SCRIPT
Act. 6

MASTERS
p. 2

1. Mademoiselle Lucas
2. Monsieur Thomas
3. Mademoiselle Duval
4. Monsieur Marty
5. Madame Maubrey
6. Mademoiselle Aziza

# Entre nous

### Expressions pour la conversation

To ask about someone's health you would use one of the following expressions:

|  |  |  |
|---|---|---|
| (to a friend) | **Comment vas-tu?** | *How are you?* |
| (to an adult) | **Comment allez-vous?** | *How are you?* |

You may explain that **Comment vas-tu?** is a little more formal than **Ça va?** Both expressions are used when talking to friends. **Comment allez-vous?** is even more formal and is used with adults.

### Mini-dialogues   OPTIONAL

Create new dialogs by replacing the underlined words with the words suggested in the pictures.

Madame Laval

PAUL: Bonjour, <u>Madame</u>.
MADAME LAVAL: Bonjour, Paul.
PAUL: <u>Comment allez-vous, Madame?</u>
MADAME LAVAL: <u>Très bien</u>. Et toi?

These expressions are given in the **Vocabulaire spécialisé** on p. 9.

| Janine | Monsieur Roland | Jean-Pierre | Mademoiselle Calmas |

QUIZ
p. 2

# Leçon 3 Combien?

The objective of this lesson is to teach numbers. These are reentered in Prélude, Leçon 4 (teaching time) and P.5 (teaching dates). If you do not intend to teach students the minutes in P.4, you could simply introduce the numbers 1–10 at this time.

Act. 1

**À Tours . . .**

**Dans une librairie**
— Donnez-moi *Paris-Match*, s'il vous plaît.
— Voici, Mademoiselle.
— C'est combien?
— Neuf francs, Mademoiselle.
— Voilà neuf francs, Monsieur.
— Merci, Mademoiselle.

**Dans un café**
— Un Coca-Cola, s'il vous plaît!
— Oui, Mademoiselle. Et pour vous, Monsieur?
— Un café, s'il vous plaît . . . et un sandwich.
— Mais oui, Monsieur!

**How much?**

**In Tours . . .**
**In a bookstore**
Give me *Paris-Match*, please.
Here you are, (Miss).
How much is it?
Nine francs, (Miss).
Here are nine francs, (Sir).
Thank you, (Miss).

**In a café**
A Coca-Cola, please.
Yes, (Miss). And for you, (Sir)?
A cup of coffee, please . . . and a sandwich.
All right, (Sir).

The château Azay-le-Rideau in the Loire Valley

## NOTES CULTURELLES  OPTIONAL

**1. Tours**  The city of Tours is located on the Loire River in a region known for its castles, its gardens, and the purity of the French spoken there. It is an excellent starting point for bicycle trips.  You may have the students locate Tours on the map of France on p. viii.

**2. Paris-Match**  *Paris-Match* is one of the most popular French magazines.  If available, you may bring a copy of *Paris-Match* to class.

**3. Le Coca-Cola**  Coca-Cola is very popular among French teenagers. Although few young people have Coke with their meals, many order it at cafés. When ordering it, one may simply ask for **un coca**.

If available, you may show pictures of well-known "châteaux de la Loire": Chenonceaux, Amboise, Azay-le-Rideau, Villandry, Chambord, etc.

Tours

# Vocabulaire spécialisé  Les achats et les nombres de 0 à 10
### *(Purchases and the numbers from 0 to 10)*

| | | | | | |
|---|---|---|---|---|---|
| 0 | **zéro** | 4 | **quatre** | 8 | **huit** |
| 1 | **un** | 5 | **cinq** | 9 | **neuf** |
| 2 | **deux** | 6 | **six** | 10 | **dix** |
| 3 | **trois** | 7 | **sept** | | |

| | |
|---|---|
| **Combien?** | *How much?* |
| **C'est combien?** | *How much is it?* |
| **C'est dix francs.** | *It's ten francs.* |
| **Oui** | *Yes* |
| **Non** | *No* |
| **Pardon.** | *Excuse me.* |
| **Merci.** | *Thank you.* |
| **s'il vous plaît** | *please* (formal form) |
| **s'il te plaît** | *please* (familiar form) |
| **Donnez-moi . . .** | *Give me . . .* (formal form) |
| **Donne-moi . . .** | *Give me . . .* (familiar form) |

Note: The French expressions corresponding to "please" and "give me" have both a
*formal* and a *familiar* form. Be sure to use the formal form when speaking to your
teacher or other adults, and the familiar form when speaking to your friends.

# NOTE CULTURELLE

## L'argent français *(French money)*

The French franc (**le franc français**) is the monetary unit of France. The franc, which is worth less than a U.S. quarter, is divided into 100 **centimes.**

French money is issued as follows:

**Pièces** *(Coins)*

  1 centime, 5 centimes, 10 centimes, 20 centimes, ½ franc (50 centimes),
  1 franc, 2 francs, 5 francs, 10 francs

**Billets** *(Bills)*

  10 francs, 50 francs, 100 francs, 500 francs

Belgium and Switzerland, where French is one of the national languages, also use the franc as the monetary unit. The value of these currencies—**le franc belge** and **le franc suisse**— is different from that of the French franc.

*Have the students note that the final **c** of **franc** is not pronounced. (This is an exception to the rule on p. 6.)*

*The 2-franc coin was introduced in the summer of 1979. The 5-franc bill has been withdrawn from circulation.*

*The approximate values of these currencies are:*
*1 franc belge = 2 cents*
*1 franc suisse = 45 cents*

Pictured on the bills are: 10 F: the composer Hector Berlioz (1803–1869); 50 F: the portrait painter Maurice Quentin de la Tour (1704–1788); 100 F: the painter Eugène Delacroix (1798–1863); 500 F: the philosopher and mathematician Blaise Pascal (1623–1662).

SUGGESTED REALIA: French money; money from other French-speaking countries.

# Prononciation

The distinction between vowel sound and consonant sound is an important one. For practice, give the students cognates and ask them to identify which words begin with a vowel sound and which begin with a consonant sound.

auto  autobus  hélicoptère  hôtel  harmonica  américain
chocolat  café  taxi  bus  radio  restaurant  télévision

Note: Students will encounter mainly the mute h; therefore, they should consider words beginning with h as beginning with a vowel sound, unless otherwise noted.

## Les nombres de 1 à 10 *(The numbers from 1 to 10)*

Numbers are used alone, for instance in counting: 1, 2, 3, etc., or they are used with nouns: **1 centime, 2 francs, 3 dollars**, etc. Note how numbers are pronounced when they are used alone and when they are used with nouns.[1]
Repeat after your teacher.

| NUMBER ALONE | NUMBER + CONSONANT SOUND | NUMBER + VOWEL SOUND |
|---|---|---|
| 1  un | un franc | un /n/ objet |
| 2  deux | deux francs | deux /z/ objets |
| 3  trois | trois francs | trois /z/ objets |
| 4  quatre | quatre francs | quatre objets |
| 5  cinq /k/ | cinq francs | cinq /k/ objets |
| 6  six /s/ | six francs | six /z/ objets |
| 7  sept /t/ | sept francs | sept /t/ objets |
| 8  huit /t/ | huit francs | huit /t/ objets |
| 9  neuf /f/ | neuf francs | neuf /f/ objets |
| 10  dix /s/ | dix francs | dix /z/ objets |

When numbers are used alone—
the final consonants of the numbers 5 to 10 are pronounced;
the **x** of **six** (6) and **dix** (10) is pronounced /s/.

When numbers are followed by nouns which begin with a consonant sound—
the final consonant of the number is *not* pronounced, except for the numbers **sept** (7) and **neuf** (9).

When numbers are followed by nouns which begin with a vowel sound, that is, **a, e, i, o, u, h,** and **y** + consonant—
the final consonant of the number is pronounced as if it were the first letter of the next word;
the **x** of **deux** (2), **six** (6), and **dix** (10) is pronounced /z/.

### ACTIVITÉ 1  Séries

Continue the following series:

1. 1, 2, 3, . . .
2. 1, 3, 5, . . .
3. 2, 4, 6, . . .
4. 10, 9, 8, . . .
5. 10, 8, 6, . . .
6. 9, 7, 5, . . .

[1]Sounds are given between diagonal lines.

LOTO  TIRAGE N° 2  DU 9 JANVIER 1980

7  9  4  6  3  2

NUMERO COMPLEMENTAIRE  10

Have students practice numbers followed by nouns by having them count in chain exercises:
un taxi  deux taxis  trois taxis. . .
un hôtel  deux hôtels  trois hôtels. . .

## ACTIVITÉ 2  La loterie *(The raffle)*

Imagine that you are attending a French school. The school has organized a raffle for the benefit of the choir, and you have been chosen to draw the winning numbers. Announce each one, beginning with **le** *(the)*.

→  8 – 0 – 2 – 9    **le huit – zéro – deux – neuf**

VARIATION: Have the students close their books, and read the numbers aloud for them to write down.

1. 4 – 0 – 5 – 8
2. 9 – 4 – 8 – 1
3. 7 – 8 – 3 – 6
4. 3 – 1 – 0 – 2

5. 7 – 0 – 5 – 2
6. 1 – 3 – 5 – 6
7. 7 – 4 – 8 – 2
8. 3 – 6 – 7 – 9

## ACTIVITÉ 3  Au café «Le Floride»

Imagine you are working in a large French café. Call out the following orders.

1. 8 cafés *(coffees)*
2. 3 chocolats
3. 5 thés *(teas)*
4. 6 sandwichs
5. 2 Coca-Colas
6. 10 chocolats
7. 5 cafés
8. 6 thés
9. 2 orangeades
10. 6 orangeades
11. 10 orangeades
12. 5 orangeades

WB
1

SCRIPT
Act. 3

MASTERS
p. 3

Make sure that the students make the liaison with **orangeade.** (**Orangeade** is a type of orange soda.)

## ACTIVITÉ 4  S'il te plaît, Papa . . .   OPTIONAL

Imagine that you want to do the following things, but you do not have any money. Estimate the price of each item in dollars, and ask your father for what you need. Follow the model.

→  to buy a record    **S'il te plaît, Papa, donne-moi cinq dollars.**

1. to buy two records
2. to buy a magazine
3. to buy a paperback
4. to go to the movies
5. to invite a friend to the movies

6. to invite two friends to the movies
7. to go out for pizza
8. to invite two friends to have ice cream
9. to buy a pair of sunglasses
10. to buy a cassette

This is a free-response exercise. Encourage several responses for each cue.

Act. 5

## Vocabulaire spécialisé    Les nombres de 11 à 60 *(The numbers from 11 to 60)*

The numbers from 61 to 1,000,000 are presented on pp. 186 and 194.

| | | | | | |
|---|---|---|---|---|---|
| 11 | **onze** | 21 | **vingt et un** | 31 | **trente et un** |
| 12 | **douze** | 22 | **vingt-deux** | 32 | **trente-deux** |
| 13 | **treize** | 23 | **vingt-trois** | 33 | **trente-trois** ... |
| 14 | **quatorze** | 24 | **vingt-quatre** | 40 | **quarante** |
| 15 | **quinze** | 25 | **vingt-cinq** | 41 | **quarante et un** |
| 16 | **seize** | 26 | **vingt-six** | 42 | **quarante-deux** ... |
| 17 | **dix-sept** | 27 | **vingt-sept** | 50 | **cinquante** |
| 18 | **dix-huit** | 28 | **vingt-huit** | 51 | **cinquante et un** |
| 19 | **dix-neuf** | 29 | **vingt-neuf** | 52 | **cinquante-deux** ... |
| 20 | **vingt** | 30 | **trente** | 60 | **soixante** |

You may have the students note the hyphen in compound numbers other than 21, 31, 41, etc.

Notes:  1. The word **et** *(and)* is used only with the numbers 21, 31, 41, 51.
   2. You have seen that the numbers 1-10 are pronounced differently, depending on how they are used. The same changes in pronunciation also occur when these numbers are used in combination.

SUGGESTED REALIA: hotel or restaurant bills; other bills.

| | | |
|---|---|---|
| six /s/ | six francs | six /z/ objets |
| trente-six /s/ | trente-six francs | trente-six /z/ objets |

As a class activity you may play "Loto" with cards bearing numbers from 1–60. ("Loto" is the French name for Bingo.)

## ACTIVITÉ 5    Nouvelles séries *(New series)*

Complete the following series:

1. 10, 20, ... 60
2. 14, 16, ... 40
3. 13, 15, ... 41
4. 11, 21, ... 51
5. 15, 25, ... 55
6. 16, 26, ... 56
7. 18, 22, 26, ... 58
8. 19, 22, 25, ... 58

VARIATION: Do each series as a chain exercise, choosing students at random.

ville de paris

alphabetique    a h

## ACTIVITÉ 6    Le standard *(The switchboard)*

WB 2, 3

SCRIPT
Act. 6

MASTERS p. 3

Imagine that you are working at the switchboard of IBM-France in Paris. Ask for the following numbers:

→ 10.20.30 à Nice    **Donnez-moi le dix-vingt-trente à Nice, s'il vous plaît.**

1. 20.23.25 à Lille
2. 30.40.60 à Tours
3. 14.18.16 à Lyon
4. 42.32.52 à Nantes
5. 50.60.40 à Annecy
6. 23.33.53 à Cannes
7. 18.28.58 à Colmar
8. 41.51.11 à Marseille

VARIATION: You may dictate the numbers for recognition, omitting the names of the cities.

In France, except for Paris, telephone numbers are given as three sets of two-digit numbers. A two-digit number beginning with "0" would be read **zéro-un, zéro-deux**, etc.

SUGGESTED REALIA: French phone directory.

## ACTIVITÉ 7 S'il te plaît, Maman . . . OPTIONAL

Imagine that you want to buy the following things, but you do not have any money. This time ask your mother to give you what you need for your purchases. Estimate the price of each item in dollars. Keep prices under $60. Encourage several responses for each cue.

→ a tennis racket **S'il te plaît, Maman, donne-moi trente dollars.**

1. a used bicycle
2. a transistor radio
3. a pair of jeans
4. running shoes
5. a bathing suit
6. a record album

# Entre nous

### Expression pour la conversation

To express *surprise,* the French often say:

**Oh là là!** *Oh dear! Wow! Whew!*

### Mini-dialogues OPTIONAL

Imagine that you are in a French café. Create new dialogs by replacing the underlined words with the words suggested in the pictures.

CLAIRE: <u>Un café</u>, s'il vous plaît.
LE GARÇON (*waiter*): Oui, Mademoiselle.
CLAIRE: C'est combien?
LE GARÇON: <u>Onze francs</u>.
CLAIRE: Oh là là! C'est cher!
(*That's expensive!*)

SUGGESTED REALIA: café check.

un café — 11 francs

un coca — 14 francs

un sandwich — 16 francs

un chocolat — 12 francs

un café et un sandwich — 27 francs

un coca et un sandwich — 30 francs

# Leçon 4

## Conversations dans un café

This lesson is in two parts. The first part and the first conversation teach how to tell time using full hours. The second part and the second conversation teach the divisions of the hour. You may wish to skip the second part and come back to it at a later time.

Act. 1

5

### À Dijon . . . dans un café

### Conversation numéro 1: Hélène et Paul

HÉLÈNE: Quelle heure est-il?
PAUL: Il est une heure.
HÉLÈNE: Et à quelle heure est le concert?
PAUL: À deux heures!
HÉLÈNE: Ça va. Nous avons le temps!

The expression **ça va** was introduced in Leçon 2 with the meaning of *I'm fine*. In a more general sense, **ça va** means *fine, good, that's okay.*

## NOTES CULTURELLES  OPTIONAL

**1. Dijon**  Dijon, in eastern France, is the capital of Burgundy (**la Bourgogne**), a region famous for its wines.

**2. Le café**  The café plays an important role in French social life. From early in the morning until late at night, people can go there to have something to drink and a roll or sandwich to eat. Mainly the café is a place where people come together to talk and where an individual can sit quietly reading a newspaper, waiting for a friend, or watching the people go by. The café has two sections: **la terrasse**, where sidewalk tables are put out in fair weather, and **la salle**, which is always open.

You may have the students locate Dijon on the map of France on p. viii.

## Conversation numéro 2: André et François

ANDRÉ: Quelle heure est-il?
FRANÇOIS: Il est deux heures.
ANDRÉ: Deux heures?
FRANÇOIS: Oui, deux heures. Pourquoi?
ANDRÉ: J'ai rendez-vous avec Michèle . . .
FRANÇOIS: À quelle heure?
ANDRÉ: À deux heures dix.
FRANÇOIS: Et Michèle est ponctuelle?
ANDRÉ: Oui, très ponctuelle . . . et très impatiente.
FRANÇOIS: Oh là là!
ANDRÉ: Au revoir, François!
FRANÇOIS: Au revoir, André!

**Conversations in a café**
**In Dijon . . . in a café**
**Conversation number 1: Hélène and Paul**
What time is it?
It's one o'clock.
And at what time is the concert?
At two.
Good. We have (the) time.

**Conversation number 2: André and François**
What time is it?
It's two o'clock.
Two o'clock?
Yes, two. Why?
I have a date with Michèle . . .
At what time?
At two ten. (At ten past two.)
And is Michèle on time?
Yes, (she is) very punctual . . . and very impatient.
Oh dear!
Good-by, François.
Good-by, André.

Act. 2

MASTERS
p. 4

6

## Vocabulaire spécialisé   L'heure *(The time)*

**Quelle heure est-il?**        *What time is it?*
**Il est . . .**                *It is . . .*

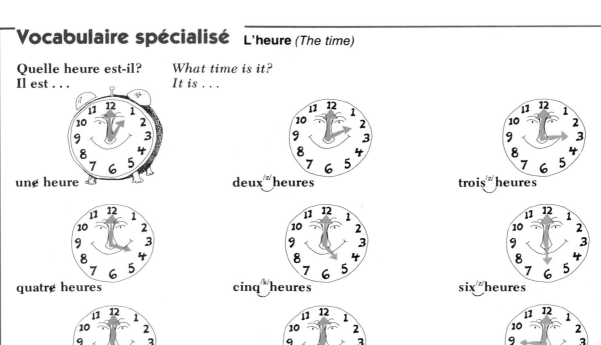

un¢ heure

deux/z/ heures

trois/z/ heures

quatr¢ heures

cinq/k/ heures

six/z/ heures

se̶p̶t/t/ heures

huit/t/ heures

neuf/v/ heures

# Prononciation

Review what constitutes a vowel sound. Words beginning with **a, e, i, o, u,** and **y** + consonant begin with a vowel sound. Words beginning with mute **h** begin with a vowel sound. (The aspirate **h** will be introduced later.)

### La liaison

As you know, the final consonant of a word is usually silent in French. However, if the next word begins with a *vowel sound,* the final consonant is sometimes pronounced as if it were the first letter of this word. This is called **liaison.** Liaison means linking two words.

Liaison occurs only after *certain* words, such as numbers followed by nouns.

In written French, liaison is not marked by any sign. As a learning aid, new liaisons will be indicated with: ‿.

In liaison, a final **s** or **x** is pronounced /z/.

   Il est trois/z/ heures.     Il est six/z/ heures.

In this book and on the tapes, only required liaisons are presented. These are the ones commonly encountered in conversational French.

Clock on the Strasbourg Cathedral

**24** Prélude

dix /z/ heures

onze heures

midi    minuit

**À quelle heure** est le concert?
**À onze heures.**

*At what time is the concert?*
*At eleven (o'clock).*

Notes: 1. In English the expression *o'clock* may be left out. In French the word **heure(s)**
may *not* be left out.

2. The word **heure(s)** is abbreviated as **h.**

Il est 3 h.

3. To distinguish between A.M. and P.M., French speakers use the following
expressions:

**du matin** *in the morning*      Il est trois heures **du matin**.
**de l'après-midi** *in the afternoon*  Il est deux heures **de l'après-midi**.
**du soir** *in the evening*        Il est dix heures **du soir**.

In telling time be sure to link the number to **heure(s)**. Note the pronunciation of the number 9: **Il est neuf** /v/ **heures.**

## *ACTIVITÉ 1*   Quelle heure est-il?

Paul has a watch that does not work very well. He often asks Hélène what
time it is. Play both roles according to the model.    Be sure students make the appropriate liaisons
and link all words together.

→  3 h.    Paul: **Quelle heure est-il?**
Hélène: **Il est trois heures.**

1. 4 h.          3. 1 h.          5. 10 h.          7. 6 h.   VARIATION with **du matin,**
2. 5 h.          4. 11 h.         6. 9 h.           8. 7 h.   **de l'après-midi, du soir.**

## *ACTIVITÉ 2*   À quelle heure?

Hélène is always well informed. This is why François asks her when certain
activities take place. Play both roles according to the model.

→  le concert: 3 h.    François: **À quelle heure est le concert?**    In this activity **le** and **la** are presented as
Hélène: **À trois heures.**    anticipatory structures. You may model
François: **Merci.**    these nouns for the students.

SCRIPT
Act. 3

1. la classe: 2 h.          4. le match *(game)* de tennis: 7 h.      7. le bus: 1 h.   /bys/
2. le récital: 6 h.         5. le match de football: 5 h.            8. le train: 11 h.
3. le film *(movie)*: 8 h.  6. le programme de télévision: 9 h.

You may introduce the notion of cognates and false cognates. Cognates have a similar spelling and meaning in both French and
English (**classe, récital, programme**); false cognates have a similar spelling but different meaning (**football** is *soccer* in French). Stress
the point that cognates are *never* pronounced the same way in French and English.

Leçon quatre  **25**

Act. 4

MASTERS
p. 4

7

# Vocabulaire spécialisé   L'heure et les minutes *(The hour and the minutes)*

Il est . . .

**une heure et quart**

**deux heures et demie**

**dix heures moins le quart**

Exceptions: **midi et demi, minuit et demi.**

To indicate the half hour and the quarter hour, the following expressions are used:

   **et quart**

   **et demie**

**moins
le quart**

Il est . . .

**trois heures dix**

**quatre heures moins vingt**

To indicate the minutes, the following are used:

   *number
(of minutes)*

**moins + *number*
*(of minutes)***

With the growing popularity of digital clocks, there is an increasing tendency to use minutes after the hour: 10 h. 52
**Il est dix heures cinquante-deux.**

## *ACTIVITÉ 3*   L'heure exacte

WB
1, 2

SCRIPT

Act. 5

MASTERS
p. 5

François checks the time with Caroline, who has a new watch. Play both
roles according to the model.

In this exercise all times fall between
the hour and the half hour.

→   1 h. 15   François: **Il est une heure et quart?**
Caroline: **Oui, il est une heure et quart.**

1. 1 h. 30
2. 2 h. 15
3. 3 h. 30

4. 5 h. 30
5. 6 h. 20
6. 8 h. 25

7. 9 h. 26
8. 10 h. 14
9. 11 h. 12

### ACTIVITÉ 4  À la gare *(At the train station)*  OPTIONAL

Imagine that you are working at the information desk
of a French train station. Travellers ask you the
departure time of the trains listed below. Answer
them according to the schedule.

| DÉPARTS | | | |
|---|---|---|---|
| Nice | 6:10 | Toulon | 9:35 |
| Lyon | 7:15 | Colmar | 10:40 |
| Cannes | 7:30 | Annecy | 10:45 |
| Tours | 8:12 | Marseille | 10:50 |
| Dijon | 8:25 | Paris | 10:55 |

→ le train de Nice
   **Le train de Nice est à six heures dix.**

1. le train de Lyon
2. le train de Cannes
3. le train de Tours
4. le train de Dijon
5. le train de Toulon

6. le train de Colmar
7. le train d'Annecy
8. le train de Marseille
9. le train de Paris

Note that in items 5–9, times fall between the half hour and the next hour so
that students may practice the construction **moins** + number of minutes.

# Entre nous

## Expressions pour la conversation

To express their *disappointment* or their *displeasure*, French speakers use
the following expressions:

> **Zut!**
> **Zut alors!**    *Darn (it)! Rats!*

## Mini-dialogues  OPTIONAL

Paul asks Anne what time it is. When she tells him, he realizes that he is
five minutes late. Read the model dialog carefully. Then create new dialogs
by replacing the underlined words, using the information contained in the
pictures. Make all necessary changes.

WB
3

SCRIPT

Act. 6

MASTERS
p. 5

QUIZ
p. 4

PAUL: Quelle heure est-il?
ANNE: Il est <u>une heure cinq</u>!
PAUL: <u>Une heure cinq</u>?
ANNE: Oui! Pourquoi? *(Why?)*
PAUL: <u>Le film</u> commence *(begins)* à <u>une heure</u>!
ANNE: Zut alors!

1:00    le film

4:30    la classe

Il est cinq heures moins
vingt-cinq.

9:50    le concert

Il est dix heures moins cinq.

10:20    l'opéra

Il est dix heures vingt-cinq.

2:20    le match

Il est deux heures vingt-cinq.

# Leçon 5

## Le calendrier de Jacqueline

**Voici Jacqueline.**

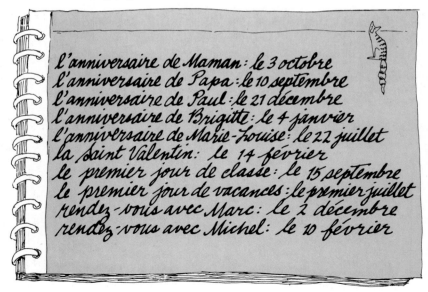

Act. 1

**Et voici le calendrier de Jacqueline.**

l'anniversaire de Maman : le 3 octobre
l'anniversaire de Papa : le 10 septembre
l'anniversaire de Paul : le 21 décembre
l'anniversaire de Brigitte : le 4 janvier
l'anniversaire de Marie-Louise : le 22 juillet
la Saint Valentin : le 14 février
le premier jour de classe : le 15 septembre
le premier jour de vacances : le premier juillet
rendez-vous avec Marc : le 2 décembre
rendez-vous avec Michel : le 10 février

Shrove Tuesday is the last day before Lent, a period of 40 days of penance and fasting that precedes Easter. Traditionally, Mardi Gras was the culmination of a period of celebration that ended abruptly on Ash Wednesday.

# NOTE CULTURELLE   OPTIONAL

## Les fêtes françaises *(The French holidays)*

Many French holidays are of Catholic origin. Here are some religious observances for which French students have one or more days of vacation:

| | | |
|---|---|---|
| **la Toussaint** | *All Saints' Day* | (November 1) |
| **Noël** | *Christmas* | (December 25) |
| **Mardi Gras** | *Shrove Tuesday* | (February or March) |
| **Pâques** | *Easter* | (March or April) |

There are also other French holidays that are not of religious origin:

| | |
|---|---|
| **le 11 novembre** | *Armistice Day* |
| **le premier mai** | *Labor Day* |
| **le 14 juillet** | *Bastille Day* (the French national holiday) |

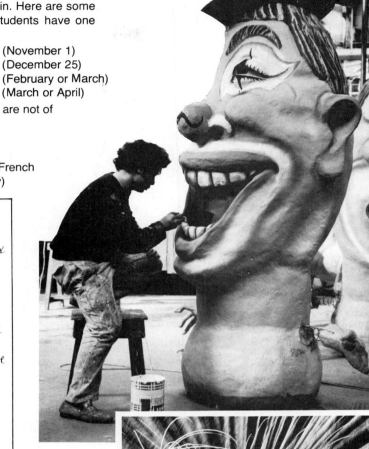

*Heureux Noël et Bonne et Heureuse Année*

**Jacqueline's date book**

**Here's Jacqueline.**

**And here's Jacqueline's date book.**

| | |
|---|---|
| Mom's birthday | October 3 |
| Dad's birthday | September 10 |
| Paul's birthday | December 21 |
| Brigitte's birthday | January 4 |
| Marie-Louise's birthday | July 22 |
| Valentine's Day | February 14 |
| the first day of class | September 15 |
| the first day of vacation | July 1 |
| date with Marc | December 2 |
| date with Michel | February 10 |

# Vocabulaire spécialisé  La date

**Les jours de la semaine** *(The days of the week)*

Point out that days of the week and months are not capitalized in French.

| | | | |
|---|---|---|---|
| **lundi** | *Monday* | **aujourd'hui** | *today* |
| **mardi** | *Tuesday* | **demain** | *tomorrow* |
| **mercredi** | *Wednesday* | | |
| **jeudi** | *Thursday* | | |
| **vendredi** | *Friday* | | |
| **samedi** | *Saturday* | | |
| **dimanche** | *Sunday* | | |

Citroën LN: la voiture qui simplifie la vie.

**Les mois de l'année** *(The months of the year)*

Review the numbers from 2–31 before teaching the dates.

| | | | |
|---|---|---|---|
| janvier | avril | juillet | octobre |
| février | mai | août | novembre |
| mars | juin | septembre | décembre |

**La date**

| | |
|---|---|
| **Quel jour est-ce?** | *What day is it?* |
| **C'est le 10 septembre.** | *It's September 10th.* |
| **Aujourd'hui, c'est le 3 octobre.** | *Today is October 3rd.* |
| **Noël est le 25 décembre.** | *Christmas is December 25th.* |
| **Mon anniversaire est le 2 mars.** | *My birthday is March 2nd.* |
| **L'anniversaire de Marc est le premier juin.** | *Marc's birthday is June 1st.* |
| **J'ai rendez-vous avec Paul le 4 juin.** | *I have a date with Paul on June 4th.* |

Notes: 1. To express a date, French speakers use the construction:

> **le** + number + month

Exception: the *first* (of the month) is **le premier.**

2. When dates are abbreviated, the day is always given before the month:

2/8   le 2 août      1/10   le premier octobre

Communication activity: **Mon anniversaire est le...** (give your birthday) **Et toi?** (point to a student)
Robert: **Mon anniversaire est le...**
Then ask another student: **Quand** *(When)* **est-ce, l'anniversaire de Robert?**
Marie: **L'anniversaire de Robert est le...**

## ACTIVITÉ 1  Un jour de retard *(A day behind)*

François has trouble keeping up with the calendar. He is always one day
behind when thinking of the date. Sylvie corrects him. Play both roles.

→ samedi      François: **Aujourd'hui, c'est samedi.**
              Sylvie: **Non, c'est dimanche.**

1. lundi   mardi
2. mardi   mercredi

3. jeudi   vendredi
4. vendredi   samedi

5. dimanche   lundi
6. mercredi   jeudi

## ACTIVITÉ 2  Un jour d'avance *(A day ahead)*

Philippe has the opposite problem. He is always one day ahead. Again
Sylvie corrects him. Play both roles.

→ 12 oct.    Philippe: **C'est le douze octobre.**
             Sylvie: **Non, c'est le onze octobre.**

1. 14 déc.
2. 24 jan.
3. 5 fév.

4. 8 avr.
5. 12 août
6. 21 oct.

7. 9 juin
8. 6 juil.
9. 2 mai  le premier mai

10. 17 sep.
11. 30 mars
12. 1 nov.   le 31 octobre

## ACTIVITÉ 3  Dates importantes   OPTIONAL

Give the following dates in French according to the model.

→ Noël (25/12)    **C'est le 25 décembre.**

1. la Saint Valentin (14/2)
2. la fête *(holiday)* nationale américaine (4/7)
3. le premier jour de l'année (1/1)
4. l'anniversaire de George Washington (22/2)
5. la fête de Christophe Colomb (12/10)
6. la fête nationale française (14/7)

In French the name **Georges**
is written with a final **s**.

# Prononciation

**Rythme et accent** *(Rhythm and stress)*

The *rhythm* of French is very *regular*. Within a group of words all syllables are short and even. There is no pause or break between words. The *stress* or accent falls on the *last syllable* of a word or group of words, making that last syllable a little longer than the others.

(This is the opposite of English, where each word of two or more syllables has its own stress pattern and where the rhythm is irregular because of long [–] and short [∪] syllables.)

Contrast:  *even rhythm and final stress*    *uneven rhythm*

Bŏnjoŭr, Mădame̸.        Goŏd morniňg, Ma͡'am.

Cŏmmeňt t'appell̸s-tu?    What ĭs yoŭr name?

## *ACTIVITÉ DE PRONONCIATION*

Act. 7

| TWO SYLLABLES | THREE SYLLABLES | FOUR SYLLABLES |
|---|---|---|
| Papa | Nathalie | Sylvie Dumas |
| Maman | Mélanie | Philippe Vallée |
| Madame | Mad∉moiselle | Madame Dulac |
| Jean-Paul | Jean-Michel | Je m'appelle Jean. |
| Bonjour | Bonjour, Paul. | Bonjour, Thomas. |
| Salut | Salut, Marc. | Salut, Suzanne. |
| Voici | Voici Lise. | Voici Michèle. |
| Voilà | Voilà Jacques. | Voilà Philippe. |
| Ça va. | Ça va mal. | Ça va très mal. |
| jeudi | un dollar | Il est midi. |
| mardi | deux dollars | Il est une heure. |
| demain | cinq dollars | Comme ci, comme ça. |

Be sure students pronounce syllables evenly. This activity reviews basic material of earlier lessons.

| FIVE SYLLABLES | SIX SYLLABLES |
|---|---|
| Voici Isabelle. | Voici Madame Lavoie. |
| Voilà Mélanie. | Voilà Sylvie Dumas. |
| C'est Monsieur Cardin. | C'est Mad∉moiselle Rochette. |
| Comment t'appelles-tu? | Je m'appelle Marc Rémi. |
| Je m'appelle Michèle. | Je m'appelle Jean-François. |
| Donne-moi un dollar. | Donne-moi vingt-cinq dollars. |
| Donnez-moi cinq francs. | Donnez-moi dix-huit francs. |
| le dix-sept avril | le vingt et un avril |
| C'est demain lundi. | C'est aujourd'hui dimanche. |

# Entre nous

## Expression pour la conversation

To express *surprise*, you may say:

**Vraiment?**    *Really?*

— Demain c'est le quinze octobre. C'est mon anniversaire.
— **Vraiment?** C'est aussi *(also)* l'anniversaire de Maman.

## Mini-dialogues   OPTIONAL

Create new dialogs, using the suggestions in the pictures to replace the
underlined words.

a) JACQUELINE: J'ai rendez-vous avec <u>Marc</u>.
    CHARLOTTE: Vraiment? Quand? *(When?)*
    JACQUELINE: <u>Le deux décembre</u>.

b)   CAROLINE: Quand est-ce, l'anniversaire de <u>Marc</u>?
    SUZANNE: C'est en <u>décembre</u>.
    CAROLINE: Quel jour?
    SUZANNE: Le <u>deux</u>.

**Marc**
**le 2 décembre**

**Brigitte**     **Marie-Louise**     **Pierre**     **Georges**
**le 4 janvier**    **le 22 juillet**    **le l avril**    **le 16 août**

WB   SCRIPT   QUIZ
3    [o—o]   p. 5
    Act. 6

# Leçon 6 La carte du temps

Act. 1

Aujourd'hui c'est le premier décembre.
Quel temps fait-il en France?
Ça dépend . . .

BORDEAUX

**À Bordeaux:**
Il fait bon.
Il fait dix degrés.

**À Toulon:**
Il fait douze degrés.
Il fait bon.
Il fait beau.
C'est magnifique!

**À Paris:**
Il fait beau à Paris en automne?
Aujourd'hui, non!
Il pleut.

**À Grenoble:**
Brrrr . . .
Il fait moins deux
   et il neige.
Oh là là! Il fait froid aujourd'hui!

---

**The weather map**

Today is December first.
How's the weather in France?
It all depends . . .

**In Bordeaux:**
The weather is (It's) fine.
It's ten degrees.

**In Toulon:**
It's twelve degrees.
The weather is (It's) fine.
The weather is (It's) nice.
It's great!

**In Paris:**
The weather is (It's) nice in Paris in the fall?
Not today!
It's raining.

**In Grenoble:**
Brrr . . .
It's minus two (two below zero)
   and it's snowing.
Oh dear! It's cold today.

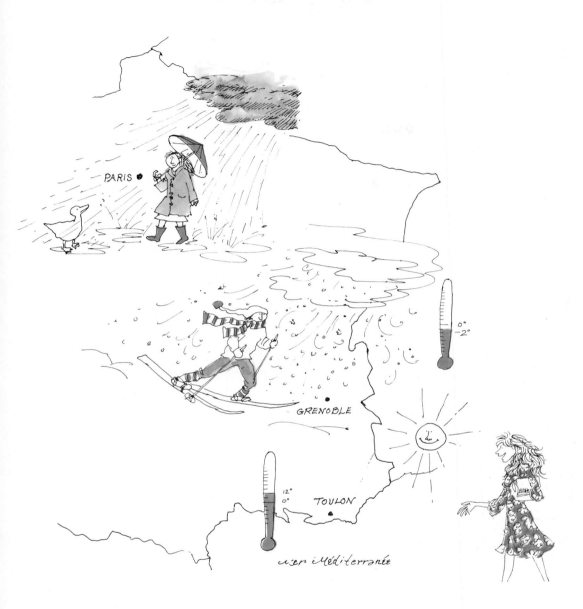

# NOTE CULTURELLE OPTIONAL

### Bonjour, la France!

Have you ever looked at a map of France? In size France is smaller than Texas, yet it is the largest country in Western Europe. It is also a land of many contrasts. It has plains, high mountains, and a long coastline. You can ski in the Alps, fish in the Atlantic, or relax on the beaches along the Mediterranean Sea. In this book you will learn more about France, its people, and the many other peoples of the world who also speak French.

Act. 2

9

## Vocabulaire spécialisé  Le temps et les saisons *(The weather and the seasons)*

**Quel temps fait-il?**     *How's the weather?*

**Il fait**
| | | |
|---|---|---|
| **beau.** | *It's nice.* |
| **bon.** | *It's fine (pleasant).* |
| **chaud.** | *It's hot.* |
| **frais.** | *It's cool.* |
| **froid.** | *It's cold.* |
| **mauvais.** | *It's bad.* |

| **en été** | *in (the) summer* |
|---|---|
| **en automne** | *in (the) fall* |
| **en hiver** | *in (the) winter* |
| **au printemps** | *in (the) spring* |

**Il pleut.**     *It's raining.*
**Il neige.**     *It's snowing.*

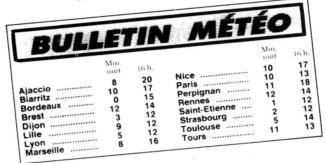

**BULLETIN MÉTÉO**

| | Min. nuit | 16 h. | | Min. nuit | 16 h. |
|---|---|---|---|---|---|
| Ajaccio | 8 | 20 | Nice | 10 | 17 |
| Biarritz | 10 | 17 | Paris | 10 | 13 |
| Bordeaux | 0 | 15 | Perpignan | 11 | 18 |
| Brest | 12 | 14 | Rennes | 12 | 14 |
| Dijon | 3 | 12 | Saint-Etienne | 1 | 12 |
| Lille | 9 | 12 | Strasbourg | 2 | 12 |
| Lyon | 5 | 12 | Toulouse | 5 | 14 |
| Marseille | 8 | 16 | Tours | 11 | 13 |

**Quelle température fait-il?**     *What's the temperature?*

| | | |
|---|---|---|
| **Il fait dix degrés.** | 10° | *It's ten degrees.* |
| **Il fait zéro.** | 0° | *It's zero.* |
| **Il fait moins cinq.** | −5° | *It's five below.* |

## NOTE CULTURELLE     OPTIONAL

### Le système métrique

Don't be surprised if a French person tells you that the weather is nice because the temperature outside has reached 15 degrees. The French use a Celsius thermometer. In fact, the French have been measuring distances in meters, liquids in liters, weights in grams, and temperatures in degrees Celsius for nearly two hundred years! They are the ones who invented the metric system!

You may want to introduce the following measurements: **un mètre, un kilomètre; un gramme, un kilogramme, une tonne; un litre.**

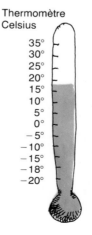

Thermomètre Celsius

| 35° |
| 30° |
| 25° |
| 20° |
| 15° |
| 10° |
| 5° |
| 0° |
| −5° |
| −10° |
| −15° |
| −18° |
| −20° |

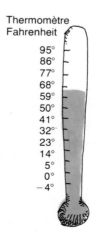

Thermomètre Fahrenheit

| 95° |
| 86° |
| 77° |
| 68° |
| 59° |
| 50° |
| 41° |
| 32° |
| 23° |
| 14° |
| 5° |
| 0° |
| −4° |

### ACTIVITÉ 1   Quel temps fait-il?

What we do often depends on the weather. We go skiing when there is snow and swimming when the weather is warm. Read what the following people are doing, and say what the weather is like.

→ Suzanne is putting on a sweater.   **Il fait froid. (Il fait frais.)**

1. Nathalie is going swimming.
2. Pierre is taking off his sweater.
3. Anne has her bathing suit on.
4. Caroline is shivering.

5. Pascal is trying to get a suntan.
6. Jacques does not want to go out.
7. Hélène is putting on her raincoat.
8. Sylvie will be able to go skiing.

### ACTIVITÉ 2   La carte du temps *(The weather map)*

Imagine that you are the weather announcer for a French TV station. Study the weather map and present the noon bulletin for each of the cities listed below.

→ À Bordeaux . . .   **À Bordeaux il fait six degrés. Il fait beau.**

1. À Lille . . .
2. À Lyon . . .
3. À Paris . . .
4. À Grenoble . . .
5. À Strasbourg . . .
6. À Toulon . . .
7. À Nice . . .
8. À Toulouse . . .
9. À Brest . . .

### ACTIVITÉ 3   Votre ville *(Your town)*

Imagine that Christine, a French girl, is planning to spend a year in your town as an exchange student. Tell her what the weather is like during the months listed below.

→ En juillet . . .   **En juillet il fait chaud.**

1. En août . . .
2. En septembre . . .
3. En novembre . . .

4. En janvier . . .
5. En mars . . .
6. En mai . . .

WB
1, 2

SCRIPT
Act. 3, 4

MASTERS
p. 7

### ACTIVITÉ 4  Les quatre saisons *(The four seasons)*   OPTIONAL

Describe the weather in the following cities for each of the four seasons.

**en été   en automne   en hiver   au printemps**

→ À Miami      **En été il fait chaud. En automne . . .**

1. À New York
2. À Chicago
3. À San Francisco
4. À Los Angeles
5. À Houston
6. À Denver

# Prononciation

## L'intonation

Act. 5

When you speak, your voice rises and falls. This is called *intonation*. In French, as in English, your voice goes down at the end of a statement. In the middle of a sentence your voice *rises* at the end of each group of words. (In English your voice levels off or drops at the end of each group of words.)

Voilà Nathalie.

L'anniversaire de Nathalie est en janvier.

L'anniversaire de Nathalie est le trente et un janvier.

Be sure that the students maintain an even rhythm and that they allow the stress to fall on the final syllable of each group of words.

### ACTIVITÉ DE PRONONCIATION

Repeat after the teacher:

Act. 5

1. Voici Paul.

   Voici Philippe.

   Voici Marie-Hélène.

   Voici Jean-François Dumas.

2. Ça va.

   Ça va mal.

   Ça va très mal.

   Ça va comme ci, comme ça.

3. Je m'appelle Anne.

   Je m'appelle Anne-Marie.

   Je m'appelle Anne-Marie Dupont.

This activity reviews some of the expressions taught in this unit.

4. Il est deux heures.

   Il est deux heures dix.

   Il est deux heures et quart.

   Il est deux heures et quart du matin.

5. Il fait mauvais.

   Il fait mauvais en hiver.

   Il fait mauvais en hiver à Toulouse.

9

# Entre nous

## Expression pour la conversation

When French speakers pause or hesitate, they often say:

**Euh ...**   *Er ... Uh ...*

## Mini-dialogues   OPTIONAL

Nathalie asks Philippe to check the weather outside.
Read the sample dialog carefully, then create new dialogs by replacing the
underlined words with the expressions suggested in the pictures.

NATHALIE: Quel temps fait-il aujourd'hui?
 PHILIPPE: Il fait beau!
NATHALIE: Et quelle température fait-il?
 PHILIPPE: Euh ... Il fait vingt degrés!

WB   MASTERS   QUIZ   WB Tests de Contrôle      TEST   pp. 7—11
3    pp. 62—64   p. 6

OBJECTIVES

To communicate and express themselves, students must have a good command of basic verb forms and verb constructions. For this reason, verbs are presented early in FRENCH FOR MASTERY. Unité 1 focuses on the following elements:

*Language*
  *verbs*
  • concept of verb-subject agreement (Because of the importance of this concept, the various verb forms are presented progressively and then summarized at the end of the unit.)
  • the present tense of **-er** verbs
  • negative and interrogative constructions
  • **être**
  *pronouns*
  • subject pronouns

*Vocabulary*
  • activities
  • some useful words

*Culture*

In this unit, the students are introduced to the French-speaking world, in its breadth and diversity.

# UNITÉ 1
# Parlez-vous français?

OPPOSITE: Mardi Gras celebration in Fort-de-France, Martinique

Each *Presentation text* contains several examples of the structures introduced in the lesson.
These STRUCTURES TO OBSERVE will be indicated at the beginning of each lesson.

# UNITÉ 1
# Leçon 1    Au Canada

STRUCTURES TO OBSERVE
• the pronoun **je** and the corresponding **-er** verb form
• the negative construction **ne. . .pas**

Act. 1

Bonjour!
Je m'appelle Suzanne Lavoie.
Je parle français.
Je parle anglais aussi.
C'est normal!
J'habite à Montréal!

Salut!
Je m'appelle Philippe Beliveau.
J'habite au Canada, mais je n'habite pas à Montréal.
J'habite à Québec.
Je parle anglais, mais je ne parle pas très bien.
Je parle français.
Vous aussi?
Magnifique!

**In Canada**
Hello!
My name is Suzanne Lavoie.
I speak French.
I also speak English.
That's logical (normal)!
I live in Montreal.

Hi!
My name is Philippe Beliveau.
I live in Canada, but I don't live in Montreal.
I live in Quebec City.
I speak English, but I don't speak very well.
I speak French.
You too?
Great!

The **CONVERSATION/OBSERVATIONS** section of each lesson constitutes the link between the *Presentation* text and the structures taught in the lesson. In the **CONVERSATION,** the students are asked to answer simple questions in which one or more structures have been used. In the **OBSERVATIONS,** the students are asked to derive these structures inductively. Most of these **CONVERSATION/OBSERVATIONS** sections are optional. If not done in class, they should be assigned as outside reading.

## CONVERSATION

Suzanne is talking about herself. Start a conversation with her by saying whether you do the same things (column A) or whether you don't (column B).

| Suzanne: | A | B |
|---|---|---|
| Je **parle** anglais. | Je **parle** anglais. | Je ne **parle** pas anglais. |
| Je **parle** français. | Je **parle** français. | Je ne **parle** pas français. |
| En hiver, je **skie**. | En hiver, je **skie**. | En hiver, je ne **skie** pas. |

## OBSERVATIONS   Str. B, D

The content of the **OBSERVATIONS** section is very important, since the concept of subject-verb agreement is basic to verb conjugation. You may want to refer to English examples *(I go, Paul goes, I am, you are)* and point out that the form of the verb is determined by who the subject is.

Most sentences have a *subject* and a *verb*. The *subject* is the word (or group of words) which tells who is doing the action. The *verb* is the word (or group of words) which tells what action is going on.

In French the *ending* of the verb depends on the subject of the sentence. Reread the above sentences in which Suzanne speaks about herself. In these sentences and in your replies the subject is **je** *(I)*, and the verb is the word in heavy type.

• Which letter does the verb end in when the subject is **je**?  -e

Now look at the suggested negative replies in column B.

• In a negative sentence, which word comes immediately *before* the verb?  ne

• Which word comes immediately *after* the verb?  pas

SUGGESTED REALIA: map of Québec; travel brochures, etc.

# NOTE CULTURELLE   OPTIONAL

### Les Canadiens français

Did you know that Montreal is the second-largest French-speaking city in the world after Paris? Over one-third of the twenty-five million citizens of Canada are of French origin and speak French. The French Canadians are very much attached to their language and their culture. This may explain why the coat of arms of the city of Quebec still bears the motto «Je me souviens» *("I remember").* The French Canadians remember their traditions.

SUPPLEMENTARY INFORMATION: You may indicate that there are many people of French-Canadian origin (**les Franco-Américains**) in the U.S., especially in New England. Some typical French-Canadian names are: Aucoin, Beaudet, Beliveau, Blanchard, Blanchette, Bourassa, Bourque, Brassard, Castonguay, Chouinard, Comeau, Coté, Cournoyer, Dionne, Dissautels, Drapeau, Giguerre, Goulet, Laflamme, Lafleur, Lajoie, Marcotte, Ouelette, Peloquin, Plante, Saintonge, Tremblay, Trottier, Santerre.

Leçon un   **43**

# Structure

## A. Les verbes en -er

When you look up a verb in the end vocabulary of this book, you will find it listed in the infinitive form: **parler** = *to speak*. The *infinitive* is the basic form of the verb. All other forms are derived from it. French verbs are grouped according to their *infinitive endings*. The most common infinitive ending is **-er**:

    **parler**   *to speak*     **skier**   *to ski*

Verbs ending in **-er** are called **-er** *verbs.*

## B. Le pronom sujet *je*

In a French sentence the ending of the verb depends on who the subject is.

| | | | |
|---|---|---|---|
| **parler** | *to speak* | Je **parle** anglais. | *I speak English.* |
| **skier** | *to ski* | Je **skie.** | *I ski.* |
| **visiter** | *to visit* | Je **visite** Québec. | *I visit Quebec City.* |

In a sentence where the subject is **je**, the verb is formed by replacing the **-er** ending of the infinitive with the ending  -e  .

SCRIPT
Act. 2

10, 13, 34

(je form)

## Vocabulaire spécialisé   Activités    You may want to model the **je** form of these verbs.

**parler**       français       anglais       espagnol       italien
   *to speak, talk*

**jouer**       au tennis       au football       au hockey
   *to play*

Have the students observe that in French **football** means *soccer.*

In French, **volleyball** is abbreviated to **volley**. Similarly, **football** and **basketball** have become **foot** and **basket**.

### ACTIVITÉ 1   Suzanne et Philippe

Suzanne tells Philippe what she does. Philippe tells her that he does different things. Play both roles according to the model.

→ parler anglais (français)

   Suzanne: **Je parle anglais.**
   Philippe: **Je parle français.**

1. parler espagnol (italien)
2. jouer au tennis (au hockey)
3. jouer au football (au volleyball)
4. téléphoner à Marc (à Denise)
5. dîner à six heures (à sept heures)
6. visiter Québec (Montréal)

Château Frontenac, Québec

**skier**
*to ski*

**dîner**
*to have dinner*

**téléphoner**   à Suzanne   à Paul
*to call, phone*

**visiter**   Paris
*to visit*

## C. L'élision

In the sentences on the left, each verb begins with a consonant sound.
In the sentences on the right, each verb begins with a vowel sound.
Compare the form of the subject in each pair of sentences.

| | |
|---|---|
| **Je** parle français. | **J'**habite à Québec. |
| **Je** téléphone à Paul. | **J'**invite Paul et Suzanne. |
| **Je** joue au hockey. | **J'**arrive de Montréal. |

> **Je** becomes **j'** before a vowel sound.

In French the final **e** of a few short words, such as **je**, is dropped when the next word begins with a *vowel sound*. In written French the dropped **e** is replaced by an *apostrophe* ('). This is called *elision*. (<u>Eli</u>sion means that the final vowel is <u>eli</u>minated.)

New instances of elision will be indicated as they occur.

Act. 2

11, 13

---

# Vocabulaire spécialisé **Activités** You may model the **je** form of these verbs for the students.

**habiter**   à Québec                          à New York
  *to live*

**arriver**   de Montréal        de Paris        **inviter**   Paul et Marie
  *to arrive, come*                                *to invite*

---

**46** Unité un

## ACTIVITÉ 2   La conférence des jeunes *(The youth conference)*

The following young people are attending the World Youth Conference.
After introducing themselves, they tell which language they speak and
where they live. Play the roles according to the model.

→   Suzanne (français / Québec)    **Je parle français.**    VARIATION: **Je m'appelle Suzanne.**
                                    **J'habite à Québec.**    **J'arrive de Québec.**

1. Paul (français / Paris)
2. Sylvie (français / Montréal)
3. Jacqueline (anglais / New York)
4. Thomas (anglais / Chicago)
5. Pietro (italien / Milan)
6. Maria (italien / Rome)
7. Teresa (espagnol / Mexico)
8. Paco (espagnol / Porto Rico)

## ACTIVITÉ 3   Nathalie

Nathalie does many things. Complete her statements with **Je** or **J'**, as
appropriate.

→   — joue au tennis.    **Je joue au tennis.**
    — invite Pierre.    **J'invite Pierre.**

1. — skie en hiver.
2. — parle italien.
3. — téléphone à Paul.
4. — dîne à six heures.
5. — arrive de Paris.
6. — habite à Montréal.
7. — parle espagnol.
8. — invite Monique.

---

## Vocabulaire spécialisé   **Mots utiles** (Useful words)

| | | |
|---|---|---|
| **à** | *at* | J'arrive **à** midi. |
| | *in* | J'habite **à** Montréal. |
| | *to* | Je parle **à** Pierre. |
| **de** | *from* | J'arrive **de** Québec. |
| | *of, about* | Je parle **de** Paris. |
| **aussi** | *also, too* | Je joue au tennis. Je joue au golf **aussi.** |
| **bien** | *well* | Je parle **bien** français.  *Usually the adverbs* **bien** *and* **mal** |
| **mal** | *poorly, badly* | Je parle **mal** espagnol.  *come immediately after the verb.* |
| **très** | *very* | Je joue **très** bien au football. |
| **et** | *and* | Voici Paul **et** voilà Sylvie. |
| **ou** | *or* | J'invite Suzanne **ou** Michèle. |
| **mais** | *but* | Je parle italien, **mais** je parle très mal. |
| **avec** | *with* | Je joue **avec** Suzanne. |

Note: There is elision with **de** when the next word begins with a vowel sound:
        J'arrive **d'**Annecy.

## D. La négation avec *ne . . . pas*

Paul does not do what Sylvie does. Compare what each one says.

Act. 3

| Sylvie: | Paul: | |
|---|---|---|
| Oui, je parle anglais. | Non, je **ne** parle **pas** anglais. | *I don't speak English.* |
| Oui, je joue au tennis. | Non, je **ne** joue **pas** au tennis. | *I don't play tennis.* |
| Oui, j'habite à Québec. | Non, je **n'**habite **pas** à Québec. | *I don't live in Quebec.* |
| Oui, j'invite Marc. | Non, je **n'**invite **pas** Marc. | *I don't invite Marc.* |

To make a sentence negative, French speakers use the following construction:

> subject   +   **ne**   +   verb   +   **pas**   +   (rest of sentence)
>                  ↓
>               **n'** (before a vowel sound)

### *ACTIVITÉ 4*   Hélas! *(Too bad!)*

Janine is a very active person. Her friend Thomas is not. Play both roles according to the model.

→ Je joue au tennis.   Janine: **Je joue au tennis.**
   Thomas: **Hélas, je ne joue pas au tennis!**

1. Je joue au volleyball.
2. Je joue avec Suzanne.
3. Je parle espagnol.
4. Je parle italien.

5. Je téléphone à Sylvie.
6. Je dîne avec Philippe.
7. Je visite Québec.
8. Je skie.

### *ACTIVITÉ 5*   Oui, mais . . .

WB
D1, D2

SCRIPT

Act. 4, 5

MASTERS
p. 8

One cannot do everything. Philippe does certain things, but he does not do others. Play the role of Philippe according to the model.

→ J'invite Suzanne. (Monique)   Philippe: **J'invite Suzanne, mais je n'invite pas Monique.**

1. Je joue au tennis. (au hockey)
2. J'habite à Québec. (à Montréal)
3. Je parle à Paul. (à Marc)
4. J'invite Hélène. (Catherine)

5. Je téléphone à Jean-Paul. (à François)
6. Je joue avec Jacques. (avec Paul)
7. Je visite Paris. (Nice)
8. Je dîne avec Michèle. (Sylvie)

Make sure that students use **n'** in items 2 and 4.

### *ACTIVITÉ 6*   Et toi?   OPTIONAL

Marie-Noëlle tells you what she does and asks whether you do the same things. Answer her according to the model.

→ Je danse très bien. Et toi?   **Je danse très bien aussi. (Non, je ne danse pas très bien.)**

1. Je parle espagnol. Et toi?
2. Je parle très bien français. Et toi?
3. J'habite au Canada. Et toi?
4. J'habite à Montréal. Et toi?

5. Je joue bien au tennis. Et toi?
6. Je joue mal au ping-pong. Et toi?
7. Je dîne à six heures et demie. Et toi?
8. Je skie en hiver. Et toi?

# Prononciation

Act. 8

**1. Le son** *(The sound)* /i/[1]

*Model word:* Phi̲lippe

*Practice words:* i̲l, Mi̲mi̲, Sylvi̲e, vi̲si̲te, dî̲ne, Y̲ves, ski̲e, hi̲ver

*Practice sentences:* Phi̲lippe vi̲si̲te l'I̲tali̲e.
Y̲ves habi̲te à Ni̲ce.

The French sound /i/ as in **Mimi** is shorter than the English vowel *e* of *me.*

Comment écrire /i/ *(How to write* /i/): **i, î, y**

**2. Le son** /a/

*Model word:* Ma̲da̲me

*Practice words:* A̲nnie, Ma̲x, Ca̲nnes, Ca̲na̲da̲, Pa̲na̲ma̲, ça̲ va̲, Ja̲cques

*Practice sentences:* Ma̲da̲me La̲va̲l ha̲bite à Pa̲na̲ma̲.
Ça̲ va̲, Na̲thalie?

The French sound /a/ is shorter and more precise than the English vowel *a* of *father.*

Comment écrire /a/: **a, à, â**

# Entre nous

SCRIPT
Act. 7

MASTERS
p. 8

QUIZ
pp. 12–13

## Expressions pour la conversation

To express their feelings about a situation French speakers often say:

| | |
|---|---|
| **Magnifique!** | *Great!* |
| **C'est magnifique!** | *That's great!* |
| **Dommage!** | *Too bad!* |
| **C'est dommage!** | *That's too bad!* |

## Mini-dialogue     OPTIONAL

There are many things that Jacques cannot do very well.

JACQUES: Je joue au tennis.
MONIQUE: Magnifique!
JACQUES: Mais je ne joue pas bien!
MONIQUE: Dommage!

## L'art du dialogue

a) Act out the dialog between Jacques and Monique.
b) Act out new dialogs where Jacques talks about his *playing volleyball,* his *speaking English,* his *speaking Spanish.* Replace **joue au tennis** and **ne joue pas** with the appropriate expressions.

---

[1]In this book French sounds are transcribed in phonetic symbols that you will find in many French dictionaries. One sound may have several different spellings. It may also happen that one letter or group of letters has several pronunciations. The sound-spelling correspondences of the French language are listed in Appendix 1.

# Leçon 2 À la Martinique

STRUCTURES TO OBSERVE
- the subject pronouns **il, elle, ils, elles** and the corresponding **-er** verb forms
- yes/no questions

Act. 1

Voici Denis.
Il habite à Fort-de-France.
Est-ce qu'il parle français?
Oui, bien sûr!
Mais il parle créole aussi.

Voici Hélène.
Elle joue au tennis.
Est-ce qu'elle habite à
    Fort-de-France?
Non, elle habite à Saint-Pierre.

Voici Antoine et Jean-Philippe.
Ils jouent au football.
Est-ce qu'ils jouent bien?
Oui, ils jouent très bien.

Voici Marie et Sylvie.
Elles habitent à Sainte-Anne.
Est-ce qu'elles dansent bien?
Ah oui! Elles dansent très,
    très bien!

**50** Unité un

Two of the favorite pastimes of Martinique young people are soccer and dancing. Fort-de-France is the capital of Martinique. Saint-Pierre, the former capital, was destroyed by a volcanic eruption in 1902. Sainte-Anne is a small town on the southeastern tip of the island.

## CONVERSATION

Are the following statements correct? If a statement is true, say **C'est vrai.**
If it is false, say **C'est faux.**

1. Denis parl**e** français.  vrai
2. **Il** habit**e** à Fort-de-France.  vrai
3. Hélène jou**e** au tennis.  vrai
4. **Elle** habit**e** à Fort-de-France.  faux

5. Antoine et Jean-Philippe jou**ent** au football.  vrai
6. **Ils** jou**ent** mal.  faux
7. Marie et Sylvie habit**ent** à Fort-de-France.  faux
8. **Elles** dans**ent** bien.  vrai

## OBSERVATIONS   Str. A

Look at the even-numbered sentences. The names of the young people have
been replaced by *pronouns.*

• Which pronoun is used to replace the following names:

  **Denis? Hélène? Antoine et Jean-Philippe? Marie et Sylvie?**
    il      elle              ils            elles

Sentences 1 to 4 tell what *one* person is doing. They have *singular* subjects.

• Which letter does each verb end in?   -e
• Is this letter pronounced?   no

Sentences 5 to 8 tell what *two* people are doing. They have *plural* subjects.

• Which three letters does each verb end in?   -ent
• Are these letters pronounced?   no

Départements are the administrative divisions of France.
You may ask your students to locate Martinique on
the map of the French-speaking world on pp. vi–vii.

## NOTE CULTURELLE   OPTIONAL

### La Martinique

Have you ever heard of Martinique? It is an island in the Caribbean Sea, south of Puerto Rico. The inhabitants of Martinique **(les Martiniquais)** are primarily of African origin. They
speak French, as well as a language of their own, **créole.**
Both Martinique and the nearby island of Guadeloupe are
French **départements,** and the people who live there are
French citizens. Did you realize that part of France is located
so close to the United States?

**In Martinique**

Here is Denis.
He lives in Fort-de-France.
Does he speak French?
Yes, of course.
But he also speaks Creole.

Here are Antoine and
  Jean-Philippe.
They play soccer.
Do they play well?
Yes, they play very well.

Here is Hélène.
She plays tennis.
Does she live in Fort-de-France?
No, she lives in Saint-Pierre.

Here are Marie and Sylvie.
They live in Sainte-Anne.
Do they dance well?
Oh yes! They dance very,
  very well!

SUGGESTED REALIA: travel brochures.
SUPPLEMENTARY INFORMATION: In the Caribbean, French is also spoken in Haiti. A former
French colony, Haiti gained its independence in 1804 and thus became the first independent black
country. Today, many Haitians have immigrated to the U.S.

Leçon deux  **51**

# Structure

The negative construction is reviewed in column C. Make sure that the students understand it. If necessary, you may ask them to translate these negative sentences.

## A. Les pronoms sujets: *il, elle, ils, elles*

In column A the subjects are *nouns*. In columns B and C these nouns have been replaced by *pronouns*. Note the forms of these pronouns and the corresponding verb endings.

| A | B | C |
|---|---|---|
| **Philippe** téléphon**e**. | **Il** téléphon**e** à Anne. | **Il** ne téléphon**e** pas à Sylvie. |
| **Mélanie** jou**e**. | **Elle** jou**e** au tennis. | **Elle** ne jou**e** pas au volleyball. |
| **Paul et Marc** parl**ent**. | **Ils** parl**ent** français. | **Ils** ne parl**ent** pas anglais. |
| **Annie et Louise** ski**ent**. | **Elles** ski**ent** bien. | **Elles** ne ski**ent** pas très bien. |
| **Paul et Anne** dans**ent**. | **Ils** dans**ent** mal. | **Ils** ne dans**ent** pas bien. |

To replace a noun subject, the French use the following subject pronouns:

Act. 2

|  | SINGULAR | PLURAL |
|---|---|---|
| *Masculine* | **il** *he* | **ils** *they* |
| *Feminine* | **elle** *she* | **elles** *they* |

➜ The French have two pronouns which correspond to the English *they*. **Ils** refers to a group of boys or a group including both boys and girls. **Elles** refers to a group composed only of girls.

➜ There is liaison after **ils** and **elles** when the next word begins with a vowel sound.

| NO LIAISON | LIAISON |
|---|---|
| Ils parlent français. | Ils̬ habitent à la Martinique. |
| Elles téléphonent à Anne. | Elles̬ invitent Anne. |

The verb is formed by replacing the **-er** ending of the infinitive with the ending which corresponds to the subject.

| When the subject is: | the ending is: |
|---|---|
| (singular) **il, elle** (*one* person) | -e |
| (plural) **ils, elles** (*two* or more people) | -ent |

➜ The endings **-e** and **-ent** are both *silent* in spoken French. Therefore the singular and plural verb forms, like **joue** (**Anne joue**) and **jouent** (**Anne et Marie jouent**), sound the same.

## ACTIVITÉ 1   Paul? ou Marc et Sylvie?

Who is doing the following things? Look carefully at the ending of each verb
and complete the sentences with **Paul** or with **Marc et Sylvie**, as appropriate.

→ — joue au tennis.    **Paul joue au tennis.**

1. — jouent au ping-pong.
2. — parle français.
3. — parlent créole.
4. — téléphonent à Denis.
5. — invite Antoine.

6. — dînent avec Jean-Philippe.
7. — habitent à la Martinique.
8. — habite à Québec.
9. — visite Montréal.
10. — dansent bien.

## ACTIVITÉ 2   Aussi

Friends often share the same interests. Read what the following people are
doing and say that their friends (indicated in parentheses) do the same things.

→ Philippe parle créole. (Marc et Antoine)    **Marc et Antoine parlent créole aussi.**

1. Hélène joue au tennis. (Lucie et Annie)
2. Paul et Jacques parlent avec Suzanne. (Denis)
3. Antoine téléphone à Paul. (Isabelle et Claire)

4. Marc invite Suzanne. (Philippe)
5. Jacques et Denis habitent à Fort-de-France. (Paul)
6. Nicole arrive à une heure. (Monique et Lise)

## ACTIVITÉ 3   Français ou anglais?

The following students speak the language of the country where they live.
Say whether they speak French or English, using subject pronouns.

→ Paul habite à New York.    **Il parle anglais.**

1. Caroline habite à Paris.
2. Jacques habite à Québec.
3. Antoine habite à Fort-de-France.
4. Sylvie habite à Chicago.

5. Denis et Charles habitent à Miami.
6. Hélène et Claire habitent à la Martinique.
7. Jacqueline et Robert habitent à Dallas.
8. Paul, Jacques et Anne habitent à Annecy.

## ACTIVITÉ 4   Avec qui? (With whom?)

The following teenagers are doing things together with their friends.
Express this according to the model, using appropriate subject pronouns.

→ Hélène joue au tennis. (avec Mélanie)    **Elle joue au tennis avec Mélanie.**

1. Paul et Jean-Marc jouent au volleyball. (avec Isabelle)
2. Annette et Sylvie parlent français. (avec Antoine)
3. Philippe et Monique dînent. (avec Jean-Pierre)
4. Marc, Sylvie et Brigitte jouent au football. (avec Thomas)

5. Jean-Claude et François habitent à Paris. (avec Paul)
6. Thérèse et Monique habitent à Québec. (avec Lucie)
7. André et Jean-Paul arrivent à New York. (avec Jacques)
8. Monique et Albert arrivent à Boston. (avec Claire)

## ACTIVITÉ 5  Oui et non

Read what the following people are doing; then say that they are not doing
something else. Use the expression in parentheses and the appropriate
subject pronoun.

→ Monsieur Ballard téléphone à Paris. (à Québec)    **Il ne téléphone pas à Québec.**

WB
A1

SCRIPT

Act. 3

MASTERS
p. 9

1. Hélène parle à Paul. (à Jacques)
2. Monique et Sylvie skient en hiver.
   (au printemps)
3. Thomas et Jean-Luc jouent au tennis.
   (au ping-pong)
4. Jacqueline dîne avec Lucie. (Anne-Marie)
5. Paul et Marc invitent Mélanie. (Thérèse)

6. Madame Beliveau habite à Québec.
   (à Paris)
7. Monsieur et Madame Vallée habitent à
   Fort-de-France. (à Montréal)
8. Suzanne arrive de San Francisco.
   (de Chicago)

Be sure students use **n'. . . pas** in items 5–8.

12, 13

## Vocabulaire spécialisé  Activités

**étudier** (le français, l'anglais, la musique)
*to study*

**danser**
*to dance*

**rentrer**
*to come back,
go back, go home*

## ACTIVITÉ 6  Les vacances sont finies. *(Vacation is over.)*

Read what the following students do during their vacation. Now that the
vacation is over, they are studying and are not doing these things anymore.
Express this according to the model.

→ Paul skie.    **Aujourd'hui il étudie.**
                **Il ne skie pas.**

Marc et Anne dansent.    **Aujourd'hui ils étudient.**
                          **Ils ne dansent pas.**

WB
A2, A3

SCRIPT

Act. 4, 5

1. Thérèse joue au tennis.
2. Henri dîne au restaurant.
3. Jean et Paul jouent au football.

4. Sylvie et Annie skient.
5. Catherine et Jacques dansent.
6. François et Robert visitent Paris.

## B. Questions à réponse affirmative ou négative *(Yes / no questions)*

The questions below ask for a *yes* or *no* answer. Such questions are called *yes/no questions*. Compare these questions with the statements on the right.

SCRIPT
Act. 7

| QUESTIONS | STATEMENTS |
|---|---|
| **Est-ce que** Denis habite à Fort-de-France? | Oui, Denis habite à Fort-de-France. |
| **Est-ce qu'il** parle français? | Oui, il parle français. |
| **Est-ce que** Marie joue au tennis? | Oui, Marie joue au tennis. |
| **Est-ce qu'elle** étudie avec Paul? | Oui, elle étudie avec Paul. |

To transform a statement into a yes/no question, French speakers use the following construction:

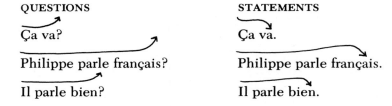

> **est-ce que**  +  (rest of statement)  ?
> ↓
> **est-ce qu'**  (+ vowel sound)

→ Note the elision **est-ce qu'** when the next word begins with a vowel sound.

→ In informal questions you can change a statement into a yes/no question by simply letting your voice rise at the end of the sentence. This is like English.

| QUESTIONS | STATEMENTS |
|---|---|
| Ça va? | Ça va. |
| Philippe parle français? | Philippe parle français. |
| Il parle bien? | Il parle bien. |

## *ACTIVITÉ 7*   Les étudiants français *(French students)*

Imagine that you are the president of the French Club. Your school is hosting the following French-speaking students for a month. Before welcoming them, you would like to know more about them. Ask questions according to the model.

→ Philippe parle anglais.   **Est-ce que Philippe parle anglais?**

VARIATION: Ask intonation questions.
**Philippe parle anglais?**

1. Jeanne parle italien.
2. Marc joue au tennis.
3. Francine skie bien.
4. Claire étudie la musique.
5. Jacqueline habite à Paris.
6. Jean-Paul habite à Lyon.
7. Lucie et Charles jouent au volleyball.
8. Paul et Louis jouent au football.

There are no examples of elision in this exercise. To practice elision, substitute names beginning with a vowel sound: Anne, Annie, Antoine, Hélène, Isabelle, Olga, Yves. **Est-ce qu'Anne parle anglais?**

***ACTIVITÉ 8*** **À la surprise-partie** *(At the party)*  This activity reviews subject pronouns and practices elision with **est-ce qu'.**

The following teenagers are at a party. Ask whether they dance well. Use subject pronouns.

→ Philippe     **Est-ce qu'il danse bien?**

1. Annie
2. Jean-Paul
3. Jacques et André
4. Nathalie et Suzanne
5. Robert et Sylvie
6. Louise et Mélanie
7. Henri
8. Lucie et Jean-Philippe

WB
B1, B2

SCRIPT

Act. 6, 8

MASTERS
p. 9

VARIATIONS: **Est-ce qu'il parle bien anglais?**
**Est-ce qu'il étudie avec Paul?** (Also, elision with **ils** and **elles**.)

# Prononciation

Act. 10

## Le son /r/

*Model word:* Pa<u>r</u>is

*Practice words:* Ma<u>r</u>c, Ma<u>r</u>ie, Pat<u>r</u>ick, a<u>rr</u>ive, <u>r</u>ent<u>r</u>e, pa<u>r</u>le

*Practice sentences:*  Ma<u>r</u>ie a<u>rr</u>ive à Fo<u>r</u>t-de-F<u>r</u>ance.
                       Ma<u>r</u>c pa<u>r</u>le c<u>r</u>éole.

The French /r/ is pronounced at the back of the throat. To pronounce a French /r/, say /ga/ and then clear your throat while keeping your tongue in the same position. The resulting sound is an /r/. Practice the French /r/ by pronouncing the French word **garage.**

# Entre nous

## Expressions pour la conversation

To attract a friend's attention you can say:

**Tiens!** *Look! Hey!* **Tiens,** voilà Marc!

There are many ways of saying *yes* or *no* in French:

| | | |
|---|---|---|
| **Oui!** | *Yes!* | **Oui,** Marc parle français. |
| **Mais oui!** | *Certainly!* | **Mais oui,** il parle français. |
| **Bien sûr!** | *Sure! Of course!* | **Bien sûr,** Marie parle français aussi. |
| | | |
| **Non!** | *No!* | **Non,** Marc n'habite pas à Montréal. |
| **Mais non!** | *Of course not!* | **Mais non,** il n'habite pas à Québec. |
| **Pas du tout!** | *Not at all!* | **Pas du tout!** Il parle très bien français. |
| **Au contraire!** | *On the contrary!* | **Au contraire!** Il danse très bien. |

## Mini-dialogue    OPTIONAL

Philippe and Annie are at a party at an international school. Annie knows
many of the guests.

PHILIPPE: Bonjour, Annie!
ANNIE: Bonjour, Philippe! Ça va?
PHILIPPE: Ça va, merci!
ANNIE: Tiens, voilà Jacqueline!
PHILIPPE: Est-ce qu'elle parle français?
ANNIE: Bien sûr! Elle habite à Montréal!
PHILIPPE: Est-ce qu'elle parle avec un accent?
ANNIE: Mais non! Au contraire, elle parle très bien!

## L'art du dialogue

SCRIPT

Act. 9

MASTERS
p. 9

QUIZ
p. 14

a) Act out the dialog between Annie and Philippe.

b) Now imagine that Patrick drops in. Patrick is from Fort-de-France. Act out the new dialog,
replacing Jacqueline by **Patrick,** and Montréal by **Fort-de-France.** Make all necessary
changes.

c) Now **Alice** and **Robert,** who are from **Québec,** show up. Act out the new dialog between
Annie and Philippe, and make all necessary changes.

# Leçon 3  Au club international

Act. 1

The International Club is having a big party.
Michèle meets several students from Africa there.

**Michèle parle à Abdou.**

MICHÈLE: Bonjour! Je m'appelle Michèle!
Et toi? Comment est-ce que tu t'appelles?
ABDOU: Je m'appelle Abdou.
MICHÈLE: Où est-ce que tu habites?
ABDOU: J'habite à Dakar.

**Michèle parle à Adjoua et à Aya.**

MICHÈLE: Est-ce que vous habitez à Dakar aussi?
ADJOUA: Non! Nous habitons à Abidjan.
MICHÈLE: Quand est-ce que vous rentrez à Abidjan?
AYA: Nous rentrons demain.
MICHÈLE: Pourquoi demain?
ADJOUA: Parce que les vacances sont finies.
MICHÈLE: Dommage!

**At the International Club**

Michèle is talking to Abdou.

Michèle: Hello! My name is Michèle!
And you? What's your name?
Abdou: My name is Abdou.
Michèle: Where do you live?
Abdou: I live in Dakar.

Michèle is talking to Adjoua and Aya.

Michèle: Do you live in Dakar also?
Adjoua: No! We live in Abidjan.
Michèle: When are you going back to Abidjan?
Aya: We are going back tomorrow.
Michèle: Why tomorrow?
Adjoua: Because vacation is over.
Michèle: Too bad!

## CONVERSATION OPTIONAL

Michèle is asking you questions. Answer her by completing the sentences.

1. **Où** est-ce que **tu habites?** (à Philadelphie? à Akron? à . . .?)
   J'habite à . . .
2. **À quelle heure** est-ce que **tu dînes?** (à cinq heures et demie? à six heures? à . . .?)
   Je dîne à . . .
3. **Quand** est-ce que **tu joues** au tennis? (en été? en hiver? au printemps? . . .?)
   Je joue au tennis . . .

## OBSERVATIONS  Str. B  OPTIONAL

Reread Michèle's questions carefully.

- How does she say *you* in her questions?  tu
- Which two letters do the verbs end in when the subject is **tu?**  -es

In these questions Michèle is asking for information.

- Which interrogative expression does she use to say *where? at what time? when?*  où  à quelle heure  quand
- What expression does she use immediately after the interrogative expression?  est-ce que

SUPPLEMENTARY INFORMATION: Among other African countries that use French as their official language are **le Zaïre** (the largest country in Africa) and **Madagascar** (a large island off the east coast of Africa).

SUGGESTED REALIA: stamps from French-speaking African countries.

## NOTE CULTURELLE  OPTIONAL

### Qui parle français en Afrique?

French is spoken in many countries of central and western Africa. These countries are former French or Belgian colonies which have maintained French as their official language. Dakar is the capital of Senegal **(le Sénégal),** a country whose inhabitants are predominantly Moslem. Abidjan is the capital of the Ivory Coast **(la Côte-d'Ivoire),** one of the most prosperous and dynamic countries of western Africa.

Although not the official language, French is also spoken by many people in the North African countries of Morocco **(le Maroc),** Algeria **(l'Algérie),** and Tunisia **(la Tunisie).**

**Abdou** is a boy's name typical of Senegal. **Adjoua** and **Aya** are girls' names typical of the Ivory Coast.

Turn to the map of the French-speaking world on pp. vi–vii.

Dakar, Sénégal

In the past, many African families used to give French names to their children. After these countries gained their independence in the 1960's, there was a return to African traditions and African names. In certain tribes, children are named after the day of the week on which they are born, such as Adjoua (Tuesday) or Aya (Friday).

# Structure

## A. Les pronoms sujets: *je, tu, nous, vous*

In Lesson 2 of this Unit you learned four subject pronouns: **il, elle, ils, elles.** The other four subject pronouns are: **je** (which you learned in Lesson 1), **tu, nous,** and **vous.** Note the verb endings that correspond to these pronouns in the sentences below.

Act. 2

| SINGULAR | | | PLURAL | | |
|---|---|---|---|---|---|
| **je** | *I* | Je parl**e** français. | **nous** | *we* | Nous parl**ons** français. |
| ↓ **j'** | (+ vowel sound) | J'habit**e** à Paris. | | | Nous habit**ons** à Dakar. |
| **tu** | *you* | Tu parl**es** français.<br>Tu habit**es** à Dakar. | **vous** | *you* | Vous parl**ez** français.<br>Vous habit**ez** à Québec. |

→ In French there are two pronouns which correspond to the English *you:*

**tu** when speaking to *one* person
**vous** when speaking to *two* or more people

→ There is liaison after **nous** and **vous** when the next word begins with a vowel sound.

→ The following **-er** verb endings are used with the above subject pronouns:

WB A1

(je) **-e** (tu) **-es** (nous) **-ons** (vous) **-ez**

The **je** and **tu** endings are silent. The **nous** and **vous** endings are pronounced.

### *ACTIVITÉ 1* Tennis?

Imagine that you are looking for tennis partners at the Roland Garros tennis club in Paris. Ask the following people if they play tennis, using **tu** or **vous,** as appropriate.

→ Charles et Émilie **Est-ce que vous jouez au tennis?**

1. Paul
2. Hélène
3. Jean-Paul et Marie-Anne
4. Claire
5. Sylvie et André
6. Suzanne, Édouard et Philippe

## Vocabulaire spécialisé  Mots utiles *(Useful words)*

| | | |
|---|---|---|
| **beaucoup** | *much, very much, a lot* | Nous étudions **beaucoup**. |
| **un peu** | *a little, a little bit* | Vous parlez **un peu** français. |
| **maintenant** | *now* | J'étudie **maintenant**. Maintenant often comes at the end of the sentence. |
| **rarement** | *rarely, seldom* | Tu joues **rarement** au tennis, Jacqueline? |
| **souvent** | *often* | Charles invite **souvent** Nathalie. |
| **toujours** | *always* | Nous skions **toujours** à Grenoble. |

You may want to review the adverbs **bien** and **mal**.

Note: The above expressions usually come after the verb. They *never* come between the subject and the verb. Compare:

Nous <u>parlons</u> **toujours** français.    *We always <u>speak</u> French.*

Tu <u>ne joues pas</u> **souvent** au tennis.    *You <u>don't</u> often <u>play</u> tennis.*

Be sure the students do *not* say "très beaucoup." Stress that **beaucoup** means *very much*.

## ACTIVITÉ 2   Dialogue

Be curious! Ask the person next to you if he or she does the following things. Use the pronoun **tu**. Your neighbor will answer you.

→  Il / elle  étudie l'espagnol?    — **Est-ce que tu étudies l'espagnol?**
    — **Oui, j'étudie l'espagnol.**
    **(Non, je n'étudie pas l'espagnol.)**

1. Il / elle danse?
2. Il / elle danse souvent?
3. Il / elle étudie la musique?
4. Il / elle joue au tennis?
5. Il / elle téléphone beaucoup?
6. Il / elle étudie rarement?
7. Il / elle parle toujours français?
8. Il / elle parle un peu français?

## ACTIVITÉ 3   En Amérique

A French journalist is writing an article about American high school students. Imagine he is asking questions about you and your friends. Answer him, using the pronoun **nous**.

→  Est-ce que vous étudiez beaucoup?
    **Oui, en Amérique nous  étudions beaucoup.**
    **(Non, en Amérique nous n'étudions pas beaucoup.)**

1. Est-ce que vous jouez au baseball?
2. Est-ce que vous jouez au golf?
3. Est-ce que vous étudiez le français?
4. Est-ce que vous skiez en hiver?
5. Est-ce que vous dansez souvent?
6. Est-ce que vous téléphonez beaucoup?

## B. Questions d'information

The questions in the chart below cannot be answered by *yes* or *no*. Since they ask for specific information, they are called *information questions*.

Act. 7

| | | | |
|---|---|---|---|
| **où?** | *where?* | — **Où** est-ce que tu habites? | — À Dakar. |
| **quand?** | *when?* | — **Quand** est-ce qu'Aya rentre? | — Le 15 août. |
| **à quelle heure?** | *at what time?* | — **À quelle heure** est-ce que nous dînons? | — À six heures. |
| **comment?** | *how?* | — **Comment** est-ce que tu joues au tennis? | — Très bien! |
| **pourquoi?** | *why?* | — **Pourquoi** est-ce que tu invites Janine? | |
| **parce que . . .** | *because . . .* | — **Parce que** Janine danse très bien. | |

There is usually liaison in the expression **quand**/t/**est-ce que. . .** ?

To form an information question, French speakers often use the following construction:

> interrogative expression  +  **est-ce que**  +  subject  +  verb  +  (rest of sentence)  ?
> ↓
> **est-ce qu'** (+ vowel sound)

→ The interrogative expression indicates what type of information is requested.

→ The expression **parce que** becomes **parce qu'** before a vowel sound.

J'invite Adjoua **parce qu'**elle danse bien.

où? quand? comment?
qui? pourquoi?
il a réponse à tout
le petit Larousse en couleurs

Short questions with **où** are often formed as follows:

## *ACTIVITÉ 4*  Le club français     | où + verb + subject |     Où habite Aya?

The president of the French Club wants to know the addresses of some of the members. The secretary tells her where each one lives. Play both roles according to the model.

→ Sylvie (à Québec)     La présidente: **Où est-ce que Sylvie habite?**
                        La secrétaire: **Elle habite à Québec.**

1. Jacques (à Montréal)     3. Aya et Adjoua (à Abidjan)     5. Jacqueline (à Paris)
2. Abdou (à Dakar)          4. Suzanne et Michèle (à Nice)   6. Louis et Antoine (à Toulouse)

## *ACTIVITÉ 5*  Curiosité

Annie says that her friends are doing certain things. Philippe wants more information. Play both roles according to the model.

→ Jacques arrive à Paris. (quand?)     Annie: **Jacques arrive à Paris.**
                                       Philippe: **Quand est-ce qu'il arrive à Paris?**

WB
B1, B2

SCRIPT

Act. 8, 9

1. Aya rentre à Abidjan. (quand?)                5. Thomas joue au tennis. (comment?)
2. Sylvie visite Abidjan. (quand?)               6. Hélène parle anglais. (comment?)
3. Louise dîne au restaurant. (à quelle heure?)  7. François étudie l'espagnol. (pourquoi?)
4. Paul téléphone à Marie. (à quelle heure?)     8. Isabelle parle avec Henri. (pourquoi?)

# Prononciation

## Le son /ɔ̃/

*Model word:* non

*Practice words:* onze, Simon, dînons, visitons, bonjour, bombe

*Practice sentences:* Bonjour, Simon!

Nous jouons avec Yvon.

The sound /ɔ̃/ is a nasal vowel. When you pronounce a nasal vowel, air passes through your nasal passages. Be sure not to pronounce an /n/ or /m/ after a nasal vowel.

Comment écrire /ɔ̃/: **on** (**om** before **b** or **p**)

# Entre nous

### Expression pour la conversation

In addition to using **est-ce que** or letting your voice rise at the end of a sentence, there is another way to make a yes/no question in French, especially when you expect the other person to agree with you. You simply add **n'est-ce pas?** to the end of the sentence.

Aya habite à Abidjan, **n'est-ce pas?**     *Aya lives in Abidjan, doesn't she?*
Vous parlez français, **n'est-ce pas?**     *You speak French, don't you?*

### Mini-dialogue    OPTIONAL

The evening before Aya's departure for Abidjan, Philippe invites her to a restaurant. Madame Leblanc, Philippe's mother, asks her son about his plans.

MME LEBLANC: Tu dînes avec *nous*, n'est-ce pas?     *us*
PHILIPPE: Non, Maman. *Ce soir* je dîne *en ville*.     *Tonight; in town*
MME LEBLANC: Avec *qui* est-ce que tu dînes?     *whom*
PHILIPPE: Je dîne avec Aya. Elle rentre demain à Abidjan.
MME LEBLANC: Où est-ce que vous dînez?
PHILIPPE: Nous dînons "Chez Simone".
MME LEBLANC: Quand est-ce que tu rentres?
PHILIPPE: À onze heures.
MME LEBLANC: Au revoir. Et *amusez-vous bien*.     *have a good time*

### L'art du dialogue

a) Act out the dialog between Madame Leblanc and Philippe.
b) Imagine that Madame Leblanc is talking to her two sons, **Philippe** and **Pascal.** Act out the new dialog.

# Leçon 4 À Bruxelles

STRUCTURES TO OBSERVE
• the choice between **tu** and **vous**
• the infinitive construction after verbs such as **aimer**

Marc, un étudiant belge, parle avec Irène Arnold, une étudiante suisse.
Marc parle aussi avec Monsieur Arnold, le père d'Irène.
Monsieur Arnold travaille pour une compagnie internationale.

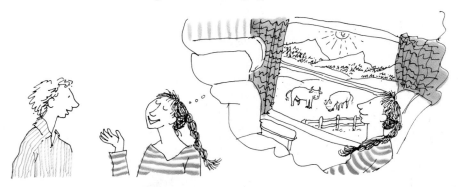

**Marc et Irène**

MARC: Irène, tu parles bien français.
IRÈNE: Je parle souvent français.
En famille nous parlons toujours français.
MARC: Tu aimes voyager?
IRÈNE: J'adore voyager. Mais hélas, je voyage rarement.

**Marc et Monsieur Arnold**

MARC: Monsieur Arnold, pourquoi est-ce que vous habitez à Bruxelles?
M. ARNOLD: Parce que je travaille pour une compagnie internationale.
MARC: Alors, vous voyagez souvent?
M. ARNOLD: Hélas oui. Je voyage souvent. Je déteste voyager.

From this point on, comprehension questions accompany the *Presentation text*.
**Est-ce qu'Irène parle français? Est-ce qu'elle aime voyager? Est-ce qu'elle voyage souvent? Où est-ce que Monsieur Arnold habite? Pourquoi est-ce qu'il habite à Bruxelles? Est-ce qu'il voyage souvent? Est-ce qu'il aime voyager?**

## CONVERSATION

Imagine that Marc, an exchange student from Belgium, is talking to you. Answer his questions.

1. Est-ce que **tu** parles français?
2. Est-ce que **tu** skies?
3. Est-ce que **tu** joues au tennis?
4. Est-ce que **tu** étudies la musique?

Now imagine that Mademoiselle Pascal, a teacher from Belgium, is talking to you. Answer her.

5. Est-ce que **vous** parlez français?
6. Est-ce que **vous** skiez?
7. Est-ce que **vous** jouez au tennis?
8. Est-ce que **vous** étudiez la musique?

## OBSERVATIONS   Str. A

Marc, the student, and Mademoiselle Pascal, the teacher, ask you the same questions, but in different ways.

Marc, like you, is a student. He talks to you in an *informal* way.

• Which pronoun does he use?   tu

Mademoiselle Pascal talks to you in a more *formal* way.

• Which pronoun does she use?   vous

You may ask your students to locate these countries on the map of the French-speaking world on pp. vi–vii.

## NOTE CULTURELLE   OPTIONAL

### Qui parle français en Europe?

Have you heard of Brussels? Geneva? Luxemburg? Monaco? These are all cities outside France where the inhabitants speak French. Brussels **(Bruxelles)** is the capital of Belgium **(la Belgique)**, a country with two national languages: French and Flemish. Since many European organizations have their offices there, Brussels is considered one of the capitals of Europe.

Geneva **(Genève)** is the second largest city in Switzerland **(la Suisse).** It is the seat of the International Red Cross and of many United Nations agencies.

In spite of its small size, Luxemburg **(le Luxembourg)** is a very prosperous and dynamic country. It is also an important international center. **Monaco** is a popular resort, located on the French Riviera. It is known for its Grand Prix car race and its casino.

SUGGESTED REALIA: stamps from these countries.

Helvetia, the Latin name for Switzerland, appears on Swiss coins and stamps.

### In Brussels

Marc, a Belgian student, is talking with Irène Arnold, a Swiss student.
Marc is also talking with Mr. Arnold, Irène's father.
Mr. Arnold works for an international company.

Marc: Irène, you speak French well.
Irène: I often speak French.
At home we always speak French.
Marc: Do you like to travel?
Irène: I adore traveling. But unfortunately (alas), I rarely travel.

Marc: Mr. Arnold, why do you live in Brussels?
M. Arnold: Because I work for an international company.
Marc: So you travel often?
M. Arnold: Unfortunately (alas), yes. I travel often. I hate to travel.

# Structure

## A. *Tu ou vous?*

In the Prélude, students learned that French speakers address one another with different degrees of formality. You may wish to review the notes on pp. 5, 9, 16 before beginning this section.

Compare the pronouns which Marc uses when he speaks to his classmate Anne and when he speaks to Madame Robert, his English teacher.

| Marc parle à Anne: | Marc parle à Madame Robert: | |
|---|---|---|
| **Tu** parles bien anglais! | **Vous** parlez bien anglais! | *You speak English well!* |
| Où est-ce que **tu** habites? | Où est-ce que **vous** habitez? | *Where do you live?* |

When talking to one person, French speakers sometimes say **tu** and sometimes **vous**.

> **Tu** is used to address a child, a member of the family, a close friend, or a classmate. **Tu** is called the *familiar* form of address.
>
> **Vous** is used to address everyone else. **Vous** is called the *formal* form of address.

→ **Vous** is also the plural of both the familiar and the formal forms:

| FAMILIAR | FORMAL |
|---|---|
| Salut, Paul! Salut, Suzanne! | Bonjour, Monsieur! Bonjour, Madame! |
| Est-ce que **vous** parlez espagnol? | Est-ce que **vous** parlez anglais? |

→ In the **Questions personnelles** and in most **Conversation** sections you will be addressed as **vous**. You should use **vous** when talking to your teacher. However, when talking to your classmates, you should use **tu**.

You may address your students as **tu**, since this form of address is being used more and more frequently by teachers in France.

### ACTIVITÉ 1  À qui est-ce qu'il parle? *(To whom is he speaking?)*

François is spending his vacation in the home of his friend Marc. Note the form of address he uses in the following questions and decide whether he is speaking to Marc or to Madame Rémi, Marc's mother.

→ Est-ce que vous jouez très bien au tennis?   **François parle à Madame Rémi.**

1. À quelle heure est-ce que tu téléphones?
2. Est-ce que vous dînez souvent au restaurant?
3. Quand est-ce que tu rentres?
4. Est-ce que vous parlez espagnol?
5. Quand est-ce que vous rentrez à Paris?
6. Pourquoi est-ce que tu étudies aujourd'hui?

### ACTIVITÉ 2  Une enquête *(A survey)*

Imagine that a French magazine has asked you to make a survey of how widely French is spoken in this country. Ask the following people if they speak French, using the familiar or formal form of address, as appropriate.

→ your cousin   **Est-ce que tu parles français?**

1. your math teacher
2. the principal
3. your best friend
4. your best friend's mother
5. your uncle
6. your neighbor's little boy
7. the student seated next to you
8. that student's father

## B. Le présent des verbes réguliers en -*er*

### Forms

You may practice the -**er** verb conjugation by asking the students to conjugate other verbs: **je chante, tu chantes. . . ; je joue, tu joues. . .**

Most verbs in **-er** form their present tense like **parler.**

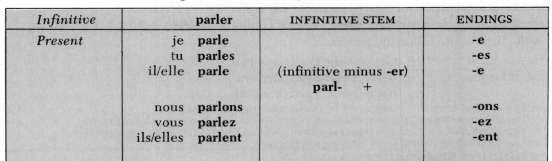

| *Infinitive* | | **parler** | INFINITIVE STEM | ENDINGS |
|---|---|---|---|---|
| *Present* | je | **parle** | | **-e** |
| | tu | **parles** | | **-es** |
| | il/elle | **parle** | (infinitive minus **-er**) | **-e** |
| | | | **parl-** + | |
| | nous | **parlons** | | **-ons** |
| | vous | **parlez** | | **-ez** |
| | ils/elles | **parlent** | | **-ent** |

The present tense forms of **parler** consist of two parts:

(1) a part which does not change: the *stem* (which is the infinitive minus **-er**)
(2) a part which changes to agree with the subject: the *ending*

Verbs conjugated like **parler** are called *regular* **-er** verbs because their forms can be predicted.

At this point you may want to prepare a list of all the -**er** verbs already taught. This activity may be set up as a game. Ask each student to take a sheet of paper and write from memory as many verbs as he/she can remember. The student with the longest correct list is the winner.

### Uses

Note the English equivalents of the French verbs in the present tense:

Irène **parle** français.
$\begin{cases} \textit{Irène \textbf{speaks} French.} \\ \textit{Irène \textbf{does speak} French.} \\ \textit{Irène \textbf{is speaking} French.} \end{cases}$

Irène **ne parle pas** anglais.
$\begin{cases} \textit{Irène \textbf{does not speak} English.} \\ \textit{Irène \textbf{is not speaking} English.} \end{cases}$

Est-ce qu'Irène **parle** italien?
$\begin{cases} \textit{\textbf{Does} Irène \textbf{speak} Italian?} \\ \textit{\textbf{Is} Irène \textbf{speaking} Italian?} \end{cases}$

→ In French the present tense consists of *one* word. It is used to describe what people *do* (regularly) or *are doing* (at the moment).

***ACTIVITÉ 3*** Voyage en France *(A trip to France)*

A group of American students are on a tour of France. During the trip they do the following things:

> **arriver à Paris / téléphoner à Paul / visiter la tour Eiffel / inviter Sylvie /**
> **parler français / arriver à Annecy / skier / visiter Toulouse / rentrer à New York**

Describe the trips of the following people.

1. Paul                            (begin with: **Il arrive à Paris.** ...)
2. Hélène et Louise            (begin with: **Elles arrivent à Paris.** ...)
3. you                             (begin with: **J'arrive à Paris.** ...)
4. you and your best friend     (begin with: **Nous arrivons à Paris.** ...)

Act. 5

12, 13

# Vocabulaire spécialisé    Activités

**chanter**
*to sing*

**écouter** (la radio)
*to listen to (the radio)*

**regarder** (la télé)
*to watch (TV)*

**regarder** (Paul)
*to look at*

**nager**
*to swim*

**travailler**
*to work*

**voyager**
*to travel*

Note: **Regarder** has two meanings: *to look at* and *to watch*.
       Paul **regarde** Sylvie.     Sylvie **regarde** la télé.

Activités 4 and 5 focus on two uses of the present tense in French: I play
tennis (in general); and, I am playing tennis (right now).

## ACTIVITÉ 4  Activités

Ask your classmates whether they do the following things.

→ jouer au tennis      — **Est-ce que tu joues au tennis?**
                       — **Bien sûr, je joue au tennis.**
                          **(Mais non, je ne joue pas au tennis.)**

1. danser            5. voyager            9. parler français
2. skier             6. regarder la télé   10. parler anglais
3. nager             7. écouter la radio   11. travailler
4. étudier           8. jouer au football  12. chanter

## ACTIVITÉ 5  Et maintenant?

B
1

RIPT

ct. 6

Ask your classmates whether they are doing the things in **Activité 4** right
now.

→ jouer au tennis      — **Et maintenant, est-ce que tu joues au tennis?**
                       — **Non! Maintenant je ne joue pas au tennis.**

## C. La construction verbe + infinitif

For preliminary practice of this construction,
you may have students conjugate the sentence:
**Je n'aime pas travailler. Tu n'aimes pas travailler.**

ct. 7

Note the use of the infinitive in the sentences of the chart below:

| | | |
|---|---|---|
| **adorer** | *to love, adore* | **J'adore nager.** |
| **aimer** | *to like* | **J'aime voyager.** |
| **désirer** | *to wish, want* | Nous **désirons visiter** Bruxelles. |
| **détester** | *to dislike, hate* | Vous **détestez regarder** la télé. |

In French the infinitive is used after verbs like those listed above. Note the English
equivalents of the French infinitive.

Nous détestons **voyager.** $\begin{cases} \textit{We hate to travel.} \\ \textit{We hate travelling.} \end{cases}$

→ In the negative the expression **ne . . . pas** goes around the first verb.

Je **n'**aime **pas** travailler.    *I don't like to work.*

## ACTIVITÉ 6  Expression personnelle

Do you have plans for the future? Say whether or not you wish to do the
following things.

→ visiter Paris      **Je désire visiter Paris.**
                     **(Je ne désire pas visiter Paris.)**

1. visiter Québec    Dakar         4. travailler à Bruxelles   à Paris
2. habiter en France  en Russie    5. étudier l'italien        l'espagnol
3. voyager en Chine  en Afrique    6. visiter le Japon         l'Italie

### ACTIVITÉ 7   Dialogue

Ask your classmates whether or not they like to do the following things.
Your friends will answer.

→ skier
    — **Est-ce que tu aimes skier?**
    — **Oui, j'aime skier. (Oui, j'adore skier.)**
      **(Non, je n'aime pas skier.) (Non, je déteste skier.)**

WB
C1

SCRIPT

Act. 8

1. nager
2. chanter
3. écouter la radio
4. regarder la télé

5. travailler
6. voyager
7. étudier
8. parler anglais

9. parler français en classe
10. jouer au tennis
11. téléphoner
12. danser

### ACTIVITÉ 8   Une excellente raison *(An excellent reason)*   OPTIONAL

Say that the following people are doing certain things because they like to do them.

→ Aya voyage.
    **Aya voyage parce qu'elle aime voyager.**

1. Monique chante.
2. Charles étudie la musique.
3. Henri téléphone.
4. Isabelle chante.
5. Marc et Sylvie nagent.
6. Annie et Paul dansent.

7. Suzanne et Claire jouent au tennis.
8. Jacques et Philippe écoutent la radio.
9. Nous travaillons.
10. Nous parlons espagnol.
11. Vous regardez la télé.
12. Vous voyagez.

Be sure students make the liaison with
**aimer** in items 5 –12.

VARIATION in the negative: **Aya ne parle pas français
parce qu'elle n'aime pas parler français.**

# Prononciation

Act. 10

## 1. Le son /u/

*Model word:* v**ou**s

*Practice words:* **où, nous, douze, Abdou, Adjoua, joue, toujours, souvent** (underlines on ou)

*Practice sentences:* Min**ou** habite à T**ou**l**ou**se.

    Abd**ou** j**ou**e avec n**ou**s.

The French sound /u/ is similar to but shorter than the vowel in the English word *do.*

    Comment écrire /u/: **ou, où**

## 2. Le son /y/

*Model word:* t**u**

*Practice words:* sal**u**t, aven**u**e, ét**u**die, min**u**te, L**u**cie, S**u**zanne, sûr

*Practice sentences:* S**u**zanne et **U**rs**u**le ét**u**dient.

    Sal**u**t, L**u**cie. Comment vas-t**u**?

    L**u**c habite aven**u**e d**u** Maine.

The sound /y/ has no English equivalent. To produce this new sound, try to
say the sound /i/ while keeping your lips rounded as if to whistle.

    Comment écrire /y/: **u, û**

# Entre nous

## Expressions pour la conversation

To get someone's attention, you can say:

| | | |
|---|---|---|
| **Eh!** | *Hey!* | **Eh,** Paul! Quand est-ce que tu rentres? |
| **Dis!** <br> **Dis donc!** } | *Say! Hey!* (**tu** form) | **Dis donc,** Nathalie, est-ce que tu aimes voyager? |
| **Dites!** <br> **Dites donc!** } | *Say! Hey!* (**vous** form) | **Dites,** Marc et Irène, pourquoi est-ce que vous travaillez? |

## Mini-dialogue     OPTIONAL

Sometimes Nicole is a bit too enthusiastic.

MARC: Dis, Nicole, est-ce que tu aimes les *surprises-parties?*     *parties*

NICOLE: Bien sûr! J'adore les surprises-parties. J'adore danser!

MARC: Est-ce que tu danses bien?

NICOLE: Je danse très, très bien.

MARC: Et Sylvie, est-ce qu'elle aime danser?

NICOLE: Oh, Sylvie *aime bien* danser, mais elle ne danse pas bien.     *really likes*

MARC: *Dans ce cas,* c'est Sylvie *que* j'invite à la surprise-partie.     *In that case; whom*

NICOLE: Pourquoi Sylvie? *Pourquoi pas moi?*     *Why not me?*

MARC: Parce que je ne danse pas très bien. Je préfère inviter une fille qui ne danse pas bien. C'est normal, non?

## L'art du dialogue

a) Act out the dialog between Marc and Nicole.

b) Imagine that Marc is thinking of playing tennis. Act out a new dialog, replacing **les surprises-parties** by **le tennis,** and **danser** by **jouer.** Leave out **à la surprise-partie.**

# Leçon 5 En vacances

Act. 1

Hélène est suisse. Elle vous parle. Écoutez.

Vous êtes étudiants, n'est-ce pas?
Moi, je ne suis pas étudiante.
Je suis interprète.
Je travaille pour Swissair.
D'habitude je suis à Genève.
Mais aujourd'hui, je ne suis pas à Genève.
Je suis à Tahiti.
Oui! À Tahiti!
Pourquoi?
Parce que je suis en vacances.
Et vous? Êtes-vous en vacances?
Non?
Où êtes-vous alors?
En classe?
Dommage!

Genève is located in the French-speaking part of Switzerland. It is the seat of many international organizations (Red Cross, UN agencies, etc.).

Pour qui est-ce qu'Hélène travaille? Où est-ce qu'elle est d'habitude?
Où est-ce qu'elle est aujourd'hui? Pourquoi est-ce qu'elle est à Tahiti?

## CONVERSATION OPTIONAL

Hélène, the young person from Switzerland, is going to ask you a few questions about your summer activities. Answer her.

1. Voyagez-vous?
2. Nagez-vous?
3. Jouez-vous au tennis?

4. Travaillez-vous?
5. Étudiez-vous?

## OBSERVATIONS   Str. D   OPTIONAL

**Est-ce que vous voyagez?** and **Voyagez-vous?** are two ways of asking the same question: *Do you travel?*

• In these two questions, which word is the *subject?* which word is the *verb?*   voyagez   vous

Reread Hélène's questions carefully.

• Which word comes first — the subject or the verb?   the verb
• Which word comes second?   the subject
• What connects the verb and the subject?   a hyphen

## NOTE CULTURELLE   OPTIONAL

### Qui parle français dans le monde?
*(Who speaks French in the world?)*

How many people in the world speak French? Maybe 100 million, maybe more. French is spoken in France, of course, but it is spoken and understood on every continent of the earth. It is spoken by many Europeans and Africans, and it is also spoken by people in Vietnam, in the Middle East, and in the Caribbean. It is spoken as far away as Tahiti, in the South Pacific, and as close as the eastern provinces of Canada. In fact, within the United States it is spoken by many families in New England and Louisiana.

Yes, French is truly an international language!

**On vacation**
Hélène is Swiss. She is speaking to you. Listen.
You are students, aren't you?
I'm not a student.
I'm an interpreter.
I work for Swissair.
Usually I am in Geneva.
But today I am not in Geneva.
I am in Tahiti.
Yes! In Tahiti!
Why?
Because I am on vacation.
And you? Are you on vacation?
No?
Where are you then?
In class?
Too bad!

You may want to refer students to the map of the French-speaking world on pp. vi–vii.

# Structure

## A. Le verbe *être*

Note the forms of **être** *(to be)* in the present tense.

Act. 2

SCRIPT

Act. 4

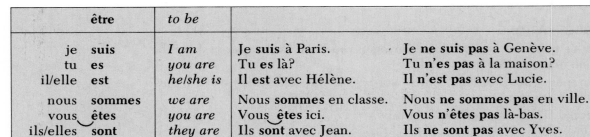

| être | | to be | | |
|---|---|---|---|---|
| je | suis | *I am* | Je **suis** à Paris. | Je **ne suis pas** à Genève. |
| tu | es | *you are* | Tu **es** là? | Tu **n'es pas** à la maison? |
| il/elle | est | *he/she is* | Il **est** avec Hélène. | Il **n'est pas** avec Lucie. |
| nous | sommes | *we are* | Nous **sommes** en classe. | Nous **ne sommes pas** en ville. |
| vous | êtes | *you are* | Vous **êtes** ici. | Vous **n'êtes pas** là-bas. |
| ils/elles | sont | *they are* | Ils **sont** avec Jean. | Ils **ne sont pas** avec Yves. |

→ The verb **être** does not follow a predictable pattern as do the regular **-er** verbs. **Être** is called an *irregular* verb.

→ Liaison is required in the form **vous êtes.**

→ Liaison is frequently heard after **est** and **sont,** and sometimes after other forms of **être.**

### ACTIVITÉ 1    En vacances!

It is vacation time. Say where the following students are. Say also that they are not in class.

→ Paul (à Toulon)    **Paul est à Toulon. Il n'est pas en classe.**

1. Suzanne (à Nice)
2. Abdou (à Dakar)
3. tu (à la Martinique)
4. je (à Montréal)
5. Pierre et Jean-Marc (à Québec)
6. nous (à Genève)
7. Aya et Adjoua (à Abidjan)
8. vous (à Tahiti)
9. Philippe et André (à Annecy)
10. Jacques (à Lyon)

Act. 5

## Vocabulaire spécialisé   Où?

| | | |
|---|---|---|
| ici | *here* | François travaille **ici.** |
| là | *there* | Pierre n'est pas **là.** |
| là-bas | *over there* | Qui est-ce, **là-bas?** |
| **à la maison** | *at home, home* | Nous regardons la télé **à la maison.** |
| **au restaurant** | *at the restaurant* | Vous dînez **au restaurant?** |
| **en classe** | *in class* | **En classe** nous parlons toujours français. |
| **en vacances** | *on vacation* | Jacques est **en vacances** à Tahiti. |
| **en ville** | *downtown, in town* | Je suis **en ville** avec Mélanie. |

## ACTIVITÉ 2   Où sont-ils?

What we do often depends on where we are. Express this, using the
appropriate form of **être** and one of the following expressions:

**en classe   en ville   en vacances   à la maison   au restaurant**

→ Paul nage.   **Il est en vacances.**

In some instances more than one response may be appropriate.
Encourage students to use their imagination.

1. Caroline regarde la télé.
2. Nous écoutons la radio.
3. Vous dînez avec Anne et Michèle.
4. Je joue au tennis.
5. Tu voyages beaucoup.

6. Philippe visite Genève.
7. Suzanne et Marc parlent avec le professeur.
8. Nous étudions.
9. Louis et Mathieu skient.
10. Vous nagez.

## B. *Qui?*

The following questions begin with **qui?** *(who?)*. Note the word order.

| | |
|---|---|
| **Qui** travaille? | Jean-Pierre travaille. |
| **Qui** joue au tennis? | Suzanne et Henri jouent au tennis. |
| **Qui** aime voyager? | Nous aimons voyager. |

To ask who is doing something, French speakers generally use the
following construction:

In **qui**-questions with **être**, the verb
agrees with the subject that follows
the verb: **Qui êtes-vous? Qui sont
les filles là-bas?**

$$\boxed{\textbf{qui} \ + \ \text{verb} \ + \ \ldots \text{(rest of sentence)} \ ?}$$

→ In **qui** questions the verb is singular, even if the expected answer is plural.

In the above constructions, **qui** is the subject of the sentence. When **qui** is the direct object, the regular interrogative
constructions (with **est-ce que** or with inversion) are used. **Qui est-ce que tu invites? Qui invites-tu?**

## ACTIVITÉ 3   Un sondage d'opinion *(An opinion poll)*

Imagine that you are taking a class survey about the leisure activities of
young Americans. Ask who does the following things.

→ écouter la radio   **Qui écoute la radio?**   You may have a student at the board count how
many in the class answer "yes" to each question.

1. voyager
2. voyager souvent
3. aimer chanter
4. danser
5. aimer danser

6. regarder la télé
7. détester regarder la télé
8. jouer au tennis
9. jouer au bridge
10. skier

## C. Expressions interrogatives avec *qui*

Note the interrogative expressions in the questions below:

| à qui | *to whom* | **À qui** est-ce que tu téléphones? |
|---|---|---|
| avec qui | *with whom* | **Avec qui** est-ce que vous voyagez? |
| de qui | *of (about) whom* | **De qui** est-ce que Pierre parle? |
| pour qui | *for whom* | **Pour qui** est-ce que Michèle travaille? |

You may indicate that in conversational English the preposition often comes at the end of the sentence. This is *never* done in French.

**Qui** *(who, whom)* may be used with prepositions such as **à, avec, de,** and **pour** *(for)*, to form interrogative expressions.

→ Information questions of this kind must *always begin with the preposition.*

### ACTIVITÉ 4   Curiosité

Hélène is telling Georges what she does. Georges wants more details. Play both roles according to the model.

→ visiter Tahiti (avec)    Hélène: **Je visite Tahiti.**
Georges: **Avec qui est-ce que tu visites Tahiti?**

1. aimer danser (avec)
2. téléphoner souvent (à)
3. voyager (avec)
4. rentrer (avec)
5. travailler (pour)
6. regarder la télé (avec)
7. chanter (pour)
8. parler beaucoup (de)
9. parler français (à)

WB
C1

### D. L'interrogation avec inversion   OPTIONAL

You may indicate that students have already encountered several questions with inversion: **Qui est-ce? Quel temps fait-il? Quelle heure est-il?**

Look at the two sets of questions below. They both ask the same thing. Compare the positions of the subject pronouns in each pair of questions.

| | |
|---|---|
| Est-ce que **vous** parlez anglais? | Parlez-**vous** anglais? |
| Où est-ce que **tu** habites? | Où habites-**tu**? |
| À quelle heure est-ce que **nous** dînons? | À quelle heure dînons-**nous**? |
| Quand est-ce qu'**il** est en vacances? | Quand est-**il** en vacances? |

In conversational French, questions are frequently formed with **est-ce que.** However, when the subject of the sentence is a pronoun, French speakers often prefer using the following construction:

This may be presented for recognition only. Inverted questions will be reviewed on p. 273 when the addition of the letter t (**parle-t-il?**) is introduced.

| interrogative expression (if any) + verb + subject pronoun + (rest of sentence) ? |
|---|

→ This is called *inversion,* since the subject and verb have been inverted, or turned around. Note that the verb and subject pronoun are connected with a hyphen.  Inversion is usually not used with **je.**

→ There is liaison before **il/elle** and **ils/elles** in inversion.

### ACTIVITÉ 5   Questions personnelles

1. Êtes-vous en vacances maintenant?
2. Aimez-vous chanter?
3. Jouez-vous bien au tennis?
4. Nagez-vous souvent en été?
5. Pourquoi regardez-vous la télé?  parce que j'aime/je déteste regarder...
6. Avec qui étudiez-vous?
7. Où habitez-vous?
8. À quelle heure arrivez-vous en classe?

VARIATION: Students may ask classmates the same questions using the **tu** form.

## ACTIVITÉ 6   Le club des sports   OPTIONAL

Imagine that you are the president of a sports club. Ask the new members (indicated in parentheses) if they can do the following. Use **tu** or **vous**, as appropriate.

→ (Pierre) nager bien     **Nages-tu bien?**
  (Anne et Suzanne) jouer au ping-pong?     **Jouez-vous au ping-pong?**

1. (Caroline) nager?
2. (André et Pierre) nager le crawl?
3. (Hélène) skier?

4. (Albert et Thomas) skier bien?
5. (Marie-Thérèse) jouer au football?
6. (Jacques et Paul) jouer au tennis?

## ACTIVITÉ 7   Interview   OPTIONAL

Olivier interviewed Charlotte, but forgot to write down his questions. Ask the questions again, using inversion and the interrogative expression in parentheses.

→ J'habite *à Tours*. (où?)     **Où habites-tu?**

1. Je travaille *à Paris*. (où?)
2. Je travaille *avec Madame Charron*. (avec qui?)
3. Je rentre à Tours *le 2 octobre*. (quand?)
4. Je voyage *en train*. (comment?)

5. J'arrive à Tours *à minuit*. (à quelle heure?)
6. J'habite à Tours *parce que j'aime Tours*. (pourquoi?)

# Prononciation

### 1. Le son /e/

*Model word:* et

*Practice words:* Léa, Mélanie, Édith, téléphoner, écoutez, Québec, télé, mai

*Practice sentences:* Léa téléphone à Édith.
Dédé déteste la télé.

The French vowel sound /e/ is much more tense than the English vowel sound in *day*. Smile when you say /e/. Keep your lips tight.

Comment écrire /e/:  **é; et, ez, er** (final); **ai** (final)

### 2. Le son /ɛ/

*Model word:* elle

*Practice words:* sept, Ève, Annette, Estelle, aime, déteste, Michel, Michèle, être

*Practice sentences:* Michel aime Estelle.
Michèle déteste être avec Annette à Québec.

The French vowel sound /ɛ/ is pronounced with the mouth somewhat more open than for /e/. It is more tense than the English vowel sound in *get*.

Comment écrire /ɛ/:  **è, ê; e** (+ pronounced final consonant); **e** (+ two consonants); **ai** (+ pronounced final consonant)

# Entre nous

**Expressions pour la conversation**

The French often begin or end sentences with:

| | | |
|---|---|---|
| **alors** | *then, well then, so* | —Sylvie n'est pas en ville.<br>—**Alors,** où est-elle? |
| **et alors?** | *so what?* | —Sylvie est avec Michel.<br>—**Et alors?** |

**Mini-dialogue**   OPTIONAL

Marc is frantically looking for his girlfriend Sylvie. He calls Sylvie's friend Annie.

MARC: Allô, Annie?

ANNIE: Oui! Allô, Marc. Ça va?

MARC: Ça va! Dis, Annie, je *cherche* Sylvie.          *am looking for*
       Est-ce qu'elle est en ville?

ANNIE: Non, elle n'est pas en ville.

MARC: Est-ce qu'elle est en classe, alors?

ANNIE: Non, elle n'est pas en classe.

MARC: Alors, elle est avec Michel?

ANNIE: Mais non, elle n'est pas avec Michel.

MARC: Tu es sûre?

ANNIE: Mais oui, elle n'est pas avec Michel.

MARC: Alors, où est-elle?

ANNIE: C'est simple. Elle est ici avec *moi*.          *me*

**L'art du dialogue**

a) Act out the phone conversation between Annie and Marc.

b) Act out a new phone conversation in which Marc is looking for his brother **Henri**.

c) Now imagine that Marc is looking for two girls: **Sylvie** and **Nathalie**. Act out the new conversation, making all the necessary changes.

SCRIPT  MASTERS  QUIZ
pp. 12;   p. 19   WB   Tests de Contrôle   TEST  pp. 20–23
65–66
Act. 9

OPPOSITE: Place de la Concorde and the Obélisque de Louxor, with the Église de la Madeleine in the background.

# SECTION MAGAZINE 1

Accès aux avions
to planes

AIR AFRIQUE
une grande compagnie dans un grand continent

AIR CANADA

AIR FRANCE

# VOYAGE!

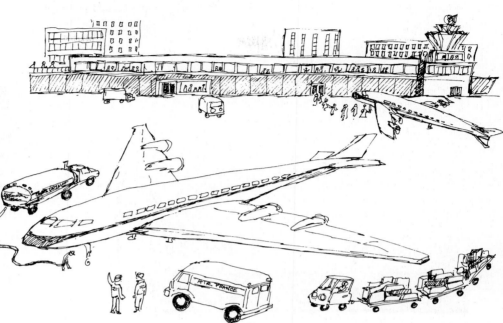

## DÉPARTS

| Bruxelles | 9h.10 |
|---|---|
| Genève | 9h.25 |
| Dakar | 9h.35 |
| Tunis | 9h.55 |
| Alger | 10h.20 |

## ARRIVÉES

| Montréal | 9h.22 |
|---|---|
| Abidjan | 9h.32 |
| Casablanca | 9h.41 |
| Luxembourg | 9h.57 |
| Fort-de-France | 10h.08 |

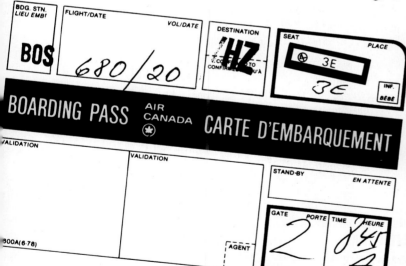

| BDG. STN. LIEU EMBI | FLIGHT/DATE | VOL/DATE | DESTINATION | SEAT | PLACE |
|---|---|---|---|---|---|

**BOS** 680/20 HZ

V. CONFIRM TO CONFIRMER JUSQU'À

3E
3E
INF. BÉBÉ

**BOARDING PASS** AIR CANADA **CARTE D'EMBARQUEMENT**

VALIDATION

VALIDATION

600A(6-78)

STAND-BY EN ATTENTE

GATE PORTE 2 TIME HEURE 8 45 A.

AGENT

swissair

Départs Departures

Départs Departures

16.58

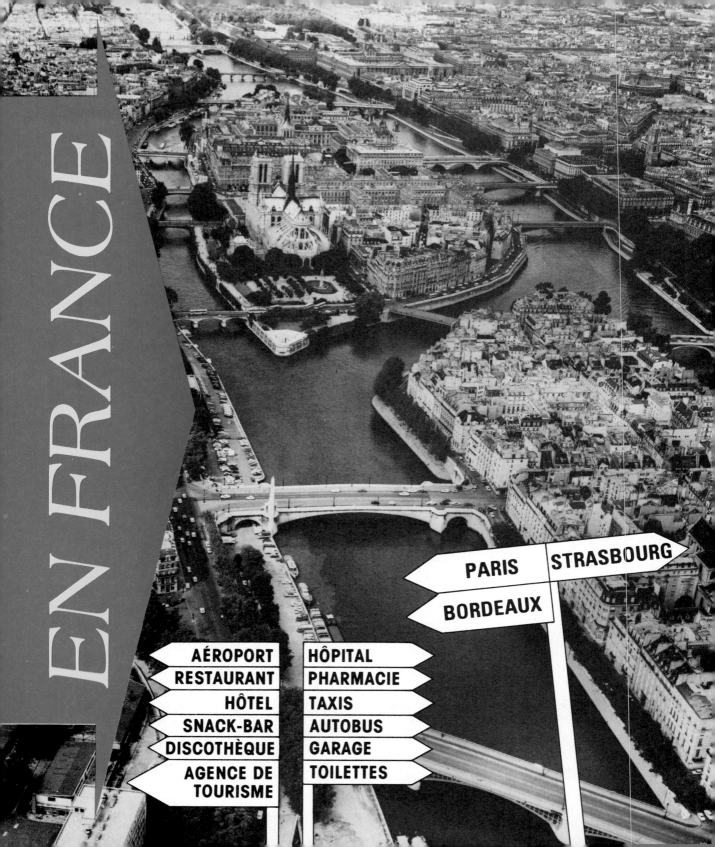

EN FRANCE

PARIS
STRASBOURG
BORDEAUX

AÉROPORT
RESTAURANT
HÔTEL
SNACK-BAR
DISCOTHÈQUE
AGENCE DE TOURISME

HÔPITAL
PHARMACIE
TAXIS
AUTOBUS
GARAGE
TOILETTES

| CAFÉ | 5 francs |
|------|----------|
| THÉ | 6 francs |
| CHOCOLAT | 7 francs |
| COCA-COLA | 9 francs |
| SANDWICH | 10 francs |

ALLÔ, MICHÈLE!

TÉLÉPHONE

AVENUE DU PRÉSIDENT WILSON

RUE FRANKLIN

16ᵐᵉ ARR

AVENUE DU PRÉSIDENT KENNEDY

DANGER

STOP

SILENCE

ATTENTION

# PARIS

# Je parle français.

## Parlez-vous français?

Est-ce que vous parlez français?
Mais oui, vous parlez français. Tous les jours!° Tous les jours vous utilisez° des° expressions d'origine française.° Voici des exemples:

| *Domaine* | *Expressions* |
|---|---|
| Unités de mesure | mètre, kilomètre, gramme, kilogramme |
| Automobile | auto, limousine, chauffeur |
| Cuisine | restaurant, café, chef, hors-d'œuvre, entrée, margarine, mayonnaise, bouillon, salade, purée, mousse, sauté, sauce, casserole |
| Mode° | chic, élégance, boutique, eau de cologne, eau de toilette |
| Art | théâtre, musique, sculpture, concert; flûte, clarinette; crayon, collage, papier-mâché |
| Danse | ballet, plié, tour-jeté, pirouette |

Combien de ces° expressions connaissez-vous?°

Et connaissez-vous les villes suivantes° aux États-Unis? °

**Bâton Rouge, la Nouvelle-Orléans, Louisville, Beaumont, Montpelier, Détroit, Terre Haute, Prairie du Chien, Des Moines, Pierre, Butte**

**Formidable!** *Great!* **Tous les jours!** *Every day!* **utilisez** *use* **des** *some* **d'origine française** *of French origin* **Mode** *Fashion* **Combien de ces** *How many of these* **connaissez-vous** *do you know* **les villes suivantes** *the following cities* **aux États-Unis** *in the United States*

# Bonjour, Christine!

Bonjour les amis!°
Je m'appelle Christine Descroix.
J'ai seize ans° et je suis une Sagittaire.
J'habite à Toulon avec mes° parents.
J'étudie l'anglais et l'espagnol
parce que je veux° travailler
dans une agence de voyages.°
J'aime voyager.
En juillet, je vais° visiter la Grèce°
avec ma famille.
J'aime aussi danser.
J'aime le jazz et la musique pop.
Mon° musicien préféré° est
Michael Jackson.
Et vous?

Christine

**les amis** *friends*  **J'ai seize ans** *I'm sixteen*  **mes** *my*  **veux** *want*  **dans une agence de voyages** *in a travel agency*  **vais** *am going*  **la Grèce** *Greece*  **ma** *my*  **mon** *my*  **préféré** *favorite*

# BOÎTE AUX LETTRES°

**JANINE LEVASSEUR**
PÉDIATRE
*Docteur en Médecine*

JEAN-PIERRE ALQUIER
**DENTISTE**

**RAYMOND CICCOLI**
INGÉNIEUR

**FRANÇOISE SIMONET**
PROFESSEUR DE PIANO

**OLIVIER MUELLER**
ARCHITECTE

SYLVIE LAMBERT
**JOURNALISTE**

Jacqueline MALLET
**PHARMACIENNE**

ALBERT DUCLOS
**PHOTOGRAPHE**

**SYLVIE LONGCHAMP**
PROGRAMMEUSE IBM

**ROBERT PECOUL**
OPTICIEN

Mademoiselle Dupuis est canadienne. Elle habite à Québec et elle travaille dans une agence de voyages.° Elle parle français et anglais.

Monsieur Lamy est français. Il habite à Fort-de-France, la capitale de la Martinique. Il est professeur d'éducation physique.

**boîte aux lettres** *mailbox* **dans une agence de voyages** *in a travel agency* **allemand** *German* **médecin** *doctor* **belge** *Belgian*

Madame Kubler est suisse. Elle habite à Genève. Elle est pharmacienne. Elle parle français et allemand.°

Monsieur Teritaau habite à Tahiti. Il travaille pour le gouvernement français. Il parle tahitien et français.

# Oui, ils parlent français!

Madame Kouadio habite à Dakar, la capitale du Sénégal. Elle est médecin.°

Monsieur Belkora est tunisien, mais il n'habite pas en Tunisie. Il habite à New York. Il est économiste et il travaille pour les Nations Unies. Il parle français, anglais et arabe.

Monsieur Pons est belge.° Il habite à Bruxelles. Il est ingénieur et il travaille pour une compagnie d'électronique. Il parle français.

# LA CARTE DU TEMPS°

## PARIS

*Température*[1]: 5°    *Temps:* pluie

## GENÈVE

*Température:* 1°    *Temps:* nuages

## DAKAR

*Température:* 15°    *Temps:* soleil

## ABIDJAN

*Température:* 24°    *Temps:* soleil

## QUÉBEC

*Température:* −12°    *Temps:* neige

*Le premier janvier dans le monde francophone.*

## MONTRÉAL

*Température:* −8°    *Temps:* neige

## FORT-DE-FRANCE

*Température:* 22°    *Temps:* soleil

## PORT-AU-PRINCE

*Température:* 16°    *Temps:* nuages

## PAPEETE
*Température:* 25°    *Temps:* soleil

[1]**Température = degrés Celsius**

**la carte du temps** *the weather map*
**dans le monde francophone** *in the French-speaking world*

# Ils parlent français!

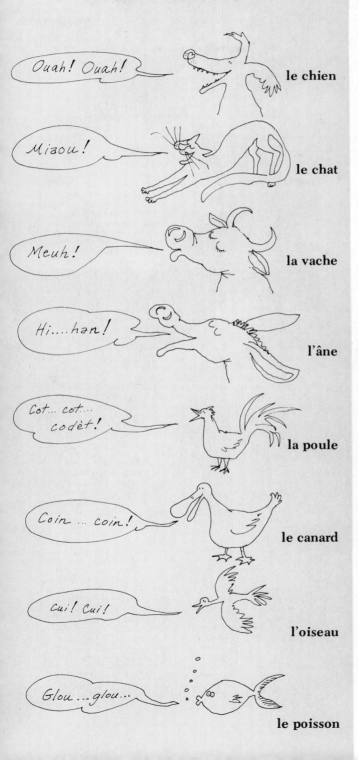

Ouah! Ouah! — le chien

Miaou! — le chat

Meuh! — la vache

Hi....han! — l'âne

Cot... cot... codèt! — la poule

Coin ... coin! — le canard

Cui! Cui! — l'oiseau

Glou...glou... — le poisson

## PROJETS CULTURELS

### Projets individuels

1. *Select a French-speaking country or area and make a poster advertising it. (Source of pictures: travel brochures, travel magazines, the travel section of the Sunday paper)*
2. *Prepare a chart listing eight countries which use French as their official language. For each country, give the following information: population, size, capital, unit of currency, principal products. (Source: almanac)*

### Projets de classe

1. *Imagine that your class is going to take a trip around the world. On this trip, you will stop in six French-speaking countries or areas (including islands). On a world map, draw the route which you will take. For each stop, prepare a display of travel brochures and plan a list of things you would like to do there. (Source: travel agencies, travel magazines, tour books)*
2. *Prepare a bulletin board exhibit of stamps from French-speaking countries. You may use a world map as a background. For each country, select stamps representing famous people and places, typical animals, flowers, plants, etc. (Source: actual stamps, reproductions of stamps from catalogs and stamp magazines)*

OBJECTIVES

In this unit, the students learn to describe themselves and to describe their environment: people and things. To help them achieve this objective, the following elements are presented:

*Language*
- **avoir**
- nouns and articles: gender and number
- descriptive adjectives: forms and uses, the noun-adjective agreement
- stress pronouns
- **c'est** vs. **il est**

*Vocabulary*
- people
- adjectives of description (physical aspect, personality, nationality)
- daily life objects
- countries

*Culture*

This unit focuses on French youth and interpersonal relationships, especially the concept of friendship.

# UNITÉ 2
## Salut, les amis!

# Leçon 1
## UNITÉ 2
### Invitations

STRUCTURES TO OBSERVE
- the indefinite article **un/une**
- the concept of gender: masculine vs. feminine
- the concept of agreement: article and noun; noun and adjective.

Act. 1

Suzanne and Michèle are organizing a party with their brothers, Marc and Alain. Whom are they going to invite? Suzanne and Marc each have special guests in mind.

### Suzanne et Michèle

SUZANNE: Est-ce que nous invitons Claude Dumas?

MICHÈLE: Claude Dumas? Qui est-ce? Un *garçon* ou une *fille?*   *boy; girl*

SUZANNE: Un garçon!

MICHÈLE: Un *ami?*   *friend*

SUZANNE: *Plus ou moins.* C'est le garçon avec qui je joue au tennis.   *More or less.*

MICHÈLE: *Comment est-il?*   *What's he like?*

SUZANNE: Il est *grand* et blond . . .   *tall*

MICHÈLE: Et bien sûr, il est très *beau* . . .   *good-looking*

SUZANNE: Euh . . . non. Mais il est *amusant* et très *sympathique.*   *amusing; nice*

MICHÈLE: Alors, d'accord! Nous invitons Claude à la surprise-partie.

Avec qui est-ce que Suzanne joue au tennis? Est-ce que Claude Dumas est blond?
Est-ce que Suzanne et Michèle invitent Claude Dumas?

## NOTES CULTURELLES   OPTIONAL

**1. Claude et Dominique**   Claude and Dominique are names that can be given either to boys or girls. There are other names that may also be given to boys or girls, but although they sound the same, they are spelled differently:

| | | | | |
|---|---|---|---|---|
| boys: | **Michel** | **Daniel** | **Joël** | **Noël** | **René** |
| girls: | **Michèle** | **Danièle** | **Joëlle** | **Noëlle** | **Renée** |

**2. Une surprise-partie**   The term **surprise-partie** is a word which French has borrowed from English. It is not a surprise party, in the American sense, but rather an informal party, usually with music and dancing. You will discover that modern French has borrowed quite a few words and expressions from English. Sometimes meanings change somewhat as a word is transferred from one language to another.

Other terms that French teenagers use to refer to parties are **une surboum** and **une boum**.

**Marc et Alain**

MARC: Est-ce que tu invites Dominique Laroche?

ALAIN: Dominique Laroche? Qui est-ce? Un garçon ou une fille?

MARC: Une fille.

ALAIN: Une amie?

MARC: Oui!

ALAIN: Est-ce que c'est la fille à qui tu téléphones *tout le temps*?     *all the time*

MARC: C'est ça!

ALAIN: Elle est grande et blonde, n'est-ce pas?

MARC: Elle est blonde, mais elle n'est pas très grande.

ALAIN: Et bien sûr elle est très belle . . .

MARC: *Pas spécialement!* Mais elle est très amusante et très     *Not especially!*
      sympathique! *C'est l'essentiel*, n'est-ce pas?     *That's the important thing*

ALAIN: D'accord! J'invite Dominique!

À qui est-ce que Marc téléphone souvent? Est-ce que Dominique est blonde?
Est-ce qu'Alain invite Dominique?

## Vocabulaire pratique

| NOM: | **une surprise-partie** | *(informal) party* | |
|---|---|---|---|
| EXPRESSIONS: | **c'est ça!** | *that's it! that's right!* | Tu arrives demain? Oui, **c'est ça!** |
| | **d'accord?** | *okay? all right?* | J'invite Paul. **D'accord?** |
| | **d'accord!** | *okay! fine!* | Oui, **d'accord!** |
| | **être d'accord** | *to agree* | Tu es **d'accord?** |

## CONVERSATION

1. Qui est Claude? **Un** <u>garçon</u> ou **une** <u>fille</u>?
2. Qui est Dominique? **Un** <u>garçon</u> ou **une** <u>fille</u>?
3. Qui êtes-vous? **Un** <u>garçon</u> ou **une** <u>fille</u>?
4. Qui enseigne (*teaches*) le français? **Un** <u>monsieur</u> (*man*) ou **une** <u>dame</u> (*woman*)?

## OBSERVATIONS    Str. A

The underlined words above are *nouns*. In French, nouns are often introduced by *articles*. The words in heavy type are called *indefinite articles*.

- Does **garçon** refer to a male or female? Which article is used to introduce it? What about **monsieur**?   male   un   un

- Does **fille** refer to a male or female? Which article is used to introduce it? What about **dame**?   female   une   une

# Structure

## A. Noms masculins, noms féminins; l'article indéfini: *un*/*une*

All French nouns have a *gender*. They are either *masculine* or *feminine*. Note the following masculine and feminine nouns:

Act. 2

| MASCULINE | |
|---|---|
| **un** garçon | *a boy* |
| **un** ami | *a friend* (male) |
| **un** artiste | *an artist* (male) |

| FEMININE | |
|---|---|
| **une** fille | *a girl* |
| **une** amie | *a friend* (female) |
| **une** artiste | *an artist* (female) |

Nouns referring to men and boys are usually masculine.
Nouns referring to women and girls are usually feminine.

Nouns are often introduced by *indefinite articles*:

> **un** (*a, an*) introduces *masculine* nouns
> **une** (*a, an*) introduces *feminine* nouns

As a listening comprehension activity, you may use the following cognate nouns and ask your students if they refer to men or women: **un/une dentiste, un/une artiste, un/une journaliste, un/une photographe, un acteur/une actrice.**

→ There is liaison after **un** when the next word begins with a vowel sound.

→ You can often determine the gender of a noun from the form of the word that introduces it. For instance:

If someone says: "Je téléphone à **un ami**," you know that person is calling a boy.
If someone says: "Je téléphone à **une amie**," you know that person is calling a girl.

This is because **un** signals that a noun is masculine, and **une** signals that a noun is feminine.

## ACTIVITÉ 1  Qui est-ce?

Can you tell which of the two people (indicated in parentheses) is being introduced? (Your clue is **un** or **une**.) Respond according to the model.

→ Voici un ami. (Philippe, Jacqueline)  **Voici Philippe.**

1. Voici une amie. (Jean-Paul, Thérèse)
2. Voici un pianiste. (Marc, Suzanne)
3. Voici une artiste. (Pierre, Stéphanie)
4. Voici un touriste. (Monsieur Smith, Madame Jones)
5. Voici une journaliste. (Walter Cronkite, Barbara Walters)

Note the pronunciations: **femme** /fam/, **fille** /fij/, **monsieur** /məsjø/

Act. 4

### Vocabulaire spécialisé  Personnes

| | | | |
|---|---|---|---|
| un ami | (close) friend | une amie | (close) friend |
| un camarade | classmate, school friend | une camarade | classmate, school friend |
| un élève | (high school) student | une élève | (high school) student |
| un étudiant | (college) student | une étudiante | (college) student, coed |
| un garçon | boy | une fille | girl |
| un homme | man | une femme | woman |
| un monsieur | gentleman, man (polite term) | une dame | lady, woman (polite term) |
| un professeur | teacher | une personne | person |

| | | | |
|---|---|---|---|
| Comment s'appelle . . .? | What's . . .'s name? | | |
| Comment s'appelle-t-il? | What's his name? | Comment s'appelle-t-elle? | What's her name? |

Notes:  1.  The noun **un professeur** is always masculine, whether it refers to a man or a woman. The noun **une personne** is always feminine, whether it refers to a male or female.

Voici **Monsieur** Brun.    Qui est-ce? C'est **un** professeur.
Voici **Madame** Lamblet.    Qui est-ce? C'est **un** professeur.

2.  To help you remember genders, the *masculine* nouns in the vocabulary sections are listed in the *left* column; the *feminine* nouns in the *right* column.

Literally, **un élève** means *pupil*. Although the term **étudiant** used to refer only to college students, its usage is now extending to high school students as well. Another term for a high school student is **un lycéen/une lycéenne**.

## ACTIVITÉ 2  À l'école *(At school)*

Imagine that you are an exchange student in a French school. Introduce the following classmates according to the model, using the suggested noun.

VARIATION: They are students.

→ Catherine (amie)    **Catherine est une amie.**    Catherine est une étudiante.

A1, A2

SCRIPT

Act. 3, 5

MASTERS
p. 13

| (ami/amie) | (camarade) | (élève) |
|---|---|---|
| 1. Jean-Paul | 5. Marie-Noëlle | 9. Suzanne |
| 2. Antoine | 6. Pierre | 10. Philippe |
| 3. Sylvie | 7. Jean-Marc | 11. Isabelle |
| 4. Nathalie | 8. Christine | 12. Thomas |

Be sure students use the appropriate article **un/une**, and use liaison with **ami** and **élève**.

## B. L'article défini: le/la

Compare the words which introduce the nouns in each pair of sentences.

Act. 2

| | |
|---|---|
| Voici **un** garçon. | Qui est **le** garçon? |
| Voici **une** fille. | Qui est **la** fille? |
| Voici **un** ami. | Qui est **l'**ami? |
| Voici **une** amie. | Qui est **l'**amie? |

If students have problems with the meaning of the article, you may want to translate the sentences.

Nouns can also be introduced by *definite articles:*

**le** *(the)*   introduces *masculine* nouns
**la** *(the)*   introduces *feminine* nouns

→ **Le** and **la** become **l'** when the next word begins with a vowel sound.

The definite article **le / la** usually corresponds to the English *the.*

→ However, French speakers also use **le / la** with nouns in a general sense, while English usually leaves *the* out.

**L'homme** aime **la liberté.**     *Man loves liberty.*
**La femme** aussi!     *Woman too!*

The use of the definite article in the general sense is presented here for recognition. It is formally introduced in Unité 5.1.

### *ACTIVITÉ 3*   Au café

Paul is looking at the people who come into the café. Express this according to the model.

→ une fille     **Paul regarde la fille.**

VARIATIONS with cognates: un/une artiste, un/une touriste, un/une journaliste, un/une photographe, un/une Américain(e)

1. un garçon
2. une dame
3. un professeur
4. une personne
5. un monsieur
6. une femme
7. un étudiant
8. une étudiante
9. un élève
10. une élève
11. une camarade
12. un homme

Items 7, 8, 9, 10, and 12 require **l'**.

### *ACTIVITÉ 4*   Comment s'appelle . . . ?

Paul and Hélène are meeting after class. As Paul points out people, Hélène wants to know their names. Play both roles according to the model.

→ garçon     Paul: **Voici un garçon.**
         Hélène: **Comment s'appelle le garçon?**

VARIATION: Hélène asks **Comment s'appelle-t-il/elle?**

1. fille
2. monsieur
3. dame
4. professeur
5. personne
6. femme
7. étudiant
8. étudiante
9. homme

The purpose of this activity is to have students provide the proper articles without looking at the **Vocabulaire** for gender. Note that items 7–9 begin with a vowel sound.

## C. L'accord des adjectifs (Adjective agreement)

Adjectives are used to describe nouns and pronouns. In the sentences below, the words in heavy type are adjectives. Compare the forms of the adjectives used to describe Marc and Suzanne.

Act. 7

| | |
|---|---|
| Marc est **blond**. | Suzanne est **blonde**. |
| Il est **grand**. | Elle est **grande**. |
| Il est **intelligent**. | Elle est **intelligente**. |

You may vary the examples with the following cognate adjectives: **indépendant, tolérant, patient.**

An *adjective* modifying a *masculine* noun or pronoun must be in the *masculine* form. An *adjective* modifying a *feminine* noun or pronoun must be in the *feminine* form. This is called *noun-adjective agreement.*

In written French, feminine adjectives are usually formed as follows:

> masculine adjective  +  **e**  → feminine adjective

→ If the masculine adjective already ends in **-e**, the feminine form is the same as the masculine form.

You may vary the examples with the following cognate adjectives: **optimiste, idéaliste, dynamique, timide.**

Marc est **sincère**.    Suzanne est **sincère**.

→ Adjectives which follow the above pattern are called *regular* adjectives. Those which do not are *irregular* adjectives.

Marc est **beau**.    Suzanne est **belle**.

The vocabulary lists all adjectives in their masculine form. However, if an adjective is irregular, the feminine form is given in parentheses.

### Notes de prononciation

1. If the masculine adjective in the written form ends in a *vowel*, the feminine and masculine adjectives sound the same:
   **sincère; bleu, bleue** *(blue)*
2. If the masculine adjective in the written form ends in a *pronounced consonant*, the masculine and feminine adjectives sound the same:
   **noir, noire** *(black)*
3. If the masculine adjective in the written form ends in a *silent consonant,* that silent consonant is pronounced in the feminine form:
   **grand, grande; intelligent, intelligente**[1]

As a listening comprehension activity, you may ask your students to determine whether the following adjectives refer to men or women: **élégant(e), patient(e), impatient(e), tolérant(e), indépendant(e).**

---

[1]If the silent consonant in the masculine form is an **n,** the masculine adjective ends in a nasal vowel. In the corresponding feminine form, which ends in **-ne,** the final vowel is not nasal, and the adjective ends in the sound /n/: **brun, brune.**

Comment est-il? (literally, *How is he?*) is the equivalent of *What's he like?*

## Vocabulaire spécialisé  La description

Voici Alain.
Comment est-il?

Voici Suzanne.
Comment est-elle?

ADJECTIFS:

| | | | |
|---|---|---|---|
| **beau (belle)** | *good-looking, beautiful* | Il est assez **beau**. | Elle est **belle**. |
| **brun** | *dark-haired* | Il est **brun**. | Elle n'est pas **brune**. |
| **blond** | *blond* | Il n'est pas **blond**. | Elle est **blonde**. |
| **grand** | *tall, big* | Il est assez **grand**. | Elle est **grande**. |
| **petit** | *short, little* | Il n'est pas **petit**. | Elle n'est pas **petite**. |
| **amusant** | *amusing* | Il est **amusant**. | Elle est **amusante**. |
| **intelligent** | *intelligent* | Il est **intelligent**. | Elle est **intelligente**. |
| **intéressant** | *interesting* | Il est **intéressant**. | Elle est **intéressante**. |
| **sincère** | *sincere* | Il est **sincère**. | Elle est très **sincère**. |
| **sympathique** | *nice, pleasant* | Il est **sympathique**. | Elle est **sympathique**. |

ADVERBES:

| | | |
|---|---|---|
| **assez** | *rather* | Tu es **assez** intelligent. |
| **très** | *very* | Je suis **très** sincère. |

VOCABULARY EXPANSION: **timide, optimiste, idéaliste, dynamique, indépendant, patient, poli** *(polite)*, **réservé**

See also the **Vocabulaire** on pp. 110–111.

Adverbs are invariable. Make sure that students do not try to make agreements with adverbs.

## ACTIVITÉ 5  Les jumeaux *(The twins)*

The following pairs of twins have the same characteristics. Describe the girl in each pair.

→ Louis est brun. (Louise)   **Louise est brune aussi.**

VARIATIONS with cognates: **romantique, loyal, tolérant, indépendant, optimiste, pessimiste.**

1. Daniel est petit. (Danièle)
2. Michel est grand. (Michèle)
3. Denis est blond. (Denise)
4. André est beau. (Andrée)
5. René est sincère. (Renée)
6. Charles est sympathique. (Charlotte)
7. François est amusant. (Françoise)
8. Martin est intelligent. (Martine)

## ACTIVITÉ 6  Personnes célèbres *(Famous people)*   OPTIONAL

Select four of the following well-known people. Describe each one in three affirmative or negative sentences.

→ Woody Allen   **Il est assez petit.  Il n'est pas très beau.  Il est très amusant.**

1. John Travolta
2. Muhammad Ali
3. Raquel Welch
4. Barbra Streisand
5. Carol Burnett
6. Burt Reynolds
7. Jane Fonda
8. Robert Redford
9. Mickey Mouse
10. Dracula
11. King Kong
12. Superman

VARIATION: Individual students can read their descriptions aloud, and the others can guess which person has been described. **Qui est-ce? C'est Woody Allen.**

# Prononciation

**Le son** /ɛ̃/

*Model word:* Al<u>ain</u>

*Practice words:* c<u>in</u>q, <u>in</u>vite, b<u>ien</u>, s<u>ym</u>pathique, <u>in</u>telligent, cous<u>in</u>

*Practice sentences:* Al<u>ain</u> <u>in</u>vite Juli<u>en</u> Dup<u>in</u>.

Mart<u>in</u> est un cous<u>in</u> améric<u>ain</u>.

The nasal vowel /ɛ̃/ sounds somewhat like the vowel sound in the American word *bank*, but it is shorter. Be sure not to pronounce an /n/ or /m/ after /ɛ̃/.

Comment écrire /ɛ̃/: **in** (**im** before **b** or **p**); **yn** (**ym** before **b** or **p**); **ain** (**aim** before **b** or **p**); **en** (in the letter combination **ien**)

# Entre nous

## Expressions pour la conversation

To express surprise, the French use:

**Ah!**   **Ah!** Voici Christophe.   **Oh!**   **Oh!** Dis donc! Il est grand!

To express doubt (or to show that they have not quite understood), the French use:

**Comment?** *What?* (polite form)   **Comment?** Tu n'es pas à la surprise-partie?
**Quoi?** *What?* (less polite)   **Quoi?** Tu n'invites pas Claude?

## Mini-dialogue   OPTIONAL

Irène is talking to Christophe about someone she has just met.

IRÈNE: Dis! *J'ai fait la connaissance d'*un garçon ...   *I met*
CHRISTOPHE: Ah? Comment est-il?
IRÈNE: Il est très beau!
CHRISTOPHE: Oh?
IRÈNE: Et très sympathique!
CHRISTOPHE: Brun ou blond?
IRÈNE: Très brun.
CHRISTOPHE: Grand ou petit?
IRÈNE: Assez grand.
CHRISTOPHE: Comment s'appelle-t-il?
IRÈNE: Claude Masson.
CHRISTOPHE: *Eh bien, tu perds ton temps.*   *Well, you're wasting your time.*
IRÈNE: Comment?
CHRISTOPHE: C'est *mon cousin.* Il est *idiot!*   *my cousin; stupid*

## L'art du dialogue

a) Act out the dialog.
b) Imagine that Claude Masson is a girl. Reverse the roles of Irène and Christophe and make the necessary changes. Note: **Comment s'appelle-t-il?** becomes **Comment s'appelle-t-elle?** **un garçon** becomes **une fille; mon cousin** becomes **ma cousine; idiot** becomes **idiote.**

STRUCTURES TO OBSERVE
• **avoir**
• gender of nouns designating objects
• the use of **de** (instead of **un/une**) after **pas**

# UNITÉ 2
# Leçon 2    Le vélomoteur de Sylvie

Act. 1

Jean-Paul has been invited to a picnic, but he has trouble finding transportation.

### Jean-Paul et Philippe

| | | |
|---|---|---|
| JEAN-PAUL: | Est-ce que tu as une bicyclette? | |
| PHILIPPE: | Non, je n'ai pas de bicyclette, | |
| | mais j'ai un *vélomoteur*! | *motorbike* |
| JEAN-PAUL: | Un vélomoteur? *Formidable!* | *Great!* |
| | Où est-ce qu'il est? | |
| PHILIPPE: | Il n'est pas *là*... | *here* |
| | Il est à la maison et... | |
| JEAN-PAUL: | Et quoi? | |
| PHILIPPE: | *Il ne marche pas!* | *It doesn't work!* |
| JEAN-PAUL: | Zut alors! | |
| PHILIPPE: | *Écoute!* Téléphone à Sylvie. | *Listen!* |
| | Elle a un vélomoteur *qui* marche. | *that* |

### Jean-Paul et Sylvie

| | | |
|---|---|---|
| JEAN-PAUL: | Dis, Sylvie! Tu as un vélomoteur, n'est-ce pas? | |
| SYLVIE: | Oui, bien sûr! J'ai un vélomoteur. Pourquoi? | |
| JEAN-PAUL: | Écoute... Je suis *invité* à un pique-nique, | *invited* |
| | et je n'ai pas de... | |
| SYLVIE: | *Un moment!* Est-ce que tu as un *permis?* | *Just a moment!;* *license* |
| JEAN-PAUL: | Euh... non! Je n'ai pas de permis! | |
| SYLVIE: | *Pas de* permis, pas de vélomoteur! | *No* |
| JEAN-PAUL: | Et pas de pique-nique! | |
| SYLVIE: | *C'est la vie!* | *That's life!* |

   Est-ce que Philippe a une bicyclette? À qui est-ce que Jean-Paul téléphone?
Est-ce que Sylvie a un vélomoteur?

## CONVERSATION

In the questions below you are asked whether you have certain things.
Answer *yes* or *no*.

1. Avez-vous une radio?
    Oui, j'ai une radio.
    (Non, je n'ai pas **de** radio.)
2. Avez-vous une guitare?
3. Avez-vous un piano?
4. Avez-vous une raquette?
5. Avez-vous un téléviseur *(TV set)?*

## OBSERVATIONS   Str. A, C

In the above questions, **radio, guitare, piano, raquette,** and **téléviseur** are
nouns referring to *things.*   piano, téléviseur

• Which of these nouns are *masculine?* Which are *feminine?*   radio, guitare, raquette

Reread the negative sentence in the model.

• What word is used instead of **un / une** after the negative word **pas?** de

# NOTE CULTURELLE   OPTIONAL

### Le vélomoteur

Very few French teenagers have cars, but many have a
moped or motorbike **(un vélomoteur).** In a country where
people are quite conscious of energy problems, the
motorbike has the advantage of being very economical . . .
and easy to handle through traffic jams. In order to drive a
motorbike, one must have a license **(un permis)** and wear a
crash helmet.

Refer students to Section Magazine, p. 174.
SUGGESTED REALIA: ads or brochures for French motorbikes, mopeds, and bicycles (Mobylette, Motobécane, Peugeot).

# Structure

## A. Le genre des noms: les objets

All French nouns, those referring to *things* as well as those referring to *people*, are either *masculine* or *feminine*. In the sentences below, note how the gender of the underlined noun is reflected in the words in heavy type.

| MASCULINE | FEMININE | |
|---|---|---|
| Voici **un** <u>vélomoteur</u>. | Voici **une** <u>bicyclette</u>. | *Here is a motorbike/bicycle.* |
| Paul regarde **le** vélomoteur. | Paul regarde **la** bicyclette. | *Paul looks at the motorbike/ bicycle.* |
| **Il** marche bien. | **Elle** marche bien. | *It works well.* |
| Est-ce qu'**il** est **grand**? | Est-ce qu'**elle** est **grande**? | *Is it big?* |
| Non, **il** est **petit**. | Non, **elle** est **petite**. | *No, it is small.* |

A *masculine* noun is introduced by a *masculine article* (**un, le,** or **l'**) and is modified by *masculine adjectives*. It can often be replaced by the *subject pronoun* **il**.

A *feminine* noun is introduced by a *feminine article* (**une, la,** or **l'**) and is modified by *feminine adjectives*. It can often be replaced by the *subject pronoun* **elle**.

→ When you learn a new noun, learn it together with the article that indicates its gender. Think of **un transistor, une bicyclette** (rather than just **transistor, bicyclette**).

Remind students that in the **Vocabulaire** sections, masculine nouns are on the left and feminine nouns are on the right.　　voiture = auto　　vélo = bicyclette

---

## Vocabulaire spécialisé　Objets courants *(Everyday things)*

NOMS:

**un appareil-photo**

**un livre**

**un transistor**

**un disque**

**un sac**

**un vélo**

**un électrophone**

**un téléviseur**

**un vélomoteur**

VERBE: **marcher**　*to work*　　Est-ce que le téléviseur **marche** bien?

Note:　When the subject is a person, **marcher** means *to walk*.
　　　Contrast:　Philippe **marche** rapidement.　*Philippe **walks** quickly.*
　　　　　　　La voiture ne **marche** pas.　*The car doesn't **work**.*

---

**Un téléviseur** (or **un poste de télévision**) is a *TV set;* **la télévision** is *TV (programming).*

**102**　Unité deux　　Also for *record player:* **un tourne-disque, une chaîne-stéréo.**

### ACTIVITÉ 1  Où?

Alain wonders where certain things are. Michèle tells him. Play both roles according to the model.

→  un sac / ici     Alain: **Où est le sac?**
                    Michèle: **Il est ici.**

1. un disque / ici
2. une guitare / là
3. une cassette / là-bas

4. une raquette / ici
5. un livre / là
6. un électrophone / là-bas

7. un vélo / à la maison
8. une voiture / à la maison
9. un vélomoteur / là-bas

### ACTIVITÉ 2  Tout marche bien. *(Everything is working well.)*

Alain shows Michèle various things he owns. Michèle asks whether these things are working well, and Alain says they are. Play both roles according to the model.

→  une radio     Alain: **Voici une radio.**
                 Michèle: **Est-ce qu'elle marche bien?**
                 Alain: **Oui, elle marche très bien.**

1. un appareil-photo
2. un électrophone

3. une mini-cassette
4. une montre

5. un transistor
6. un téléviseur

7. une auto
8. une moto

Another term for **mini-cassette** is **un magnétophone à cassettes**.
Make sure that students differentiate between **caméra** and **appareil-photo**.

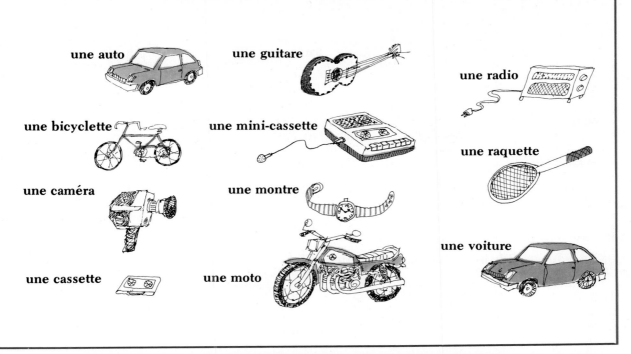

une auto

une guitare

une radio

une bicyclette

une mini-cassette

une raquette

une caméra

une montre

une cassette

une moto

une voiture

VOCABULARY EXPANSION: **un crayon, un stylo, un cahier, une gomme, une bande, un magnétophone, une calculatrice**
At this point you may wish to introduce the classroom vocabulary given in Part Four of the teacher's manual and included in the Activity Masters.

## ACTIVITÉ 3    En ville

Alain and Michèle are window-shopping. Whenever Michèle points out
something, Alain gives his opinion. Play both roles according to the model.
Be sure to use the appropriate form of the adjective in parentheses.

WB
A2, A3

SCRIPT

Act. 3, 4

MASTERS
p. 15

→  une guitare (beau)    Michèle: **Regarde la guitare!**
                          Alain: **Elle est belle!**

1.  un sac (grand)               4.  une montre (petit)        7.  une raquette (beau)
2.  un livre (amusant)           5.  un téléviseur (grand)     8.  un électrophone (petit)
3.  une radio (petit)            6.  une caméra (petit)        9.  un appareil-photo (beau)

**Vocabulaire spécialisé**  **Les couleurs**

blanc (blanche)

gris

bleu

noir

rouge

vert

jaune

**de quelle couleur?**  *what color?*  —**De quelle couleur** est la radio?
                                        —Elle est blanche et noire.

WB
V1

## ACTIVITÉ 4    De quelle couleur . . .?

Give the colors of the following items which you have at home or in class.
Be sure to make the necessary agreements.

→  la radio    **Elle est bleue (blanche, verte . . .).**

(à la maison)                (en classe)          Additional cues: **le crayon, le stylo, le cahier**

1.  le téléviseur            4.  la table
2.  la voiture               5.  la lampe
3.  le téléphone             6.  le livre de français

VOCABULARY EXPANSION: **brun** (red-brown), **violet/violette** (purple), **orange, rose** (pink). For
recognition only: **bleu pâle** (light blue), **bleu foncé** (dark blue). Note that colors expressed with
**pâle** and **foncé** are invariable. They do not agree with the nouns they modify.

## B. Le verbe avoir

The verb **avoir** *(to have, own)* is irregular. Note the forms of this verb in the present tense.

| avoir | to have | |
|---|---|---|
| j'    **ai** | *I have* | **J'ai** un ami à Québec. |
| tu    **as** | *you have* | **As**-tu une guitare? |
| il/elle   **a** | *he/she has* | Est-ce que Philippe **a** une radio? |
| nous **avons** | *we have* | Nous **avons** un électrophone. |
| vous **avez** | *you have* | **Avez**-vous une montre? |
| ils/elles **ont** | *they have* | Ils n'**ont** pas la caméra. |

→ There is liaison in the forms **nous avons, vous avez, ils ont, elles ont.**

### ACTIVITÉ 5   Qui a une guitare?

Jean-Paul wants to borrow a guitar. Tell him that each of the following people has one.

→ Roger      **Roger a une guitare.**   VARIATION: **Est-ce que Roger a un transistor?**

1. Lucie
2. Marc et François
3. nous
4. vous
5. Isabelle
6. Denise et Sylvie
7. je
8. tu

### ACTIVITÉ 6   Qui a le téléphone?   Avoir le téléphone is the French expression that corresponds to *to have a phone.*

Marc is trying to reach his friends, but they don't all have a telephone. Tell him who has a phone and who does not.

→ François / non      **François n'a pas le téléphone.**

1. Sylvie / oui
2. André / non
3. Anne et Suzanne / oui
4. Jean et Louis / non
5. nous / oui
6. vous / non
7. je / oui
8. tu / non

## C. L'article indéfini dans les phrases négatives

Note the form of the indefinite article in negative sentences:

| pas un | becomes | pas de | (un sac?) | Tu n'as **pas de** sac. |
|---|---|---|---|---|
| pas une | | ↓ pas d' (+ vowel sound) | (une radio?) | Il n'a **pas de** radio. |
| | | | (un électro-phone?) | Je n'ai **pas d'**électro-phone. |

Exception: After **être**, **pas un** and **pas une** do not change.

Dominique n'est **pas un** garçon. Dominique est une fille!

For extra practice with **pas de**, ask the class whether they have the items listed in the **Vocabulaire** on pp. 102–103. Have them imagine they are on a desert island and they have nothing. **Avez-vous un appareil-photo? Non, nous n'avons pas d'appareil-photo.**

## ACTIVITÉ 7 Dialogue

Ask your classmates if they own the following things (1-4) or have the following pets at home (5-8).

→ une caméra  — **Est-ce que tu as une caméra?**
            — **Oui, j'ai une caméra. (Non, je n'ai pas de caméra.)**

1. un appareil-photo
2. un hélicoptère
3. une Mercédès
4. une trompette
5. un boa
6. un cobra
7. un éléphant
8. un canari

## ACTIVITÉ 8 Oui et non

Anne owns the following things. Pierre does not. Express this according to the model.

→ un sac  **Anne a un sac. Pierre n'a pas de sac.**

1. un vélo
2. une radio
3. un électrophone
4. une guitare
5. une caméra
6. un vélomoteur
7. un appareil-photo
8. une raquette

## ACTIVITÉ 9 Oui ou non?

We need certain objects to do certain things. Read what the following people are or are not doing. Then say whether or not they have the objects indicated in parentheses. This exercise offers practice in cognate recognition.

→ Paul ne joue pas au tennis. (une raquette?)  **Il n'a pas de raquette.**
   Henri joue au ping-pong. (une raquette?)  **Il a une raquette.**

1. François étudie. (un livre?)
2. Sylvie n'étudie pas. (un livre?)
3. Suzanne écoute la symphonie. (une radio?)
4. Jacques n'écoute pas le concert. (un transistor?)
5. Albert regarde le film. (un téléviseur?)
6. Nathalie ne regarde pas la comédie. (un téléviseur?)
7. Jean-Pierre est ponctuel. (une montre?)
8. Jean-Paul n'est pas ponctuel. (une montre?)

WB
C1

SCRIPT

Act. 6, 7

# Prononciation

Act. 9

## Le son /ã/

*Model word:* qu<u>an</u>d

*Practice words:* gr<u>an</u>d, Fr<u>an</u>ce, d<u>an</u>ser, H<u>en</u>ri, <u>An</u>dré, l<u>am</u>pe

*Practice sentences:* <u>An</u>dré et Fr<u>an</u>cine d<u>an</u>sent.
                   <u>An</u>dré r<u>en</u>tre <u>en</u> Fr<u>an</u>ce <u>en</u> déc<u>em</u>bre.

The sound /ã/ is a nasal vowel. Be sure not to pronounce an /n/ or /m/ after a nasal vowel.

   Comment écrire /ã/: **an** (or **am** before **b** or **p**); **en** (or **em** before **b** or **p**)

# Entre nous

**Expressions pour la conversation**

To express admiration or appreciation, the French use words like:

**Fantastique!**
**Formidable!** } *Great! Terrific!*     Tu as une voiture? **Formidable!**
**Sensationnel!**

## Mini-dialogue     OPTIONAL

Christophe, who is in charge of the class picnic, thought that he had solved the transportation problem.

CHRISTOPHE: Dis, Albert, tu as un vélo?

ALBERT: Non, je n'ai pas de vélo, mais j'ai une voiture.

CHRISTOPHE: Formidable! Elle marche?

ALBERT: Oui, elle marche très bien.

CHRISTOPHE: Sensationnel! Dis, *tu peux l'amener au*        *can you bring it to the*
pique-nique?

ALBERT: C'est impossible.

CHRISTOPHE: Impossible? Pourquoi?

ALBERT: Elle n'est pas ici.

CHRISTOPHE: Où est-elle?

ALBERT: Elle est *chez ma grand-mère* qui habite en        *at my grandmother's*
Alaska.

CHRISTOPHE: Zut alors!

## L'art du dialogue

a) Act out the dialog between Christophe and Albert.

b) Write out a new dialog in which you replace **un vélo** by **une moto**, and **une voiture** by **un vélomoteur.** Make all other necessary changes.

WB
Vos
possessions

SCRIPT
[cassette icon]
Act. 8

MASTERS
p. 15

QUIZ
pp. 26–27

Leçon deux  **107**

# Leçon 3

UNITÉ 2

# Leçon 3 **Dans l'autobus**

STRUCTURES TO OBSERVE
• the position of adjectives: before and after the noun
• the constructions **il est** and **c'est**

Act. 1

The students of the Lycée Carnot are going on a bus trip. Everyone is looking out the window, except Jean-Pierre and Catherine, who are busy looking at the people in the bus.

Qui est le garçon là-bas?
Ah, c'est Antoine.
Il est beau.
Il est amusant.
C'est un garçon sympathique.
C'est un garçon formidable.
C'est aussi le *petit ami* de Claire.     *boyfriend*
Dommage!

**Est-ce qu'Antoine est sympathique? Qui est Antoine?**

**Catherine**

## CONVERSATION

1. Êtes-vous une personne **intelligente?**
2. Êtes-vous une personne **sincère?**
3. Avez-vous un ami **sympathique?**
4. Avez-vous une amie **sympathique?**

## OBSERVATIONS   Str. A

In the above questions, nouns are used with adjectives.

• Do the adjectives come *before* or *after* the nouns?   after

• Is this the same as in English?   No. In English they come before.

Où est Claire?
Ah, elle est là-bas.
Elle est très *jolie*.                    *pretty*
Elle est *drôle*.                          *funny*
C'est une fille sympathique.
C'est une fille extraordinaire . . .
    mais c'est la *petite amie* d'Antoine.   *girlfriend*
Zut alors!

**Claire**

**Antoine**

**Est-ce que Claire est jolie?
Qui est Claire?**

**Jean-Pierre**

OPTIONAL

# NOTES CULTURELLES

**1. Les amis**   Who is a friend? For French teenagers, **un ami** or **une amie** is much more than just an acquaintance. It is a close friend, a person with whom you enjoy spending time now and with whom you will keep in touch over the years.

   **Le meilleur ami** *(best male friend)* or **la meilleure amie** *(best female friend)* is the person with whom you share your problems as well as your joys, the person who is always there when you need someone to talk to.

   **Le petit ami** *(boyfriend)* or **la petite amie** *(girlfriend)* is the very special person whom you are dating exclusively.

   A classmate or friend whom you see often is **un camarade** or **une camarade**.

**2. Le lycée**   The **lycée** is the equivalent of the American senior high school. The school corresponding to the American junior high school is **le C.E.S.** (**Collège d'Enseignement Secondaire**). Most French lycées bear the names of famous people. Lycée Carnot is named after Lazare Carnot (1753–1823), a famous French revolutionary. For a more detailed explanation of the French lycée, see p. 363.

# Structure

## A. La place des adjectifs

In French, descriptive adjectives generally come *after* the noun they modify.

> Suzanne est une fille **intelligente** et **sympathique**.
> Paul a une bicyclette **bleue** et une guitare **noire**.

Only *a few* adjectives come *before* the noun. Here are some of these adjectives:

SCRIPT
Act. 2

| | | | |
|---|---|---|---|
| **beau (belle)** | *beautiful, handsome* | Antoine est un **beau** garçon. | The special form **bel** is introduced in Unité 4.3. |
| **joli** | *pretty* | Sylvie est une **jolie** fille. | |
| **grand** | *big, large* | J'ai un **grand** /ᵗ/ électrophone. | |
| **petit** | *little, small* | J'ai un **petit** appareil-photo. | |
| **bon (bonne)** | *good* | Nous avons un **bon** électrophone. | |
| **mauvais** | *bad* | Vous avez un **mauvais** /ᶻ/ appareil-photo. | |

→ There is liaison between **grand, petit, bon,** and **mauvais,** and the noun which follows. In liaison, **-d** is pronounced /t/, and **-s** is pronounced /z/. Also, in liaison, **bon** is pronounced like **bonne.**

→ Note the special meanings: **un petit ami** *(boyfriend),* **une petite amie** *(girlfriend).*

### ACTIVITÉ 1 Photos

Paul is showing pictures of his friends and commenting on each one. Play the role of Paul according to the model. Use the nouns **garçon** and **fille,** as appropriate.

→ Jacques (drôle)    **Jacques est un garçon drôle.**
  Mélanie (intelligente)    **Mélanie est une fille intelligente.**

1. Marie-Noëlle (amusante)
2. Jacqueline (sympathique)
3. Jean-François (sincère)

4. Isabelle (intéressante)
5. Henri (optimiste)
6. Suzanne (indépendante)

VARIATIONS with **timide, idéaliste, pessimiste, dynamique, romantique.**

Act. 3

17

## Vocabulaire spécialisé La personnalité

**joli**
*pretty*

**bon (bonne)**
*good*

**mauvais**
*bad*

Joli is used with girls; beau is used with boys.

### *ACTIVITÉ 2* Les amies

The following boys have girlfriends with similar characteristics.
Describe the girls.

→ Paul est sympathique.  **Il a une amie sympathique.**

1. Pierre est brun.
2. Charles est blond.
3. Philippe est amusant.

4. Jean-François est sincère.
5. Robert est intelligent.
6. Denis est élégant *(well-dressed)*.

### *ACTIVITÉ 3* La course de vélos *(The bicycle race)*

A group of friends have organized a bicycle race. Describe the bicycle of
each participant, using the adjectives in parentheses and the noun **vélo**.

→ Mélanie (vert)  **Mélanie a un vélo vert.**
  Michel (mauvais)  **Michel a un mauvais vélo.**

WB
A1, A2

SCRIPT

Act. 4, 5

1. François (rouge)
2. Caroline (petit)
3. Isabelle (beau)
4. Robert (bleu)
5. Claire (bon)

6. Philippe (blanc)
7. Catherine (grand)
8. Albert (jaune)
9. Sylvie (joli)
10. Sophie (mauvais)

**drôle**
*funny*

**pénible**
*annoying*

**bête**
*silly, stupid*

Another term for **pénible** is **embêtant**.
Another term for *stupid* is **idiot**.

## B. *Il est* ou *c'est*?

The distinction between **il est** and **c'est** is an important but difficult concept. You may present it here for recognition only.

The sentences below describe **Paul** and **Anne**. Note the constructions in heavy type.

|  | Comment est-il/elle? | Qui est-ce? |  |
|---|---|---|---|
| Paul | **Il est** amusant<br>**Il est** intelligent. | **C'est** un ami.<br>**C'est** un élève. | **C'est** un ami amusant.<br>**C'est** un élève intelligent. |
| Anne | **Elle est** sympathique.<br>**Elle est** intelligente. | **C'est** une amie.<br>**C'est** une élève. | **C'est** une amie sympathique.<br>**C'est** une élève intelligente. |

In descriptions French speakers use **être** in the following constructions:

> **Il est**
> **Elle est** } + adjective    and    **C'est** + article + noun + adjective (if any)

➜ The above constructions are used to describe things as well as people.

| Voici un vélo. | **Il est** grand. | **C'est** un vélo français. |
|---|---|---|
| Voilà une voiture. | **Elle est** belle. | **C'est** une voiture américaine. |

➜ In negative sentences **c'est** becomes **ce n'est pas.**

**Ce n'est pas** Paul.    **Ce n'est pas** le professeur.

The adjective may also precede the noun: **C'est une belle voiture.**

➜ **C'est** is also used with the names of people.

**C'est** Nicole!    **C'est** Madame Lamblet!

## *ACTIVITÉ 4*   D'accord!

Alain and Suzanne are often of the same opinion when they discuss people they know. Play both roles according to the model.

➜ Philippe est un ami sympathique.

Alain: **C'est un ami sympathique!**
Suzanne: **D'accord! Il est sympathique!**

1. Paul est un garçon intelligent.
2. Thérèse est une fille amusante.
3. Richard est un beau garçon.
4. Annie est une jolie fille.
5. Monsieur Bouffon est un professeur amusant.
6. Madame Chouette est une femme sympathique.
7. Mademoiselle Callet est une personne intelligente.
8. Monsieur Gentil est une personne sincère.

## *ACTIVITÉ 5*   Descriptions

Complete the following descriptions with **Il/Elle est** or **C'est**, as appropriate.

**A.   Antoine**
1. —— grand.
2. —— blond.
3. —— un garçon sympathique.
4. —— un mauvais élève.

**B.   Suzanne**
5. —— une fille blonde.
6. —— une camarade sympathique.
7. —— très amusante.
8. —— assez petite.

**C.   La moto d'Antoine** *(Antoine's motorcycle)*
9. —— une moto confortable.cognate
10. —— une bonne moto.
11. —— rouge et jaune.
12. —— très moderne.cognate

**D.   Le vélomoteur de Suzanne**
13. —— gris et bleu.
14. —— très économique. cognate
15. —— un joli petit vélomoteur.
16. —— assez moderne.

WB
B1, B2

SCRIPT

Act. 7, 8

MASTERS
p. 16

Act. 6

**ACTIVITÉ 6**  **Le salon de la voiture** *(The car show)* OPTIONAL

Imagine that you are attending the annual car show as a reporter for an automobile magazine. You look at the following cars. First say that each one has the characteristic indicated in parentheses. Then give your opinion of each one, using **bonne** or **mauvaise** and the noun **voiture**.

→  Voici une Cadillac. (grande)    **Elle est grande. C'est une bonne (mauvaise) voiture.**

1. Voici une Renault. (petite)
2. Voici une Fiat. (jolie)
3. Voici une Toyota. (économique)
4. Voici une Rolls Royce. (élégante)
5. Voici une Citroën. (moderne)
6. Voici une Peugeot. (belle)

# Prononciation

## Le son /ɔ/

t. 10

*Model word:*  b<u>o</u>nne

*Practice words:*  P<u>au</u>l, R<u>o</u>ger, téléph<u>o</u>ne, m<u>o</u>derne,  électroph<u>o</u>ne

*Practice sentences:*  Yv<u>o</u>nne est b<u>o</u>nne et j<u>o</u>lie.
À N<u>o</u>ël, Nic<u>o</u>le téléph<u>o</u>ne à C<u>o</u>lette.

The sound /ɔ/ is pronounced somewhat like the *o* in the English word *model*, but the French sound /ɔ/ is both shorter and more tense.

Comment écrire /ɔ/: **o**; (sometimes) **au**

# Entre nous

## Expression pour la conversation

To emphasize a statement or an answer, you may say:

**Eh bien!**  *Well!*   — **Eh bien**, François, est-ce que tu as un vélomoteur?
— **Eh bien**, non!

## Mini-dialogue   OPTIONAL

Suzanne is at the window describing someone she sees in the street.
Alain is trying to guess who it is.

SUZANNE: Tiens! Voilà un garçon. Il arrive *en* voiture.          *by*
ALAIN: Est-ce que c'est une grande voiture?
SUZANNE: Non, elle est petite.
ALAIN: Est-ce qu'elle est rouge?
SUZANNE: Non, elle est bleue.
ALAIN: Eh bien, c'est Robert. Il a une petite voiture bleue!
SUZANNE: Eh bien, non! Ce n'est pas Robert. C'est Paul.

## L'art du dialogue

a)  Act out the dialog between Alain and Suzanne.
b)  Act out a new dialog in which Suzanne sees **Sophie** (and not **Thérèse**) coming on a small motorbike (**un vélomoteur**). Make the necessary changes.

WB
B3; La
voiture . . .

SCRIPT
Act. 9

MASTERS
p. 16

QUIZ
pp. 28–29

Leçon trois  **113**

STRUCTURES TO OBSERVE
• plural forms of nouns
• plural forms of definite and indefinite articles
• plural forms of adjectives

# UNITÉ 2
# Leçon 4   Le bal du Mardi Gras

Act. 1

For Mardi Gras the International Club has organized a costume party. Everyone is trying to identify the guests.

JEANNE: Regarde les clowns là-bas!
SOPHIE: Qui est-ce?
JEANNE: Paul et David!
SOPHIE: Des étudiants américains?
JEANNE: Non, des étudiants anglais!
SOPHIE: Ils sont très drôles!
JEANNE: Oui, mais . . . Ils sont un peu snobs!
SOPHIE: Dommage!

**Est-ce que Paul et David sont français? Est-ce qu'ils sont américains? Est-ce qu'ils sont anglais?**

ROBERT: Regarde les filles là-bas!
JULIEN: Les filles *en* rouge? Qui est-ce?
ROBERT: C'est Monique et Marie.
JULIEN: Elles sont américaines?
ROBERT: Non, ce sont des étudiantes françaises . . . de la Guadeloupe!
JULIEN: Elles sont très jolies!
ROBERT: . . . et très sympathiques aussi!
JULIEN: *Tant mieux!*

*in*

**Est-ce que Monique et Marie sont américaines? Est-ce qu'elles sont françaises? Où est-ce qu'elles habitent?**

*So much the better!*

## CONVERSATION

Do you have many good friends? Of course you do! Answer the following questions in the affirmative.

1. Avez-vous **des amis sympathiques?**
2. Avez-vous **des amies sympathiques?**
3. Avez-vous **des amis intéressants?**
4. Avez-vous **des amies intéressantes?**

## OBSERVATIONS   Str. B, C

Reread the above questions.

- What is the *plural* of **ami?** of **amie?**   amis/amies
  Which letter do plural nouns end in? Is this letter pronounced?   no
- Which indefinite article comes before **amis?** before **amies?**   des/des
  What is the *plural* of **un?** of **une?**   des/des
- What is the *plural* of **sympathique?** of **intéressant?** of **intéressante?**   sympathiques/intéressants/intéressantes
  Which letter do plural adjectives end in? Is this letter pronounced?   no

## NOTES CULTURELLES   OPTIONAL

**1. Mardi Gras**   When you see children in costumes going from door to door in the United States, you know it's Halloween. In France you will not see children out in costumes until February or March for the celebration of **Mardi Gras.** In some parts of the French-speaking world (New Orleans, Quebec, Haiti, Martinique, as well as Nice and Cannes in France) **Mardi Gras** or **Carnaval** is celebrated with a ten-day pageant, which has been prepared for many months. In other parts of France, **Mardi Gras** may simply be the occasion for a big costume party.

**2. La Guadeloupe**   Guadeloupe is a small Caribbean island close to Martinique. The inhabitants of Guadeloupe and Martinique are French citizens, primarily of African ancestry.
You may refer the students to the map of the French-speaking world on pp. vi–vii.

guadeloupe
martinique

Literally, **Mardi Gras** means "Fat Tuesday." It is the last day before **le Carême** *(Lent),* the traditional 40-day period of fasting before Easter in the Catholic religion.
SUGGESTED REALIA: Mardi Gras travel brochures.

# Structure

You may want to have the students practice the pronunciation of the feminine and masculine forms of the following adjectives of nationality.

anglais /e/     anglaise /ɛz/       français, japonais
canadien /jɛ̃/   canadienne /jɛn/     italien, égyptien
américain /ɛ̃/   américaine /ɛn/      mexicain

## A. L'article défini avec les noms géographiques

Note the use of the definite article in the following sentences:

**Le Canada** est un pays américain.     *Canada is an American country.*
**La Californie** est jolie.     *California is pretty.*

In French most *geographical* names are introduced by a definite article. It is used with *countries, states, rivers,* and *mountains,* but not with *cities.*

**Paris** est la capitale de **la France**.     *Paris is the capital of France.*

Exceptions: **Israël, Panama** (no articles); **la Nouvelle-Orléans, Le Havre**

Act. 2

1, 2,
3

## Vocabulaire spécialisé   Pays et nationalités

| un pays | *country* | une nationalité |
|---|---|---|
| l'Amérique | *America* | |
| le Canada | *Canada* | **canadien (canadienne)** |
| les États-Unis | *United States* | **américain** |
| le Mexique | *Mexico* | **mexicain** |
| l'Europe | *Europe* | |
| l'Allemagne | *Germany* | **allemand** |
| l'Angleterre | *England* | **anglais** |
| la Belgique | *Belgium* | **belge** |
| l'Espagne | *Spain* | **espagnol** |
| la France | *France* | **français** |
| l'Italie | *Italy* | **italien (italienne)** |
| la Suisse | *Switzerland* | **suisse** |
| l'Asie | *Asia* | |
| la Chine | *China* | **chinois** |
| le Japon | *Japan* | **japonais** |
| l'Afrique | *Africa* | |
| l'Égypte | *Egypt* | **égyptien (égyptienne)** |

You may remind students that adjectives of nationality take the same endings as other adjectives.

l'Australie   *Australia*

Notes: 1. Most countries whose names *end* in **-e** are feminine.

This applies to states also: le Colorado, le Texas, la Californie, la Virginie.

**la France   la Suisse**     Exception: **le Mexique**

All other countries are masculine.

**le Japon   le Canada**

2. Adjectives of nationality are not capitalized in French.

J'ai un ami **français** et une amie **anglaise.**

However, when these adjectives are used as *nouns* to refer to people, they are capitalized.

Paul parle avec un **Français** et     *Paul is talking with a Frenchman and*
une **Anglaise.**     *an English woman.*

The names of languages are not capitalized: **l'anglais, l'allemand.**

In French, **l'Amérique** is considered as one continent. It is subdivided into **l'Amérique du Nord, l'Amérique centrale,** and **l'Amérique du Sud.**

## ACTIVITÉ 1 Aimez-vous la géographie?

Give the continents where the following countries are located:

**en Asie   en Amérique   en Europe   en Afrique**

You may refer the students to a world map and ask them to locate these countries.

→ France   **La France est en Europe.**

1. Allemagne
2. Chine
3. Italie
4. Japon
5. Mexique
6. Angleterre
7. Espagne
8. Canada
9. Danemark
10. Sénégal
11. Viêt-nam
12. Portugal
13. Tunisie
14. Algérie
15. Côte-d'Ivoire *(Ivory Coast)*
16. Suisse

## ACTIVITÉ 2 Une question de nationalité

The following people own things which were made in the countries where they live. Express this according to the model.

→ Luisa habite à Séville. (une guitare)
   **Elle a une guitare espagnole.**

1. François habite à Paris. (un téléviseur)
2. Nathalie habite à Québec. (un disque)
3. Michèle habite à New York. (une voiture)
4. Pietro habite à Rome. (une moto)
5. Birgit habite à Munich. (une caméra)
6. Tatsuo habite à Tokyo. (une auto)
7. Lin habite à Hong-Kong. (une bicyclette)
8. Pedro habite à Mexico. (une guitare)

WB
A1

VARIATION: Give each person's nationality.
**Luisa est espagnole.**

### B. Le pluriel: les noms et les articles

When referring to several objects, the French use the subject pronouns **ils/elles**.
**Voici des montres. Elles marchent bien.**

Compare the *singular* and *plural* forms of the articles and nouns in the sentences below:

| SINGULAR | PLURAL |
|---|---|
| Où est **le garçon?** | Où sont **les garçons?** |
| Qui est **la fille** là-bas? | Qui sont **les filles** là-bas? |
| J'invite **l'étudiant.** | J'invite **les étudiants.** |
| Je parle à **un garçon.** | Je parle à **des garçons.** |
| Nous invitons **une fille.** | Nous invitons **des filles.** |
| Paul est **un ami.** | Paul et Charles sont **des amis.** |
| C'est **une amie.** | Ce sont **des amies.** |

#### Plural nouns

In written French the plural of most nouns is formed as follows:

$$\boxed{\text{singular noun} \quad + \quad \text{s} \quad \rightarrow \quad \text{plural noun}}$$

If the noun ends in **-s** in the singular, the singular and plural forms are the same.

> Voici **un Français.**     Voici **des Français.**

➜ In spoken French the final **-s** of the plural is always *silent*. Therefore, singular and plural nouns sound the same. You can tell, however, if the noun is singular or plural by listening to the article which introduces it.

> Voici **une amie.**     Voici **des amies.**

In English, one usually listens to the noun in order to tell if it is singular or plural: the girl, the girls. However, in a few cases one must listen to the word which introduces the noun: this fish, these fish.

#### Plural articles

The forms of the plural articles are summarized in the chart below.

| | SINGULAR | PLURAL | | |
|---|---|---|---|---|
| *Definite Article* | le (l') <br> la (l') | les | **les** garçons <br> **les** filles | **les** amis <br> **les** amies |
| *Indefinite Article* | un <br> une | des | **des** sacs <br> **des** montres | **des** électrophones <br> **des** autos |

➜ There is liaison after **les** and **des** when the next word begins with a vowel sound.

### Les Peugeot Diesel. D'abord des Peugeot.

In French, family names and proper nouns do not usually take an **-s**.

→ **Des** corresponds to the English article *some*. While *some* is often omitted in English, **des** *must* be expressed in French. Contrast:

| Voici | **des** | livres. | | J'invite | **des** | amis. |
|-------|---------|---------|---|----------|---------|-------|
| *Here are* | *some* | *books.* | | *I'm inviting* | . . . | *friends.* |

→ In *negative* sentences, except after **être**:

SCRIPT
Act. 3

> **pas des** becomes **pas de**        (**des** disques?)   Marc n'a **pas de** disques.
> ↓
> **pas d'** (+ vowel sound)   (**des** amis?)   Tu n'as **pas d'**amis.

Note the construction with **être: Vous n'êtes pas des étudiants.**

→ The plural of **c'est (ce n'est pas)** is **ce sont (ce ne sont pas).**

**C'est** une amie.          **Ce sont** des amies.
**Ce n'est pas** un ami.          **Ce ne sont pas** des amis.

**C'est** is used instead of **ce sont** before names of people: **C'est Henri et Pierre.**
**C'est Monsieur et Madame Dupont.**

## ACTIVITÉ 3   Présentations *(Introductions)*

Introduce the following young people as friends of yours. Use **un, une,** or **des.**

→ Jacqueline          **Jacqueline est une amie.**
  Paul et Marc          **Paul et Marc sont des amis.**

1. Caroline
2. Jean-Philippe
3. Suzanne et Hélène
4. Henri et Charles
5. Georges, Louis et Simon
6. Sylvie, Nicole et Michèle

## ACTIVITÉ 4   Imitations

Say that Paul and Henri are doing the same things their cousin Philippe does. Follow the model, using *plural* forms.

→ Philippe parle à une amie.          **Paul et Henri parlent à des amies.**

1. Philippe invite une amie.
2. Il dîne avec un ami.
3. Il parle à un journaliste.
4. Il joue au tennis avec un garçon.
5. Il joue au tennis avec une fille.
6. Il invite un camarade.
7. Il parle à un professeur.
8. Il écoute un professeur.

## ACTIVITÉ 5   Dans un grand magasin *(In a department store)*

Sylvie is in a department store. The salesperson tells her that the things she is looking for are over there. Play both roles.

→ une montre          Sylvie: **Je désire une montre.**
                      L'employé(e): **Les montres sont là-bas.**

1. une caméra
2. un téléviseur
3. une guitare
4. une raquette
5. un livre
6. un disque
7. un électrophone
8. un appareil-photo

Note the liaison in items 7 and 8. The plural of **appareil-photo** is **appareils-photo.**

### ACTIVITÉ 6   Dans un petit magasin

This time Sylvie is shopping in a small store. Whenever she asks for certain items, the salesperson says that they do not have them. Play both roles.
(Note: **Je regrette** means *I am sorry*.)

→   une caméra      Sylvie: **Avez-vous des caméras?**
L'employé(e): **Je regrette . . .   Nous n'avons pas de caméras.**

1. un transistor
2. une cassette
3. une radio
4. une raquette
5. un appareil-photo
6. un électrophone

## C. Le pluriel: les adjectifs

Note the *plural* forms of the adjectives in the sentences below.

Roger est **américain**.          Jim et Bob sont **américains**.
Anne est une amie **française**.   Louise et Claire sont des amies **françaises**.
Marc est un élève **français**.    Paul et Michel sont des élèves **français**.

In written French the plural of an adjective is formed as follows:

> singular adjective   +   s   →   plural adjective

If the adjective ends in -s in the singular, the singular and plural forms are the same.

→  In spoken French the final -s of plural adjectives is silent.

→  There is liaison when a plural adjective comes *before* a noun that begins with a vowel sound:

les‿élèves            les bons‿élèves
les‿appareils-photo   les petits‿appareils-photo

The plural forms of **beau** are taught in Unité 4.3.

Liaison is not required after a plural noun followed by an adjective beginning with a vowel sound: **les livres italiens** or **les livres‿italiens**

### ACTIVITÉ 7   Le client

You are going shopping. Ask whether the store carries the items you are looking for.

→  un disque américain     **Avez-vous des disques américains?**

1. un disque français
2. un vélo anglais
3. une moto italienne
4. un livre canadien
5. un sac rouge
6. une montre suisse
7. un vélomoteur bleu
8. une cassette espagnole
9. une grande bicyclette
10. un petit électrophone
11. un bon appareil-photo
12. un petit téléviseur

The use of **de** instead of **des** before an adjective is not taught at this level. In conversational French it is common to use **des**. *Avez-vous des grands sacs?* / *Avez-vous de grands sacs?*

## *ACTIVITÉ 8* L'école internationale

Read where the following students at an international school normally live and say what their nationalities are.

→ Suzanne et Mélanie habitent à Paris. **Elles sont françaises.**

1. Thomas et Daniel habitent à Bordeaux.
2. Marie et Anne habitent à Québec.
3. Paul et François habitent à Québec.
4. Jim et Bob habitent à Chicago.
5. Linda et Louise habitent à Boston.
6. Pietro et Mario habitent à Rome.
7. Rafael et Carlos habitent à Mexico.
8. Jane et Silvia habitent à Liverpool.

## D. L'expression *il y a*

Note the use of **il y a** in the sentences below:

| Dans la classe . . . | *In the class . . .* |
|---|---|
| **il y a** un professeur intéressant, | *there is an interesting teacher,* |
| **il y a** une fille française, | *there is a French girl,* |
| **il y a** des élèves intelligents. | *there are intelligent students.* |

**Il y a** (*there is, there are*) has only one form. It is used with both *singular* and *plural* nouns.

→ Note the interrogative and negative constructions with **il y a:**

**Est-ce qu'il y a** un téléviseur ici?  Non, **il n'y a pas** de téléviseur ici.
**Est-ce qu'il y a** des disques?  Non, **il n'y a pas** de disques.

Remind students that **pas un/une/des** becomes **pas de (d')** after **il y a.**
The inverted form **y a-t-il** is not taught at this level.

## *ACTIVITÉ 9* Dans la classe

Ask your classmates if the following items (1-7) and people (8-14) are in the classroom. Your classmates will answer as appropriate.

→ un téléviseur  —**Est-ce qu'il y a un téléviseur?**
  —**Mais oui! Il y a un téléviseur.**
  (**Mais non! Il n'y a pas de téléviseur.**)

1. un électrophone
2. une mini-cassette
3. des disques
4. des cassettes
5. des livres
6. des livres français
7. un appareil-photo

8. des garçons
9. des filles
10. des garçons sympathiques
11. des filles sympathiques
12. des élèves français
13. des élèves canadiens
14. des élèves intelligents

If items 1, 7, 12 –14 are answered in the negative, be sure **pas d'** is used.

Remember that liaison is required *before* the noun. It is optional after a plural noun, and never occurs after a singular noun. les_élèves   les bons_élèves   les_élèves_américains

## E. Récapitulation: la forme des adjectifs

Here is a form chart for the endings of regular adjectives:

| | SINGULAR | PLURAL | | |
|---|---|---|---|---|
| *Masculine* | — | -s | un ami **intelligent** | des_amis **intelligents** |
| *Feminine* | -e | -es | une amie **intelligente** | des_amies **intelligentes** |

WB
E1

### *ACTIVITÉ 10*   Similarités      OPTIONAL

The children in Alain's family are all alike. Describe (a) his sister Suzanne, (b) his brothers Pierre and Paul, (c) his older sisters Nicole and Yvonne.

→ Alain est grand.   (a) **Suzanne est grande.**
(b) **Pierre et Paul sont grands.**
(c) **Nicole et Yvonne sont grandes.**

This activity may be performed by dividing the class into three parts: one responds with (a), the second with (b), and the third with (c).

1. Alain est brun.
2. Alain est intelligent.
3. Alain est français.
4. Alain est drôle.

5. Alain est sympathique.
6. Alain est intéressant.
7. Alain n'est pas embêtant *(annoying)*.
8. Alain n'est pas pénible.

# Prononciation

Act. 11

### Les lettres: voyelle + n (m)

The letter group "vowel+n" ("vowel+m") represents a nasal vowel, unless it is followed by a vowel or another **n** (**m**).

Contrast the pronunciation of the nasal and non-nasal vowels in the following words. (Be sure not to pronounce an /n/ after a nasal vowel.)

NASAL VOWELS
/ã/ Jean, Antoine, Christian
/ɛ̃/ Martin, cousin
    canadien, américain
/œ̃/ un, brun

NON-NASAL VOWELS
/an/ Jeanne, Anatole, Christiane
/in/ Martine, cousine
/ɛn/ canadienne, américaine
/yn/ une, brune

# Entre nous

## Expression pour la conversation

When you are not sure, or when you want to avoid saying yes or no, you can say:

**peut-être** *maybe, perhaps*  —Tu as dix dollars?
—**Peut-être** . . . Pourquoi?

## Mini-dialogue   OPTIONAL

Marc wonders why Sylvie is wearing glasses.

MARC: Tiens, tu as des *lunettes?*   *glasses*
SYLVIE: Bien sûr!
MARC: Est-ce que tu es *myope* maintenant?   *nearsighted*
SYLVIE: Non, je ne suis pas myope.
MARC: Alors, pourquoi est-ce que tu as des lunettes?
SYLVIE: Parce que c'est la *mode,* idiot!   *style*
MARC: Tu as des idées bizarres!
SYLVIE: Peut-être . . .   Mais *toi,* tu n'as pas d'idées!   *you*

## L'art du dialogue

Act out the dialog between Marc and Sylvie.

WB
Votre
chambre

SCRIPT
Act. 10

MASTERS
p. 17

QUIZ
pp. 30–31

# Leçon 5

# À la Maison des Jeunes

Act. 1

Un groupe d'amis arrive à la Maison des Jeunes.

### Tennis

NICOLAS: Tu aimes jouer au tennis?
CAROLINE: Bien sûr! C'est formidable, non?
NICOLAS: Tu joues avec moi?
CAROLINE: Avec toi? D'accord!

**Est-ce que Caroline aime jouer au tennis?**

### Basketball

PIERRE: Qui joue au basket?
PHILIPPE: Moi!
CLAIRE: Moi aussi!
PIERRE: Et André? Il ne joue pas avec *nous*?  *us*
CLAIRE: Non. Il joue avec Isabelle!
PIERRE: Avec *elle*?  *her*
CLAIRE: Pourquoi pas? Elle joue très bien.
PIERRE: C'est vrai!

**Avec qui est-ce qu'André joue au basketball?**
**Comment est-ce qu'Isabelle joue?**

### Monopoly

SYLVIE: Tiens! Voilà Marc et voilà Paul!
BÉATRICE: Nous jouons au Monopoly avec *eux*?  *them*
SYLVIE: Est-ce qu'ils jouent bien?
BÉATRICE: Euh, non . . . Marc joue mal . . .
SYLVIE: Et Paul?
BÉATRICE: *Lui, il triche!*  *He cheats!*
SYLVIE: Alors, je ne joue pas avec eux.
BÉATRICE: *Moi non plus!*  *Me neither!*

**Est-ce que Marc joue bien au Monopoly? Est-ce que Paul joue bien?**
**Est-ce que Sylvie et Béatrice jouent avec Marc et Paul?**

## CONVERSATION

Let's talk about your best male friend: **votre meilleur ami.**

1. Est-ce que vous parlez français avec **lui**?
2. Est-ce que vous étudiez avec **lui**?
3. Est-ce que vous jouez au tennis avec **lui**?

Now let's talk about your best female friend: **votre meilleure amie.**

4. Est-ce que vous parlez français avec **elle**?
5. Est-ce que vous étudiez avec **elle**?
6. Est-ce que vous jouez au tennis avec **elle**?

## OBSERVATIONS    Str. B

Reread the above questions, paying special attention to the pronouns that follow the word **avec.** These are called *stress pronouns.*

- Which stress pronoun is used to refer to your best *male* friend? lui
  Is this the same as the subject pronoun **il**? no
- Which stress pronoun is used to refer to your best *female* friend? elle
  Is this the same as the subject pronoun **elle**? yes

## NOTES CULTURELLES    OPTIONAL

**1. La Maison des Jeunes**   Most French cities have a public youth center called **La Maison des Jeunes et de la Culture** or, simply, **La Maison des Jeunes.** There young people gather to practice their favorite sports, to play cards, to watch movies, to listen to folk music, to dance, and to have a good time together. They can also develop their artistic talents by participating in plays or by taking art or pottery lessons. Often **La Maison des Jeunes** also offers practical training for useful skills such as car repair, shop, typing, sewing . . . and English!

**2. Le Monopoly**   Monopoly is as popular in France as it is in the United States. The French **Monopoly** board uses Paris street names, and naturally millionaires are millionaires in French francs!

SUGGESTED REALIA: French Monopoly game.

MAISON DES JEUNES ET DE LA CULTURE
49 rue des martyrs
JOUÉ LES TOURS

Les spectacles
Modern'Jazz Danse

### FEVRIER

| DANSE | Samedi 4 | 21 h. | Ballet de "Modern'Jazz". Direction S. ALZETTA. |
| DANSE | Samedi 4 Dimanche 5 | | Stage de danse - "Modern'Jazz" avec S. ALZETTA. |
| RENCONTRE | Mardi 7 | 21 h. | Conférence   FRANCE - URSS |
| SEJOUR | Samedi 11 | 19 h. | Départ Séjour SKI |

# Structure

## A. Les expressions impersonnelles avec c'est

Act. 2

Note the use of **c'est** in the sentences below:
(modification)

| | | |
|---|---|---|
| **vrai** | *true, right* | Tu parles italien? **C'est vrai?** |
| **faux (fausse)** | *false, wrong* | Non, **c'est faux!** |
| **facile** | *easy* | Je parle anglais. **C'est facile.** |
| **difficile** | *hard, difficult* | J'étudie le chinois. **C'est difficile.** |

French speakers often use impersonal expressions formed as follows:

> **C'est**
> **Ce n'est pas** } + masculine adjective

→ Impersonal expressions are sometimes formed with adverbs, such as **bien** and **mal**.

**C'est bien!**  *That's good (fine).*  Tu étudies? **C'est bien!**
**C'est mal!**  *That's bad.*  Alain n'étudie pas. **C'est mal!**

### ACTIVITÉ 1   Vrai ou faux?

Imagine your little cousin is making statements about geography. Tell him whether his statements are right or wrong. Use: **Oui, c'est vrai!** or **Non, ce n'est pas vrai!**

→  Paris est en France.     **Oui, c'est vrai!**     After **en** the definite article is not used with names of countries.

1. Miami est en Floride.
2. San Francisco est en Californie.
3. Berlin est en Italie.
4. Rome est en France.
5. La Tunisie est en Amérique.
6. Abidjan est en Afrique.
7. Fort-de-France est en Suisse.
8. Genève est en Suisse.

### ACTIVITÉ 2   Expression personnelle     OPTIONAL

Say whether or not you like to do the following things and why. Use **C'est** or **Ce n'est pas** with adjectives such as **amusant, intéressant, drôle, pénible, facile, difficile.**

WB
A1

SCRIPT

Act. 3

→  nager     **J'aime nager parce que c'est amusant (ce n'est pas difficile).**
            **Je n'aime pas nager parce que c'est pénible (ce n'est pas amusant).**

1. téléphoner
2. parler français
3. parler français en classe
4. danser
5. voyager
6. regarder la télé
7. dîner en ville
8. jouer au golf
9. écouter la musique classique

## B. Les pronoms accentués

Stress pronouns are sometimes called disjunctive pronouns.

In each sentence below, the first pronoun is a *stress pronoun,* and the second is a *subject pronoun.* Compare the two sets of pronouns.

|  | STRESS PRONOUN | SUBJECT PRONOUN |  |
|---|---|---|---|
| *Singular* | Moi, | je | parle français. |
|  | Toi, | tu | étudies l'espagnol. |
|  | Lui, | il | a un vélomoteur. |
|  | Elle, | elle | joue au tennis. |
| *Plural* | Nous, | nous | sommes américains. |
|  | Vous, | vous | habitez en France. |
|  | Eux, | ils | ont une petite voiture. |
|  | Elles, | elles | dansent très bien. |

Point out that four stress pronouns have the same forms as the corresponding subject pronouns: **elle, nous, vous, elles.** Four stress pronouns have different forms: **moi, toi, lui, eux.**

Stress pronouns occur frequently in French. They are used—

1. in short statements where there is no verb:

Qui danse bien?    **Moi!**　　　　　　*Me! (I do!)*
Qui parle italien?    **Pas lui!**　　　　*Not him! (He doesn't.)*

2. to reinforce a subject pronoun:

**Moi,** j'adore danser.　　　　　　　*I love to dance.*

3. after words like **avec** and **pour:**

Marie joue avec **lui.**　　　　　　　*Marie plays with him.*
Il travaille pour **nous.**　　　　　　*He works for us.*

4. before and after **et** and **ou:**

**Toi et moi,** nous étudions beaucoup.　*You and I, we study a lot.*
Qui rentre maintenant? **Eux ou vous?**　*Who is going back now? They or you?*

5. After **c'est** and **ce n'est pas:**

C'est Pierre?    Oui, c'est **lui!**　　　　*Is it Pierre? Yes, it's him (he).*
C'est Claire?    Non, ce n'est pas **elle!**　*Is it Claire? No, it's not her (she).*

## ACTIVITÉ 3　Une enquête *(A survey)*

A French magazine is making a survey. Answer the questions affirmatively or negatively.

→　Qui parle français?　　**Moi! (Pas moi!)**

1. Qui étudie le français?　　l'espagnol
2. Qui a des amis français?　　allemands
3. Qui a des amis en Californie?　en Floride
4. Qui a des disques?　cassettes
5. Qui aime nager?　marcher
6. Qui adore danser?　chanter

### ACTIVITÉ 4  La photo

Alain and Suzanne are looking at a photograph of their kindergarten class.
Alain tries to remember everyone's name. Suzanne lets him know if he is
right or wrong. Play both roles.

WB
B1, B2,
B3

SCRIPT
Act. 6, 7

→ Henri (oui)  Alain: **C'est Henri?**       Michèle (non)  **C'est Michèle?**
  Suzanne: **Oui, c'est lui!**          **Non, ce n'est pas elle!**

1. Antoine (oui)                    5. Louise et Claire (non)
2. Martine (oui)                    6. Monsieur Duval (oui)
3. Jean-Pierre (non)                7. Madame Lemoine (non)
4. Marc et André (oui)              8. Mademoiselle Thomas (oui)

### ACTIVITÉ 5  Non!   OPTIONAL

Answer the questions below in the negative, and then give the correct
information (in parentheses). Reinforce your answers with stress pronouns.

→ Pierre habite à Abidjan? (à Dakar)   **Non! Lui, il habite à Dakar!**

1. Christine parle anglais? (espagnol)      5. Nous jouons bien? (vous / mal)
2. Charles chante mal? (bien)               6. Tu joues au tennis? (je / au golf)
3. Paul et Georges étudient souvent?        7. Vous habitez à Paris? (nous / à Dijon)
   (rarement)                               8. J'étudie l'espagnol? (tu / l'anglais)
4. Alice et Michèle voyagent rarement?
   (souvent)

### ACTIVITÉ 6  Pourquoi?

WB
B4

SCRIPT

Act. 5

MASTERS
p. 18

Suzanne wants to know why Paul does the following things. Play the role of
Suzanne, using stress pronouns in your questions.

→ Je joue avec Pierre.    Suzanne: **Pourquoi est-ce que tu joues avec lui?**

1. Je rentre avec Pierre et Antoine.      4. Je travaille pour Monsieur Moreau.
2. J'étudie avec Paul.                    5. Je travaille aussi pour Madame Lasalle.
3. Je dîne avec Jeannette et Isabelle.    6. Je danse avec Hélène.

# Prononciation

Act. 9

### Le son /wa/

*Model word:* t<u>oi</u>

*Practice words:* m<u>oi</u>, v<u>oi</u>ci, v<u>oy</u>age, Mademois<u>e</u>lle, v<u>oi</u>là

*Practice sentences:* Ben<u>oî</u>t v<u>oy</u>age avec m<u>oi</u>.
                      V<u>oi</u>là Mademois<u>oi</u>elle Descr<u>oi</u>x.

Comment écrire /wa/: **oi, oî, oy**

# Entre nous

## Expressions pour la conversation

To introduce a mild reproach, you can say:

| | | | |
|---|---|---|---|
| **Écoute!** | (tu form) | *Listen!* | Écoute, Alain! Tu es pénible aujourd'hui. |
| **Écoutez!** | (vous form) | *Listen!* | Écoutez, vous deux! Vous jouez mal! |

## Mini-dialogue   OPTIONAL

Alain is at a party. He would like to invite Dominique to dance, but he has a problem.

ALAIN: Avec qui est-ce que tu danses maintenant?

DOMINIQUE: Avec Jacques.

ALAIN: Avec lui? Écoute, Jacques est sympathique,
mais il n'est pas très drôle. Pourquoi est-ce que
tu ne danses pas avec moi? Moi, *au moins* . . .     *at least*

DOMINIQUE: C'est vrai! Jacques n'est pas *spécialement*     *especially*
drôle, mais il danse très bien!

ALAIN: Et moi?

DOMINIQUE: Toi?

ALAIN: Oui, moi!

DOMINIQUE: Écoute, Alain. Tu es sympathique, mais quand
je danse avec toi, *tu me marches toujours sur*     *you always step on my feet*
*les pieds.* Alors . . .

## L'art du dialogue

a) Act out the dialog between Alain and Dominique.

b) Now imagine that it is **Dominique** who would like to dance with **Alain**. Reverse the roles of Alain and Dominique. Replace Jacques with **Jacqueline** and make the necessary changes. Act out the new dialog.

c) Now imagine that **Alain** and **Paul** would like to dance with **Dominique** and **Sylvie**. Write a new dialog in which you replace Alain by **Alain et Paul**, Dominique by **Dominique et Sylvie**, Jacques by **Jacques et Thomas**, and **tu me marches** by **vous nous marchez**. Make all other necessary changes.

WB
Occupations
SCRIPT
Act. 8
MASTERS
pp. 18;
67–68
QUIZ
p. 32
WB Tests de contrôle
TEST pp. 33–37
Leçon cinq  **129**

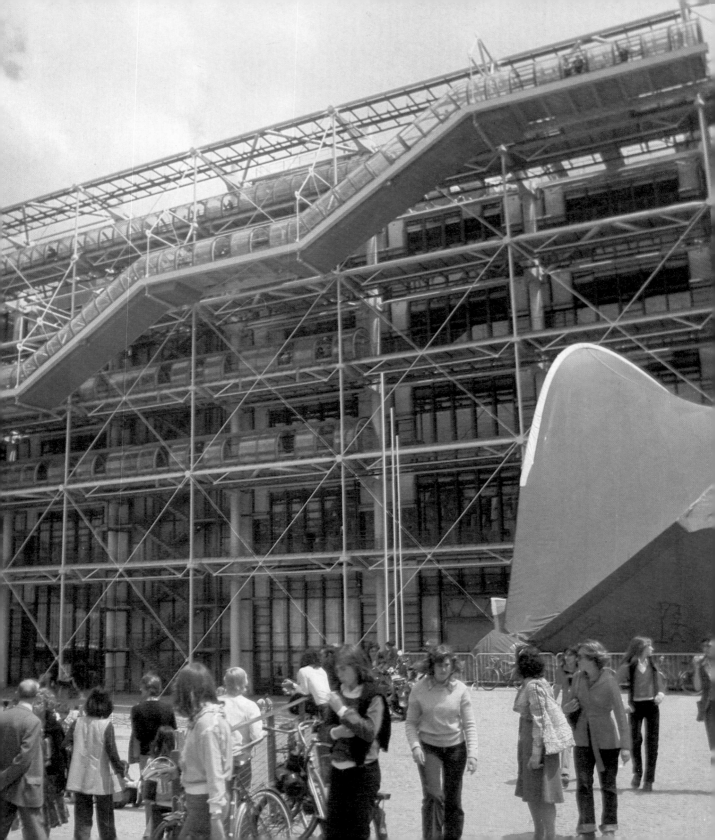

OBJECTIVES
In this unit, the students will learn to talk about their recreational activities, especially sports and music, and to discuss their future plans. They will also learn to describe their family, their family relationships, and their personal belongings.

*Language*
- **aller**
- **aller** + *infinitive* and the near future
- contracted forms of the definite article with à and **de; jouer à** and **jouer de**
- **chez**
- various ways of describing ownership and relationship: **de, être à,** possessive adjectives

*Vocabulary*
- the family and relatives
- the city and places in the city
- recreational activities

*Culture*
This unit focuses on certain aspects of the life of young people in France, especially leisure-time activities and vacations.

# UNITÉ 3
# Loisirs et vacances

OPPOSITE: The Centre Pompidou (Beaubourg) in Paris

# Leçon 1

## Week-end à Paris

STRUCTURES TO OBSERVE
• **aller**
• the contraction **au**
• the future construction **aller** + infinitive

Act. 1

18

Aujourd'hui, c'est samedi.
Les élèves *ne vont pas* en classe.
Où est-ce qu'ils vont alors?
*Ça dépend!*

*aren't going*

*It depends!*

Voici Jean-Michel et voici Nathalie.
Jean-Michel va au concert.
Nathalie va au théâtre.

Voici Pierre.
Où est-ce qu'il va?
Est-ce qu'il va au concert?
Au théâtre?
Au cinéma?
Non! Il va au café.
Il a rendez-vous avec Élisabeth.

Voici Martine.
Elle a un grand sac et des lunettes de soleil.
Est-ce qu'elle va à un rendez-vous secret?
Non!
Elle va au Centre Pompidou.
Elle va regarder les acrobates.
Et *après*, elle va *aller* à la bibliothèque.

*afterwards; to go*

Voici Jean-Claude.
Est-ce qu'il va visiter le Centre Pompidou?
Est-ce qu'il va regarder les acrobates?
Est-ce qu'il va écouter un concert?
Est-ce qu'il va aller au cinéma?
*Hélas*, non!
Il va rester à la maison.
Pourquoi?
Parce qu'il est malade.
Pauvre Jean-Claude!
Il fait *si* beau *dehors!*

*Alas*

*so; outside*

Quel jour est-ce aujourd'hui? Où va Jean-Michel? Où va Nathalie? Où va Pierre? Avec qui est-ce que Pierre a rendez-vous? Où va Martine? Est-ce que Jean-Claude va au Centre Pompidou? Pourquoi est-ce qu'il reste à la maison?

Jean-Claude is asking you if you are going to do certain things next weekend.

1. Est-ce que vous allez étudier?
   Oui, **je vais** étudier.
   (Non, **je ne vais pas** étudier.)
2. Est-ce que vous allez travailler?

3. Est-ce que vous allez voyager?
4. Est-ce que vous allez skier?
5. Est-ce que vous allez rester à la maison?

**OBSERVATIONS**   Str. C

The above questions refer to next Saturday and Sunday.
- Do they concern *present* or *future* events?   future events
- What expression did you use to say *I am going* (to do something)?   je vais
  *I am not going* (to do something)?   je ne vais pas
- Are the verbs which follow these expressions in the *infinitive?*   yes

## NOTE CULTURELLE   OPTIONAL
### Le Centre Pompidou

What place in Paris attracts more visitors than the Eiffel Tower, the Louvre Museum, and Notre Dame Cathedral? It is **Le Centre Pompidou** (also known as **Beaubourg**), an immense cultural center, which is free and open to the public.

On the large modern plaza in front of the building one can be entertained by mimes, jugglers, and acrobats. From the glass-encased escalators one has a magnificent view of Paris. Special exhibits focus on modern art and architecture. But the most popular section by far is the library! It is the first large library in France to offer open access to books, slides, cassettes, and videotape materials, and to provide audio-visual rooms where visitors can work with television cameras.

The Centre Pompidou is named after Georges Pompidou, president of France from 1969–1974.

## Vocabulaire pratique

| | | | |
|---|---|---|---|
| NOMS: | **un rendez-vous** | *date, appointment* | **les lunettes de soleil**   *sunglasses* |
| ADJECTIFS: | **malade** | *sick* | Vous n'êtes pas **malades**! |
| | **riche** ≠ **pauvre** | *rich* ≠ *poor* | **Pauvre** Alain! Il est très malade. |
| VERBE: | **rester** | *to stay* | Il déteste **rester** à la maison. |
| EXPRESSION: | **en classe** | *in class* | Aujourd'hui les élèves sont **en classe**. |
| | | *to class* | Quand les élèves sont malades, ils ne vont pas **en classe**. |

You should stress that **rester** means *to stay,* and not *to rest.* You may want to explain the concept of false cognates, using **rester** as an example.
One may say either **avoir rendez-vous** or **avoir** *un* **rendez-vous**.

# Structure

## A. Le verbe *aller*

**Aller** *(to go)* is the only *irregular* verb ending in **-er**. Note the forms of **aller** in the present tense.

Act. 2

| Infinitive | | **aller** | *to go* | J'aime **aller** en France. |
|---|---|---|---|---|
| *Present* | je | **vais** | *I go, I am going* | Je **vais** à la maison. |
| | tu | **vas** | *you go, you are going* | **Vas**-tu à Québec? |
| | il/elle | **va** | *he/she goes, he/she is going* | Paul **va** à Paris. |
| | nous | **allons** | *we go, we are going* | Nous **allons** en ville. |
| | vous | **allez** | *you go, you are going* | Est-ce que vous **allez** là-bas? |
| | ils/elles | **vont** | *they go, they are going* | Ils ne **vont** pas en classe. |

The verb **aller** is usually accompanied by a word or phrase indicating a place.
(After the verb *to go* in English, the place is often left out.)
Compare:

Quand est-ce que **tu vas** à **Paris?**       *When **are you going to Paris?***
**Je vais** à **Paris** en septembre.        *I **am going (to Paris)** in September.*

### *ACTIVITÉ 1*   Lundi et dimanche

On Monday the following students are going to class. On Sunday they are not going. Express this according to the model.

→ Charles   **Lundi, Charles va en classe. Dimanche, il ne va pas en classe.**

1. Philippe
2. Suzanne
3. moi
4. toi

5. Michèle et Denise
6. les élèves
7. nous
8. vous

VARIATION: **Mardi, Charles va en ville. Mercredi, il ne va pas en ville.**

### *ACTIVITÉ 2*   Les vacances

The following students at a Swiss boarding school are going home for vacation. To which of the following cities is each one going?

WB
A1

SCRIPT
Act. 3

MASTERS
p. 19

**à Paris?   à Québec?   à Boston?   à Tokyo?**

→ Jean-Michel est canadien.   **Jean-Michel va à Québec.**

1. Je suis français.
2. Charlotte est américaine.
3. Nous sommes japonais.
4. Tu es canadienne.

5. Vous êtes françaises.
6. Tatsuo est japonais.
7. Mike et Susan sont américains.
8. Vous êtes canadiens.

# Vocabulaire spécialisé    Ville et campagne

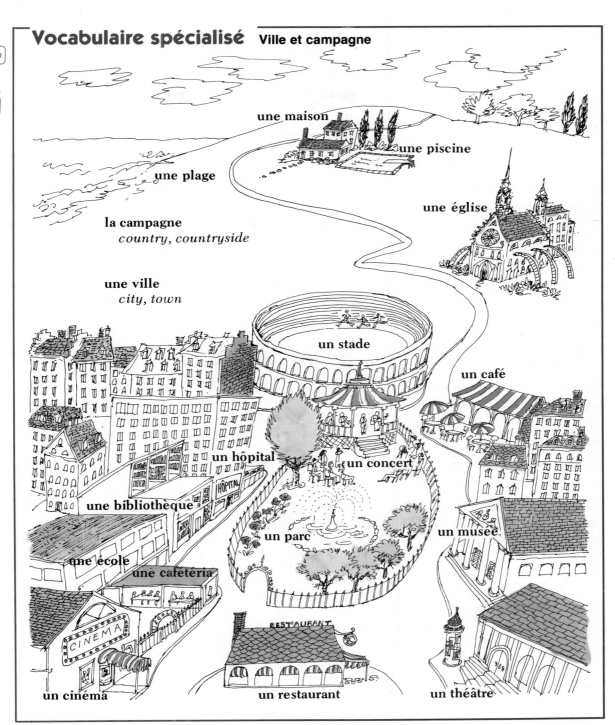

une maison

une piscine

une plage

une église

la campagne
*country, countryside*

une ville
*city, town*

un stade

un café

un hôpital

un concert

une bibliothèque

un parc

un musée

une école

une cafétéria

CINEMA

RESTAURANT
HÔPITAL

un cinéma

un restaurant

un théâtre

Review **à la maison** *(at home)*.
VOCABULARY EXPANSION: **un hôtel, un magasin, une boutique; un temple (église protestante), une synagogue**

## *ACTIVITÉ 3*   Là où j'habite   OPTIONAL

Indicate whether the following places are found in your neighborhood.

→ un cinéma   **Il y a un cinéma. (Il n'y a pas de cinéma.)**   You may remind the students that **un/une** becomes **de (d')** after **pas**.

1. un stade
2. une plage
3. un théâtre
4. un restaurant

5. une église
6. une piscine
7. un hôpital
8. une bibliothèque

9. un parc
10. une école
11. un musée
12. une cafétéria

You may wish to review the various meanings of **à** with these examples:

*at*   **Nous sommes à la plage.**
*to*   { **Nous allons à la campagne.**
{ **Nous parlons à Paul.**
*in*   **Nous habitons à Paris.**

## B. À + l'article défini

The preposition **à** has several meanings: *in, at, to.*

Note the forms of **à** + *definite article* in the sentences below:

| | | |
|---|---|---|
| Voici le cinéma. | Paul est **au** cinéma. | Françoise va **au** cinéma. |
| Voici la piscine. | Sylvie est **à la** piscine. | Jacques va **à la** piscine. |
| Voici l'hôpital. | Henri est **à l'**hôpital. | Marie va **à l'**hôpital. |
| Voici les Champs-Élysées. | Anne est **aux** Champs-Élysées. | Lise va **aux** Champs-Élysées. |

The preposition **à** contracts with **le** and **les,** but *not* with **la** and **l'**.

| à + le → au | à + les → aux |
|---|---|

→ There is liaison after **aux** when the next word begins with a vowel sound.
Le professeur parle **aux élèves.**

## *ACTIVITÉ 4*   À Paris

The following students are visiting Paris. Say where each one is going.

→ Monique: le théâtre   **Monique va au théâtre.**   VARIATION: They are now at these places.
**Monique est au théâtre**

1. Paul: le café
2. Jacqueline: le cinéma
3. Nicole: le restaurant
4. Suzanne: le musée

5. Charles: le concert
6. Philippe: la bibliothèque
7. Louis: le Centre Pompidou
8. Anne: les Invalides[1]

9. Alain: le Louvre[2]
10. Marc: l'Arc de Triomphe
11. Sylvie: les Champs-Élysées
12. Étienne: la tour Eiffel

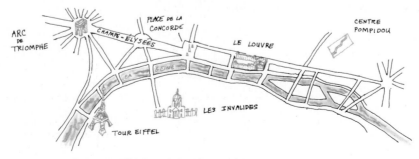

[1]Formerly a hospital for disabled veterans (**les invalides**); now housing a military museum and the tomb of Napoleon (1769-1821).
[2]Former royal palace begun in 1204 and finished under Louis XIV (1638-1715); now a national museum housing the "Mona Lisa" and the "Vénus de Milo."

## ACTIVITÉ 5  Dialogue

Ask your classmates if they often go to the following places and events.

→ le restaurant  Élève 1: **Est-ce que tu vas souvent au restaurant?**
Élève 2: **Oui, je vais souvent au restaurant.**
**(Non, je ne vais pas souvent au restaurant.)**

VARIATION in the plural:
–Allez-vous. . . ?
–Oui, nous allons. . .

WB
B1, B2,
B3

SCRIPT
Act. 5, 6

MASTERS
p. 19

1. le théâtre
2. la plage
3. la piscine
4. la campagne
5. le stade
6. le musée
7. l'église
8. la bibliothèque
9. l'hôpital
10. le parc
11. le cinéma
12. le concert

## ACTIVITÉ 6  Le bon endroit *(The right place)*   OPTIONAL

Can you tell where the following people are? Read the first sentence. Then complete the second sentence with an appropriate place.

→ Paul regarde un film. Il est . . .   **Il est au cinéma.**

1. Janine dîne. Elle est . . .
2. Hélène nage. Elle est . . .
3. Charles joue au football. Il est . . .
4. Jean regarde les sculptures modernes. Il est . . .
5. Annie étudie. Elle est . . .
6. Robert est très malade. Il est . . .

VARIATION: Have a student name a place. E.g. **Je suis à l'école.** Have other students suggest what that classmate might be doing. **Tu étudies. Tu écoutes le professeur. Tu regardes les filles/les garçons,** etc.

## C. *Aller* + l'infinitif

The following sentences describe *future* events. Note the words in heavy type.

Nathalie **va nager.**
Paul et Marc **vont jouer** au tennis.
Nous **allons rester** à la maison.

*Nathalie is going to swim.*
*Paul and Marc are going to play tennis.*
*We are going to stay at home.*

To express the near future, the French use the following construction:

> present of **aller**  +  infinitive

This construction corresponds to the English construction: *to be going* (to do something). Note the interrogative and negative forms:

**Est-ce que tu vas** visiter Paris?
Non, **je ne vais pas** visiter Paris.

*Are you going to visit Paris?*
*No, I'm not going to visit Paris.*

→ In negative sentences the word **ne** comes before the verb **aller,** and the word **pas** comes between **aller** and the infinitive.

## ACTIVITÉ 7  Tourisme

Say where the following people are going this summer and what they are going to visit.   À is used with names of cities; **en** is used with feminine countries or states.

→ Monique (à Paris / la tour Eiffel)   **Monique va à Paris. Elle va visiter la tour Eiffel.**

The French Quarter.

1. Alice (à New York / la statue de la Liberté)
2. nous (en Égypte / les pyramides)
3. vous (à Rome / le Vatican)
4. toi (à la Nouvelle-Orléans / le Vieux Carré)
5. moi (à San Francisco / Alcatraz)
6. les élèves (en Floride / le Cap Canaveral)

### ACTIVITÉ 8   Dialogue

Ask your classmates if they are going to do the following things this weekend.

WB
C1, C2

SCRIPT
Act. 7, 8, 9

MASTERS
p. 19

→ étudier    Élève 1: **Est-ce que tu vas étudier?**
             Élève 2: **Oui, je vais étudier. (Non, je ne vais pas étudier.)**

1. travailler
2. écouter la radio
3. regarder la télé
4. visiter un musée
5. jouer au volleyball
6. nager
7. inviter des amis
8. danser
9. aller à la campagne
10. aller à la bibliothèque
11. jouer au tennis
12. rester à la maison

### RÉVISION: *avoir* et *être*   OPTIONAL

**être:   je suis, tu es, il est, nous sommes, vous êtes, ils sont**
**avoir:  j'ai, tu as, il a, nous avons, vous avez, ils ont**

### ACTIVITÉ DE RÉVISION   Vacances à Paris   OPTIONAL

Say that the following people are on vacation, that they have a car, are going to Paris, and are going to visit **le Centre Pompidou.**

→ Charles    Élève 1: **Charles est en vacances.**
             Élève 2: **Il a une voiture.**
             Élève 3: **Il va à Paris.**
             Élève 4: **Il va visiter le Centre Pompidou.**

1. vous
2. moi
3. Hélène
4. Monsieur Rémi
5. Colette et Marie
6. Paul et Robert
7. toi
8. nous

### UN JEU   (A game)   OPTIONAL

Activities entitled **UN JEU** can be challenge activities. The winner is the student with the most logical and grammatically correct sentences. These activities can also be given as written assignments.

How many logical sentences can you make in five minutes, using elements of columns A, B, and C? Be sure to use the appropriate forms of **aller,** as shown in the models below.

| A | B | C |
|---|---|---|
| je | le restaurant | nager |
| tu | le café | marcher |
| Philippe | la cafétéria | dîner |
| nous | la plage | jouer au volleyball |
| vous | la piscine | jouer au football |
| Michèle et Sophie | le musée | regarder les garçons et les filles |
| | le parc | danser |
| | la campagne | parler avec des amis |
| | le stade | écouter un concert |
| | la discothèque | visiter une exposition (*exhibit*) |

→ **Tu vas au café. Tu vas parler avec des amis.**
→ **Michèle et Sophie vont à la piscine. Elles vont nager.**

# Prononciation

Act. 11

**Le son /ʒ/**

*Model word:* <u>j</u>e

*Practice words:* <u>J</u>ean, <u>J</u>acques, <u>G</u>i<u>g</u>i, <u>G</u>eor<u>g</u>es, <u>G</u>ilbert, <u>j</u>aune, rou<u>g</u>e

*Practice sentences:* <u>G</u>i<u>g</u>i <u>j</u>oue avec <u>G</u>eor<u>g</u>es et <u>G</u>ilbert.

<u>J</u>eudi, <u>J</u>ean-<u>J</u>acques va voya<u>g</u>er.

The sound /ʒ/ is pronounced like the **g** of **rouge**. The sound /ʒ/ is almost never introduced by the sound /d/ as in the English name *John*.

Comment écrire /ʒ/: **j**; **g** (before **e, i, y**); **ge** (before **a, o**)

# Entre nous

## Expressions pour la conversation

The following expressions are often used in conversation:

| | |
|---|---|
| **Allons!** | *Let's go!* |
| **Allons . . !** | *Let's go (somewhere)!* |
| **Ça n'a pas d'importance.** | *It doesn't matter.* |

## Mini-dialogue     OPTIONAL

Bill is spending the summer vacation with a French family. It is Sunday and his friends are discussing where to go that afternoon.

MICHÈLE: Où est-ce que nous allons aujourd'hui?

JACQUES: Allons au cinéma! Il y a un très bon film.

ANDRÉ: Au cinéma? C'est *ridicule!*　　　　　　　　　*ridiculous*
Il fait très beau aujourd'hui. Allons à la plage.

BRIGITTE: Moi, je préfère aller au café.

MICHÈLE: Et toi, Bill, où est-ce que tu préfères aller? Au cinéma, à la plage ou au café?

BILL: Ça n'a pas d'importance.

JACQUES: Pourquoi est-ce que ça n'a pas d'importance?

BILL: Parce qu'en France, il y a des jolies filles *partout!*　　　　　　*everywhere*

## L'art du dialogue

a) Act out the dialog between Bill and his friends.

b) Imagine that the scene takes place in Paris. André wants to go to **les Champs-Élysées**, and Brigitte wants to go to **le Centre Pompidou**. Act out the new dialog, making all the necessary changes.

# Leçon 2 Marie-Noëlle

STRUCTURES TO OBSERVE
• possession with **de**
• the contraction **du**
• constructions with **chez**

Marie-Noëlle est une fille sympathique, mais . . .
   elle a une mauvaise *habitude.*           *habit*
Elle emprunte toujours tout.

Elle a la montre de Jacqueline,
     le skate-board de Philippe,
     les disques de Pierre . . .

Elle va à la plage avec le transistor d'Antoine,
                le sac de Françoise,
                le bikini de Nathalie.

Et quand elle joue au tennis,
     elle emprunte le short de Sylvie,
          le tee-shirt de la cousine de Sylvie,
          la raquette du cousin de Sylvie.

Où est Marie-Noëlle aujourd'hui?
Est-ce qu'elle est *chez elle?*             *at home*
Non, elle est *chez Thérèse!*           *at Thérèse's*
Est-ce parce que Thérèse a un *nouveau* vélomoteur?    *new*
Non, c'est parce que Thérèse a un frère très intelligent,
   très beau et très sympathique!
C'est *plus* important *que* le vélomoteur, non?      *more . . . than*

  **Quelle est la mauvaise habitude de Marie-Noëlle? Où est Marie-Noëlle aujourd'hui?
Pourquoi est-ce qu'elle est chez Thérèse?**

## CONVERSATION OPTIONAL

Imagine that someone is asking you who has the following objects.
Answer that Marie-Noëlle has them.

1. Qui a **la montre de Jacqueline?**
   Marie-Noëlle a la montre de Jacqueline.
2. Qui a les disques de Pierre?
3. Qui a le sac de Françoise?
4. Qui a le short de Sylvie?
5. Qui a le skate-board de Philippe?

## OBSERVATIONS    Str. B    OPTIONAL

Reread the first question.

• How do you say *Jacqueline's watch* in French?
• Which noun comes *first?* **la montre** or **Jacqueline?**
  Which noun comes *second?*
  Which little word comes between the two nouns?
  la montre de Jacqueline/la montre/Jacqueline/de

# NOTE CULTURELLE    OPTIONAL

### L'américanisation

In many ways French teenagers have adopted an American
life style. They drink Coca-Cola, wear T-shirts and jeans, and
play basketball and volleyball.

Just as people borrow customs from one another, so languages borrow words. Most French sports terms are of
English origin: **le volleyball, le football, le basketball, le
golf,** etc. Recently many other new words have been borrowed by the French: **le short, le tee-shirt, le skate-board,**
etc. Often the French shorten these borrowed words. They
talk of **le volley, le foot, le basket, le skate,** and they give
these words a French pronunciation.

Of course, English has also borrowed many words from
French: **boutique, restaurant, rendez-vous, chic,** . . . you
can probably extend this list without difficulty!

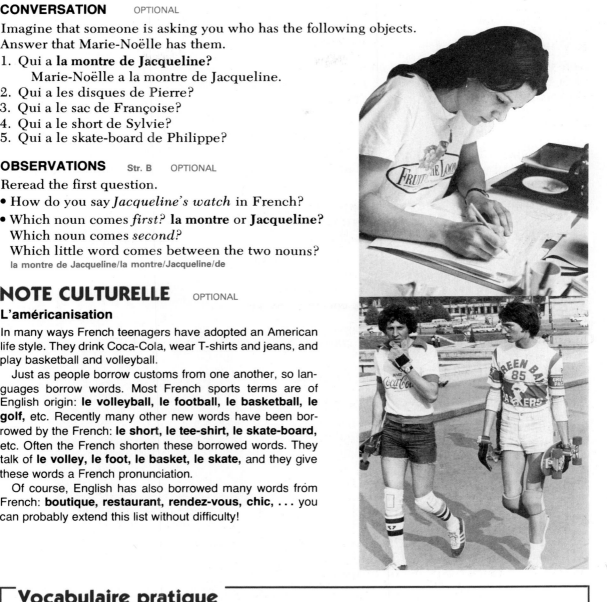

---

# Vocabulaire pratique

| NOMS: | **un cousin** | *cousin* (male) | **une cousine** | *cousin* (female) |
|---|---|---|---|---|
| | **un frère** | *brother* | **une sœur** | *sister* |
| VERBE: | **emprunter** | *to borrow* | J'**emprunte** des livres à la bibliothèque. | |
| EXPRESSION: | **tout** | *all, everything* | **Tout** est intéressant. | |

# Structure

Chez is used only with nouns or pronouns referring to people. In Unité 4.5 students will learn to differentiate between:
**Je vais chez le pharmacien.** *I am going to the pharmacist's.*
**Je vais à la pharmacie.** *I am going to the pharmacy.*

## A. Chez

Act. 2

Note the English equivalents of **chez** in the following sentences:

| | |
|---|---|
| Je suis **chez moi.** | *I am (at) home (at my house).* |
| Tu es **chez Marie-Noëlle.** | *You are at Marie-Noëlle's (house).* |
| Paul va **chez lui.** | *Paul is going home (to his house).* |
| Henri va **chez Jacques.** | *Henri is going to Jacques' (house).* |
| Annette va **chez une amie.** | *Annette is going to a friend's (house).* |

Students may have already seen **chez** in the names of restaurants: **Chez Pierre.**

**Chez** cannot stand alone. It must be followed by a *noun*, a *stress pronoun*, or **qui**. Note the word order in questions:

**Chez qui** vas-tu? { *To whose house are you going?* / *Whose house are you going to?* }

→ There is liaison after **chez** when the next word begins with a vowel sound.

Marie-Noëlle n'est pas chez elle. Elle est chez une amie.
There is never liaison between **chez** and a proper name: chez Alice.

## ACTIVITÉ 1 Les visites de Marie-Noëlle

Before leaving for a summer in the United States, Marie-Noëlle visits her friends to say good-by. Say where she is going.

→ Charles **Marie-Noëlle va chez Charles.**

1. Françoise
2. Thérèse
3. Paul et André
4. un ami suisse
5. une amie canadienne
6. des amis américains
7. le professeur
8. Madame Dupont

## ACTIVITÉ 2 Le championnat de football

The soccer championship is on TV tonight, and everyone is staying home to watch it. Express this, using **rester chez** and the appropriate stress pronoun.

WB
A1, A2

→ Paul **Paul reste chez lui.** Review the stress pronouns if necessary.

SCRIPT
Act. 3, 4

1. Marie-Noëlle
2. Monsieur Duroc
3. le professeur
4. Pierre et Jean
5. Anne et Julie
6. Ève et moi  **Ève et moi, nous restons chez nous.**
7. nous
8. vous
9. toi
10. moi

MASTERS
p. 20

VARIATIONS: Everyone is home. **Paul est chez lui.** Everyone is going home. **Paul va chez lui.**
**142** Unité trois  Everyone is going back home: **Paul rentre chez lui.**

### ACTIVITÉ 3  Où sont-ils?  OPTIONAL

There are things we do when we are at home, and other things we do someplace else.
Read the following sentences and say whether the people are at home or not.

→  Paul nage.  **Il n'est pas chez lui.**  You may encourage different responses:
   Anne étudie.  **Elle est chez elle.**  **Paul est chez lui. Il a une piscine.**

1. André skie.
2. Tu voyages.
3. Caroline regarde la télévision.
4. Jean et Louis écoutent des disques.
5. Je téléphone.
6. Lise et Annie jouent au tennis.
7. Vous dînez au restaurant.
8. Nous empruntons un livre à la bibliothèque.

## B. La possession avec *de*

Remind students that the French do not use ' or 's
to indicate possession or relationship.

To indicate possession or relationship, French speakers use the construction:

| noun + **de** + noun | **la guitare de Paul** | *Paul's guitar* |
|---|---|---|
| ↓ | | |
| **d'** ( + vowel sound) | **les amies d'Anne** | *Anne's friends* |

➜  To remember the word order, think of **de** as meaning *of* or *which belongs to*.

### ACTIVITÉ 4  Un tapeur *(A leech)*

If more than one person is indicated as the owner, the word **de**
must be repeated. **Voici la voiture de Michel et de Jean.**

Jacques borrows everything from his friends. Indicate who owns the things he has.

→  la caméra (Pierre)  **Il a la caméra de Pierre.**

1. l'électrophone (Paul)
2. la radio (Marc)
3. la moto (Albert)
4. les lunettes de soleil (Alain)
5. les disques (Robert)
6. les cassettes (Julien)

### ACTIVITÉ 5  Les objets trouvés *(Lost and found)*

The following things have been turned into the lost and found office.
Identify their owners.

→  le livre (Antoine)  **C'est le livre d'Antoine.**

1. le sac (Sylvie)
2. la raquette (Sophie)
3. la mini-cassette (René)
4. l'électrophone (Olivier)
5. les lunettes (Isabelle)  Be sure students use
6. les livres (Philippe)  **ce sont** in items 5 and 6.

### ACTIVITÉ 6  Présentations *(Introductions)*

Imagine you are hosting a French party. Introduce the following people.

→  Isabelle (cousine / Marc)  **Isabelle est la cousine de Marc.**  Make sure students use appropriate articles.

1. Jacques (cousin / Sylvie)
2. Marc (ami / Caroline)
3. Pauline (amie / Pierre)
4. Philippe (camarade / Charles)
5. Suzanne (petite amie / Paul)
6. Robert (frère / Marc)
7. Thomas (frère / Christine)
8. Jeannette (sœur / Pascal)

WB
B1

SCRIPT
⊙━⊙
Act. 5, 6

MASTERS
p. 20

## C. *De* + l'article défini

The preposition **de** has several meanings: *of, from, about.*
Note the forms of **de** + *definite article* in the sentences below:

| | | |
|---|---|---|
| le concert | Nous arrivons **du** concert. | Nous parlons **du** concert. |
| la tour Eiffel | Nous arrivons **de la** tour Eiffel. | Nous parlons **de la** tour Eiffel. |
| l'opéra | Nous arrivons **de l'**opéra. | Nous parlons **de l'**opéra. |
| les Champs-Élysées | Nous arrivons **des** Champs-Élysées. | Nous parlons **des** Champs-Élysées. |

The preposition **de** contracts with **le** and **les**, but *not* with **la** and **l'**.

| de + le → du | de + les → des |
|---|---|

➜ There is liaison after **des** when the next word begins with a vowel sound.

Où sont les livres des‿élèves?

**MOZART**
**"Don Giovanni"**
**Chœurs et Orchestre du Théâtre National de l'Opéra de Paris**
**Dir. : Lorin Maazel**
Coffret 3 disques ou 3 cassettes CBS 79321

### *ACTIVITÉ 7*  Rendez-vous

After visiting Paris, the following students are meeting in a café. Say from which place each one is coming.

➜ Jacques: l'Arc de Triomphe    **Jacques arrive de l'Arc de Triomphe.**

1. Sylvie: la tour Eiffel
2. Isabelle: le théâtre
3. Jean-Paul: le Centre Pompidou
4. François: le Quartier Latin

5. Nicole: l'Opéra
6. Marc: le Louvre
7. André: les Champs-Élysées
8. Pierre: les Invalides

VARIATION to review **à** + *definite article:*  **Jacques va à l'Arc de Triomphe.**

### *ACTIVITÉ 8*  Non!

Paul is accused of having borrowed the following items from the people indicated in parentheses. He insists that he does not have them. Play the role of Paul.

➜ la guitare (le cousin de Marc)    **Non! Je n'ai pas la guitare du cousin de Marc.**

1. le vélo (le cousin de Suzanne)
2. les disques (la cousine de Charles)
3. la caméra (l'élève américain)

4. l'appareil-photo (l'élève américaine)
5. le livre (le professeur)
6. la raquette (l'amie de Denise)

## D. *Jouer à* et *jouer de*

Note the constructions with **jouer** in the sentences below:

Chantal **joue au** tennis.     *Chantal **plays** tennis.*
Elle **joue de la** guitare.     *She **plays** the guitar.*

French speakers use the following constructions with **jouer:**

| **jouer à** | + | definite article | + | sport, game |
|---|---|---|---|---|

| **jouer de** | + | definite article | + | instrument |
|---|---|---|---|---|

In conversational French, words are often shortened. **J'aime jouer au volley. Martine joue du saxo.**
l'appareil-photo → l'appareil photographique     la moto → la motocyclette     l'auto → l'automobile

# Vocabulaire spécialisé     Les sports, les jeux et les passe-temps
*(Sports, games, and hobbies)*

**jouer à (+ le sport)**

   **jouer au basket(ball)**

    **au foot(ball)**

    **au volley(ball)**

**jouer de (+ l'instrument)**

   **jouer du piano**

    **du violon**

    **du saxo(phone)**

  **jouer de la flûte**

    **de la guitare**

    **de la clarinette**

**jouer à (+ le jeu [ *game* ])**

  **jouer aux cartes**

   **au Monopoly**

   **aux échecs**

VOCABULARY EXPANSION: **sports: jouer au hockey, au baseball, au squash, au golf**
**jeux: jouer aux dames** *(checkers),* **au trictrac** or **jacquet** *(backgammon),* **au bridge**
**instruments: jouer du violoncelle** *(cello),* **du hautbois** *(oboe),* **de la**
**trompette, du tuba, de la batterie** *(drums, drum set)*

## ACTIVITÉ 9  Dialogue

Ask your classmates if they play the following instruments and games.

VARIATION in the plural:
–Est-ce que vous jouez. . .?
–Oui, nous jouons. . .

→ le ping-pong      Élève 1: **Est-ce que tu joues au ping-pong?**
                   Élève 2: **Oui, je joue au ping-pong.**
                            **(Non, je ne joue pas au ping-pong.)**

   le piano         Élève 1: **Est-ce que tu joues du piano?**
                   Élève 2: **Oui, je joue du piano.**
                            **(Non, je ne joue pas du piano.)**

WB
D1

SCRIPT

Act. 9

| | | | |
|---|---|---|---|
| 1. le volley | 4. la clarinette | 7. le Monopoly | 10. la trompette |
| 2. le basket | 5. le saxo | 8. les cartes | 11. le banjo |
| 3. le football | 6. la flûte | 9. les échecs | 12. le violon |

### UN JEU

The people in column A are talking to friends and relatives of the people in column C. Using the expression **parler à**, form sentences similar to the models below. How many sentences can you make in five minutes?

| A | B | C |
|---|---|---|
| Adèle | le cousin | Charles |
| Jean-Pierre | la cousine | Jacqueline |
| Jacques et Pierre | le frère | le garçon italien |
| Hélène et Béatrice | la sœur | la fille espagnole |
| | le meilleur (*best*) ami | les étudiants canadiens |
| | la meilleure amie | |

→ **Jean-Pierre parle au frère du garçon italien.**

→ **Hélène et Béatrice parlent à la cousine des étudiants canadiens.**

# Prononciation

Act. 11

## Le son /ʃ/

*Model word:*  c<u>h</u>ez

*Practice words:*  <u>Ch</u>arles, Mi<u>ch</u>el, Ra<u>ch</u>el

*Practice sentences:*  <u>Ch</u>arles a une moto blan<u>ch</u>e.
                       Ra<u>ch</u>el et Mi<u>ch</u>èle dînent <u>ch</u>ez <u>Ch</u>arlotte.

The sound /ʃ/ is pronounced like the *ch* of the English word *machine*.
Do not pronounce a /t/ before /ʃ/, unless the **t** appears in the French word.

*Contrast:* /ʃ/ ma<u>ch</u>ine      /tʃ/ ma<u>tch</u>

   Comment écrire /ʃ/: **ch**

# Entre nous

## Expression pour la conversation

**au moins**  *at least*     Pierre a **au moins** cinquante disques de musique classique.

## Mini-dialogue     OPTIONAL

PIERRE: Où vas-tu?
ANDRÉ: Je vais chez Jacques.
PIERRE: Pourquoi chez lui? Pourquoi pas chez moi?
ANDRÉ: Parce que lui, au moins, il a une sœur sympathique.
PIERRE: Eh bien, j'ai une mauvaise *nouvelle* pour toi!          *piece of news*
       *Sa* sœur n'est pas là. Elle est à Montréal où elle          *His*
       va *passer* les vacances chez des amis.          *to spend*

## L'art du dialogue

a)  Act out the dialog between Pierre and André.
b)  Imagine that **Pierre** and his brother **Paul** meet André. In Pierre's lines replace **je** and **moi** by **nous** and make the necessary changes.
c)  Write and act out a new dialog between **Colette** and **Marie**. Marie wants to visit **Chantal**, who has a good-looking brother (**frère; son frère**).

WB     SCRIPT     MASTERS     QUIZ
Et     ▭           p. 20        pp. 39–40
vous?  Act. 10

Leçon deux   **147**

STRUCTURES TO OBSERVE
• the possessive adjectives
  **mon, ma, mes** and **ton, ta, tes**
• how to state someone's age

# UNITÉ 3
# Leçon 3 Christine a un petit ami.

Act. 1

Christine a deux passions: le ski et la *photo*.                    *photography*
En hiver elle va en vacances à La Plagne, une *station de ski*      *ski resort*
dans les Alpes. Et, bien sûr, elle *prend* beaucoup de photos.      *takes*

Un jour Hélène regarde l'album de photos de Christine.

| | |
|---|---|
| HÉLÈNE: Qui est la fille *en* bleu? Est-ce que c'est *ta* sœur? | *in; your* |
| CHRISTINE: Non. C'est *ma* cousine Suzanne. | *my* |
| HÉLÈNE: Et les garçons dans la voiture de sport? Ce sont tes frères? | |
| CHRISTINE: Non! Ce sont mes cousins. | |
| HÉLÈNE: *Quel âge ont-ils?* | *How old are they?* |
| CHRISTINE: Jean-François *a vingt et un ans* et Gérard a dix-neuf ans. | *is 21* |
| Ils sont très sympathiques. | |
| HÉLÈNE: Ah . . . Et le garçon en jaune? Il *a l'air* sympathique aussi! | *seems* |
| Qui est-ce? | |
| CHRISTINE: Écoute, Hélène! Tu es trop *curieuse!* | *curious* |
| HÉLÈNE: Ah, ah! C'est ton petit ami, *je parie!* | *I bet* |

stages
chamois
ÉCOLE DE SKI été
hiver
LA PLAGNE

E.S.F. LA PLAGNE
E.S.F. PLAGNE-VILLAGES    Tél. (79) 09 00 40
73210 LA PLAGNE           (79) 09 04 40

Où va Christine en hiver? Où est La Plagne?
Comment s'appelle la cousine de Christine?
Comment s'appellent les cousins de Christine?
Qui est le garçon en jaune?

## CONVERSATION    OPTIONAL

Let's be on very friendly terms. In the following questions you will be addressed as **tu**. The questions are about people you know.

1. Comment s'appelle **ton** père (*your father*)?    Il s'appelle . . .
2. Comment s'appelle **ta** mère (*your mother*)?    Elle s'appelle . . .
3. Comment s'appelle **ton** meilleur ami?    Il . . .
4. Comment s'appelle **ta** meilleure amie?    Elle . . .
5. Comment s'appellent **tes** cousins?    Ils . . .
6. Comment s'appellent **tes** cousines?    Elles . . .

## OBSERVATIONS    Str. A    OPTIONAL

Reread the above questions. The words in heavy type all mean *your*.
They are called *possessive adjectives*.

- Which possessive adjective is used before a *masculine singular* noun (**père**)?    ton
  before a *feminine singular* noun (**mère**)?    ta
  before a *masculine plural* noun (**cousins**)?    tes
  before a *feminine plural* noun (**cousines**)?    tes

# NOTES CULTURELLES    OPTIONAL

**1. Le ski en France**    How far do you live from a ski area? In France skiing is a very popular sport, and many teenagers spend Christmas and February vacations on the slopes. Some schools have organized special **classes de neige,** where entire school groups go to a ski area and combine classes in the morning with skiing in the afternoon.

The most popular ski resorts are located in the Alps and the Pyrenees. **La Plagne,** at an altitude of about 6,000 feet, is one of the highest and most modern ski areas in the Alps.

**2. La photo (la photographie)**    The art of photography was discovered by two Frenchmen: **Nicéphore Niepce** and **Jacques Daguerre.** In fact, the first photographs were called "daguerreotypes" (1839). Today photography is a favorite pastime of many French young people.

SUGGESTED REALIA: travel brochures advertising ski areas in France or Switzerland. You may obtain these brochures at your local travel agency and bring them to class. Some popular French ski resorts are Val d'Isère, Chamonix, and Courchevel.

## Vocabulaire pratique

| NOMS: | **un album** | *album* | **une photo** | *photograph, picture* |
|---|---|---|---|---|
| | | | **les vacances** | *vacation* |
| | **un petit ami** | *boyfriend* | **une petite amie** | *girlfriend* |
| | **un meilleur ami** | *best friend* (male) | **une meilleure amie** | *best friend* (female) |
| EXPRESSIONS: | **dans** | *in* | La photo est **dans** l'album. | |
| | **trop** | *too, too much* | Tu parles **trop.** Tu es **trop** curieux. | |

# Structure

## A. Les adjectifs possessifs: *mon, ma, mes; ton, ta, tes*

One way of indicating possession and relationship is to use *possessive adjectives*.
Note the forms of the possessive adjectives **mon** *(my)* and **ton** *(your)*
in the chart below:

Act. 4

|  | SINGULAR | PLURAL | | |
|---|---|---|---|---|
| *Masculine* | mon | mes | mon cousin | mes cousins |
|  |  |  | mon ami | mes amis |
| *Feminine* | ma ↓ mon (+ vowel sound) | mes | ma cousine | mes cousines |
|  |  |  | mon amie | mes amies |
| *Masculine* | ton | tes | ton disque | tes disques |
|  |  |  | ton album | tes albums |
| *Feminine* | ta ↓ ton (+ vowel sound) | tes | ta sœur | tes sœurs |
|  |  |  | ton amie | tes amies |

Possessive adjectives agree with the nouns they introduce.

→ French speakers use **ton, ta, tes** with people whom they address as **tu.**
Paul, tu as **tes** livres avec toi?

→ **Ma** and **ta** become **mon** and **ton** when the next word begins with a vowel sound.
Hélène est **mon** amie.      Où est **ton** auto?

→ There is liaison after **mon, ton, mes, tes** when the next word begins with a vowel sound.

## ACTIVITÉ 1   Le tour de l'école *(Around school)*

Marc is showing his school to his cousin Michèle. Play the role of Marc.

→ l'école      **Voici mon école.**

1. le camarade
2. la camarade
3. l'ami Charles
4. l'amie Élisabeth
5. la classe
6. les livres
7. les professeurs
8. les amis

### ACTIVITÉ 2  Départ *(Departure)*

Pierre is packing his suitcase and cannot find the things listed below. His sister Annie tells him that she does not have them. Play both roles.

→ la raquette   Pierre: **Où est ma raquette?**
            Annie: **Je n'ai pas ta raquette.**

1. le short
2. la caméra
3. l'appareil-photo
4. la guitare

5. les lunettes de soleil   *où sont*
6. le transistor
7. les disques   *où sont*
8. le tee-shirt

### ACTIVITÉ 3  Expression personnelle   OPTIONAL

Say what your favorites are, according to the model. (Note: **préféré** means *favorite*.)

→ la ville préférée   **Ma ville préférée est San Francisco (Boston, Atlanta, . . .)**

1. le disque préféré
2. le livre préféré
3. le film préféré
4. le programme de télé préféré
5. le jour préféré
6. le mois préféré
7. la saison préférée
8. le restaurant préféré

Additional cues: **la couleur préférée, l'acteur préféré, l'actrice préférée, le musée préféré, l'instrument préféré**

# Vocabulaire spécialisé   La famille

NOMS:  **La famille proche** (*Immediate family*)

| | | | | | |
|---|---|---|---|---|---|
| **un père** | *father* | **une mère** | *mother* | **les parents** | *parents* |
| **un grand-père** | *grandfather* | **une grand-mère** | *grandmother* | **les grands-parents** | *grand-parents* |
| **un fils** /fis/ | *son* | **une fille** | *daughter* | **les enfants** | *children* |
| **un frère** | *brother* | **une sœur** | *sister* | | |

## ACTIVITÉ 4   La famille de Christine

Hélène is looking at Christine's photograph album. Hélène asks whether the people in the pictures are members of her family, and Christine says that they are. Play the two roles.

→  la cousine Lucie       Hélène:  **C'est ta cousine Lucie?**
Christine:  **Oui, c'est ma cousine Lucie.**

1. le père
2. la tante
3. le grand-père
4. l'oncle André
5. la grand-mère
6. la mère
7. les cousins
8. les cousines

WB
A1, A2

SCRIPT
Act. 3, 5

MASTERS
p. 21

NOMS: **La famille éloignée** *(Distant family)*

| | | |
|---|---|---|
| **un oncle**  *uncle* | **une tante**  *aunt* | **les parents**  *relatives* |
| **un cousin**  *cousin* (male) | **une cousine**  *cousin* (female) | |

ADJECTIFS: **jeune** ≠ **âgé**  *young* ≠ *old*

Note: **Les parents** may mean either *parents* or *relatives*.

## B. L'âge

To ask someone's age, the French say:

**Quel âge avez-vous?**  or  **Quel âge as-tu?**

To state how old someone (or something) is, the French use the following expression:

| | | |
|---|---|---|
| **avoir ... ans** | Mon père **a 42 ans.** | *My father is 42 (years old).* |
| | Mes cousines **ont 16 ans.** | *My cousins are 16 (years old).* |

➔ Although the words *years old* may be left out in an English expression of age, the equivalent French sentence can *never* omit the word **ans**.

## *ACTIVITÉ 5*  Expression personnelle

Say how old the following people are by completing the sentences below. If you do not know for sure, make a guess!

1. Moi, j'ai ...
2. Mon père ...
3. Ma mère ...
4. Mon meilleur ami ...

5. Ma meilleure amie ...
6. Mon oncle préféré ...
7. Ma cousine préférée ...
8. Le professeur ...

## C. La construction: nom + *de* + nom

Compare the word order in French and English.

| J'ai une raquette. | C'est une **raquette de tennis.** | *It's a tennis racket.* |
| Paul a une voiture. | C'est une **voiture de sport.** | *It's a sports car.* |
| Tu as une classe. | C'est une **classe d'anglais.** | *It's an English class.* |
| Qui est le professeur? | C'est le **professeur de musique.** | *He's the music teacher.* |

When a noun modifies another noun, French speakers frequently use the construction:

> main noun  +  **de**  +  modifying noun
> ↓
> **d'**  ( +  vowel sound)

→ In French the *main noun* comes *first*. In English the main noun comes second.

→ There is no article after **de.**

## ACTIVITÉ 6  Complétez...

Complete the following sentences with an expression made up of **de** + underlined noun.

→ J'aime le sport. J'ai une voiture . . .    **J'ai une voiture de sport.**

1. Claire aime le ping-pong. Elle a une raquette . . .
2. Nous adorons le jazz. Nous écoutons un concert . . .
3. Jacques aime la musique classique. Il écoute un programme . . .
4. Vous étudiez l'anglais. Vous avez un livre . . .
5. Tu étudies le piano. Aujourd'hui tu as une leçon . . .
6. Thomas et Paul aiment l'espagnol. Ils ont un bon professeur . . .
7. Je regarde mes photos. J'ai un album . . .

WB
C1

SCRIPT

Act. 7, 8

## UN JEU    OPTIONAL

Form logical sentences similar to the models below, using elements of columns A, B, C, and D. How many sentences can you make in five minutes or less?

| A | B | C | D | |
|---|---|---|---|---|
| je | avoir | des disques | tennis | volley |
| Paul | écouter | un concert | musique disco | ping-pong |
| Christine | regarder | un programme | musique classique | sport |
| nous | | un match (*game*) | piano | français |
| | | une classe | basket | |
| | | une raquette | | |

→ **Nous regardons un match de volley.**
→ **J'ai une raquette de ping-pong.**

# Prononciation

## Le son /ø/

*Model word:* d<u>eu</u>x

*Practice words:* <u>eu</u>x, bl<u>eu</u>, pl<u>eu</u>t, curi<u>eu</u>se, <u>Eu</u>gène, j<u>eu</u>, j<u>eu</u>di

*Practice sentences:* <u>Eu</u>génie est trop curi<u>eu</u>se.

Ils ont d<u>eu</u>x livres bl<u>eu</u>s avec <u>eu</u>x.

The sound /ø/ is pronounced with the lips rounded and tense. The tip of the tongue touches the lower front teeth.

Comment écrire /ø/: **eu**

# Entre nous

## Expression pour la conversation

To say that someone (or something) is attractive (or interesting), the French often use the following expression:

**pas mal**  —Cette fille est jolie, n'est-ce pas?

—Oui, elle est **pas mal**.

*Pas mal is invariable. In conversational style, the negative ne is often omitted before the verb, although pas mal is a negative expression.*

## Mini-dialogue    OPTIONAL

Henri regarde les photos de Monique. Il *trouve que* la    thinks that
cousine de Monique est très jolie, mais . . .

HENRI: Qui est-ce, *cette* fille? C'est ta sœur?    that
MONIQUE: Non, c'est ma cousine.
HENRI: Elle est pas mal. Quel âge est-ce qu'elle a?
MONIQUE: Elle a seize ans.
HENRI: Dis, Monique . . .
MONIQUE: Oui?
HENRI: Quel est le numéro de téléphone de ta cousine?
MONIQUE: C'est le 70-22 . . . à Tahiti![1]

WB
Famille

SCRIPT
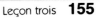
Act. 9

MASTERS
p. 21

QUIZ
pp. 41–42

## L'art du dialogue

a) Act out the dialog between Monique and Henri.
b) Now the roles are reversed. It is **Monique** who is asking about **Henri's** cousin. Act out the new dialog, replacing **cette fille** by **ce garçon**, **sœur** by **frère**, and **cousine** by **cousin**. Make the necessary changes.

[1]Tahiti is a French island in the South Pacific.

UNITÉ 3

# Leçon 4

## Vive les grandes vacances!

Act. 1

23

Bonjour!
Je m'appelle Olivier Pécoul.
Nous habitons à Paris, mais en été nous allons en vacances
   à La Grande-Motte.
Voici l'*immeuble* où nous habitons là-bas.

*apartment house*

Monsieur Moreau habite au premier *étage*
   avec *sa femme* et sa fille.

*floor*
*his wife*

Mademoiselle Lamblet habite au
   deuxième étage avec son père et sa
   mère.

Paul, mon meilleur ami, habite au
   troisième étage avec sa sœur et ses
   parents.

Comment s'appelle le meilleur
ami d'Olivier? Où est-ce qu'il
habite?

Mademoiselle Imbert habite au quatrième
   étage avec son chien Malice, ses deux
   chats Neptune et Pompon, son
   *perroquet* Coco et son canari Froufrou.
   (Je *pense que* c'est une personne très
   intéressante, mais mon père pense
   qu'elle est un peu bizarre.)

*parrot*
*think that*

Pourquoi est-ce que le père
d'Olivier pense que Mademoiselle
Imbert est bizarre?

Monsieur et Madame Martinot habitent au
   cinquième étage avec *leur* fils et leurs
   deux filles.

*their*

Et au sixième étage habite un garçon
   super-intelligent et très sympathique!
   Et *ce* garçon . . . c'est moi!

À quel étage habite Olivier?

*that*

**156** Unité trois

On a detailed map of France, you may want to locate the following popular beach resorts:
On the Atlantic: La Baule, Trouville, Deauville, Les Sables-d'Olonne, Bayonne, Biarritz, Saint-Jean-de-Luz
On the Mediterranean: Cannes, Nice, Saint-Tropez

## CONVERSATION

How well do you know the families of your best friends? Let's see.
(If you are not sure of an answer, use your imagination!)

A. Qui est ton meilleur ami?

1. Comment s'appelle **son** père?
2. Comment s'appelle **sa** mère?
3. Comment s'appellent **ses** frères
   (ou **ses** sœurs)?

B. Qui est ta meilleure amie?

4. Comment s'appelle **son** père?
5. Comment s'appelle **sa** mère?
6. Comment s'appellent **ses** frères
   (ou **ses** sœurs)?

## OBSERVATIONS   Str. A

Reread the questions above. Compare the possessive adjectives in heavy type used in parts A and B.

- How do you say *his* father? *her* father?   son père   son père
- How do you say *his* mother? *her* mother?   sa mère   sa mère
- How do you say *his* brothers? *her* brothers?

ses frères   ses frères

# NOTE CULTURELLE   OPTIONAL

## Les grandes vacances

Do you go away for summer vacation (**les grandes vacances**)? Or do you stay at home and look for a job? In France very few teenagers work during the summer, for vacation time is devoted strictly to relaxation. Most young people spend their vacations with their families away from home. Many go to the country or to the mountains, but the favorite vacation spots are the beaches along the Atlantic (**l'Atlantique**) and the Mediterranean (**la Méditerranée**). **La Grande-Motte** is a new summer resort in southern France.

Act. 2

# Vocabulaire spécialisé   Les animaux domestiques

| | |
|---|---|
| un animal | *animal* |
| un chat | *cat* |
| un chien | *dog* |
| un cheval | *horse* |
| un oiseau | *bird* |
| un poisson | *fish* |
| un poisson rouge | *goldfish* |

Note: Nouns which end in **-al** form their plural in **-aux: des animaux, des chevaux.**
Nouns which end in **-eau** form their plural in **-eaux: des oiseaux.**

VOCABULARY EXPANSION: **un canari, un perroquet** *(parrot)*, **une perruche** *(parakeet)*, **un serpent**, **un cochon d'Inde** *(guinea pig)*, **un hamster** (no liaison), **une souris blanche** *(white mouse)*

# Structure

## A. L'adjectif possessif: *son, sa, ses*

Note the forms of the possessive adjective **son** (*his*, *her*, *its*):

Act. 3

|  |  | SINGULAR | PLURAL |  |  |
|---|---|---|---|---|---|
| *Masculine* |  | son | ses | son vélo<br>son ami | ses disques<br>ses amis |
| *Feminine* |  | sa<br>↓<br>son (+ vowel sound) | ses | sa radio<br>son amie | ses photos<br>ses amies |

➔ **Sa** becomes **son** before a vowel sound.

➔ There is liaison after **son** and **ses** when the next word begins with a vowel sound.

Note the uses of the possessive adjective:

| le vélo de Marc: | **son** vélo | *his bicycle* |
| le vélo de Christine: | **son** vélo | *her bicycle* |
| la radio de Marc: | **sa** radio | *his radio* |
| la radio de Christine: | **sa** radio | *her radio* |
| les photos de Marc: | **ses** photos | *his pictures* |
| les photos de Christine: | **ses** photos | *her pictures* |

It is possible to distinguish between *his* and *her* by adding **à lui** or **à elle** after the noun.

➔ The choice between **son, sa, ses** depends on the *gender* (masculine or feminine) and the *number* (singular or plural) of the *following* noun. It does *not* depend on the gender of the owner.

The same pattern holds true for things:
**la radio de la voiture**    **sa radio**    *its radio*
**les photos du livre**    **ses photos**    *its pictures*

## ACTIVITÉ 1   Chez Marc

Paul wants to know whether the following things belong to Marc. Olivier answers *yes*. Play the two roles.

➔ le vélo    Paul: **Est-ce que c'est le vélo de Marc?**
              Olivier: **Oui, c'est son vélo.**

1. la guitare
2. les disques
3. l'électrophone
4. les livres
5. le téléviseur
6. les posters
7. l'album de photos
8. la photo
9. la caméra
10. les lunettes de soleil
11. l'appareil-photo
12. la moto

Use **ce sont** with items 2, 4, 6, 10.

**VOUS AVEZ UNE AUTOMOBILE**

**AVEZ-VOUS UN VÉLO?**

**LE VÉLO, C'EST LA SANTÉ**

## ACTIVITÉ 2  Chez Marie et Christophe

The animals or things in part A belong to **Marie**. Those in part B belong to
her brother **Christophe**. Point them out, as in the models.

Be sure students use **ce sont** with plural items.

**A: Marie**  |  **B: Christophe**

→ le vélo   **C'est son vélo.**          → le disque   **C'est son disque.**

1. la radio            5. le poisson rouge      9. la guitare          13. les livres
2. le sac              6. la guitare           10. l'électrophone      14. les oiseaux
3. le chien            7. les disques          11. le chat             15. les photos
4. l'album             8. les cassettes        12. le cheval           16. les disques

## ACTIVITÉ 3  Invitations

The following people are each inviting a friend or relative to the school
dance. Express this according to the model.

→  Michel: la petite amie     **Michel invite sa petite amie.**

1. André: la cousine          4. Pascal: l'amie Sophie      7. Guillaume: l'amie Janine
2. Jean-Claude: la sœur       5. Monique: le cousin         8. Paul: l'amie Thérèse
3. Marie-Noëlle: le frère     6. Nathalie: l'ami Antoine

## B. L'adjectif possessif: *leur, leurs*

The possessive adjective **leur** *(their)* has the following forms:

|            | SINGULAR | PLURAL |                              |                              |
|------------|----------|--------|------------------------------|------------------------------|
| *Masculine* | leur     | leurs  | **leur** cousin  **leur** album | **leurs** livres  **leurs** amis |
| *Feminine*  | leur     | leurs  | **leur** cousine  **leur** école | **leurs** photos  **leurs** amies |

→  There is liaison after **leurs** before a vowel sound.

→  The use of **leur** or **leurs** depends on whether the noun introduced is *singular* or *plural*.

le chien de Paul et de Philippe:   **leur** chien   *their dog*
les chats de Paul et de Philippe:   **leurs** chats   *their cats*

## ACTIVITÉ 4  Les millionnaires

Monsieur and Madame Richard are millionaires. Imagine you are showing
their estate to a friend. Point out the items below.

→  la maison     **Voici leur maison.**

1. la piscine          3. la Rolls Royce      5. les chiens          7. l'hélicoptère
2. la Mercédès         4. le parc             6. les chevaux         8. le court de tennis

Cognates are sometimes introduced into the activities so that students learn to recognize and handle them.
These words are not considered active vocabulary.

The **x** of **deuxième, sixième, dixième,** etc. is pronounced /z/.
There is no liaison before **huitième** and **onzième: un huitième (onzième) étage.**
With numbers ending in **un,** the regular pattern is followed: **le vingt et unième président.**

## C. Les nombres ordinaux   This may be presented for recognition only.

Numbers like *first*, *second*, and *third* are used to rank persons or things, to put them in a given order. They are called *ordinal numbers*. Compare the ordinal numbers with the regular numbers.

| (2) | **deux** | **deuxième** | Février est le **deuxième** mois de l'année. |
| (3) | **trois** | **troisième** | Mercredi est le **troisième** jour de la semaine. |
| (4) | **quatre** | **quatrième** | J'habite au **quatrième** étage *(floor)*. |
| (12) | **douze** | **douzième** | Qui habite au **douzième** étage? |

To form ordinal numbers, the French use the following pattern:

> number   (minus final **e**, if any)   +   **ième**

For extra practice with ordinals you may have students rank:
   – the days of the week: **Mardi est le deuxième jour.**
   – the months of the year: **Mars est le troisième mois.**
   – the US presidents: **Lincoln est le seizième président.**
   – team standings: **Les Red Sox sont la première équipe** *(team).*

Exceptions:   **un (une)** → **premier (première)**
            **cinq** → **cinquième**
            **neuf** → **neuvième**

➔ Ordinal numbers are adjectives and come *before* the noun.

***ACTIVITÉ 5***   **La course de bicyclettes** *(The bicycle race)*

Give the order of arrival of the following participants in the bicycle race.

➔ Jacques (6)      **Jacques est sixième.**

1. Catherine (4)   3. Paul (8)   5. Thomas (1)   7. Isabelle (11)
2. Henri (7)   4. Marie-Françoise (2)   6. Jacqueline (10)   8. Marc (12)

## UN JEU

The people in column A cannot do the things in column B, because they do not have the things in column C. Express this in logical sentences, as in the models below. How many different sentences can you make in five minutes?

| A | B | C |
|---|---|---|
| Paul | jouer au ping-pong | le téléviseur |
| Suzanne | jouer au tennis | la radio |
| Charles et Henri | regarder le match | l'électrophone |
| Annie et Pauline | écouter le concert | la voiture |
| mes cousins | voyager | la raquette |
| mes amies | danser | les disques |
| mon meilleur ami | aller à la campagne | la moto |
| ma sœur | écouter la musique | |

➔ **Annie et Pauline ne vont pas à la campagne parce qu'elles n'ont pas leur voiture.**

➔ **Ma sœur ne joue pas au ping-pong parce qu'elle n'a pas sa raquette.**

# Prononciation

## Le son /œ/

*Model word:* h**eu**re

*Practice words:* n**eu**f, l**eu**r, s**œu**r, act**eu**r, profess**eu**r, j**eu**ne

*Practice sentence:* L**eu**r s**œu**r arrive à n**eu**f h**eu**res.

Comment écrire /œ/: usually **eu**; sometimes **œu**

Note: The letters **eu** are usually pronounced /œ/ before a final pronounced
consonant other than /z/ (as in the ending **-euse**).

Contrast: /œ/ **leur**          /ø/ curi**euse**

# Entre nous

### Expression pour la conversation

To show that you understand, or agree with a statement, you can say:

**Ah bon!** *All right!*          **Ah bon!** Je comprends (*understand*) maintenant.

### Mini-dialogue          OPTIONAL

SUZANNE: Où est Philippe?

CLAIRE: Il est avec son oncle, dans son *bateau*.          *boat*

SUZANNE: Dans son bateau? Philippe a un bateau
maintenant? Formidable!

CLAIRE: Mais non, c'est son oncle qui a le bateau.

SUZANNE: Ah bon! Je comprends maintenant.

### L'art du dialogue

a) Act out the dialog between Suzanne and Claire.

b) Now imagine that Philippe is with his aunt. Replace **oncle** by **tante,** and make all
necessary changes.

WB          SCRIPT   MASTERS   QUIZ
La          ▭●▬     p. 22     pp. 43–44
famille. . .  Act. 9                                            Leçon quatre   **161**

# Leçon 5 **L'album de timbres**

STRUCTURES TO OBSERVE
• the construction **être à** to indicate possession
• the possessive adjectives **notre, nos** and **votre, vos**

Act. 1

### Scène 1

Un jour, Pierre va dans le *grenier* et trouve un album de timbres.
«*À qui est-il?*» demande Pierre à ses cousins.
Il y a beaucoup de candidats pour *cet* album.

*attic*
*"To whom does it belong?"*
*this*

| | |
|---|---|
| PIERRE: | À qui est l'album? |
| BERNARD: | Je pense qu'il est à mon frère. |
| JACQUES: | Non, il n'est pas à lui. Il est à moi. |
| PHILIPPE: | Non, il n'est pas à toi. Il est à moi. |
| PAUL ET HENRI: | Ce n'est pas vrai! Il est à nous! |
| | Regardez! Il y a *nos* initiales sur la *couverture*. |
| PIERRE: | S'il y a *vos* initiales, il est à vous! |
| | *Tenez!* Voilà votre album! |

*our; cover*
*your*
*Look!*

### Scène 2

Paul et Henri regardent l'album et *découvrent* . . . qu'il est *vide*.

*discover; empty*

| | |
|---|---|
| PAUL: | Eh Pierre! Ce n'est pas notre album de timbres. |
| | Il n'est pas à nous. Est-ce qu'il est à toi, Jacques? |
| JACQUES: | Non, il est au frère de Bernard! |
| BERNARD: | Non, il n'est pas à lui! Il est à toi, Philippe. |
| PHILIPPE: | Il n'est pas à moi! |
| PIERRE: | Alors, à qui est-il? |
| HENRI: | Eh bien, *il n'est à personne!* |

*it doesn't belong to anyone*

Où est-ce que Pierre trouve un album de timbres? Qui sont les candidats pour l'album? Est-ce qu'il y a beaucoup de timbres dans l'album?

In the following questions you are asked if you have certain things
with you now.
1. Avez-vous **votre** livre de français avec vous?
2. Avez-vous **votre** radio avec vous?
3. Avez-vous **vos** disques?
4. Avez-vous **vos** photos?

**OBSERVATIONS**   Str. A      OPTIONAL

In the above questions the words in heavy type are the possessive
adjectives which correspond to **vous.**
• What is the form of this possessive adjective before a *singular* noun?   votre
• What form is used before a *plural* noun?   vos

# NOTE CULTURELLE   OPTIONAL
## Les timbres français

Do you collect stamps? For many French people, young and
old, stamp collecting is a favorite hobby. Indeed, French post-
age stamps are very beautiful. Many of them have an educational value: they depict famous persons, monuments,
buildings, landscapes, and works of art. Special issues com-
memorate historical and scientific events. A study of French
stamps is, in fact, an excellent introduction to French culture.

SUGGESTED REALIA: French stamps.

# Vocabulaire pratique

| | | | |
|---|---|---|---|
| NOM: | **un timbre** | *stamp* | |
| VERBES: | **demander** (à) | *to ask* | Paul **demande:** Où est l'album? |
| | **penser** | *to think* | Je **pense** que c'est l'album de Philippe. |
| | **trouver** | *to find* | Nous ne **trouvons** pas ton album. |
| EXPRESSIONS: | **que** | *that* | Paul pense **que** c'est son album. |
| | **si** | *if* | Je ne sais pas **si** Jean va téléphoner. |
| | **sur** | *on* | Les initiales sont **sur** l'album. |

Note: **Si** becomes **s'** before **il** and **ils.** However, no elision occurs with **elle** or **elles.**
Contrast:
    Je demande à Paul **s'**il a mon album.
    Je demande à Marie **si** elle a mon livre de français.

# Structure

## A. Les adjectifs possessifs: *notre, nos; votre, vos*

The possessive adjectives **notre** *(our)* and **votre** *(your)* have the following forms:

|  | SINGULAR | PLURAL |  |  |
|---|---|---|---|---|
| *Masculine/ Feminine* | **notre** | **nos** | **notre** cousin **notre** amie | **nos** cousins **nos** amies |
| *Masculine/ Feminine* | **votre** | **vos** | **votre** album **votre** sœur | **vos** albums **vos** sœurs |

➡ There is liaison after **nos** and **vos** before a vowel sound.

➡ The French use **votre** and **vos** when speaking to —

several people:  (aux élèves) 
{ Voici **votre** école.
{ Voici **vos** livres.

one person whom they address as **vous:**  (au professeur)
{ Voici **votre** école.
{ Voici **vos** livres.

Be sure students pronounce the **o** in **notre** and **votre** like the **o** in **bonne**.
Note: When **notre** and **votre** come before a vowel sound, the **e** is dropped.
This is similar to the pronunciation of **quatre heures**.

## ACTIVITÉ 1   Là-bas

In a big department store a customer is looking for various things. The person at the information desk points out where they are to be found. Play both roles.

➡ les disques

Le client (La cliente):  **Où sont vos disques?**
L'employé (L'employée):  **Nos disques sont là-bas.**

1. les livres
2. les posters
3. les radios
4. les cassettes
5. le restaurant
6. la cafétéria
7. les albums de timbres
8. les caméras

**MAISON-LOISIRS**
verrerie, vaisselle, électroménager - 3ᵉ ét.
radio - t.v. - photo : r.-c.
ameublement, éclair : 3ᵉ ét.
tapis : 4ᵉ ét.
sport, loisirs, jardin : 4ᵉ ét.
centre de bricolage : 4ᵉ ét.
**HOME-LEISURE**
glassware, table-ware,
household appliances 3rd f.
radio, TV, photo. ; g.-f.
furniture, light fittings :
3rd floor
carpeting - 4th floor
sport, leisure, garden. 4th f.
Do-it-yourself centre : 4th f.

**CADEAUX**
souvenirs et articles de
Nice, parfums, bijoux,
disques, livres et articles
de fumeurs :
rez-de-chaussée
orfèvrerie : 3ᵉ étage
**GIFTS**
souvenirs of Nice,
perfumes, jewelry,
records, books
and gifts for the smoker
ground floor
golds and silverware :
3rd floor

## B. Récapitulation: les adjectifs possessifs

Review the possessive adjectives in the chart below:

| THE OWNER | THE POSSESSIVE ADJECTIVE | | | ENGLISH EQUIVALENT |
|---|---|---|---|---|
| | before a singular noun | | before a plural noun | |
| | *Masculine* | *Feminine* | | |
| je<br>tu<br>il, elle | **mon**<br>**ton**<br>**son** | **ma** (mon +vowel)<br>**ta** (ton +vowel)<br>**sa** (son +vowel) | **mes**<br>**tes**<br>**ses** | *my*<br>*your*<br>*his, her, its* |
| nous<br>vous<br>ils, elles | **notre**<br>**votre**<br>**leur** | | **nos**<br>**vos**<br>**leurs** | *our*<br>*your*<br>*their* |

→ The gender and the number of a possessive adjective are determined only by the *noun it introduces.*

Voici Monique et **sa** collection.     *Here is Monique and **her** collection.*
Voici Robert et **sa** collection.      *Here is Robert and **his** collection.*

## ACTIVITÉ 2   Au revoir!

The following people are taking a trip to Canada, and their friends and family are seeing them off. Say with whom each person is arriving at the airport.

→ Monique (le petit ami et les cousines)
**Monique arrive avec son petit ami et ses cousines.**

1. Jacques (le père et la mère)
2. Pauline (la sœur et le frère)
3. Henri (l'oncle et la tante)
4. Isabelle (les cousins et les cousines)
5. Pierre (les parents et la grand-mère)
6. Monsieur Dumas (la fille et les fils)
7. moi (les amis et la sœur)
8. toi (les amies et le frère)
9. Louis et André (le père et la tante)
10. Hélène et Sylvie (la mère et l'oncle)
11. vous (les amis et la cousine)
12. nous (les amies et le cousin)

## ACTIVITÉ 3   La surprise-partie   OPTIONAL

Say what everyone is bringing to the party. Use the appropriate possessive adjectives.

→ vous (un électrophone et des disques)
**Vous arrivez avec votre électrophone et vos disques.**

1. moi (une guitare)
2. toi (un livre et des disques)
3. nous (une voiture)
4. vous (des cassettes et un banjo)
5. Paul (une clarinette)
6. Michèle (des photos)
7. Jacqueline et Anne (des disques)
8. Marc et Philippe (un appareil-photo)

## C. Être à

Review the contractions au and aux. Le livre est au professeur. Il n'est pas aux élèves.

To indicate possession the French also use the expression **être à** *(to belong to).*

| être à + | noun | La caméra **est à Marie.** | *The movie camera **belongs to Marie.*** |
|---|---|---|---|
| | | Les timbres **sont à Pierre.** | *The stamps **belong to Pierre.*** |
| | stress | L'album n'est pas **à lui.** | *The album does not **belong to him.*** |
| | pronoun | Les photos **sont à moi.** | *The pictures **belong to me.*** |

Note the use of **être à** in questions:

**À qui est** le livre?  { *To whom does the book **belong?*** / *Whose book is it?* }

**À qui sont** les timbres?  { *To whom do the stamps **belong?*** / *Whose stamps are they?* }

Remind the students that in questions, the preposition *always* comes at the beginning of the sentence:
À qui est la montre?
*To whom does the watch belong? (Whom does the watch belong to?)*

**ACTIVITÉ 4**  **Rendez à César . . .** *(Render unto Caesar . . .)*

Give back the things listed below to their rightful owners.
(Remember: **à + le → au; à + les → aux**)

→ les timbres (Pierre)    **Les timbres sont à Pierre.**

1. l'appareil-photo (Jacques)
2. les photos (Sylvie)
3. la raquette (Philippe)
4. le chien (la fille)
5. le chat (le garçon)
6. les livres (le professeur)
7. la caméra (les cousins de Denise)
8. les cartes (les amis de Chantal)

**ACTIVITÉ 5**  **Une guitare**

Monique has found a guitar. She asks Marc if it belongs to the following people. Marc says *no*. Play both roles, using a stress pronoun in Marc's answers.

→ Paul    Monique: **Est-ce qu'elle est à Paul?**
         Marc: **Non, elle n'est pas à lui.**

VARIATION with **les timbres: Est-ce qu'ils sont à Paul?**

1. Philippe
2. Élisabeth
3. Hélène
4. Georges

5. Paul et Jacques
6. Lucie et Charlotte
7. toi
8. vous

WB
C1

SCRIPT
Act. 6

MASTERS
p. 23

## UN JEU    OPTIONAL

Tell what the people in column A are doing, selecting activities from
column B. Then decide which objects of column C might belong to them.
Be sure to use the expression **être à** according to the models below. How
many sets of sentences can you make in five minutes?

| A | B | C |
|---|---|---|
| je | skier | les livres |
| tu | voyager | les disques |
| Anne-Marie | écouter un concert | l'album |
| mon cousin | regarder un match | la radio |
| mes amis | jouer au tennis | le téléviseur |
| Louise et Anne | jouer au football | la voiture |
| nous | jouer au volleyball | le ballon (*ball*) de foot |
| vous | étudier | le ballon de volley |
| | collectionner les timbres | la raquette |
| | | les skis |

→ **Tu étudies. Les livres sont à toi.**

→ **Anne-Marie joue au volleyball. Le ballon de volley est à elle.**

# Prononciation

ct. 8

## Le son /o/

*Model word:* au

*Practice words:* beau, jaune, piano, radio, faux, vélo, drôle, hôtel, nos, vos

*Practice sentences:*   Margot a un beau piano.

Voici vos vélos jaunes.

The sound /o/ is pronounced somewhat like the *o* in the English word *noble,*
although it is shorter and more tense.

Comment écrire /o/: **o, ô; au, eau**

Note de Prononciation: The letter o is pronounced:
/o/ at the end of a word, before a final silent consonant, and in the ending **-ose**; /ɔ/ otherwise.
*Contrast:* /o/ idiot, vélo, piano, nos, vos
  /ɔ/ idiote, école, Noël, notre, votre

Leçon cinq   **167**

# Entre nous

## Expression pour la conversation

To disagree with a request, you may say:

**Pas question!** *Nothing doing! No way!*

## Mini-dialogue    OPTIONAL

La générosité d'Henri a des limites.

MONIQUE: Où est ton frère, Henri?

HENRI: Il n'est pas *là*. Il est en vacances.      *here*

MONIQUE: Dis, *est-ce que je peux* emprunter son      *may I*
électrophone?

HENRI: Bien sûr.

MONIQUE: Et ses disques?

HENRI: Ses disques aussi!

MONIQUE: Et ses cassettes?

HENRI: Bien sûr.

MONIQUE: Et sa guitare?

HENRI: Sa guitare! Mais mon frère n'a pas de guitare.

MONIQUE: Et la guitare là-bas?

HENRI: Ah *ça*, pas question! Elle n'est pas à lui.      *that*
Elle est à moi!

## L'art du dialogue

a) Act out the dialog between Monique and Henri.

b) Now imagine that instead of looking for Henri's brother, Monique is looking for his sister. Replace **ton frère** by **ta sœur** and make the necessary changes. Act out the new dialog.

c) Imagine that Henri has two brothers and that Monique is looking for them. Replace **ton frère** by **tes frères** and make the necessary changes. Act out the new dialog.

d) Suppose that Monique is interested in Henri's banjo rather than his guitar. Act out the new dialog, replacing **sa guitare** by **son banjo**. Make the necessary changes.

WB Objets   SCRIPT Act. 7   MASTERS pp. 23; 69–70   QUIZ p. 45   WB Tests de contrôle   TEST pp. 46–49

**168**   Unité trois

Le monde de
tous les jours

# SECTION
# MAGAZINE 2

# Le langage des COULEURS

Est-ce que les couleurs parlent?
Bien sûr!
Chaque° couleur a une signification.
Voici le langage des couleurs:

| | | |
|---|---|---|
| **ROUGE** | | Courage. Passion. |
| **ORANGE** | | Courage. Initiative. |
| **JAUNE** | | Dynamisme. |
| **VERT** | | Patience. |
| **BLEU** | | Calme. Optimisme. |
| **VIOLET** | | Mélancolie. |
| **BLANC** | | Idéalisme. Sincérité. |
| **NOIR** | | Romantisme. Mystère. |

Est-ce que vous avez une couleur préférée?°
Est-ce que votre couleur préférée correspond à votre personnalité?

**Chaque** *Each*　**préférée** *favorite*

# Petit catalogue
# des compliments . . .
# et des insultes

sympa = sympathique   mignon *cute*   génie *genius*

# Les noms à la mode°

Comment est-ce que vous vous appelez?°
Jim, Bob ou Carl? Linda, Annie ou Sylvia?
Est-ce que votre nom est un nom à la mode?
En France, il y a des noms à la mode . . . et les modes° changent.

| filles | | | | | | | | | |
|---|---|---|---|---|---|---|---|---|---|
| | | Chantal | Brigitte | | Stéphanie | | | Carine Delphine | |
| Clémentine | | Marie-Laure | Sylvie | Nathalie | Christelle | Aurélie Valérie | | Vanessa | ? |
| **1900** | | **1950** | **1960** | **1965** | **1970** | **1975** | | **1980** | **2000** |
| Gaston | | Jean-Paul Jean-François | Bruno Gérard | Éric Thierry | Olivier Laurent | Christophe Nicolas | | Benjamin | ? |
| garçons | | | | | | | | | |

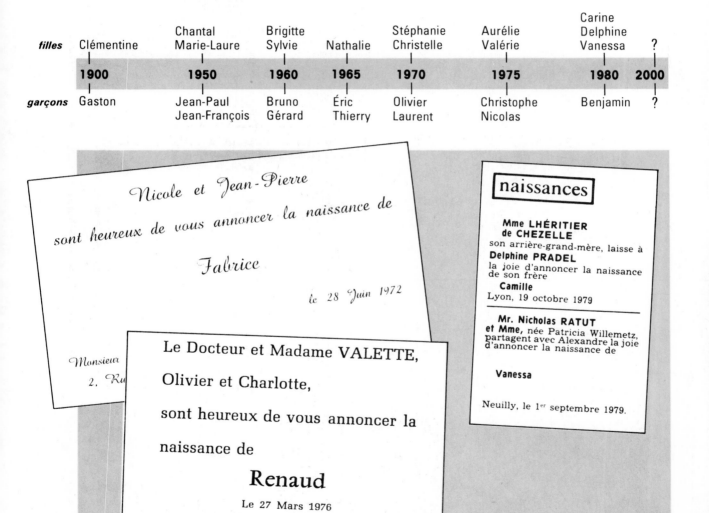

*Nicole et Jean-Pierre*
*sont heureux de vous annoncer la naissance de*
*Fabrice*
*le 28 Juin 1972*

*Monsieur*
*2, Ru*

Le Docteur et Madame VALETTE,
Olivier et Charlotte,
sont heureux de vous annoncer la
naissance de

**Renaud**

Le 27 Mars 1976

135, rue de l'Ermitage          37100 Tours

## naissances

**Mme LHÉRITIER de CHEZELLE**
son arrière-grand-mère, laisse à
**Delphine PRADEL**
la joie d'annoncer la naissance
de son frère
**Camille**
Lyon, 19 octobre 1979

**Mr. Nicholas RATUT**
et Mme, née Patricia Willemetz,
partagent avec Alexandre la joie
d'annoncer la naissance de

**Vanessa**

Neuilly, le 1er septembre 1979.

**Les noms à la mode** *Popular names*   **Comment est-ce que vous vous appelez?** *What's your name?*
**les modes** *fashions*     ILLUSTRATIONS: **heureux** *happy*   **naissance** *birth*

# Les secrets du VISAGE°

Regardez-vous° dans la glace!°
Regardez la forme de votre visage!
Avez-vous un visage ovale? rond? carré?°
C'est une question importante.

Certaines° personnes disent° en effet
que la forme de votre visage détermine
votre personnalité.

## Vous avez un visage ovale . . .

Vous êtes très romantique . . .
Comme° les personnes ro-
mantiques, vous êtes
généreux,° mais vous êtes
aussi impressionnable.
Vous êtes un peu timide et
vous n'êtes pas toujours très
patient.
Vous aimez la musique et
vous aimez danser. Vous
adorez voyager.

## Vous avez un visage carré . . .

Vous êtes réaliste . . .
Vous avez aussi une grande
curiosité intellectuelle.
Vous avez un sens pratique
très développé.
En général, vous aimez
commander . . . mais vous
n'aimez pas être commandé.

## Vous avez un visage rond . . .

Vous avez beaucoup de sens
pratique.
Vous êtes sérieux et vous
aimez l'action. Mais vous
n'êtes pas très tolérant.
Vous aimez les sports.

## Vous avez un visage triangulaire . . .

Vous êtes une personne intellectuelle et vous
avez aussi un tempérament d'artiste.
Vous aimez exprimer° vos opinions et vous
aimez discuter° avec vos amis.
Vous avez beaucoup
d'imagination, mais vous
n'êtes pas très organisé. Vous
êtes aussi assez superstitieux.
Vous avez beaucoup d'amis,
mais vous n'êtes pas toujours
très patient avec eux.
Vous détestez l'ordre et la
discipline.

Et maintenant analysez la personnalité de ces° Français célèbres.°

**Napoléon,** *empereur*

**Brigitte Bardot,** *actrice*

**Jacques Cousteau,** *explorateur*

MASTERS
p. 90

**visage** *face*   **Regardez-vous** *Look at yourself*   **glace** *mirror*   **carré** *square*   **Certaines** *Some*   **disent** *say*
**Comme** *Like*   **généreux** *generous*   **exprimer** *to express*   **discuter** *to argue*   **ces** *these*   **célèbres** *famous*

# Vive le vélomoteur!

Quel est le véhicule qui° a un moteur, deux roues,° et deux pédales? Le vélomoteur, bien sûr!

Le vélomoteur est très populaire en France. Chaque° jour des milliers° de jeunes Français utilisent° leur vélomoteur pour aller° à l'école … En été, ils utilisent leur vélomoteur pour aller à la plage ou à la campagne.

Le vélomoteur a beaucoup d'avantages:
     Il est très pratique.
     Il est très économique.
     Et il n'est pas dangereux …
       si vous êtes prudent!

Vive le vélomoteur!

**qui** *that*   **roues** *wheels*   **Chaque** *Every*   **des milliers** *thousands*   **utilisent** *use*   **pour aller** *to go*
ILLUSTRATION: **Stationnement: ne payez plus le droit de vous arrêter** *Parking: stop paying for the right to stop*

# L'ART DES CADEAUX°

Choisir° un cadeau est souvent un problème.
Qu'est-ce que° vous allez choisir pour l'anniversaire d'un ami? pour
l'anniversaire d'une amie?
Ça dépend de° leur personnalité.
Voici des suggestions:

| **Pour un garçon** | **Pour une fille** |
|---|---|

Si le garçon est . . .                     Si la fille est . . .

 élégant
**un pull,°**
**une cravate°**

 élégante
**un pull,**
**un foulard°**

 sportif
**un tee-shirt**

 sportive
**un tee-shirt**

 intellectuel
**un livre**

 intellectuelle
**un livre**

 musicien
**un disque**

 musicienne
**deux billets° d'opéra
(un pour elle et un
pour vous)**

 romantique
**une plante**

 romantique
**une plante, des fleurs°**

 bon avec les animaux
**un chien**

votre meilleure amie
**votre photo**

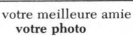

 votre meilleur ami
**votre photo**

**L'art des cadeaux** *The art of gift-giving*   **Choisir** *Choosing*   **Qu'est-ce que** *What*   **Ça dépend
de** *That depends on*   **pull** *pullover*   **cravate** *tie*   **foulard** *scarf*   **billets** *tickets*   **fleurs** *flowers*

# L'album de photos de Brigitte

Bonjour! Je m'appelle Brigitte Martinot. J'ai dix-sept ans et j'habite à Annecy. Je vais au lycée° Berthollet où je suis élève de première.° Voici quelques° photos de famille:

La fille avec le vélo, c'est moi. Je vais souvent à la campagne à vélo.

Voici mon père. Il est dentiste. Il a des lunettes drôles, n'est-ce pas?

Voici Maman. Elle aussi, elle travaille. Elle est chef° du personnel dans une banque. Elle a beaucoup de responsabilités.

Voici ma sœur Annie sur son vélomoteur.

Voici Pierre, mon frère. Il aime skier, mais ce n'est pas un champion...

Qui est-ce? Non, ce n'est pas mon cousin. C'est... mon petit ami! Comment s'appelle-t-il? Ah ça,° c'est un secret!

lycée *high school*   de première *11th grade*
quelques *some*   chef *head*   ça *that*

Avez-vous une bicyclette?   une radio?   un appareil-photo?

Voici la proportion de jeunes Français qui ont ces° objets:

radio        80%        appareil-photo        60%        électrophone        55%

bicyclette        65%        vélomoteur        18%

Viens, c'est la foire aux jouets

5.00 prix fous jusqu'au 14 Juin

**AU BON MARCHÉ**
*Rive Gauche*
Métro: Sèvres-Babylone. Parking.

MASTERS
p. 92

**possessions** *belongings*    **ces** *these*    ILLUSTRATION: **foire** *market*    **jouets** *toys*

# Nos meilleurs amis

Quel est le meilleur ami de l'homme?
C'est le chien, naturellement!
Voici le portrait de quatre chiens
populaires en France.

**Le terrier**     Il y a de nombreuses
espèces° de terriers: les fox-terriers, les
terriers irlandais,° les terriers écossais,°
les bull-terriers. Les terriers sont des
chiens de chasse.° Ils sont de couleur
blanche et noire ou blanche et jaune. Ils
ont beaucoup de personnalité. Ce sont
des chiens très intelligents . . . et
souvent capricieux!

**Le Saint-Bernard**     Le Saint-Bernard
est un chien très grand, très fort° et très
musclé. Son courage est légendaire.

**Le caniche**     Il y a des caniches noirs,
des caniches blancs, des caniches gris
et des caniches bruns.° Le caniche est
un chien extrêmement° intelligent et très
loyal.

**Le basset**     Il s'appelle «basset» parce
que c'est un chien bas sur pattes.°
Le basset est un chien petit et très
musclé. Il a la réputation d'être très
courageux.

de nombreuses espèces *many kinds*   irlandais *Irish*   écossais *Scottish*   de chasse *hunting*
bruns *brown*   extrêmement *extremely*   fort *strong*   bas sur pattes *short-legged*

# VIVE L'ÉCOLE!

À l'âge de onze ans, les jeunes Français entrent au collège, ou plus exactement° au C.E.S. (Collège d'Enseignement Secondaire). À l'âge de dix-sept ou dix-huit ans, ils passent° le « bac » (ou baccalauréat). En France, le baccalauréat représente la fin° des études° secondaires.

Voici la correspondance approximative entre° les études secondaires en France et aux États-Unis.

| EN FRANCE | | | AUX ÉTATS-UNIS | |
|---|---|---|---|---|
| *Âge* | *École* | *Classe* | *École* | *Classe* |
| 11 ans | | sixième | elementary school | 6th |
| 12 ans | C.E.S. | cinquième | | 7th |
| 13 ans | | quatrième | junior high school | 8th |
| 14 ans | | troisième | | 9th |
| 15 ans | | seconde | | 10th |
| 16 ans | lycée | première | high school | 11th |
| 17 ans | | terminale | | 12th |

## PROJETS CULTURELS

### *Projets individuels*

1. *Get a French newspaper (Le Figaro, France-Soir) and look at the birth and wedding announcements. Make a list of the first names which are popular now (birth announcements) and those which were popular about twenty years ago (wedding announcements).*
2. *Using pictures of people in French magazines and newspapers, describe their personalities according to the shapes of their faces. Use the texts in Les secrets du visage as models.*

### *Projets de classe*

1. *Prepare a bulletin board exhibit about French cars. Use advertisements from French and American magazines, newspaper clippings, and (if you wish) model cars.*
2. *Using pictures from French magazines (Paris-Match, Jours de France, etc.), make a display which shows French people at work and at play. Write a short caption (in French) for each picture.*

plus exactement *more exactly*  passent *take*  fin *end*  études *studies*  entre *between*
ILLUSTRATIONS: langue vivante *modern language*  renforcé *intensive*  TP = travaux pratiques *lab*
SN = sciences naturelles

OBJECTIVES

In this unit, the students will learn to express themselves in simple shopping situations. They will learn how to use French money and how to make comparisons concerning people and things.

*Language*
- **acheter**
- **-ir** and **-re** verbs
- demonstrative and interrogative pronouns
- the comparative and the superlative forms
- expressions with **avoir**
- the impersonal subject pronoun **on**

*Vocabulary*
- clothing
- shops and shopping
- money

*Culture*

This unit introduces shopping customs, especially with respect to clothing, and stresses the importance of personal appearance.

# UNITÉ 4
## En ville

| | |
|---|---|
| **4.1** | **Au Bon Marché** |
| **4.2** | **Rien n'est parfait!** |
| **4.3** | **Comment acheter une robe** |
| **4.4** | **Un gourmand** |
| **4.5** | **Ici, on n'est pas en Amérique.** |

# Leçon 1
## UNITÉ 4
### Au Bon Marché

STRUCTURES TO OBSERVE
• regular verbs in **-ir**
• the expression **qu'est-ce que?**
• numbers

Dans deux mois les vacances *commencent!*                                    *begin*
Aujourd'hui, Brigitte et Michèle vont en ville.
Elles vont dans un grand magasin *qui* s'appelle « Au Bon Marché ».          *which*
Pourquoi? *Pour regarder* les bikinis, bien sûr!                             *To look at*

**Scène 1.** Brigitte, Michèle

| | | |
|---|---|---|
| BRIGITTE: | Alors, Michèle, *qu'est-ce que tu choisis?* | *what are you choosing* |
| | le bikini jaune ou le bikini bleu? | |
| MICHÈLE: | Le bikini rouge! Regarde, il est *mignon!* | *cute* |
| BRIGITTE: | Peut-être, . . . mais il est trop petit pour toi! | |
| MICHÈLE: | Ça n'a pas d'importance! | |
| BRIGITTE: | Comment! Ça n'a pas d'importance? | |
| MICHÈLE: | Je suis au régime . . . Je vais *maigrir!* | *to lose weight* |

**Scène 2.** Brigitte, Michèle, une employée

| | | |
|---|---|---|
| L'EMPLOYÉE: | Vous choisissez le bikini rouge? | |
| MICHÈLE: | Oui, Madame! Combien est-ce qu'il *coûte?* | *cost* |
| L'EMPLOYÉE: | Il coûte *cent* francs, Mademoiselle. | *one hundred* |
| MICHÈLE: | Euh . . . Et le bikini bleu? | |
| L'EMPLOYÉE: | *Quatre-vingts* francs. | *eighty* |
| BRIGITTE *(à Michèle):* | Et *combien d'argent* as-tu? | *how much money* |
| MICHÈLE: | Euh . . . Quatre-vingts francs . . . | |
| | *(à l'employée)* Excusez-moi, Madame. Je ne choisis | |
| | pas le bikini rouge . . . Je choisis le bikini bleu. | |
| BRIGITTE: | Dommage, le bikini rouge est vraiment très joli! | |
| MICHÈLE: | *Voyons,* Brigitte! Il est trop petit pour moi! | *Come on* |

**Où vont Brigitte et Michèle? Comment s'appelle le magasin où elles vont? Quel bikini est-ce que Michèle choisit dans la scène 1? Pourquoi? Quel bikini est-ce que Michèle choisit dans la scène 2? Pourquoi?**

How good are you at arithmetic? Do you remember the numbers in French?
Let's see.

1.  How much is *four times twenty* in English?
2.  How do you say *four* in French? How do you say *twenty*?   quatre/vingt
3.  What do you think the number **quatre-vingts** means?   eighty
4.  How much is *eighty* plus *ten* in English?
5.  What do you think the number **quatre-vingt-dix** means?   ninety
6.  How much is *eighty* plus *fifteen*?
7.  What do you think the number **quatre-vingt-quinze** means?   ninety-five

## NOTE CULTURELLE          OPTIONAL

### Le grand magasin

Where would you buy a tennis racket? a pair of shoes? a bicycle? a camera? Probably in a department store. To buy these items, many French people go to the **grand magasin.** One of the oldest and most famous **grands magasins** in Paris is **Au Bon Marché**. It was founded in the nineteenth century by a man who wanted to give everyone a chance to buy good but inexpensive items. **Bon marché** means *inexpensive*.

*la tente*   1850ᶠ **1340ᶠ** 5 places*

**AU BON MARCHÉ** *Rive Gauche*

## Vocabulaire pratique

| | | |
|---|---|---|
| NOMS: | **un magasin** | *store, shop* |
| | **un grand magasin** | *department store* |
| | **un régime** | *diet* |
| EXPRESSION: | **être au régime** | *to be on a diet*   Je ne **suis** pas **au régime.** |

# Structure

If your students find that **choisir** is too much of a tongue twister, you may practice the forms of -ir verbs with **finir**: **Je finis à midi,** etc.
You may also want to use a clock and review times: **Tu finis à trois heures,** etc.

## A. Les verbes réguliers en *-ir*

Many French verbs end in **-ir.** Most of these verbs are conjugated like **choisir** *(to choose).* Note the forms of this verb in the present tense, paying special attention to the *endings.*

Act. 2

| Infinitive | choisir | | STEM | ENDINGS |
|---|---|---|---|---|
| Present | je **choisis** | un livre | | **-is** |
| | tu **choisis** | des disques | | **-is** |
| | il/elle **choisit** | des photos | (infinitive minus **-ir**) | **-it** |
| | nous **choisissons** | un vélo | **chois-**+ | **-issons** |
| | vous **choisissez** | une voiture | | **-issez** |
| | ils/elles **choisissent** | une caméra | | **-issent** |

Note that all final consonants are silent.

Act. 2

## Vocabulaire spécialisé  Verbes réguliers en *-ir*

| | | |
|---|---|---|
| choisir | *to choose* | Est-ce que tu **choisis** le bikini bleu? |
| finir | *to finish* | Les classes **finissent** à midi. |
| grossir | *to get fat, gain weight* | Marc **grossit** parce qu'il n'est pas au régime. |
| maigrir | *to get thin, lose weight* | Je **maigris** parce que je suis au régime. |
| réussir | *to succeed, pass* (a test) | Nous **réussissons** parce que nous étudions. |
| ne réussir pas | *to fail, flunk* (a test) | Vous **ne réussissez pas** parce que vous n'étudiez pas. |

The negative form of the infinitive is **ne pas réussir**. The form **ne réussir pas** is given here so as not to confuse students at this point.

### ACTIVITÉ 1  L'examen

Some students finish the exam and pass the course. Others do not finish and fail. Express this according to the models.

→ Paul finit.     **Il réussit.**
   Catherine ne finit pas.     **Elle ne réussit pas.**

1. Je finis.
2. Tu ne finis pas.
3. Mes amis finissent.
4. Les mauvais élèves ne finissent pas.
5. Nous finissons.
6. Vous ne finissez pas.
7. Philippe ne finit pas.
8. Michèle finit.
9. Mes amies ne finissent pas.
10. Ils finissent.

## ACTIVITÉ 2   Le régime

Some of Michèle's friends have decided to go on a diet and are losing weight. The others are not on a diet and are gaining weight. Describe what is happening to each of the people mentioned below according to the models.

→ Monique est au régime.     **Elle maigrit. Elle ne grossit pas.**
    André n'est pas au régime.     **Il grossit. Il ne maigrit pas.**

1. Nous sommes au régime.
2. Vous n'êtes pas au régime.
3. Danièle et Nicole sont au régime.
4. Paul et Jacques ne sont pas au régime.

5. Je suis au régime.
6. Tu n'es pas au régime.
7. Albert est au régime.
8. Sylvie n'est pas au régime.

## ACTIVITÉ 3   Questions personnelles

WB
A1, A2

SCRIPT

Act. 3

1. À quelle heure finissent les classes aujourd'hui?
2. À quelle heure finit la classe de français?
3. Quand finit l'école cette année (*this year*)?
4. Quand vous allez au restaurant avec vos amis, est-ce que vous choisissez un restaurant cher (*expensive*)?
5. Quand vous êtes au restaurant avec votre famille, qui choisit le menu?

## B. L'expression interrogative *qu'est-ce que*

Note the use of the interrogative expression **qu'est-ce que** (*what*) in the sentences below.

    **Qu'est-ce que** Michèle choisit?     Elle choisit un bikini.
    **Qu'est-ce qu'**André regarde?     Il regarde un film.

To ask *what* people are doing, etc., the French use the following construction:

**Qu'est-ce que**   +   subject   +   verb   +   (rest of sentence)   ?
    ↓
**Qu'est-ce qu'** (+  vowel sound)

→ Note also the expression: **Qu'est-ce que c'est?**   *What is it? What's this?*
    **Qu'est-ce que c'est?**     C'est une Renault. C'est une voiture française.

With inverted questions only, **que** is used: **Que choisit-elle? Que regardez-vous?**

## ACTIVITÉ 4   Le transistor de Georges

Because Georges is always listening to his radio, he has trouble hearing what Sophie tells him. He asks her to repeat what she said. Play both roles.

→ Je finis . . . (la leçon)     Georges: **Qu'est-ce que tu finis?**
                           Sophie: **Je finis la leçon.**

WB
B1

SCRIPT

Act. 4

1. Je choisis . . . (des cassettes)
2. Je choisis . . . (un short)
3. Je regarde . . . (un match de tennis)
4. Je regarde . . . (un western)

5. J'écoute . . . (un concert)
6. Je visite . . . (un musée)
7. J'étudie . . . (le piano)
8. J'ai . . . (une guitare)

## RÉVISION: les nombres

Review the numbers from 0 to 60 in Appendix 2.A.

### *ACTIVITÉ DE RÉVISION* **Problèmes de maths** OPTIONAL

Do the following multiplications out loud. (**Fois** means *times*.)

You may want to use **font** for this exercise:
**deux fois deux font quatre.**

→ $2 \times 2$  **deux fois deux, quatre**

| | | | | |
|---|---|---|---|---|
| 1. $3 \times 6$ | 4. $6 \times 10$ | 7. $3 \times 7$ | 10. $15 \times 3$ | 13. $2 \times 14$ |
| 2. $2 \times 11$ | 5. $7 \times 7$ | 8. $3 \times 13$ | 11. $12 \times 3$ | 14. $5 \times 11$ |
| 3. $4 \times 8$ | 6. $8 \times 7$ | 9. $2 \times 8$ | 12. $3 \times 17$ | 15. $6 \times 9$ |

### C. Les nombres de 60 à 100

You may practice these numbers by having the students count in sequence around the classroom: 60, 61, 62...: 60, 62, 64...; 60, 63, 66...

Read the numbers from 60 to 100, paying special attention to the way the French express the numbers 70, 80, and 90.

The ending **s** in **quatre-vingts** occurs only with the number 80.

| | | | |
|---|---|---|---|
| 60 | soixante | 80 | quatre-vingts |
| 61 | soixante et un | 81 | quatre-vingt-un |
| 62 | soixante-deux | 82 | quatre-vingt-deux |
| 63 | soixante-trois | 83 | quatre-vingt-trois |
| 64 | soixante-quatre | 84 | quatre-vingt-quatre |
| 65 | soixante-cinq | 85 | quatre-vingt-cinq |
| 66 | soixante-six | 86 | quatre-vingt-six |
| 67 | soixante-sept | 87 | quatre-vingt-sept |
| 68 | soixante-huit | 88 | quatre-vingt-huit |
| 69 | soixante-neuf | 89 | quatre-vingt-neuf |
| 70 | soixante-dix[1] | 90 | quatre-vingt-dix |
| 71 | soixante et onze | 91 | quatre-vingt-onze |
| 72 | soixante-douze | 92 | quatre-vingt-douze |
| 73 | soixante-treize | 93 | quatre-vingt-treize |
| 74 | soixante-quatorze | 94 | quatre-vingt-quatorze |
| 75 | soixante-quinze | 95 | quatre-vingt-quinze |
| 76 | soixante-seize | 96 | quatre-vingt-seize |
| 77 | soixante-dix-sept | 97 | quatre-vingt-dix-sept |
| 78 | soixante-dix-huit | 98 | quatre-vingt-dix-huit |
| 79 | soixante-dix-neuf | 99 | quatre-vingt-dix-neuf |
| | | 100 | cent |

$4 \times 20 = 80$

$4 \times 20 + 10 = 90$

$60 + 10 = 70$

To practice listening comprehension, you may play "Loto" (Bingo).

WB
C1, C2

SCRIPT

Act. 5,6

MASTERS
p. 24

### *ACTIVITÉ 5* **Week-end**

The following students are spending the weekend in the country. Say how much money each one has.

→ Philippe (60 F)  **Philippe a soixante francs.**

| | | | |
|---|---|---|---|
| 1. Michèle (65 F) | 3. Marc (80 F) | 5. Annette (85 F) | 7. Alain (73 F) |
| 2. Sylvie (75 F) | 4. Antoine (95 F) | 6. Robert (100 F) | 8. Isabelle (91 F) |

[1]In Switzerland, numbers from 70 to 99 follow the pattern from 20 to 69: 70 is **septante** (71 is **septante et un**, 72 is **septante-deux**, etc.), 80 is **octante**, and 90 is **nonante**.

## ACTIVITÉ 6   Les bikinis     OPTIONAL

Several bikinis are for sale. Each girl buys the most expensive one she can afford.

bikini bleu = 80 F      bikini jaune = 90 F      bikini rouge = 95 F

→ Suzanne (93 F)     **Suzanne a quatre-vingt-treize francs.**
                     **Elle choisit le bikini jaune.**

1. vous (87 F)          3. tu (100 F)            5. Marie (83 F)
2. elles (98 F)         4. Paulette (92 F)       6. Yvette (99 F)

---

# Vocabulaire spécialisé   L'argent

| | | |
|---|---|---|
| NOMS: | **l'argent** *money* | **une pièce** *coin* |
| | **un billet** *bill, bank note* | You may introduce **la monnaie** *(change).* |
| ADJECTIFS: | **cher (chère)** *expensive* | La raquette est **chère.** |
| | **bon marché** *inexpensive* | Les disques sont **bon marché.** |
| VERBES: | **coûter** *to cost* | Les cassettes **coûtent** vingt francs. |
| | **dépenser** *to spend* | Je n'aime pas **dépenser** mon argent. |

Note:  The expression **bon marché** is invariable. It never takes endings to agree with the noun it modifies.

**Bon marché** is invariable because **marché** is a noun. Literally, the expression means *good deal* or *good bargain.*

---

## ACTIVITÉ 7   Leur argent     OPTIONAL

Help the following people count their money.

→ Albert a un billet de 50 francs et 3 pièces de 5 francs.
   **Albert a soixante-cinq francs.**

1. Sylvie a 2 billets de 50 francs.
2. Charles a 8 billets de 10 francs.
3. Michèle a 9 billets de 10 francs.
4. Marc a 8 billets de 10 francs et 2 pièces de 1 franc.
5. Annie a 8 billets de 10 francs et 11 pièces de 1 franc.
6. Paul a 9 billets de 10 francs et 1 pièce de 5 francs.

## D. Les expressions interrogatives *combien* et *combien de*

Note the use of **combien** and **combien de** in the following sentences:

| | | For simplicity the questions below use inversion. It is also possible to use **est-ce que**: Combien est-ce que les disques coûtent? Combien de timbres est-ce que tu as? | |
|---|---|---|---|

**combien** + verb

   *how much*         **Combien** coûte le livre?        *How much does the book cost?*

                     **Combien** coûtent les disques?     *How much do the records cost?*

**combien de** + noun

   *how much*         **Combien** d'argent dépenses-tu?   *How much money are you spending?*

   *how many*        **Combien de** timbres as-tu?     *How many stamps do you have?*

➔ **Combien de** becomes **combien d'** before a vowel sound.

The construction **Combien est-ce que tu as de disques?** is not presented here.
Expressions of quantity are introduced in Unité 8.2.

### ACTIVITÉ 8 Questions personnelles

1. Combien de frères avez-vous? combien de sœurs?
2. Combien de cassettes avez-vous? combien de disques?
3. Combien de garçons est-ce qu'il y a dans la classe? combien de filles?

Be sure students repeat the noun in their answers: **J'ai 20 cassettes.**

### ACTIVITÉ 9 Les collections de Jean-Louis

Jean-Louis collects the following things. Sylvie asks him how many items
he has in each collection and how much they cost. Play both roles.

SCRIPT
Act. 7

➔ des disques     Jean-Louis: **J'ai des disques.**
                  Sylvie: **Combien de disques as-tu?**
                             **Combien coûtent tes disques?**

1. des posters      3. des pièces américaines      5. des disques de jazz
2. des timbres      4. des disques de musique disco    6. des photos

### UN JEU    OPTIONAL

The people in column A are spending the amounts of money indicated in
parentheses. Say how many items from column B they are choosing. Many
combinations are possible. How many sentences similar to the models
below can you make in five minutes?

| A | B |
|---|---|
| moi (75 francs) | un magazine (5 francs) |
| toi (60 francs) | un livre (15 francs) |
| Nicole (55 francs) | un disque (30 francs) |
| nous (100 francs) | une cassette (25 francs) |
| vous (95 francs) | |
| Pierre et Alain (90 francs) | |

➔ **Nous dépensons 100 francs. Nous choisissons trois disques et deux magazines.**

➔ **Je dépense 75 francs. Je choisis deux disques et un livre.**

# Prononciation

Act. 9

**Le son** /k/

*Model word:* <u>qu</u>'est-ce <u>qu</u>e

*Practice words:* <u>C</u>olette, <u>qu</u>and, <u>Qu</u>ébec, cin<u>q</u>, <u>qu</u>inze

*Practice sentences:* <u>Qu</u>'est-ce <u>qu</u>e <u>C</u>atherine choisit?

Claude a quatre-vingt-quatorze francs.

Hold a piece of paper in front of your mouth and pronounce the English words
*cat* and *scat*. The paper moves when you say *cat* because you produce a puff of
air as you pronounce the sound /k/. The paper does not move when you say
*scat*. The French /k/ is always pronounced like the *k*-sound in *scat*, without a
puff of air.

Comment écrire /k/: **c** (before **a, o, u,** or consonant); **k, qu,** final **q**

Note: The letters **qu** practically always represent the sound /k/: **qui.**

# Entre nous

**Expression pour la conversation**

**Ça dépend!** *It depends!* —Tu choisis le vélo vert ou le vélo blanc?
—Je ne sais pas . . . **Ça dépend!**

**Mini-dialogue** OPTIONAL

Les *échanges* d'Henri ne sont pas toujours très *équitables.*  *trades; fair*

HENRI: Dis, Monique, combien de disques de jazz as-tu?
MONIQUE: Soixante-quinze!
HENRI: Très bien. *Je te propose* un échange.  *I propose to you*
MONIQUE: Qu'est-ce que tu désires *échanger?*  *to trade*
HENRI: Ta collection de disques de jazz *contre* ma collection de  *against*
    musique pop. Es-tu d'accord?  *(in exchange for)*
MONIQUE: Ça dépend! Combien de disques de musique pop as-tu?
HENRI: Cinq ou six.

**L'art du dialogue**

a) Act out the dialog between Henri and Monique.
b) Henri proposes another trade: his French stamps (**les timbres français**) against Monique's
American stamps (**les timbres américains**). Act out the new dialog, making the appropriate
changes.

# UNITÉ 4
# Leçon 2   Rien n'est parfait!

Act. 1

*Cet après-midi,* François et André sont dans un magasin de vêtements. *Ce* magasin s'appelle «Tout pour les jeunes».

*This afternoon*

*clothing; This*

  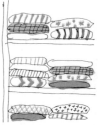

### Scène 1.

FRANÇOIS:  Je vais *acheter* un *pull.*

ANDRÉ:  Quel pull est-ce que tu achètes? Ce pull noir?

FRANÇOIS:  Non, ce pull bleu.

ANDRÉ:  Il est très chaud.

FRANÇOIS:  . . . et très chic!

ANDRÉ *(qui regarde le prix):*  Il est aussi très cher.

FRANÇOIS:  Combien est-ce qu'il coûte?

ANDRÉ:  Trois cents francs!

FRANÇOIS:  *Oh mon Dieu! Quelle horreur!*

*to buy; sweater*

*My goodness!*
*How awful!*

### Scène 2.

ANDRÉ:  *Comment trouves-tu* cette *veste?*

FRANÇOIS:  Quelle veste? Cette veste-ci?

ANDRÉ:  Non. Cette veste-là!

FRANÇOIS:  Elle est très chic!

ANDRÉ:  . . . et elle n'est pas chère!

FRANÇOIS:  Mais elle est trop grande!

ANDRÉ:  *Rien n'*est parfait!

*What do you think of;*
*jacket*

*Nothing*

  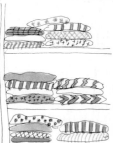

Qu'est-ce que François va acheter? Combien coûte le pull? Est-ce qu'il est cher? Qu'est-ce que François pense de la veste? Est-ce que la veste est chère? Pourquoi est-ce que la veste n'est pas parfaite?

## CONVERSATION

Let's discuss what you think about this class. Answer affirmatively or negatively.

1. Est-ce que vous aimez **ce** livre?
2. Est-ce que vous aimez **cette** classe?
3. Est-ce que vous aimez **ces** illustrations?

## OBSERVATIONS

In the above questions, the words in heavy type are used to point out specific things. They are called *demonstrative adjectives* and correspond to *this (these)* and *that (those)* in English.

- What is the form of the demonstrative adjective before a masculine
  singular noun (**livre**)?   ce
  before a feminine singular noun (**classe**)?   cette
  before a plural noun (**illustrations**)?   ces

## NOTE CULTURELLE

### L'élégance française

Have you heard of **Pierre Cardin, Yves Saint-Laurent, Chanel?** These French designers have made French fashions known all over the world. French people, in general, tend to be rather fashion-conscious and pay careful attention to their personal appearance. For a French teenager, being well-dressed does not mean wearing expensive clothes, but wearing clothes that are well cut and colors that do not clash. It also means dressing to fit the occasion. Shorts and sneakers are fine for the beach, but not for going shopping or going out to eat. As for jeans, they are the uniform of French youth . . . as long as they fit well and are clean!

## Vocabulaire pratique

| | | |
|---|---|---|
| NOMS: | **les jeunes** | *young people* |
| | **le prix** | *price* |
| ADJECTIVES: | **chaud** | *warm, hot*   |
| | **chic** | *elegant, in style* |
| | **parfait** | *perfect* |

Note: The adjective **chic** is invariable: **un pull chic, une veste chic.**

Other clothing items are presented on p. 200.

Act. 3

24

# Vocabulaire spécialisé
(modification)

## Les vêtements *(Clothing)*

Les vêtements is active vocabulary.

**Pour la campagne . . .**

un anorak

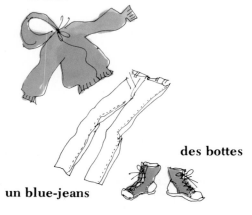

des bottes

un blue-jeans

**Pour la ville . . .**

des lunettes

un pull(-over)

un pantalon

des chaussures

une veste

**Pour le sport . . .**

un tee-shirt

un short

des chaussettes

**Pour la plage . . .**

un maillot de bain

des lunettes de soleil

des sandales

VERBE: **porter**   *to wear*   Qu'est-ce que vous **portez** aujourd'hui?

## ACTIVITÉ 1 Expression personnelle: De quelle couleur?

Describe what you wear at the following times. Give the color of each item.

You may want to review weather expressions on p. 36.

1. Quand je vais au stade, je porte . . .
2. Quand je joue au tennis, je porte . . .
3. Quand je vais à la plage, je porte . . .
4. Quand je vais à la montagne, je porte . . .
5. Quand il fait froid, je porte . . .
6. Quand il fait chaud, je porte . . .

# Structure

## A. Acheter

Note the forms of the verb **acheter** *(to buy)* in the present tense, paying special attention to the **e** of the stem.

| Infinitive | acheter | | | |
|---|---|---|---|---|
| Present | j' **achète** une veste | tu **achètes** un pull | il/elle **achète** un anorak | nous **achetons** des sandales<br>vous **achetez** des bottes<br>ils/elles **achètent** des lunettes de soleil |

Many verbs which end in **e** + consonant + **er** have the following stem change:

> **e** → **è** in the **je, tu, il,** and **ils** forms of the present

Point out that the endings are regular. You may also point out that the stem change occurs only when the **e** is accented: **il achète** but **nous achetons.** The contrast between /ɛ/ and /ə/ is reviewed in the **Prononciation** section.

## ACTIVITÉ 2 Achats *(Purchases)*

The following people all received money for Christmas. Say what each one is buying.

→ Pierre (des skis)    **Pierre achète des skis.**

1. Monique (un bikini)
2. Jacqueline et Denise (des sandales)
3. moi (un appareil-photo)
4. Jean-Claude (un anorak)
5. nous (un chien)
6. vous (des poissons rouges)
7. Henri et moi (des bottes)   nous. . .
8. Hélène et toi (des lunettes de soleil)   vous. . .

VARIATION in the negative: **Pierre n'achète pas de skis.**
For additional practice, introduce **amener** *(to bring).*
These people are bringing a friend to a picnic. **Pierre amène un ami.**

Mille is always invariable. Multiples of **cent** only take an **-s** when **cent**
is the last word of the number: **trois cents** *but* **trois cent dix.**

## B. Les nombres de 100 à 1.000.000

Act. 8, 9

MASTERS
p. 25

| | | | | | |
|---|---|---|---|---|---|
| 100 | cent | 200 | deux cents | 1.000 | mille |
| 101 | cent un | 201 | deux cent un | 2.000 | deux mille |
| 102 | cent deux | 202 | deux cent deux | 10.000 | dix mille |
| 103 | cent trois | 203 | deux cent trois | 100.000 | cent mille |
| 110 | cent dix | 900 | neuf cents | 1.000.000 | un million |

In writing numbers the French use periods where the Americans use commas,
and vice versa.

Stress that 100 is **cent** (and not *un cent*); 101 is **cent un** (and not *cent et un*), etc.

### ACTIVITÉ 3   À la banque *(At the bank)*   OPTIONAL

As a warm-up, practice numbers in chain
activities: 100, 200, 300, etc.; 110, 120,
130, etc.; 125, 150, 175, etc.

Help the bank teller add the following amounts of money.

→ 100 F + 10 F   **Cent francs plus dix francs égalent** *(equal)* **cent dix francs.**

1. 100 F + 50 F
2. 100 F + 100 F
3. 100 F + 150 F
4. 100 F + 500 F
5. 100 F + 225 F
6. 500 F + 400 F
7. 500 F + 500 F
8. 1.000 F + 9.000 F

For additional practice, read a page number from this book (e.g., p. 215). When students have found
the page, hold your book open to that page so they can check if they are right.

## C. L'adjectif interrogatif *quel?*

The interrogative adjective **quel** *(what? which?)* is used in *questions.* It
agrees with the noun it introduces and has the following forms:

| | SINGULAR | PLURAL | | |
|---|---|---|---|---|
| *Masculine* | **quel** | **quels** | **Quel** garçon? | **Quels** amis invites-tu? |
| *Feminine* | **quelle** | **quelles** | **Quelle** fille? | **Quelles** amies invites-tu? |

→ There is liaison after **quels** and **quelles** when the next word begins with
a vowel sound.

Except in liaison, the four forms of **quel** sound the same.

You may remind students that they have already seen **quel** in
expressions such as: **Quelle heure est-il? Quel temps fait-il?**

### ACTIVITÉ 4   Achats *(Purchases)*

André is shopping for the following items before going on a summer trip to
France. Françoise asks him which ones he is buying. Play both roles.

→ un maillot de bain   André: **J'achète un maillot de bain.**
                       Françoise: **Quel maillot de bain est-ce que tu achètes?**

1. un short
2. des chaussettes
3. une guitare
4. un pantalon
5. des sandales
6. des lunettes de soleil

VARIATIONS: a) with **choisir**: Je choisis un maillot de bain.
b) with inversion: Quel maillot de bain achètes-tu?

### ACTIVITÉ 5   Questions personnelles

1. Quelle ville habitez-vous?
2. À quelle école allez-vous?
3. À quel cinéma allez-vous?
4. À quelle plage allez-vous?
5. Dans quel magasin achetez-vous vos vêtements?
6. Dans quel magasin achetez-vous vos chaussures?
7. Quels programmes regardez-vous à la télé?
8. Quelles langues *(languages)* parlez-vous?

WB
C1

## D. L'adjectif démonstratif ce

The demonstrative adjective **ce** *(this, that)* agrees with the noun it introduces.
It has the following forms:

|  | SINGULAR *(this, that)* | PLURAL *(these, those)* | | |
|---|---|---|---|---|
| *Masculine* | **ce** ↓ **cet** (+ vowel sound) | **ces** | **ce** pantalon **cet** anorak | **ces** pantalons **ces** anoraks |
| *Feminine* | **cette** | **ces** | **cette** guitare **cette** auto | **ces** guitares **ces** autos |

→ There is liaison after **cet** and **ces** when the next word begins with a vowel sound.

→ To distinguish between a person or an object which is close by and one which is further away, the French sometimes use **-ci** or **-là** after the noun.

André achète **ces** chaussures-**ci**.      *André is buying **these** shoes (over here).*
Françoise achète **ces** chaussures-**là**.   *Françoise is buying **those** shoes (over there).*

You may point out that **-ci** and **-là** stand for **ici** *(here)* and **là** *(there).*

## ACTIVITÉ 6   Combien?

Imagine that you are shopping in a French department store and are
interested in buying the following objects. Ask the prices.

→  le maillot de bain      **Combien coûte ce maillot de bain?**  VARIATION: Another student provides a price.

1. les chaussures
2. le tee-shirt
3. la cassette
4. les sandales
5. le short

6. les lunettes de soleil
7. la guitare
8. l'anorak  cet
9. l'appareil-photo  cet
10. l'électrophone  cet

## ACTIVITÉ 7   Différences d'opinion

Whenever they go shopping together, Paul and Brigitte cannot agree on
what they like. Play both roles according to the model.

→  un short      Paul: **J'aime ce short-ci.**
                 Brigitte: **Eh bien, moi, j'aime ce short-là.**

1. une chemise *(shirt)*
2. un pantalon
3. des chaussures
4. des sandales

5. une cassette
6. des disques
7. une bicyclette
8. un anorak

## Vocabulaire spécialisé  Quand?

un matin:  ce matin          demain matin

un soir:  ce soir           demain soir

un après-midi:  cet après-midi   demain après-midi

une nuit *(night):*  cette nuit

ce week-end, cette semaine, ce mois-ci, cette année
cet été, cet automne, cet hiver, ce printemps

**ACTIVITÉ 8**  **Projets** *(Plans)*  OPTIONAL     This activity may be assigned as written homework.

Describe your plans — real or imaginary — by completing the sentences below.

1. Demain matin, je vais...
2. Demain après-midi, je vais...
3. Ce soir, je vais...
4. Ce week-end, je vais...
5. Ce mois-ci, je vais...
6. Cet hiver, je vais...
7. Cet été, je vais...
8. Cette année, je vais...

**UN JEU**  OPTIONAL

When you see what people are wearing, you can often tell what they are going to do. How many different logical sentences can you make in five minutes? Follow the models below:

| A | B | C |
|---|---|---|
| André | un maillot de bain | nager |
| Françoise | des lunettes de soleil | skier |
| Sylvie | un short | aller à la plage |
| Henri | des chaussettes blanches | aller à un concert |
| Michèle | des chaussures de ski *(ski boots)* | jouer au tennis |
| | un anorak | jouer au football |
| | un pantalon très chic | aller à la campagne |
| | des chaussures noires | |
| | des bottes | |

→ **Sylvie porte un short. Elle va jouer au football.**

→ **Françoise porte un anorak. Elle va skier.**

# Prononciation

ct. 11

**Les sons /ə/ et /ɛ/**

| Contrast: /ə/ | ce | de | je | le | ne | que | acheter |
|---|---|---|---|---|---|---|---|
| /ɛ/ | cette | Odette | Germaine | Colette | Ginette | quelle | achète |

The letter **e** at the end of a one-syllable word or when followed by a single consonant is pronounced with the lips slightly rounded: /ə/.
In the middle of a word the sound /ə/ is often dropped. Practice the following words:

Mad~e~moiselle  maint~e~nant  nous ach~e~tons  vous ach~e~tez

Remember that the letter **e** with a grave accent or followed by two consonants is pronounced /ɛ/.

It is important that students distinguish between the two pronunciations of the **acheter** stem.

/ə/ ach~e~ter  ach~e~tons  ach~e~tez
/ɛ/ achète  achètes  achètent

# Entre nous

### Expression pour la conversation

To correct someone, you can say:

**Voyons!**  *Come on! Come now!*

—Qui est cette fille? C'est Monique?
—Mais non, **voyons!** C'est Colette.

### Mini-dialogue  OPTIONAL

François has trouble identifying people in an old photograph.

FRANÇOIS: Qui est ce monsieur?
MME RÉMI: Quel monsieur? Ah, ce monsieur-ci?
C'est Papa, voyons!
FRANÇOIS: Et ce monsieur-là avec ces moustaches?
MME RÉMI: Mais c'est l'oncle Alain.
FRANÇOIS: Et cet horrible petit garçon avec ce
pantalon *ridicule*?  *ridiculous*
MME RÉMI: Ce petit garçon-là? Voyons, François.
C'est toi!

### L'art du dialogue

a) Act out the dialog between François and his mother.
b) Imagine and act out a similar dialog between **Colette** and her mother. Change **garçon** to **fille**.

WB        SCRIPT      MASTERS   QUIZ
Projets               p. 25     pp. 52–53

Act. 10

STRUCTURES TO OBSERVE
• the comparative construction
• the irregular adjectives **beau** and **nouveau**

# UNITÉ 4
# Leçon 3  Comment acheter une robe

Act. 1

Aujourd'hui Madame Simonet et sa fille Brigitte regardent
les *nouveaux manteaux* et les nouvelles *robes*.

*new coats; dresses*

| | |
|---|---|
| BRIGITTE: | Oh, la belle robe! | |
| MME SIMONET: | C'est vrai, elle est assez jolie! Combien est-ce qu'elle coûte? | |
| BRIGITTE: | Quatre cents francs! | |
| MME SIMONET: | Dans ce *cas*, je préfère cette robe-là. | *case* |
| BRIGITTE: | Mais Maman, elle est moins jolie que *l'autre*. | *the other one* |
| MME SIMONET: | Elle est peut-être moins jolie, mais elle est moins chère . . . et elle est *plus longue!* | *longer* |
| BRIGITTE: | Voyons, Maman! Les robes sont *courtes* cette année! | *short* |
| MME SIMONET: | Eh bien, moi, je n'aime pas la *mode* des robes courtes! | *fashion* |

Brigitte n'insiste pas.

Elle pense: «Demain je vais *revenir* avec Papa. Il est moins
conservateur que Maman . . . et il est plus généreux!»

*to come back*

Avec qui est-ce que Brigitte va dans les magasins? Combien coûte la robe? Est-ce que Brigitte est
d'accord avec sa mère? Pourquoi pas? Avec qui est-ce que Brigitte va revenir? Pourquoi?

Let's make some comparisons.

Comment s'appelle votre meilleur ami?

1. Êtes-vous **plus grand (grande) que** cet ami?
2. Êtes-vous **plus généreux (généreuse) que** lui?
3. Êtes-vous **plus drôle que** lui?

**OBSERVATIONS**    Str. B    OPTIONAL

In the above questions you are asked to *compare yourself* to your best friend.

• How do you say *taller than* in French?    plus grand(e) que
  How do you say *more generous than?*    plus généreux (généreuse) que
• In all the above comparisons, which word comes *before* the adjective?    plus
  Which word comes *after* the adjective?    que

In questions 2 and 3 **cet ami** has been replaced by a pronoun.

• Is this pronoun a *subject* pronoun or a *stress* pronoun?    stress

SUGGESTED REALIA: ads for clothes, mail-order catalogues.

## NOTE CULTURELLE    OPTIONAL

**L'achat des vêtements** *(Buying clothes)*

Do you buy your own clothes? For a French teenager, shopping for clothes may be a problem . . . especially when mother comes along. In general, French young people do not receive enough allowance to buy their own clothes. Since clothes are fairly expensive, they have to rely on their parents' generosity, and also on their tastes, which may not be the same as their own.

---

## Vocabulaire pratique

| | | |
|---|---|---|
| ADJECTIFS: | **conservateur (conservatrice)** | *conservative* |
| | **généreux (généreuse)** | *generous* |
| EXPRESSIONS: | **plus ≠ moins** | *more ≠ less* |

---

# Vocabulaire spécialisé   La mode

(nouns only)

un chapeau

un chemisier

une cravate

une chemise

un costume

un manteau

une jupe

une veste

des bas

un pantalon

une robe

le style
  **élégant**                                    *elegant*
  **court ≠ long (longue)**                       *short ≠ long*
  **nouveau (nouvelle) ≠ vieux (vieille)**        *new ≠ old*

la mode   *fashion*
  **être à la mode**    *to be in fashion*        Cette robe n'**est** pas **à la mode!**
                        *to be fashionable*        Brigitte **est** toujours **à la mode.**

Note:  Words which end in **-eau** form their plural in **-eaux.**
  **un chapeau   des chapeaux        un manteau   des manteaux**

VOCABULARY EXPANSION: **un bonnet** *(wool hat),* **une casquette** *(cap),* **des gants** *(gloves),* **un foulard** *(scarf),* **un mouchoir** *(handkerchief),* **un imperméable** *(raincoat),* **des collants** *(tights),* **une ceinture** *(belt)*
**les accessoires: une bague** *(ring),* **un collier** *(necklace),* **une boucle d'oreille** *(earring)*

## *ACTIVITÉ 1*   Questions personnelles

1. Qu'est-ce que vous portez aujourd'hui?
2. Qu'est-ce que vous portez quand vous allez à un concert?
3. Qu'est-ce que vous portez quand vous allez à une surprise-partie?
4. Qu'est-ce que le professeur porte aujourd'hui? et l'élève à côté de *(next to)* vous?

# Structure

## A. Les adjectifs *vieux, nouveau* et *beau*

Note the position and forms of the irregular adjectives **vieux** *(old)*, **nouveau** *(new)*, and **beau** *(beautiful, good-looking)*.

.ct. 4

|  | BEFORE A CONSONANT SOUND | BEFORE A VOWEL SOUND |
|---|---|---|
| *Masculine Singular* | un **vieux** manteau<br>un **nouveau** manteau<br>un **beau** manteau | un **vieil** /j/ anorak<br>un **nouvel** anorak<br>un **bel** anorak |
| *Feminine Singular* | une **vieille** robe<br>une **nouvelle** robe<br>une **belle** robe | une **vieille** auto<br>une **nouvelle** auto<br>une **belle** auto |
| *Masculine Plural* | des **vieux** manteaux<br>des **nouveaux** manteaux<br>des **beaux** manteaux | des **vieux** /z/ anoraks<br>des **nouveaux** /z/ anoraks<br>des **beaux** /z/ anoraks |
| *Feminine Plural* | des **vieilles** robes<br>des **nouvelles** robes<br>des **belles** robes | des **vieilles** /z/ autos<br>des **nouvelles** /z/ autos<br>des **belles** /z/ autos |

The adjectives **vieux, nouveau,** and **beau** usually come before the noun. When this occurs, there is liaison between the adjective and the noun if the noun begins with a vowel sound.

Remind students of other adjectives that come before the noun: **grand, petit, bon, mauvais, joli.**

## ACTIVITÉ 2  Les soldes de printemps *(Spring sales)*

The following people are taking advantage of the big spring sale at "Au Bon Marché" to replace their old things with new ones. Express this according to the model.

→ Jacqueline (une jupe)  **Jacqueline a une vieille jupe.**  VARIATION: **Jacqueline trouve une belle jupe.**
 **Elle achète une nouvelle jupe.**

1. Henri (un costume)
2. Brigitte (un manteau)
3. Paul (une cravate)
4. Sylvie (des bas)
5. Michèle (un chemisier)

6. Philippe (des chemises)
7. Jean-Claude (un chapeau)
8. Georges (un anorak)  vieil/nouvel
9. Catherine (un électrophone)  vieil/nouvel
10. Vincent (un appareil-photo)  vieil/nouvel

In formal French, **des** becomes **de** when the adjective precedes the noun. This form is not presented at this level: **des manteaux rouges/de beaux manteaux.**

## ACTIVITÉ 3   Différences d'opinion

Paul shows Sylvie the new things he bought. Sylvie says she likes the old ones better. (Note: **mieux** means *better.*)

➡ un maillot de bain

Paul: **Regarde mon nouveau maillot de bain.
Il est beau, n'est-ce pas?**
Sylvie: **Moi, j'aime mieux ton vieux maillot de bain.**

| | | |
|---|---|---|
| 1. une veste | 4. une cravate | 7. des tee-shirts |
| 2. un pantalon | 5. un anorak | 8. des chaussures |
| 3. une chemise | 6. un short | 9. des lunettes de soleil |

## B. La comparaison avec les adjectifs

Note how *comparisons* are expressed in French.

Act. 5

| | |
|---|---|
| Cette robe est **plus élégante que** ce manteau. | *more elegant than* |
| Ce pull est **plus joli que** cette chemise. | *prettier than* |
| Paul est **moins intelligent que** Richard. | *less intelligent than* |
| Il est **moins amusant que** lui. | *less amusing than* |
| Je suis **aussi sympathique que** mes amis. | *as nice as* |
| Je ne suis **pas aussi riche qu'**eux. | *(not) as rich as* |

To make comparisons, French speakers use the following constructions:

| $\left.\begin{array}{l} more \dots than \\ \dots \text{-}er \, than \end{array}\right\}$ (+) **plus** | (if expressed) |
|---|---|
| $\begin{array}{ll} less \dots than & (-) \textbf{ moins} \\ as \dots as & (=) \textbf{ aussi} \end{array}$ $\Big\} + $ adjective | $+$ **que** $+$ $\left\{\begin{array}{l} \text{noun} \\ \text{stress pronoun} \end{array}\right.$ <br> **qu'** $+$ (a vowel sound) |

➡ There is liaison after **plus** and **moins** when the next word begins with a vowel sound.

➡ In comparisons the adjective always agrees with the noun or pronoun it modifies.

**Le chemisier** est plus **cher** que la jupe.

**Les vestes** sont moins **chères** que les manteaux.

➡ After **que**, *stress pronouns* must be used.

Note the following irregular comparative form:

> The comparative of **bon (bonne)** is **meilleur (meilleure)**.

Brigitte est **meilleure** en tennis que Paul.

*but:* En classe, elle est **moins bonne** en anglais que lui.

The irregular comparative **pire** is not taught, since this form is used less and less frequently.

## ACTIVITÉ 4  Comparaisons

How much do you think the following items cost? Give your opinion, saying whether you think the first one is more expensive, less expensive, or as expensive as the second one. VARIATION: Have students use additional expressions of their choice. **Une très bonne guitare est plus chère qu'une raquette de ping-pong.**

→ une guitare / une raquette  **Une guitare est plus (moins, aussi) chère qu'une raquette.**

1. un vélo / une auto
2. un transistor / une caméra
3. un électrophone / un appareil-photo
4. un anorak / un manteau
5. une veste / un pantalon

6. un costume / une robe
7. un blue-jeans / un maillot de bain
8. des chaussettes / des bas
9. une voiture / une maison
10. des bottes / des sandales

## ACTIVITÉ 5  Expression personnelle

*This activity uses the definite article in the general sense. This use will be presented in more detail in Unité 5.1.*

Compare the following by using the adjectives suggested. Give your personal opinion.

→ les hommes (généreux) les femmes
**Les hommes sont plus (moins, aussi) généreux que les femmes.**

1. le tennis (intéressant) le ping-pong
2. le français (difficile) l'espagnol
3. le livre de français (bon) le livre de maths
4. la classe de musique (amusante) la classe d'anglais
5. New York (beau) Chicago
6. la Floride (belle) le Texas
7. la Nouvelle Angleterre (jolie) la Californie
8. les Français (intelligents) les Américains
9. les Françaises (élégantes) les Américaines
10. les garçons (sympathiques) les filles

VARIATION: Begin sentences with **Je pense que**...

## ACTIVITÉ 6  Questions personnelles

Use the appropriate stress pronouns in answering the questions below.

→ Êtes-vous plus grand(e) que votre meilleur ami?
**Oui, je suis plus grand(e) que lui.**
**Non, je suis moins grand(e) que lui.**
**Je suis aussi grand(e) que lui.**

1. Êtes-vous plus grand(e) que votre meilleure amie?
2. Êtes-vous plus riche que votre frère (si vous avez un frère)?
3. Êtes-vous plus riche que votre sœur (si vous avez une sœur)?
4. Êtes-vous plus généreux (généreuse) que vos amis?
5. Êtes-vous plus conservateur (conservatrice) que vos parents?
6. Êtes-vous meilleur(e) en français que vos camarades?
7. Êtes-vous meilleur(e) en maths que vos camarades?
8. Êtes-vous meilleur(e) en sport que vos amis?

In items 6–8, note the forms **moins/aussi bon(ne) que.**

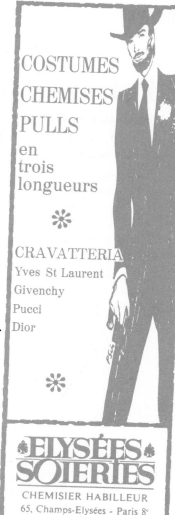

COSTUMES
CHEMISES
PULLS
en
trois
longueurs

✳

CRAVATTERIA
Yves St Laurent
Givenchy
Pucci
Dior

✳

♣ELYSÉES♣
SOIERIES
CHEMISIER HABILLEUR
65, Champs-Elysées - Paris 8ᵉ

B
1, B2

CRIPT

ct. 6, 7

ASTERS
27

*UN JEU*  OPTIONAL

If Pierre is taller than Nathalie, then she is shorter than he is. Make as many sets of logical sentences as you can in five minutes. Use the appropriate stress pronouns as in the models below.

| A | B | C | D |
|---|---|---|---|
| je | grand | Robert | mauvais |
| tu | riche | Jacqueline | bête |
| Alain | libéral (libéraux) | mes cousins | conservateur |
| Hélène | intelligent | mes amies | pauvre |
| mes amis | amusant | Nathalie | petit |
| mes cousines | bon en sport | | pénible |
| Pierre | bon en anglais | | |

→ **Je suis plus libéral que mes amies. Elles sont plus conservatrices que moi.**

→ **Tu es meilleur en anglais que mes cousins. Ils sont plus mauvais que toi.**

# Prononciation

Act. 9

### Révision: la liaison

There is liaison between a word introducing a noun and the noun, if it begins with a vowel sound.

| **les, des, ces** | les_élèves, des_écoles, ces_églises, les_Anglais, ces_Américains |
| **mes, tes, ses** | mes_amis, tes_amies, ses_enfants, ses_élèves |
| **nos, vos** | nos_amis, nos_amies, vos_élèves, vos_enfants |
| **leurs** | leurs_élèves, leurs_écoles, leurs_oncles, leurs_enfants |

There is liaison between an adjective that comes before a noun and the noun, if the noun begins with a vowel sound.

| **bon, mauvais** | un bon_ami, un mauvais_élève, les meilleurs_amis |
| **vieux, nouveau** | nos vieux_amis, les nouveaux_appareils-photo, les nouvelles_élèves |
| **beau, joli** | les beaux_anoraks, les jolis_enfants, les belles_autos |
| **grand, petit** | un grand_électrophone, un petit_anorak, les grandes_autos |

There is liaison between **plus** and **moins** and the adjective which follows, if it begins with a vowel sound.

| **plus** | plus_intéressant, plus_intelligent, plus_amusant, plus_indépendant |
| **moins** | moins_intéressant, moins_intelligent, moins_amusant, moins_indépendant |

# Entre nous

## Expression pour la conversation

To express their agreement with a question, French speakers often use the following expression:

**évidemment** *of course*
/evidamã/

—Vous parlez français en classe?
— **Évidemment!**

## Mini-dialogue OPTIONAL

Paul, Marc et Brigitte regardent le nouveau vélo de Guillaume.

PAUL: Regardez le nouveau vélo de Guillaume!

BRIGITTE: Il est beau!

MARC: Eh bien, moi, j'aime *mieux* son vieux vélo.          *better*

PAUL: Mais il n'est pas aussi joli!

BRIGITTE: Et il est moins *rapide!*          *fast*

MARC: Évidemment! Mais Guillaume est plus généreux
avec ses vieilles *affaires* qu'avec ses *nouvelles.*          *things; new ones*

PAUL: C'est vrai!

## L'art du dialogue

a) Act out the dialog between Paul, Marc, and Brigitte.
b) Now imagine that Guillaume has just bought a new motorcycle (**une nouvelle moto**). Act out the new dialog, making the necessary changes.

SCRIPT          MASTERS          QUIZ
Act. 8          p. 27          p. 54

# Leçon 4 Un gourmand

STRUCTURES TO OBSERVE
• expressions with **avoir**
• the superlative construction

Act. 1

### Scène 1. Dans la rue

Paul et Brigitte sont en ville. Il fait chaud aujourd'hui.

BRIGITTE: *J'ai chaud* et je suis fatiguée.  
    PAUL: Et moi, *j'ai faim.*  
BRIGITTE: Tu as très faim?  
    PAUL: Oh, oui!  
BRIGITTE: Bon. Allons dans une pâtisserie.  
    PAUL: *Qui est-ce qui paie?*  
BRIGITTE: Aujourd'hui, c'est moi.  
    PAUL: Brigitte, tu es une fille formidable . . . et tu as des idées sensationnelles!  
BRIGITTE: Comme toujours?  
    PAUL: Oui, comme toujours.

*I'm hot*  
*I'm hungry*

*Who's paying?*  
**Où sont Paul et Brigitte?**  
**Où vont-ils? Pourquoi?**  
**Qui va payer?**

### Scène 2. À la pâtisserie

Paul regarde les pâtisseries avec *envie*. Il y a des gâteaux, des tartes, des éclairs, des *croissants* . . .

    PAUL: Alors, Brigitte, quel gâteau choisis-tu?  
BRIGITTE: Le plus petit!  
    PAUL: Pourquoi le plus petit?  
BRIGITTE: Parce que je *n'ai pas envie* d'être malade!  
    PAUL: Eh bien, moi, je choisis *le plus gros!*  
BRIGITTE: *Comment* le plus gros?  
    PAUL: Écoute, Brigitte! Moi, je n'ai pas de problème avec mon appétit.  
BRIGITTE: Oui, mon cher Paul. Mais tu vas avoir un gros problème avec ta *silhouette!*

*desire*  
*crescent rolls*

*don't want*  
*the biggest*  
*How come*

*figure*

**Quel gâteau est-ce que Brigitte choisit? Pourquoi? Quel gâteau est-ce que Paul choisit?**

## CONVERSATION OPTIONAL

In the questions below you will be asked who in your family is *the youngest,*
*the tallest, the funniest,* and *the most generous.*

1. Qui est la personne **la plus** jeune de votre famille?
2. Qui est la personne **la plus** grande?
3. Qui est la personne **la plus** drôle?
4. Qui est la personne **la plus** généreuse?

## OBSERVATIONS   Str. C   OPTIONAL

In the above questions you are comparing one person to the
others in a group (your family).

• Which words come before the adjective?  la plus
• Is an article used before the adjective?  yes
• Is this article the same as the one which introduces the noun?
  yes

## NOTE CULTURELLE   OPTIONAL

### Les croissants et la cuisine française

Have you ever eaten a **croissant** or an **éclair? Croissants**
are delicious pastries, shaped like crescents, which the
French order with coffee when they go out for breakfast. **Éclairs** are long cream puffs with vanilla filling and
chocolate frosting. The French are famous for their cuisine,
which many people consider the best in the world. It is
therefore not surprising that the English language has borrowed many words from the French to designate food. Do you
know the following: **hors-d'oeuvre, filet mignon, mousse,
crêpe, bouillon, soufflé, omelette?**

SUGGESTED REALIA: bilingual French-English menu.

instructions

1° mettez les pièces
demandées
- attendez la chute

## Vocabulaire pratique

| | | | |
|---|---|---|---|
| NOMS: | **un gâteau** *(pl.* **gâteaux)** | *cake* | **une idée**    *idea* |
| | **un problème** | *problem* | **une pâtisserie**    *pastry; pastry shop* |
| ADJECTIFS: | **cher (chère)** | *dear* | |
| | **fatigué** | *tired* | |
| | **gros (grosse)** ≠ **mince** | *fat* ≠ *slim, slender, thin* | |
| VERBE: | **payer**    *to pay, pay for* | Est-ce que tu **paies** les pâtisseries? | |
| EXPRESSION: | **comme**    *like, as* | Mais oui, **comme** toujours! | |

Note: Verbs which end in **-yer,** like **payer,** have the following stem change:
     **y → i**  in the **je, tu, il,** and **ils** forms: **je paie**  *but:* **nous payons**

You may want to present the complete conjugation of **payer.**
Another verb conjugated like **payer** is **envoyer** *(to send).*

# Structure

## A. Expressions avec *avoir*

Note the use of **avoir** in the following sentences:

Before teaching these expressions, you may want to review the forms of avoir: **Quel âge avez-vous? Paul, quel âge a Betty?**

|  |  |
|---|---|
| Paul **a faim**. | *Paul is hungry.* |
| Brigitte **a chaud**. | *Brigitte is hot.* |

French speakers use **avoir** in many expressions where English speakers use the verb *to be*.

SCRIPT
Act. 2

## Vocabulaire spécialisé  Expressions avec *avoir*

| | | |
|---|---|---|
| **avoir chaud** | *to be (feel) warm* | Quand j'**ai chaud** en été, je vais à la plage. |
| **avoir froid** | *to be (feel) cold* | **As-tu froid** maintenant? Voici ton pull. |
| **avoir faim** | *to be hungry* | Il est midi. Nous **avons faim**. |
| **avoir soif** | *to be thirsty* | Mes amis vont au café quand ils **ont soif**. |
| **avoir raison** | *to be right* | Est-ce que vous **avez** toujours **raison**? |
| **avoir tort** | *to be wrong* | Paul n'étudie pas. Il **a tort**! |
| **avoir de la chance** | *to be lucky* | J'**ai de la chance**. J'ai des parents généreux. |

You may want to review **il fait froid/chaud,** and contrast these expressions with **avoir froid/chaud.**

## ACTIVITÉ 1   L'examen de géographie

Imagine you are teaching geography in France. Listen to the following statements made by your students and tell them if they are *right* or *wrong*.

→ New York est la capitale des États-Unis.   **Vous avez tort.**

1. Washington est la capitale des États-Unis.
2. Ottawa est la capitale du Canada.
3. La Nouvelle-Orléans est une ville de Louisiane.
4. Québec est une ville en France.
5. En Floride, il fait chaud.
6. En Alaska, il fait froid en hiver.
7. À Chicago, il fait chaud en hiver.
8. Les Mexicains parlent espagnol.

## ACTIVITÉ 2   Pourquoi?

Explain why the people mentioned below are doing what they are doing. Complete each sentence with **parce que** and the appropriate form of one of the following expressions: **avoir faim, avoir soif, avoir chaud, avoir froid.**

WB
A1, A2
SCRIPT
Act. 3, 4
MASTERS
p. 28

→ Georges achète un gâteau . . .   **Georges achète un gâteau parce qu'il a faim.**

1. Nous achetons un Coca-Cola . . .
2. Tu achètes un manteau . . .
3. Jacqueline va à la piscine . . .
4. Mes amis achètent des sandwichs . . .
5. Philippe va au café . . .
6. J'achète une pizza . . .
7. Vous nagez . . .
8. Mes cousins achètent un Pepsi . . .

## B. Les expressions *avoir envie de, avoir besoin de*

Note how the expressions **avoir envie de** *(to want, feel like)* and **avoir besoin de** *(to need)* are used in the sentences below.

**avoir envie de**

| | | |
|---|---|---|
| + noun | J'ai envie d'une pizza. | *I want (feel like having) a pizza.* |
| + infinitive | J'ai envie de nager. | *I want to swim (feel like swimming).* |

**avoir besoin de**

| | | |
|---|---|---|
| + noun | J'ai besoin de 5 dollars. | *I need 5 dollars.* |
| + infinitive | J'ai besoin d'étudier. | *I need to study.* |

→ Note the interrogative and negative constructions with these expressions:

**Est-ce que vous avez envie de** travailler?     **Est-ce que vous avez besoin d'**argent?
Nous **n'avons pas envie de** travailler.     Nous **n'avons pas besoin d'**argent.

## *ACTIVITÉ 3*   Dialogue

Ask your classmates if they feel like doing the following things.

→ voyager       Élève 1: **Est-ce que tu as envie de voyager?**
                Élève 2: **Oui, j'ai envie de voyager.**
                        **(Non, je n'ai pas envie de voyager.)**

1. visiter Paris
2. visiter Québec
3. travailler en France
4. aller au cinéma ce soir
5. aller à la piscine aujourd'hui
6. étudier cet après-midi
7. parler français
8. acheter une voiture de sport

votre machine
a besoin
de calgon !

VARIATION with the plural: **–Avez-vous envie de voyager?**
                        **–Oui, nous avons envie de voyager.**

## *ACTIVITÉ 4*   Combien?   OPTIONAL

The following students are shopping for certain things. Say how much money you think each one needs.   Elicit several responses with different prices.

→ Hélène achète un blue-jeans.   **Elle a besoin de dix-sept (quinze, vingt) dollars.**

1. Sylvie achète des chaussures.
2. Paul achète un gâteau.
3. Nous achetons un album de timbres.
4. Vous achetez un maillot de bain.
5. J'achète un anorak.
6. Tu achètes un pantalon.
7. Jacqueline achète une raquette.
8. Mon cousin achète une veste.

VARIATION: The people are in France. Give approximate prices in francs: $1 ≅ 7 francs.

## *ACTIVITÉ 5*   Questions personnelles

1. Maintenant avez-vous chaud? Avez-vous froid?
2. Maintenant avez vous faim? Avez-vous soif?
3. En général, avez-vous de la chance?
4. En général, avez-vous besoin d'argent?
5. Avez-vous besoin d'amis?
6. Avez-vous besoin de compliments?
7. Avez-vous besoin d'étudier beaucoup?
8. Avez-vous envie d'être professeur?
9. Avez-vous envie de voyager?

WB
B1
SCRIPT
Act. 5, 7
MASTERS
p. 28

## C. Le superlatif

To compare somebody or something to a larger group, the *superlative construction* is used. Note this construction in the following sentences:

Paul est le garçon **le plus intelligent** de la classe.   *the most intelligent boy in the class*
Louise est la fille **la moins dynamique.**   *the least energetic girl*

Où est le restaurant **le plus cher** de la ville?   *the most expensive restaurant in town*
Où sont les magasins **les moins chers?**   *the least expensive stores*

In French the superlative is expressed as follows:

| the most / the least | le, la, les + | plus / moins | + adjective | (if expressed) + de + name of reference group |
| --- | --- | --- | --- | --- |

The position of the superlative adjective is the same as that of the simple adjective. **Paul est le plus jeune garçon de la famille.**

→ There is liaison after **plus** and **moins** before a vowel sound.

→ The superlative form of **bon (bonne)** is **le meilleur (la meilleure).**

En français, Jeanne est **la meilleure** élève de la classe.
En anglais, Paul est **le meilleur.**

### ACTIVITÉ 6   À Montréal

Paul and Brigitte are visiting Montréal. Paul wants to go to the most expensive places, and Brigitte to the least expensive. Play both roles.

→ le café       Paul: **Où est le café le plus cher?**
                Brigitte: **Où est le café le moins cher?**

1. le restaurant
2. les magasins   Où sont
3. la boutique
4. l'hôtel
5. le cinéma
6. la cafétéria

VARIATION: **Où est le meilleur café?**

### ACTIVITÉ 7   Un sondage *(An opinion poll)*      OPTIONAL

Name the best person, place, or thing in each category. Follow the model.

→ le comédien: drôle     **Le comédien le plus drôle est (Woody Allen).**

1. la comédienne: amusante
2. l'acteur: beau
3. l'actrice *(actress)*: intelligente
4. les musiciens: bons
5. le programme de télé: drôle
6. l'équipe *(team)* de football: bonne
7. la voiture: confortable
8. la voiture: bonne
9. la ville: belle
10. la couleur: jolie

As a class activity, you may want to tabulate the results of the students' votes, and perhaps compare them with other French classes.

In order to do certain things we need other things. Express this in logical sentences, using elements from columns A, B, and C. How many different sentences can you make in five minutes? Be sure to use the expressions **avoir envie de** and **avoir besoin de,** as in the models below.

| A | B | | C | |
|---|---|---|---|---|
| je | écouter le concert | danser | un dollar | une voiture |
| tu | acheter un vélo | nager | cinq dollars | un maillot de bain |
| Pierre | aller à la campagne | skier | cent dollars | un transistor |
| nous | acheter un sandwich | voyager | un passeport | un électrophone |
| vous | acheter un disque | | un anorak | un ballon *(ball)* |
| mes amis | jouer au volley | | | |

→ **Nous avons envie d'acheter un disque. Nous avons besoin de cinq dollars.**
→ **Pierre a envie de voyager. Il a besoin d'un passeport.**

# Prononciation

Act. 9

## Le son /j/

*Model word:* p̲iano
*Practice words:* P̲ierre, v̲iolon, étud̲ier, janv̲ier, fi̲lle, fami̲lle, trava̲iller
*Practice sentences:*   Dan̲iel est canad̲ien. Il joue du p̲iano.
Cette fi̲lle ital̲ienne trava̲ille en janv̲ier.

The French sound /j/ is similar to the *y*-sound in the word *yes*. It is very short and tense.
Comment écrire /j/: **i**+vowel; **ll**; **ill**

# Entre nous

## Expression pour la conversation

To show that you heard what someone has said,
but do not want to answer, you can say:

**Hm!**

### Mini-dialogue   OPTIONAL

Pourquoi *est-ce que Pierre flatte* Nathalie?                           *is Pierre flattering*

PIERRE:   Tu es la fille la plus sympathique de la classe.
NATHALIE:   Hm!
PIERRE:   Tu es aussi la fille la plus jolie ...
NATHALIE:   Hm, Hm!
PIERRE:   Et la plus généreuse! Tiens, *prête-moi* dix francs!          *lend me*
NATHALIE:   Alors, là, mon cher Pierre, tu as tort! Je suis la fille la moins généreuse
... et toi, tu es le garçon le plus *innocent!* Au revoir, Pierre!      *naive*

### L'art du dialogue

a)  Act out the dialog between Pierre and Nathalie.
b)  Imagine that the roles are reversed. **Nathalie** is flattering **Pierre.** Act out the new dialog.

STRUCTURES TO OBSERVE
• verbs in -**re** (**vendre**)
• the impersonal pronoun **on**

# UNITÉ 4
# Leçon 5    Ici, on n'est pas en Amérique.

Act. 1

Jim passe l'été en France chez ses amis Brigitte et Philippe.
Est-ce qu'il aime sa nouvelle existence? Oui, bien sûr! Mais
*de temps en temps*, il a un petit problème d'adaptation.
Aujourd'hui, *par exemple* . . .

*from time to time*

*for instance*

BRIGITTE: Où vas-tu, Jim?

JIM: Je vais à la pharmacie.

PHILIPPE: À la pharmacie? Tu es malade?

JIM: Mais non, je ne suis pas malade! Je vais acheter le
journal et des bonbons!

BRIGITTE: Voyons, Jim! *On ne vend pas* le journal à la
pharmacie!

PHILIPPE: Et on ne vend pas de bonbons *non plus!*

BRIGITTE: En France, *on* achète le journal *chez le marchand
de journaux.*

PHILIPPE: Et on achète les bonbons *chez l'épicier!*

JIM: Mais en Amérique, on . . .

BRIGITTE: Écoute Jim! Ici, *on* n'est pas en Amérique!

JIM: Oh là là! *La vie* est compliquée!

*One doesn't sell*

*neither*
*people; at the
    newsstand*
*at the grocer's*

*you*
*Life*

## CONVERSATION

Let's talk about the kinds of things *one* can buy in an American drugstore.

1. Est-ce qu'**on achète** le journal à la pharmacie?
   Oui, **on achète** . . . (Non, on n'achète pas . . .)
2. Est-ce qu'**on achète** des magazines?
3. Est-ce qu'**on achète** l'aspirine?
4. Est-ce qu'**on achète** les médicaments *(medicine)?*

## OBSERVATIONS    Str. B

on achète

• How do you say *one buys* in French? Which pronoun corresponds to *one?*    on

• Is this pronoun followed by a *singular* or *plural* verb?    singular

Où est-ce que Jim passe l'été? Où est-ce qu'il va? Pourquoi est-ce qu'il veut *(wants)* aller à la pharmacie?
Où est-ce qu'on achète le journal en France? Où est-ce qu'on achète les bonbons?

# NOTE CULTURELLE   OPTIONAL

## Le shopping et les petits commerçants
*(Shopping and shopkeepers)*

Where do you go to buy the newspaper? Probably to a newsstand or to the neighborhood drugstore. In France you would go to the newsstand **(chez le marchand de journaux)** or to the tobacco shop **(le bureau de tabac)** which, in addition to cigarettes, often carries magazines, newspapers, matches, and stamps. You would certainly not go to the pharmacy, which sells only medicine.

Shopping habits change from country to country. Thus, in France many people go to different stores to buy individual food items. Imagine, for instance, that you are shopping for today's meal. You would go to the butcher's **(chez le boucher)** for the meat, to the baker's **(chez le boulanger)** for the bread, to the grocer's **(chez l'épicier)** for the soft drinks, to the dairy **(chez le crémier)** for the milk, to the fruit stand **(chez le marchand de fruits)** for the fruits. Of course, if you had a car, you could also go to the supermarket **(le supermarché)** or to a huge shopping center (called **l'hypermarché**) and buy everything on your list there. Many people in France still prefer the friendly atmosphere of the small individual shops, and also the quality of their products. Thus, to have fresh bread, some people still go to the local baker three times a day: before breakfast, before lunch, and before dinner.

---

# Vocabulaire pratique

| | | |
|---|---|---|
| NOMS: | **des bonbons** | *candy* |
| | **un journal** (*pl.* **journaux**) | *newspaper* |
| ADJECTIFS: | **compliqué ≠ simple** | *complicated ≠ simple* |
| VERBE: | **passer** (+ time) | *to spend* (time) |

# Structure

## A. Les verbes réguliers en -re

Many French verbs end in **-re**. Most of these are conjugated like **vendre** *(to sell)*. Note the forms of this verb in the present tense, paying special attention to the endings.

Act. 2

| Infinitive | vendre | | STEM | ENDINGS |
|---|---|---|---|---|
| Present | je **vends** | ma raquette | | -s |
| | tu **vends** | tes disques | | -s |
| | il/elle **vend** | son violon | (infinitive minus -re) | — |
| | nous **vendons** | nos livres | vend- + | -ons |
| | vous **vendez** | vos cassettes | | -ez |
| | ils/elles **vendent** | leurs vélos | | -ent |

➜ The **d** of the stem is silent in the singular forms, but it is pronounced in the plural forms.

Act. 2

> ## Vocabulaire spécialisé  Verbes réguliers en -re
>
> | | | |
> |---|---|---|
> | **attendre** | *to wait, wait for* | Yvette **attend** Michèle au café. |
> | **entendre** | *to hear* | Est-ce que vous **entendez** la radio? |
> | **perdre** | *to lose, waste* | Je n'ai pas envie de **perdre** mon argent. |
> | **vendre** | *to sell* | **Vendez**-vous votre vélomoteur? |
>
> **Répondre**, another **-re** verb, is introduced on p. 287.

Be sure students understand that **attendre** means *to wait for*; **pour** is never used with **attendre**.

### ACTIVITÉ 1  Rendez-vous

The following people are waiting for their dates at a café. Express this, using the appropriate form of **attendre**.

➜ Jim (Michèle)    **Jim attend Michèle.**

1. nous (nos amis)
2. vous (vos cousines)
3. moi (Paul)
4. toi (Brigitte)
5. Louis et Éric (Claire et Sylvie)
6. les étudiants (les étudiantes)
7. Jacques et moi (Louise et Hélène)
8. Annette et toi (François)

WB
A1

SCRIPT

Act. 3

Jacques et moi, nous. . .
Annette et toi, vous. . .

## B. Le pronom *on*

The subject pronoun **on** is often used in French. Note its English equivalents in the sentences below.

| | |
|---|---|
| **On** achète l'aspirine à la pharmacie. | *One buys (**You** buy) aspirin at the drugstore.* |
| **On** vend des magazines au bureau de tabac. | *One sells (**They** sell) magazines at the tobacco shop.* |
| En France, **on** parle français. | *In France **people** (**you, they**) speak French.* |

The impersonal pronoun **on** does not refer to a specific person. It corresponds to the English pronouns *one*, *you* (in general), *they* (in general), or *people* (in general).

→ The pronoun **on** is always used with the **il/elle** form of the verb.

→ There is liaison after **on** when the next word begins with a vowel sound.

→ In conversation, **on** is often used instead of **nous:**

Est-ce qu'**on** regarde la télé ce soir?
*Are **we** watching TV tonight?*

Sometimes a construction with **on** is used in French where English would use the passive.
**On parle français ici.** *French is spoken here.*

On est bien dans la laine.
On est bien dans un pull Starcot.

### ACTIVITÉ 2   En hiver ou en été?

Do the following happen mainly in winter or in summer?

→ aller à la piscine     **On va à la piscine en été.**

1. nager
2. skier
3. jouer au tennis
4. jouer au football
5. aller à la plage
6. porter des lunettes de soleil
7. porter un manteau
8. organiser des pique-niques
9. être en vacances
10. avoir chaud
11. avoir froid
12. avoir la grippe *(the flu)*

### ACTIVITÉ 3   En France et en Amérique

French customs are sometimes different from American customs. First describe the French custom. Then describe the American custom, using the expression in parentheses. Use **on** in both sentences.

→ Les Français parlent français. (anglais)     **En France, on parle français.**
     **En Amérique, on parle anglais.**

1. Les Français jouent au football. (au baseball)
2. Les Français jouent au rugby. (au basketball)
3. Les Français ont des petites voitures. (des grandes voitures)
4. Les Français dînent à huit heures. (à six heures)
5. Les Français achètent les magazines au bureau de tabac *(tobacco shop)*.  (à la pharmacie)
6. Les Français ont un mois de vacances. (deux semaines)

# Vocabulaire spécialisé

**Les magasins et les commerçants**
*(Shops and shopkeepers)*

une pharmacie

une librairie

une pâtisserie

une épicerie

la libraire

le libraire

la pharmacienne
le pharmacien

la pâtissière
le pâtissier

l'épicière
l'épicier

un magasin de disques

un magasin de chaussures

un magasin de vêtements

le marchand de disques

la marchande de chaussures

le marchand de vêtements

Note: **Chez** is used with names of shopkeepers, whereas **à** is used with names of shops.
Contrast:

| | |
|---|---|
| Je vais **chez le pharmacien.** | *I am going to the pharmacist's.* |
| Je vais **à la pharmacie.** | *I am going to the pharmacy.* |

---

VOCABULARY EXPANSION: **boucherie: boucher/bouchère**
**boulangerie: boulanger/boulangère**
**charcuterie: charcutier/charcutière**

You may want to present these nouns with the corresponding foods on p. 229.

## ACTIVITÉ 4  Le shopping

Imagine that you are living in Paris, and an American friend is visiting you.
This friend wants to buy the following things. Tell him/her in whose shop
these items are sold according to the model. Use the nouns given in the
**Vocabulaire spécialisé.**

→  des disques       **On vend des disques chez le marchand de disques.**

1. des livres
2. des cassettes
3. des bonbons
4. des cachets *(tablets)* d'aspirine
5. des chemises
6. des journaux
7. des blue-jeans
8. des sandales
9. des tee-shirts
10. des gâteaux
11. des éclairs
12. des médicaments *(medicine)*

WB
V1
SCRIPT
Act. 8
MASTERS
p. 29

## C. Les prépositions avec les noms de pays     Review names of countries on p. 116.

Note the *prepositions* used with names of countries in the sentences below.

| | | |
|---|---|---|
| **le** Canada | Pierre habite **au** Canada. | Jacqueline va **au** Canada. |
| **la** France | Nous sommes **en** France. | Nous allons **en** France. |
| **les** États-Unis | Vous habitez **aux** États-Unis. | Quand vas-tu **aux** États-Unis? |

To express location *in* or movement *to* a country, French speakers use:

| | | |
|---|---|---|
| **au** | if the name of the country is *masculine singular* | **au** Canada |
| **en** | if the name of the country is *feminine singular* | **en** France |
| **aux** | if the name of the country is *plural* | **aux** États-Unis |

Have the students note the liaison: **aux**/z/**États-Unis.**

## ACTIVITÉ 5  Langues internationales *(International languages)*

Say which of the following languages is spoken in each of the countries
listed below.

**anglais  français  espagnol**

Remember: countries with names that end in **-e** are feminine.

WB
C1
SCRIPT
Act. 9

→  l'Angleterre       **En Angleterre, on parle anglais.**

| | | | |
|---|---|---|---|
| 1. l'Australie | 3. le Canada | 5. la France | 7. la Belgique |
| 2. le Pérou | 4. les États-Unis | 6. le Sénégal | 8. le Guatemala |

## UN JEU   OPTIONAL

What we wear often depends on what we are doing or how we feel. Express this in logical sentences similar to the models, using elements of columns A and B. How many different sentences can you make in five minutes?

| A | B |
|---|---|
| nager | un pull |
| skier | des vêtements élégants |
| jouer au tennis | un anorak |
| jouer au football américain | un maillot de bain |
| aller à la plage | un short |
| aller dans un restaurant élégant | des sandales |
| avoir froid | un casque *(helmet)* |
| avoir chaud | |

→ **Quand on a froid, on porte un pull.**

→ **Quand on joue au tennis, on porte un short.**

# Prononciation

Act. 11

### Voyelles nasales

When you say a nasal vowel followed by a consonant sound, be sure not to pronounce an /n /.

Practice the following words:

/ā/   ve<u>nd</u>, atte<u>nd</u>, e<u>nt</u>e<u>nd</u>

/ād/   ve<u>nd</u>ent, atte<u>nd</u>ent, e<u>nt</u>e<u>nd</u>ent

# Entre nous

## Expression pour la conversation

To ask someone how to say something, you use the expression:

**Comment dit-on . . .?**   *How do you say . . .?*   **Comment dit-on** « snack bar » en français?

## Mini-dialogue    OPTIONAL

Jim visite Paris avec son ami Philippe. Il *découvre* que le français n'est pas trop difficile.

       *discovers*

JIM: J'ai faim!

PHILIPPE: Moi aussi.

JIM: Alors, allons dans un . . . Dis, comment dit-on «snack bar» en français?

PHILIPPE: On dit «snack-bar».

JIM: Et comment dit-on «hot dog»?

PHILIPPE: On dit «hot-dog».
Le français est une *langue* très simple, n'est-ce pas?

       *language*

## L'art du dialogue

a) Act out the dialog between Jim and Philippe.

b) Imagine that the conversation is taking place in the United States, and the roles are reversed. Philippe wants to know how to say **restaurant** and **omelette** *(omelet)*. Replace **français** with **anglais**.

# APPENDICES

# Appendix 1 Sound-Spelling Correspondences

| SOUND | SPELLING | EXAMPLES |
|---|---|---|
| *Vowels* | | |
| /a/ | a, à, â | Madame, là-bas, théâtre |
| /i/ | i, î | visite, Nice, dîne |
| | y (initial, final, or between consonants) | Yves, Guy, style |
| /u/ | ou, où, oû | Toulouse, où, août |
| /y/ | u, û | tu, Luc, sûr |
| /o/ | o (final or before silent consonant) | piano, idiot, Margot |
| | au, eau | jaune, Claude, beau |
| | ô | hôtel, drôle, Côte-d'Ivoire |
| /ɔ/ | o | Monique, Noël, jolie |
| | au | Paul, restaurant, Laure |
| /e/ | é | Dédé, Québec, télé |
| | e (before silent final z, t, r) | chez, et, Roger |
| | ai (final or before final silent consonant) | j'ai, mai, japonais |
| /ɛ/ | è | Michèle, Ève, père |
| | ei | seize, neige, tour Eiffel |
| | ê | tête, être, Viêt-nam |
| | e (before two consonants) | elle, Pierre, Annette |
| | e (before pronounced final consonant) | Michel, avec, cher |
| | ai (before pronounced final consonant) | française, aime, Maine |
| /ə/ | e (final or before single consonant) | je, Denise, venir |
| /ø/ | eu, œu | deux, Mathieu, œufs |
| | eu (before final se) | nerveuse, généreuse, sérieuse |
| /œ/ | eu (before final pronounced consonant except /z/) | heure, neuf, Lesieur |
| | œu | sœur, cœur, œuf |
| | œ | œil |
| *Nasal vowels* | | |
| /ɑ̃/ | an, am | France, quand, lampe |
| | en, em | Henri, pendant, décembre |
| /ɔ̃/ | on, om | non, Simon, bombe |
| /ɛ̃/ | in, im | Martin, invite, impossible |
| | yn, ym | syndicat, sympathique, Olympique |
| | ain, aim | Alain, américain, faim |
| | (o) + in | loin, moins, point |
| | (i) + en | bien, Julien, viens |
| /œ̃/ | un, um | un, Lebrun, parfum |

| SOUND | SPELLING | EXAMPLES |
|---|---|---|

*Semi-vowels*

| /j/ | **i, y** (before vowel sound) | b<u>i</u>en, p<u>i</u>ano, L<u>y</u>on |
|  | **-il, -ill** (after vowel sound), **ll** | œ<u>il</u>, trava<u>ill</u>e, Marse<u>ill</u>e, fi<u>ll</u>e |
| /ɥ/ | **u** (before vowel sound) | l<u>u</u>i, S<u>u</u>isse, j<u>u</u>illet |
| /w/ | **ou** (before vowel sound) | <u>ou</u>i, L<u>ou</u>is, j<u>ou</u>er |
| /wa/ | **oi, oî** | v<u>oi</u>ci, Ben<u>oî</u>t |
|  | **oy** (before vowel) | v<u>oy</u>age |

*Consonants*

| /b/ | **b** | <u>B</u>arbara, <u>b</u>anane, <u>B</u>elgique |
|---|---|---|
| /k/ | **c** (before **a, o, u,** or consonant) | <u>C</u>oca-<u>C</u>ola, <u>c</u>uisine, <u>c</u>lasse |
|  | **ch**(r) | <u>Ch</u>ristine, <u>Ch</u>ristian, <u>Ch</u>ristophe |
|  | **qu, q** (final) | <u>Qu</u>ébec, <u>qu</u>'est-ce <u>qu</u>e, cin<u>q</u> |
|  | **k** | <u>k</u>ilo, <u>K</u>iki, <u>k</u>etchup |
| /ʃ/ | **ch** | <u>Ch</u>arles, blan<u>ch</u>e, <u>ch</u>ez |
| /d/ | **d** | <u>D</u>idier, <u>d</u>ans, mé<u>d</u>ecin |
| /f/ | **f** | <u>F</u>élix, <u>f</u>ranc, neu<u>f</u> |
|  | **ph** | <u>Ph</u>ilippe, télé<u>ph</u>one, <u>ph</u>oto |
| /g/ | **g** (before **a, o, u,** or consonant) | <u>G</u>abriel, <u>g</u>orge, lé<u>g</u>umes, <u>g</u>ris |
|  | **gu** (before **e, i, y**) | va<u>gu</u>e, <u>Gu</u>illaume, <u>Gu</u>y |
| /ɲ/ | **gn** | mi<u>gn</u>on, champa<u>gn</u>e, Allema<u>gn</u>e |
| /ʒ/ | **j** | <u>j</u>e, <u>J</u>érôme, <u>j</u>aune |
|  | **g** (before **e, i, y**) | rou<u>g</u>e, <u>G</u>i<u>g</u>i, <u>g</u>ymnastique |
|  | **ge** (before **a, o, u**) | oran<u>ge</u>ade, <u>G</u>eorges, na<u>ge</u>ur |
| /l/ | **l** | <u>L</u>ise, e<u>ll</u>e, cheva<u>l</u> |
| /m/ | **m** | <u>M</u>aman, <u>m</u>oi, to<u>m</u>ate |
| /n/ | **n** | ba<u>n</u>ane, <u>N</u>ancy, <u>n</u>ous |
| /p/ | **p** | <u>p</u>eu, <u>P</u>apa, <u>P</u>ierre |
| /r/ | **r** | a<u>rr</u>ive, <u>r</u>ent<u>r</u>e, Pa<u>r</u>is |
| /s/ | **c** (before **e, i, y**) | <u>c</u>e, <u>C</u>écile, Nan<u>c</u>y |
|  | **ç** (before **a, o, u**) | <u>ç</u>a, gar<u>ç</u>on, dé<u>ç</u>u |
|  | **s** (initial or before consonant) | <u>s</u>ac, <u>S</u>ophie, re<u>s</u>te |
|  | **ss** (between vowels) | boi<u>ss</u>on, de<u>ss</u>ert, Sui<u>ss</u>e |
|  | **t** (before **i** + vowel) | atten<u>t</u>ion, Na<u>t</u>ions Unies, nata<u>t</u>ion |
|  | **x** | di<u>x</u>, si<u>x</u>, soi<u>x</u>ante |
| /t/ | **t** | <u>t</u>rop, <u>t</u>élé, <u>T</u>ours |
|  | **th** | <u>Th</u>érèse, <u>th</u>é, Mar<u>th</u>e |
| /v/ | **v** | <u>V</u>iviane, <u>v</u>ous, nou<u>v</u>eau |
| /gz/ | **x** | e<u>x</u>amen, e<u>x</u>emple, e<u>x</u>act |
| /ks/ | **x** | Ma<u>x</u>, Me<u>x</u>ique, e<u>x</u>cellent |
| /z/ | **s** (between vowels) | dé<u>s</u>ert, Loui<u>s</u>e, télévi<u>s</u>ion |
|  | **z** | Su<u>z</u>anne, <u>z</u>ut, <u>z</u>éro |

# Appendix 2 Numbers

## A. Cardinal numbers

| | | | | | |
|---|---|---|---|---|---|
| 0 | zéro | 18 | dix-huit | 82 | quatre-vingt-deux |
| 1 | un (une) | 19 | dix-neuf | 90 | quatre-vingt-dix |
| 2 | deux | 20 | vingt | 91 | quatre-vingt-onze |
| 3 | trois | 21 | vingt et un (une) | 100 | cent |
| 4 | quatre | 22 | vingt-deux | 101 | cent un (une) |
| 5 | cinq | 23 | vingt-trois | 102 | cent deux |
| 6 | six | 30 | trente | 200 | deux cents |
| 7 | sept | 31 | trente et un (une) | 201 | deux cent un |
| 8 | huit | 32 | trente-deux | 300 | trois cents |
| 9 | neuf | 40 | quarante | 400 | quatre cents |
| 10 | dix | 41 | quarante et un (une) | 500 | cinq cents |
| 11 | onze | 50 | cinquante | 600 | six cents |
| 12 | douze | 60 | soixante | 700 | sept cents |
| 13 | treize | 70 | soixante-dix | 800 | huit cents |
| 14 | quatorze | 71 | soixante et onze | 900 | neuf cents |
| 15 | quinze | 72 | soixante-douze | 1.000 | mille |
| 16 | seize | 80 | quatre-vingts | 2.000 | deux mille |
| 17 | dix-sept | 81 | quatre-vingt-un (une) | 1.000.000 | un million |

**Notes:**
1. The word **et** occurs only in the numbers 21, 31, 41, 51, and 61: vingt et un
2. **Un** becomes **une** before a feminine noun: trente et une filles
3. **Quatre-vingts** becomes **quatre-vingt** before another number: quatre-vingt-cinq
4. **Cents** becomes **cent** before another number: trois cent vingt
5. **Mille** never adds an -s: quatre mille

## B. Ordinal numbers

| | | | | | |
|---|---|---|---|---|---|
| 1er (ère) | premier (première) | 5e | cinquième | 9e | neuvième |
| 2e | deuxième | 6e | sixième | 10e | dixième |
| 3e | troisième | 7e | septième | 11e | onzième |
| 4e | quatrième | 8e | huitième | 12e | douzième |

Note: **Premier** becomes **première** before a feminine noun: **la première histoire**

# Appendix 3 Verbs

## A. Regular verbs

| INFINITIVE | PRESENT | |
|---|---|---|
| **parler** *(to talk, speak)* | je **parle** <br> tu **parles** <br> il **parle** | nous **parlons** <br> vous **parlez** <br> ils **parlent** |
| **finir** *(to finish)* | je **finis** <br> tu **finis** <br> il **finit** | nous **finissons** <br> vous **finissez** <br> ils **finissent** |
| **vendre** *(to sell)* | je **vends** <br> tu **vends** <br> il **vend** | nous **vendons** <br> vous **vendez** <br> ils **vendent** |

## B. -er verbs with stem changes

| INFINITIVE | PRESENT | |
|---|---|---|
| **acheter** *(to buy)* | j'**achète** <br> tu **achètes** <br> il **achète** | nous **achetons** <br> vous **achetez** <br> ils **achètent** |
| **payer** *(to pay, pay for)* | je **paie** <br> tu **paies** <br> il **paie** | nous **payons** <br> vous **payez** <br> ils **paient** |

## C. Irregular verbs

| INFINITIVE | PRESENT | |
|---|---|---|
| **avoir** *(to have, own)* | j'**ai** <br> tu **as** <br> il **a** | nous **avons** <br> vous **avez** <br> ils **ont** |
| **être** *(to be)* | je **suis** <br> tu **es** <br> il **est** | nous **sommes** <br> vous **êtes** <br> ils **sont** |
| **aller** *(to go)* | je **vais** <br> tu **vas** <br> il **va** | nous **allons** <br> vous **allez** <br> ils **vont** |

# VOCABULARIES

French-English Vocabulary
English-French Vocabulary

# French-English Vocabulary

The French-English Vocabulary for BONJOUR! contains both the active and passive words from the text, as well as the important words of the illustrations used within the units. Obvious passive cognates have not ordinarily been listed. Illustrations in the Sections Magazines are glossed where used.

The numbers following an entry indicate the unit and lesson in which the word or phrase is activated. (**P** stands for **Prélude**.) Passive meanings are separated from active meanings by a semicolon.

*Nouns*: If the article of a noun does not indicate gender, the noun is followed by *m. (masculine)* or *f. (feminine)*. If the plural (*pl.*) is irregular, it is given in parentheses.

*Adjectives*: Adjectives are listed in the masculine form. If the feminine form is irregular, it is given in parentheses. Irregular plural (*pl.*) forms are also given in parentheses.

*Verbs*: Verbs are listed in the infinitive form. An asterisk (*) in front of an active verb means that it is irregular. (For forms, see the verb charts in Appendix 3.C.) Irregular present tense forms are listed when they are used before the verb has been activated. Irregular past participle (*p. part.*) forms are listed separately.

Words beginning with an **h** are preceded by a bullet (•) if the **h** is aspirate, that is, if the word is treated as though it begins with a consonant sound.

## a

**a: il y a** there is, there are (**2.1**)

**à** at, to, in (**1.1**); from **à…heure(s)** at . . . (o'clock) (**P.4**) **à quelle heure?** (at) what time? (**P.4**) **à qui** to whom (**1.5**) **à qui est/sont…?** whose . . . is it/ are they?, to whom does/do . . . belong? (**3.5**)

**abord: d'abord** first

**un accent** accent mark, accent, stress

**accentué: un pronom accentué** stress pronoun

**un accord** agreement **d'accord** okay, all right (**2.1**) **être d'accord** to agree (**2.1**)

**un achat** purchase

**acheter** to buy (**4.2**)

**un acteur** actor

**une activité** activity

**une actrice** actress

**un adjectif** adjective

**adorer** to love, adore (**1.4**)

**une adresse** address

**un adverbe** adverb

**un aéroport** airport

**une affaire** business, concern **des affaires** things, personal belongings

**affirmatif (affirmative)** affirmative, "yes"

**l' Afrique** *f.* Africa (**2.4**)

**un âge** age **quel âge as-tu (avez-vous)?** how old are you? (**3.3**)

**âgé** old (**3.3**)

**une agence** agency **une agence de tourisme** tourist agency **une agence de voyages** travel agency

**ah!** ah! oh! (**2.1**) **ah bon!** all right! (**3.4**)

**ai: j'ai** I have

**aimer** to like (**1.4**) **aimer bien** to really like

**l' air** *m.* air **avoir l'air** to seem

**un album** album (**3.3**)

**l' Algérie** *f.* Algeria (*country in North Africa*)

**l' Allemagne** *f.* Germany (**2.4**)

**allemand** German (**2.4**)

**l' allemand** *m.* German (*language*)

* **aller** to go (**3.1**) **aller à vélo** to go by bicycle **allez: comment allez-vous?** how are you? (**P.2**)

**allô** hello (*used to answer the telephone*)

**allons!** let's go (**3.1**) **allons…!** let's go (*somewhere*)! (**3.1**) alors  then, well then, so (1.5)  **et alors?**  so what? (1.5)  **zut alors!**  darn (it)! rats! (**P.4**)

amener  to bring

américain  American (2.4)

un **Américain, une Américaine**  American (2.4)

l' **américanisation** f.  americanization

l' **Amérique** f.  America (2.4)

un **ami, une amie**  (close) friend (2.1)  **un petit ami**  boyfriend (2.3)  **une petite amie**  girlfriend (2.3)

amusant  amusing (2.1)

amuser  to amuse  **amusez-vous bien**  have a good time

un **an**  year  **avoir...ans**  to be . . . (years old) (3.3)

analyser  to analyze

un **âne**  donkey

anglais  English (2.4)

l' **anglais** m.  English (language)

un **Anglais, une Anglaise**  English person (2.4)

l' **Angleterre** f.  England (2.4)

un **animal** (pl. **animaux**)  animal (3.4)

l' **année** f.  year (**P.5**)  **cette année**  this year (4.2)

un **anniversaire**  birthday  **l'anniversaire de (Marc) est**  (Marc's) birthday is (**P.5**)  **mon anniversaire est...**  my birthday is . . . (**P.5**)

un **anorak**  (ski) jacket, parka (4.2)

août  August (**P.5**)

un **appareil-photo** (pl. **appareils-photo**)  (still) camera (2.2)

appelez: vous vous appelez  your name is

appelle: comment s'appelle...?  what's . . .'s name? (2.1)  **comment s'appelle-t-il/elle?**  what's his/her name? (2.1)  **comment t'appelles-tu?**  what's your name? (**P.2**)  **je m'appelle**  my name is (**P.2**)  **...s'appelle . . .**  is called, . . .'s name is

un **appétit**  appetite

approximatif (approximative)  approximate

après  afterwards

un **après-midi**  afternoon (4.2)  **cet après-midi**  this afternoon (4.2)  **de l'après-midi**  in the afternoon, P.M. (**P.4**)  **demain après-midi**  tomorrow afternoon (4.2)

l' **arabe** m.  Arabic (language)

l' **Arc de Triomphe** m.  triumphal arch in Paris, commemorating Napoleon's victories

l' **argent** m.  money (4.1)

une **arrivée**  arrival

arriver  to arrive, come (1.1)

l' **art** m.  art

un **artiste, une artiste**  artist

l' **Asie** f.  Asia (2.4)

assez  rather (2.1)

attendre  to wait, wait for (4.5)

une **attention**  attention  **attention!**  careful!

au  at (the), to (the), in (the) (3.1)  **au contraire**  on the contrary (1.2)  **au moins**  at least (3.2)  **au printemps**  in (the) spring (**P.6**)  **au revoir**  good-by (**P.1**)

aujourd'hui  today (**P.5**)

aussi  also, too (1.1);  so  **aussi...que**  as . . . as (4.3)  **moi aussi**  me too (**P.2**)

une **auto**  car, automobile (2.2)

l' **automne** m.  fall, autumn (4.2)  **cet automne**  this fall (autumn) (4.2)  **en automne**  in (the) fall, autumn (**P.6**)

autre  other  **l'autre**  the other one

aux  at (the), to (the), in (the) (3.1)

avance: d'avance  ahead

avant  before

avec  with (1.1)  **avec qui**  with whom (1.5)

* avoir  to have, own (2.2)  **avoir...ans**  to be . . . (years old) (3.3)  **avoir besoin de**  to need (4.4)  **avoir chaud**

to be (feel) warm (4.4)  **avoir de la chance**  to be lucky (4.4)  **avoir envie de**  to want, feel like (having) (4.4)  **avoir faim**  to be hungry (4.4)  **avoir froid**  to be (feel) cold (4.4)  **avoir l'air**  to seem  **avoir raison**  to be right (4.4)  **avoir soif**  to be thirsty (4.4)  **avoir tort**  to be wrong (4.4)

avons: nous avons  we have

avril  April (**P.5**)

# b

le **bac, baccalauréat**  diploma given at the end of secondary school

bain: un maillot de bain  bathing suit, swimsuit (4.2)

un **bal**  dance, ball

un **ballon**  ball

une **banane**  banana

une **banque**  bank

des **bas**  stockings (4.3)  **bas sur pattes**  short-legged

le **basket, basketball**  basketball (3.2)

un **basset**  basset-hound

beau (bel, belle; beaux)  good-looking, beautiful (2.1) (4.3)  **il fait beau**  it's nice (weather) (**P.6**)

beaucoup  much, very much, a lot (1.3)

bel (see **beau**)  good-looking, beautiful (4.3)

belge  Belgian (2.4)

la **Belgique**  Belgium (2.4)

belle (see **beau**)  good-looking, beautiful (2.1) (4.3)

besoin: avoir besoin de  to need (4.4)

bête  silly, stupid (2.3)

une **bibliothèque**  library (3.1)

une **bicyclette**  bicycle (2.2)

bien  well (1.1)  **bien sûr**

sure, of course (**1.2**)
**ça va (très) bien** I'm/ everything's (very) well (**P.2**) **c'est bien** that's good (fine) (**2.5**) **eh bien!** well! (**2.3**)

un **billet** bill, bank note (**4.1**); ticket

**bizarre** bizarre, strange

**blanc (blanche)** white (**2.2**)

**bleu** blue (**2.2**)

**blond** blond (**2.1**)

un **blue-jeans** (pair of) jeans (**4.2**)

une **boîte** box **une boîte aux lettres** mailbox

une **bombe** bomb

**bon (bonne)** good (**2.3**); right **ah bon!** all right! (**3.4**) **bon marché** inexpensive (**4.1**) **bon voyage!** have a good trip! **il fait bon** it's fine (pleasant) (weather) (**P.6**)

des **bonbons** *m.* candy (**4.5**)

**bonjour** hello, good morning, good afternoon (**P.1**)

une **botte** boot (**4.2**)

un **boucher, une bouchère** butcher

un **boulanger, une boulangère** baker

une **boutique** boutique, shop

**brun** dark-haired (**2.1**); (dark) brown

un **bureau** (*pl.* **bureaux**) desk **un bureau de tabac** tobacco shop

| c |

**c'** (*see* **ce**)

**ça** that, it **ça dépend** it depends (**4.1**) **ça n'a pas d'importance** it doesn't matter (**3.1**) **ça va?** how are you? how's everything? (**P.2**) **ça va** everything's

fine (going well); fine, I'm OK, everything's all right (**P.2**); good **c'est ça!** that's it! that's right! (**2.1**)

**comme ci, comme ça** so-so (**P.2**)

un **cachet** tablet

un **cadeau** (*pl.* **cadeaux**) gift, present

le **café** coffee

un **café** café (*French coffee shop*) (**3.1**)

une **cafétéria** cafeteria (**3.1**)

un **calendrier** date book

le **calme** calm, calmness

un **camarade, une camarade** classmate, school friend (**2.1**)

une **caméra** movie camera (**2.2**)

la **campagne** country, country-side (**3.1**)

le **Canada** Canada (**2.4**) **canadien (canadienne)** Canadian (**2.4**)

un **canard** duck

un **canari** canary

un **caniche** poodle

une **capitale** capital

**capricieux (capricieuse)** capricious

le **Carnaval** *winter carnival celebration in Nice and other French-speaking cities, held at Mardi Gras*

**carré** square **le Vieux Carré** *the French Quarter in New Orleans*

une **carte** map, card **jouer aux cartes** to play cards (**3.2**)

un **cas** case **dans ce cas** in that case

un **casque** helmet

une **cassette** cassette (**2.2**)

**ce (c')** this, that, it **ce sont** these are, those are, they are (**2.4**) **c'est** that's, it's (**P.1**) he's, she's (**2.3**) **c'est ça!** that's it! that's right! (**2.1**) **c'est combien?** how much is it? (**P.3**) **c'est...francs** it's . . . francs (**P.3**) **c'est le (10 septembre)** it's (September 10th) (**P.5**) **qu'est-ce que c'est?** what is it?

what's this? (**4.1**)

**ce (cet, cette; ces)** this, that, these, those (**4.2**) **ce...-ci** this (over here) (**4.2**) **ce...-là** that (over there) (**4.2**) **ce soir** tonight, this evening (**4.2**)

**célèbre** famous

**cent** one hundred (**4.1**)

un **centime** centime (*1/100 of a franc*)

un **centre** center

**certain** certain **certains** some, some people

**ces** these, those (**4.2**)

**c'est** (*see* **ce**)

**cet** this, that (**4.2**)

**cette** this, that (**4.2**)

un **champion, une championne** champion

un **championnat** championship

les **Champs-Élysées** *m.* *avenue in Paris*

**chance: avoir de la chance** to be lucky (**4.4**)

**changer** to change

**chanter** to sing (**1.4**)

un **chapeau** (*pl.* **chapeaux**) hat (**4.3**)

**chaque** each, every

la **chasse** hunting

un **chat** cat (**3.4**)

**chaud** warm, hot (**4.2**) **avoir chaud** to be (feel) warm (**4.4**) **il fait chaud** it's hot (weather) (**P.6**)

une **chaussette** sock (**4.2**)

une **chaussure** shoe (**4.2**) **des chaussures de ski** ski boots

un **chef** head, chef

une **chemise** shirt (**4.3**)

un **chemisier** blouse (**4.3**)

**cher (chère)** expensive (**4.1**) dear (**4.4**)

**chercher** to look for

un **cheval** (*pl.* **chevaux**) horse (**3.4**)

**chez** at/to . . .'s (house) (**3.2**); in **chez (le pharmacien)** at/to (the pharmacist's) (**4.5**) **chez moi (toi, lui...)** (at) home (**3.2**)

**chic** nice; elegant, in style (**4.2**)

un **chien** dog (**3.4**)
la **Chine** China (**2.4**)
 **chinois** Chinese (**2.4**)
un **chocolat** chocolate, cocoa
 **choisir** to choose (**4.1**)
 **ci: ce...-ci** this . . . (over here) (**4.2**) **ce mois-ci** this month (**4.2**)
un **cinéma** movie theater (**3.1**)
 **cinq** five (**P.3**)
 **cinquante** fifty (**P.3**)
 **cinquième** fifth (**3.4**)
une **clarinette** clarinet (**3.2**)
une **classe** class, classroom **en classe** in class (**1.5**) to class (**3.1**)
 **classique** classical
un **client, une cliente** client, customer
un **coca** Coke (Coca-Cola)
une **coïncidence** coincidence
 **collectionner** to collect
un **collège (un Collège d'Enseignement Secondaire)** junior high school
 **combien** how much (**P.3**) **c'est combien?** how much is it? (**P.3**) **combien de** how much, how many (**4.1**)
une **comédie** comedy
un **comédien, une comédienne** comedian
 **commander** to command
 **comme** like, as (**4.4**) **comme ci, comme ça** so-so (**P.2**)
 **comment** how (**1.3**) what (**2.1**) **comment allez-vous?** how are you? (**P.2**) **comment dit-on?** how do you say? (**4.5**) **comment est-il/elle?** what's he/she like? what does he/she look like? (**2.1**) **comment s'appelle...?** what's . . .'s name? (**2.1**) **comment s'appelle-t-il/elle?** what's his/her name? (**2.1**) **comment t'appelles-tu?** what's your name? (**P.2**) **comment vas-tu?** how are you? (**P.2**)
un **commerçant, une commerçante** shopkeeper

une **compagnie** company
une **comparaison** comparison
 **compléter** to complete
 **compliqué** complicated (**4.5**)
 **comprendre** to understand
un **concert** concert (**3.1**)
 **confortable** comfortable
une **connaissance** acquaintance **faire la connaissance de** to meet
 **connaissez: vous connaissez** you know
 **conservateur (conservatrice)** conservative (**4.3**)
le **contraire** opposite **au contraire** on the contrary (**1.2**)
 **contre** against, in exchange for
une **correspondance** correspondence
 **correspondre** to correspond, match
un **costume** suit (**4.3**)
la **Côte d'Azur** Riviera (*southern coast of France on the Mediterranean*)
la **Côte-d'Ivoire** Ivory Coast (*French-speaking country in West Africa*)
 **côté: à côté de** next to
une **couleur** color **de quelle couleur?** what color? (**2.2**)
une **coupe** cup
 **courageux (courageuse)** courageous, brave
 **courant** everyday
un **cours** street, drive, parkway
une **course** race
 **court** short (**4.3**)
un **court de tennis** tennis court
un **cousin, une cousine** cousin (**3.2**)
 **coûter** to cost (**4.1**)
une **couverture** cover
une **cravate** tie (**4.3**)
un **crémier, une crémière** dairy person
le **créole** Creole (*French dialect spoken in Louisiana and the Caribbean*)
un **crétin, une crétine** cretin, idiot
un **croissant** crescent roll

la **cuisine** cuisine, cooking
 **culturel (culturelle)** cultural
 **curieux (curieuse)** curious
la **curiosité** curiosity

| d |

 **d'** (*see* **de**) (**1.1**)
 **d'abord** first
 **d'accord** okay, all right (**2.1**) **être d'accord** to agree (**2.1**)
une **dame** lady, woman (*polite term*) (**2.1**)
 **dangereux (dangereuse)** dangerous
 **dans** in (**3.3**)
 **danser** to dance (**1.2**)
la **date** date (**P.5**)
 **d'avance** ahead
 **de** from, of, about (**1.1**) **de l'après-midi** in the afternoon, P.M. (**P.4**) **de qui** of (about) whom (**1.5**) **pas de** not a, not any, no (**2.2**)
 **décembre** December (**P.5**)
 **découvrir** to discover
 **défini** definite
un **degré** degree **il fait... degrés** it's . . . degrees (**P.6**)
 **dehors** outside
 **demain** tomorrow (**P.5**) **demain matin (après-midi, soir)** tomorrow morning (afternoon, evening/night) (**4.2**)
 **demander (à)** to ask (**3.5**)
 **demi: ...heure(s) et demie** half past . . . (**P.4**)
 **démonstratif (démonstrative)** demonstrative
un **dentiste, une dentiste** dentist
un **départ** departure, leaving
 **dépend: ça dépend** it depends (**4.1**)
 **dépenser** to spend (**4.1**)
 **des** some, any (**2.4**) of (the), from (the), about (the) (**3.2**)

une **description** description
**désirer** to wish, want (**1.4**)
**déterminer** to determine
**détester** to dislike, hate (**1.4**)
**deux** two (**P.3**)
**deuxième** second (**3.4**)
**développé** developed
**d'habitude** usually
**Dieu** *m.* God **mon Dieu!**
my goodness!
une **différence** difference
**difficile** hard, difficult (**2.5**)
**dimanche** *m.* Sunday (**P.5**)
**dîner** to have (eat) dinner
(**1.1**)
le **dîner** dinner, supper
**dis (donc)!** say! hey! (**1.4**)
la **discrétion** discretion
**discuter** to argue
**disent** (they) say
un **disque** record (**2.2**)
**dit: comment dit-on?** how do
you say? (**4.5**) **on dit**
people say
**dites: dites (donc)!** say! hey!
(**1.4**)
une **division** division
**dix** ten (**P.3**)
**dix-huit** eighteen
(**P.3**)
**dixième** tenth
(**3.4**)
**dix-neuf** nineteen
(**P.3**)
**dix-sept** seventeen
(**P.3**)
un **docteur** doctor
un **domaine** domain, area
**domestique** domestic
**dommage** too bad (**1.1**)
**c'est dommage** that's too
bad (**1.1**)
**donc: dis (dites) donc!** say!
hey! (**1.4**)
**donner** to give **donne-moi,
donnez-moi** give me (**P.3**)
**douze** twelve (**P.3**)
**douzième** twelfth (**3.4**)
**drôle** funny (**2.3**)
**du** of (the), from (the), about
(the) (**3.2**) **du matin** in
the morning, A.M. (**P.4**)
**du soir** in the evening,
P.M. (**P.4**)

| e |

l' **eau** *f.* water **l'eau de
cologne** cologne
un **échange** trade, exchange
**échanger** to trade, exchange
les **échecs** *m.* chess (**3.2**)
un **éclair** eclair (*pastry*)
une **école** school (**3.1**)
**économique** economical
un **économiste, une économiste**
economist
**écossais** Scottish
**écouter** to listen (to) (**1.4**)
**écoute! écoutez!** listen!
(**2.5**)
l' **éducation** *f.* education
**l'éducation physique** physical education
**effet: en effet** in effect,
indeed
**égaler** to equal
une **église** church (**3.1**)
l' **Égypte** *f.* Egypt (**2.4**)
**égyptien (égyptienne)** Egyptian (**2.4**)
**eh!** hey! (**1.4**) **eh bien!**
well! (**2.3**)
l' **électronique** *f.* electronics
un **électrophone** record player
(**2.2**)
l' **élégance** *f.* elegance, style
**élégant** well-dressed; elegant
(**4.3**)
un **élève, une élève** (high school)
student (**2.1**)
l' **élision** *f.* elision (*in French,
the dropping of a final vowel*)
**elle** she (**1.2**) it (**2.2**)
her (**2.5**)
**elles** they (**1.2**) them (**2.5**)
**éloignée: la famille éloignée**
distant family (**3.3**)
**embêtant** annoying
un **empereur** emperor
un **employé, une employée**
employee, salesperson
**emprunter** to borrow (**3.2**)
**en** in, to (**4.5**); by **en
automne (hiver, été)** in (the)
fall (winter, summer) (**P.6**)

**en classe** in class (**1.5**) to
class (**3.1**) **en vacances**
on vacation (**1.5**) **en ville**
downtown, in town (**1.5**)
un **endroit** place
des **enfants** *m.* children (**3.3**)
une **enquête** survey
l' **enseignement** *m.* teaching
**enseigner** to teach
**entendre** to hear (**4.5**)
**entre** between
une **entrée** first course (*of a meal*)
**entrer** to enter
l' **envie** *f.* desire **avoir envie
de** to want, feel like
(having) (**4.4**)
une **épicerie** grocery (**4.5**)
un **épicier, une épicière** grocer
(**4.5**)
une **équipe** team
**équitable** fair
l' **Espagne** *f.* Spain (**2.4**)
**espagnol** Spanish (**2.4**)
l' **espagnol** *m.* Spanish
(*language*)
une **espèce** kind
l' **essentiel** *m.* important thing
**est: il/elle est** he/she/it is
**est-ce que** *phrase used to
introduce a question* (**1.2**)
**n'est-ce pas?** no? isn't it
(so)? right? (**1.3**) **quel
jour est-ce?** what day is
it? (**P.5**) **qui est-ce?**
who's that? who is it? (**P.1**)
**et** and (**P.3**) **et alors?** so
what? (**1.5**)
un **étage** floor
les **États-Unis** *m.* United States
(**2.4**)
l' **été** *m.* summer (**4.2**) **cet
été** this summer (**4.2**)
**en été** in (the) summer
(**P.6**)
\* **être** to be (**1.5**) **être à** to
belong to (**3.5**) **être
d'accord** to agree (**2.1**)
une **étude** study
un **étudiant, une étudiante** (college) student (**2.1**)
**étudier** to study (**1.2**)
**euh...** er..., uh... (**P.6**)
l' **Europe** *f.* Europe (**2.4**)
**eux** them (**2.5**)

évidemment   of course (**4.3**)
exactement   exactly
un examen   exam, test
excuser   to excuse   **excusez-moi**   excuse me
un exemple   example   **par exemple**   for example, for instance
un explorateur, une exploratrice   explorer
une exposition   exhibit
une expression   expression
exprimer   to express
extra, extraordinaire   extraordinary, great
extrêmement   extremely

# f

facile   easy (**2.5**)
la faim   hunger   **avoir faim**   to be hungry (**4.4**)
fait: il fait (beau, bon, chaud, frais, froid, mauvais)   it's (nice, fine, hot, cool, cold, bad) weather (**P.6**)   **il fait...degrés**   it's . . . degrees (**P.6**)   **il fait moins...**   it's . . . (degrees) below (zero) (**P.6**)   **il fait zéro**   it's 0° (**P.6**)   **quel temps fait-il?**   how (what) is the weather? (**P.6**)   **quelle température fait-il?**   what's the temperature? (**P.6**)
une famille   family (**3.3**)   **en famille**   at home   **la famille éloignée**   distant family (**3.3**)   **la famille proche**   immediate family (**3.3**)
fantastique   fantastic; great, terrific (**2.2**)
fatigué   tired (**4.4**)
faux (fausse)   false, wrong (**2.5**)
féminin   feminine
une femme   woman (**2.1**); wife
une fête   holiday

février   February (**P.5**)
une fille   girl (**2.1**)   daughter (**3.3**)
un film   movie
un fils   son (**3.3**)
la fin   end
fini   over, finished
finir   to finish (**4.1**)
flatter   to flatter
une fleur   flower
une flûte   flute (**3.2**)
fois   times
le foot, football   soccer (**3.2**)   **jouer au football**   to play soccer (**3.2**)
une forme   form
formidable   great, terrific (**2.2**)
fort   strong
un foulard   scarf
frais: il fait frais   it's cool (weather) (**P.6**)
un franc   franc (*monetary unit of France, Belgium, and Switzerland*)
français   French (**2.4**)
le français *m.*   French (*language*)
un Français, une Française   French person (**2.4**)
la France   France (**2.4**)
francophone   French-speaking
un frère   brother (**3.2**)
froid   cold   **avoir froid**   to be (feel) cold (**4.4**)   **il fait froid**   it's cold (weather) (**P.6**)

# g

une galerie   gallery
un garçon   boy (**2.1**)
une gare   train station
un gâteau (*pl.* gâteaux)   cake (**4.4**)
général: en général   in general
généreux (généreuse)   generous (**4.3**)
la générosité   generosity
un génie   genius
le genre   gender

la géographie   geography
géographique   geographic
une glace   mirror
un gourmand, une gourmande   person who likes to eat
grand   tall, big (**2.1**)   **un grand magasin**   department store (**4.1**)
une grand-mère   grandmother (**3.3**)
un grand-père   grandfather (**3.3**)
les grands-parents   grandparents (**3.3**)
la Grèce   Greece
un grenier   attic
gris   gray (**2.2**)
gros (grosse)   fat (**4.4**); big
grossir   to get fat, gain weight (**4.1**)
un groupe   group
la Guadeloupe   Guadeloupe (*a French island in the West Indies*)
une guitare   guitar (**2.2**)

# h

h. = heure(s) (**P.4**)
habiter   to live (**1.1**)
une habitude   habit   **d'habitude**   usually
hélas   too bad
un hélicoptère   helicopter
un• héros   hero
l' heure *f.*   time, hour   **à...heure(s)**   at . . . (o'clock) (**P.4**)   **à quelle heure?**   (at) what time? (**P.4**)   **...heure(s) (dix)**   (ten) past . . . (**P.4**)   **...heure(s) et demie**   half past . . . (**P.4**)   **...heure(s) et quart**   quarter past . . . (**P.4**)   **...heure(s) moins (dix)**   (ten) of . . . (**P.4**)   **...heure(s) moins le quart**   quarter of . . . (**P.4**)   **il est...heure(s)**   it is . . .

(o'clock) (**P.4**) **quelle heure est-il?** what time is it? (**P.4**)

l' **hiver** *m.* winter (**4.2**) **cet hiver** this winter (**4.2**) **en hiver** in (the) winter (**P.6**)

• **hm!** *used to show you hear what is said, but you do not want to answer* (**4.4**)

le• **hockey** hockey **jouer au hockey** to play hockey

un **homme** man (**2.1**)

un **hôpital** (*pl.* **hôpitaux**) hospital (**3.1**)

l' **horreur** *f.* horror **quelle horreur!** how awful!

• **huit** eight (**P.3**)

• **huitième** eighth (**3.4**)

un **hypermarché** shopping center

## | i |

**ici** here (**1.5**)

l' **idéalisme** *m.* idealism

une **idée** idea (**4.4**)

**idiot** stupid

**il** he (**1.2**) it (**2.2**) **il y a** there is, there are (**2.4**)

**ils** they (**1.2**)

un **immeuble** apartment house

l' **importance** *f.* importance **ça n'a pas d'importance** it doesn't matter (**3.1**)

**indépendant** independent

**individuel** (**individuelle**) individual

un **infinitif** infinitive

l' **information** *f.* information

un **ingénieur** engineer

**innocent** naive

**insister** to insist

un **instrument** instrument (**3.2**)

**intellectuel** (**intellectuelle**) intellectual

**intelligent** intelligent (**2.1**)

**intéressant** interesting (**2.1**)

**international** (*pl.* **internationaux**) international

un **interprète,** une **interprète** interpreter, translator

**interrogatif** (**interrogative**) interrogative

l' **interrogation** *f.* interrogation, asking questions

les **Invalides** *m.* *monument in Paris, Napoleon's tomb*

une **inversion** inversion, turning around

une **invitation** invitation

**invité** invited

**inviter** to invite (**1.1**)

**irlandais** Irish

l' **Italie** *f.* Italy (**2.4**)

**italien** (**italienne**) Italian (**2.4**)

l' **italien** *m.* Italian (*language*)

## | j |

**j'** (*see* **je**) (**1.1**)

**janvier** January (**P.5**)

le **Japon** Japan (**2.4**)

**japonais** Japanese (**2.4**)

le **japonais** Japanese (*language*)

**jaune** yellow (**2.2**)

**je** I (**1.1**)

un **jeu** (*pl.* **jeux**) game (**3.2**)

**jeudi** *m.* Thursday (**P.5**)

**jeune** young (**3.3**)

les **jeunes** *m.* young people (**4.2**)

**joli** pretty (**2.3**)

**jouer** to play (**1.1**) **jouer à** + *sport, game* to play (**3.2**) **jouer de** + *instrument* to play (**3.2**)

un **jour** day (**P.5**) **quel jour est-ce?** what day is it? (**P.5**) **tous les jours** every day

un **journal** (*pl.* **journaux**) paper, newspaper (**4.5**) **chez le marchand de journaux** at the newsstand

un **journaliste,** une **journaliste** journalist

**juillet** July (**P.5**)

**juin** June (**P.5**)

un **jumeau,** une **jumelle** twin

une **jupe** skirt (**4.3**)

## | k |

un **kilomètre** kilometer

## | l |

l' (*see* **le, la**) (**2.1**)

la the (**2.1**)

**là** there (**1.5**); here **ce...-là** that . . . (over there) (**4.2**) **oh là là!** oh dear! wow! whew! (**P.3**)

**là-bas** over there (**1.5**)

un **lac** lake

la **laine** wool

une **lampe** lamp

le **langage** language

une **langue** language

le the (**2.1**)

une **leçon** lesson

**légendaire** legendary

les the (**2.4**)

**leur, leurs** their (**3.4**)

la **liaison** *linking of two words*

**libéral** (*pl.* **libéraux**) liberal

la **liberté** liberty

un **libraire,** une **libraire** bookseller, bookstore owner (**4.5**)

une **librairie** bookstore (**4.5**)

une **limite** limit

un **livre** book (**2.2**)

un **loisir** leisure activity

**long** (**longue**) long (**4.3**)

une **loterie** raffle

le **loto** lotto, lottery, bingo

le **Louvre** *museum in Paris*

**lui** him (**2.5**)

**lundi** *m.* Monday (**P.5**)

des **lunettes** *f.* glasses (4.2)
   **des lunettes de soleil**
   sunglasses (3.1)
un **lycée** high school

# | m |

**M.** Mr. (P.1)
**ma** my (3.3)
**Madame (Mme)** Mrs. (P.1)
**Mademoiselle (Mlle)** Miss
   (P.1)
un **magasin** store, shop (4.1)
   **un grand magasin** department store (4.1)
**magnifique** great (1.1)
   **c'est magnifique** that's great
   (1.1)
**mai** May (P.5)
**maigrir** to get thin, lose
   weight (4.1)
un **maillot de bain** bathing suit,
   swimsuit (4.2)
**maintenant** now (1.3)
**mais** but (1.1) **mais non**
   of course not (1.2) **mais**
   **oui** all right; certainly (1.2)
une **maison** house (3.1) **à la**
   **maison** at home, home
   (1.5) **la Maison des**
   **Jeunes** Youth Center
**mal** badly, poorly (1.1)
   **ça va (très) mal** I'm/
   everything's (very) bad (P.2)
   **c'est mal** that's bad (2.5)
   **pas mal** not bad (3.3)
**malade** sick (3.1)
un **manteau** (*pl.* **manteaux**) coat
   (4.3)
**m'appelle: je m'appelle** my
   name is (P.2)
un **marchand, une marchande**
   merchant, storekeeper,
   dealer (4.5) **chez le**

**marchand de journaux** at
   the newsstand
un **marché** market **bon**
   **marché** inexpensive (4.1)
   **Au Bon Marché** *depart-*
   *ment store in Paris*
**marcher** to work (*function*),
   walk (2.2); to step on
**mardi** *m.* Tuesday (P.5)
   **Mardi Gras** *m.* Shrove
   Tuesday
**mars** March (P.5)
un **Martiniquais, une Martini-**
   **quaise** *person from Marti-*
   *nique*
la **Martinique** Martinique
   (*French island in the West*
   *Indies*)
**masculin** masculine
un **match** game, (sports) match
les **maths** *f.* math
un **matin** morning (4.2) **ce**
   **matin** this morning (4.2)
   **demain matin** tomorrow
   morning (4.2) **du matin**
   in the morning, A.M.
   (P.4)
**mauvais** bad (2.3) **il fait**
   **mauvais** it's bad (weather)
   (P.6)
**me** (to) me
un **médecin** doctor
les **médicaments** *m.* medicine
**meilleur** better (4.3) **le**
   **meilleur** best (4.4) **un**
   **meilleur ami, une meilleure**
   **amie** best friend
   (3.3)
la **mélancolie** melancholy
une **mer** sea
**merci** thank you (P.3)
**mercredi** *m.* Wednesday
   (P.5)
une **mère** mother (3.3)
**mes** my (3.3)
une **mesure** measurement
la **météo** weather report
un **mètre** meter
**métrique** metric
**mexicain** Mexican (2.4)
le **Mexique** Mexico (2.4)
**midi** noon (P.4)
**mieux** better **tant mieux**
   so much the better

**mignon (mignonne)** cute
**mille** one thousand (4.2)
des **milliers** *m.* thousands
un **million** one million (4.2)
un **millionnaire, une millionnaire**
   millionaire
**mince** slim, slender, thin
   (4.4)
une **mini-cassette** cassette
   recorder (2.2)
**minuit** midnight (P.4)
**Mlle** Miss (P.1)
**Mme** Mrs. (P.1)
la **mode** fashion (4.3); style
   **à la mode** popular; in fashion, fashionable (4.3)
**moderne** modern
**moi** me (2.5) **moi aussi**
   me too (P.2)
**moins** less (4.3) **au moins**
   at least (3.2) **...heure(s)**
   **moins (dix)** (ten) of . . .
   (P.4) **...heure(s) moins**
   **le quart** quarter of . . .
   (P.4) **il fait moins...**
   it's . . . (degrees) below
   (zero) (P.6) **le moins**
   the least (4.4) **moins**
   **...que** less . . . than
   (4.3)
un **mois** month (P.5) **ce mois-**
   **ci** this month (4.2)
un **moment** moment **un**
   **moment!** just a moment
   (minute)!
**mon (ma; mes)** my (3.3)
le **monde** world
**Monsieur (M.)** Mr. (P.1)
un **monsieur** (*pl.* **messieurs**)
   gentleman, man (*polite*
   *term*) (2.1)
la **montagne** mountain(s)
une **montre** watch (2.2)
un **mot** word
un **moteur** motor
une **moto** motorcycle (2.2)
**muet (muette)** silent
**musclé** muscular
un **musée** museum (3.1)
un **musicien, une musicienne**
   musician
la **musique** music
**myope** nearsighted
le **mystère** mystery

# n

n' (see ne...) (1.1)
nager to swim (1.4)
national (pl. nationaux) national
une nationalité nationality (2.4)
les Nations Unies f. United Nations
naturellement naturally
ne...pas not (1.1) n'est-ce pas? no? isn't it (so)? right? (1.3)
négatif (négative) negative, "no"
neige: il neige it's snowing (P.6)
la neige snow
n'est-ce pas? no? isn't it (so)? right? (1.3)
neuf nine (P.3)
neuvième ninth (3.4)
un niveau (pl. niveaux) level
Noël m. Christmas
noir black (2.2)
un nom name, noun
un nombre number
nombreux (nombreuse) numerous, many
non no (P.3) mais non of course not (1.2) non plus neither
normal (pl. normaux) logical c'est normal that's logical (normal)
nos our (3.5)
une note note
notre (pl. nos) our (3.5)
nous we (1.3) us (2.5); (to) us
nouveau (nouvel, nouvelle; nouveaux) new (4.3)
nouvel (see nouveau) new (4.3)
nouvelle (see nouveau) new (4.3)
une nouvelle piece of news
novembre November (P.5)
un nuage cloud

une nuit night (4.2) cette nuit tonight (4.2)
un numéro number

# o

un objet object, thing les objets trouvés lost and found
un océan ocean
octobre October (P.5)
oh là là! oh dear! wow! whew! (P.3)
un oiseau (pl. oiseaux) bird (3.4)
une omelette omelet
on one, you, they, people, we (4.5)
un oncle uncle (3.3)
onze eleven (P.3)
onzième eleventh (3.4)
l' Opéra m. the Paris Opera
l' optimisme m. optimism
optimiste optimistic
une orangeade orange drink, orange soda
ordinal (pl. ordinaux) ordinal
un ordre order
organisé organized
organiser to organize
une origine origin
ou or (1.1)
où where (1.3)
oui yes (P.3) mais oui all right; certainly (1.2)

# p

un pantalon (pair of) pants (4.2)
Pâques f. Easter
par per par exemple for example, for instance
un parc park (3.1)
parce que because (1.3)
pardon excuse me (P.3)
un parent parent, relative (3.3)
parfait perfect (4.2)
parier to bet

parler to speak, talk (1.1)
partout everywhere
pas not ne...pas not (1.1) pas de not a, no, not any (2.2) pas du tout not at all (1.2) pas mal not bad (3.3) pas question! nothing doing! no way! (3.5)
passer to spend (time) (4.5); to take (a test)
un passe-temps hobby
une pâtisserie pastry, pastry shop (4.4)
un pâtissier, une pâtissière pastry cook, baker (4.5)
pattes: bas sur pattes short-legged
pauvre poor (3.1)
payer to pay, pay for (4.4)
un pays country (2.4)
une pêche peach
une pédale pedal
un pédiatre pediatrician
pénible annoying (2.3)
penser to think (3.5)
perdre to lose, waste (4.5) perdre son temps to waste one's time
un père father (3.3)
un permis license
un perroquet parrot
une personnalité personality
personne (not) anyone
une personne person (2.1) des personnes people
personnel (personnelle) personal
petit short, little (2.1)
un petit ami boyfriend (2.3) une petite amie girlfriend (2.3)
peu: un peu a little, a little bit (1.3)
peut-être maybe, perhaps (2.4)
peux: je peux I may, can tu peux you can
une pharmacie pharmacy, drugstore (4.5)
un pharmacien, une pharmacienne pharmacist (4.5)
la photo photography
une photo photograph, picture (3.3)

un **photographe, une photographe** photographer

la **photographie** photography

une **phrase** sentence

**physique** physical

un **piano** piano (**3.2**)

une **pièce** coin (**4.1**)

un **pied** foot

un **pique-nique** picnic

une **piscine** swimming pool (**3.1**)

une **place** (town) square, place

une **plage** beach (**3.1**)

**plaît: s'il te (vous) plaît** please (**P.3**)

une **plante** plant

**pleut: il pleut** it's raining (**P.6**)

la **pluie** rain

le **pluriel** plural form

**plus** more (**4.3**) **le plus** the most (**4.4**) **moi non plus** me neither **non plus** neither **plus...que** more than, . . .-er than (**4.3**)

un **poisson** fish (**3.4**)

un **poisson rouge** goldfish (**3.4**)

**ponctuel (ponctuelle)** punctual, on time

**populaire** popular

**porter** to wear (**4.2**)

une **position** position

**possessif (possessive)** possessive

des **possessions** *f.* possessions, belongings

une **poule** hen

**pour** for (**1.5**); in order to **pour qui** for whom (**1.5**)

**pourquoi** why (**1.3**)

**pratique** practical

**préféré** favorite

**préférer** to prefer

**premier (première)** first (**P.5**) (**3.4**)

la **première** *eleventh school year in France*

**prendre** to take

le **présent** present (tense)

une **présentation** introduction

**prêter** to lend, loan

le **printemps** spring (**4.2**) **au printemps** in (the) spring (**P.6**) **ce printemps** this spring (**4.2**)

un **prix** price (**4.2**)

un **problème** problem (**4.4**)

**proche: la famille proche** immediate family (**3.3**)

un **professeur** teacher (**2.1**)

un **programme** program

un **programmeur, une programmeuse** (computer) programmer

un **projet** project, plan

un **pronom** pronoun

**proposer** to propose

**prudent** prudent, careful

un **pull, pull-over** sweater, pullover (**4.2**)

## q

**qu'** (*see* que) (**1.2**)

**quand** when (**1.3**)

**quarante** forty (**P.3**)

**quart: ...heure(s) et quart** quarter past . . . (**P.4**) **...heure(s) moins le quart** quarter of . . . (**P.4**)

le **Quartier Latin** *section of Paris where many students and artists live*

**quatorze** fourteen (**P.3**)

**quatre** four (**P.3**)

**quatre-vingt dix** ninety (**4.1**)

**quatre-vingts** eighty (**4.1**)

**quatrième** fourth (**3.4**)

**que** that (**3.5**) than, as (**4.3**); whom **est-ce que** *phrase used to introduce a question* (**1.2**) **qu'est-ce que** what (**4.1**) **qu'est-ce que c'est?** what is it? what's this? (**4.1**)

**quel (quelle)** what, which (**4.2**) **à quelle heure?** (at) what time? (**P.4**) **quel...!** what a . . . ! **quel âge as-tu (avez-vous)?**

how old are you? (**3.3**) **quel jour est-ce?** what day is it? (**P.5**) **quel temps fait-il?** how (what) is the weather? (**P.6**) **quelle heure est-il?** what time is it? (**P.4**) **quelle température fait-il?** what's the temperature? (**P.6**)

**quelque** some, a few

une **question** question **pas question!** nothing doing! no way! (**3.5**)

**qui** who, whom (**1.5**); that, which **à qui** to whom (**1.5**) **avec qui** with whom (**1.5**) **de qui** of (about) whom (**1.5**) **pour qui** for whom (**1.5**) **qui est-ce?** who's that? who is it? (**P.1**)

**quinze** fifteen (**P.3**)

**quoi?** what? (**2.1**)

## r

une **radio** radio (**2.2**)

une **raison** reason **avoir raison** to be right (**4.4**)

**rapide** fast

**rapidement** rapidly, quickly

une **raquette** racket (**2.2**)

**rarement** rarely, seldom (**1.3**)

**réaliste** realistic

une **récapitulation** review, summary

**regarder** to watch, look at (**1.4**)

un **régime** diet (**4.1**) **être au régime** to be on a diet (**4.1**)

**regretter** to be sorry

**régulier (régulière)** regular

une **rencontre** encounter

un **rendez-vous** date, appointment (**3.1**) **j'ai rendez-vous avec** I have a date with (**P.5**)

**rendre** to render

**rentrer** to come back, go back, go home (**1.2**)

une **réponse** answer
**représenter** to represent
une **responsabilité** responsibility
un **restaurant** restaurant (**3.1**)
**au restaurant** at the restaurant (**1.5**)
**rester** to stay (**3.1**)
**retard: de retard** behind, late
**réussir** to succeed, pass (*a test*) (**4.1**) **ne réussir pas** to fail, flunk (*a test*) (**4.1**)
**revenir** to come back
une **révision** review
**revoir: au revoir** good-by (**P.1**)
**riche** rich (**3.1**)
**ridicule** ridiculous
**rien de** nothing
une **robe** dress (**4.3**)
**romantique** romantic
le **romantisme** romanticism
**rond** round
une **roue** wheel
**rouge** red (**2.2**)
une **rue** street, road

| s |

**sa** his, her, its (**3.4**)
un **sac** bag, handbag (**2.2**)
le **Sagittaire** Sagittarius
**sais: je ne sais pas** I don't know (**P.1**) **je sais** I know (**P.1**)
une **saison** season
la **salle** *inside section of a café*
**salon: le salon de la voiture** car show
**salut** hi (**P.1**)
une **salutation** greeting
**samedi** *m.* Saturday (**P.5**)
une **sandale** sandal (**4.2**)
la **santé** health
**s'appelle: comment s'appelle...?** what's . . . 's name? (**2.1**) **comment s'appelle-t-il/elle?** what's his/her name? (**2.1**)

un **saxo(phone)** saxophone (**3.2**)
la **scène** scene
**secondaire** secondary
un **secrétaire, une secrétaire** secretary
**seize** sixteen (**P.3**)
une **semaine** week (**P.5**) **cette semaine** this week (**4.2**)
le **Sénégal** Senegal (*French-speaking country in West Africa*)
un **sens** sense
**sensationnel** sensational; great, terrific (**2.2**)
**sept** seven (**P.3**)
**septembre** September (**P.5**)
**septième** seventh (**3.4**)
une **série** series
**sérieux (sérieuse)** serious
**ses** his, her, its (**3.4**)
un **short** (pair of) shorts (**4.2**)
**si** if (**3.5**) **s'il te (vous) plaît** please (**P.3**)
**si** so
un **signe orthographique** spelling mark
une **signification** significance, meaning
**s'il te (vous) plaît** please (**P.3**)
une **silhouette** figure
une **similarité** similarity, likeness
**simple** simple (**4.5**)
**sincère** sincere (**2.1**)
la **sincérité** sincerity
**six** six (**P.3**)
**sixième** sixth (**3.4**)
un **skate-board** skateboard
le **ski** skiing
**skier** to ski (**1.1**)
une **sœur** sister (**3.2**)
**soif: avoir soif** to be thirsty (**4.4**)
un **soir** evening (**4.2**) **ce soir** tonight, this evening (**4.2**) **demain soir** tomorrow evening (night) **du soir** in the evening, P.M. (**P.4**)
**soixante** sixty (**P.3**)
**soixante-dix** seventy (**4.1**)
un **solde** (clearance) sale
le **soleil** sun
**son (sa; ses)** his, her, its (**3.4**); one's
un **son** sound

un **sondage** poll **un sondage d'opinion** opinion poll
**sont: ils/elles sont** they are
**souvent** often (**1.3**)
**souviens: je me souviens** I remember
**spécialement** especially
**spécialisé** specialized
un **spectacle** show
un **sport** sport (**3.2**)
**sportif (sportive)** sportive, who likes sports, athletic
un **stade** stadium (**3.1**)
un **stage** course of instruction
un **standard** switchboard
une **station de ski** ski resort
la **structure** structure
le **style** style (**4.3**)
**suisse** Swiss (**2.4**)
la **Suisse** Switzerland (**2.4**)
**suivant** following
**sujet** subject
**super** great, terrific
le **superlatif** superlative
un **supermarché** supermarket
**superstitieux (superstitieuse)** superstitious
**sur** on (**3.5**); about
**sûr** sure, certain **bien sûr** sure, of course (**1.2**)
une **surprise-partie** (informal) party (**2.1**)
**sympa, sympathique** nice, pleasant (**2.1**)
une **symphonie** symphony
un **système** system

| t |

**ta** your (**3.3**)
**tabac: un bureau de tabac** tobacco shop
**Tahiti** Tahiti (*French island in the South Pacific*)
le **tahitien** Tahitian (*language*)
**tant mieux** so much the better
une **tante** aunt (**3.3**)

un **tapeur** leech
**t'appelles: comment t'appelles-tu?** what's your name? (**P.2**)
une **tarte** tart, pie
**te** (to) you
un **tee-shirt** tee shirt (**4.2**)
la **télé** TV (**2.2**)
un **téléphone** telephone
**téléphoner** to call, phone (**1.1**)
un **téléviseur** TV set (**2.2**)
la **télévision** television, TV
la **température** temperature
**quelle température fait-il?** what's the temperature? (**P.6**)
le **temps** time, weather **de temps en temps** from time to time **perdre son temps** to waste one's time **quel temps fait-il?** how (what) is the weather? (**P.6**) **tout le temps** all the time
**tenez!** look!
**tennis: jouer au tennis** to play tennis
la **terminale** *twelfth school year in France, last year of lycée*
la **terrasse** *sidewalk section of a café*
**tes** your (**3.3**)
le **thé** tea
un **théâtre** theater (**3.1**)
un **thermomètre** thermometer
**tiens!** look! hey! (**1.2**)
un **timbre** stamp (**3.5**)
**timide** timid
un **tirage** drawing
**toi** you (**2.5**) **et toi?** and you? (**P.2**)
la **toilette** toilet
**ton (ta; tes)** your (**3.3**)
**tort: avoir tort** to be wrong (**4.4**)
**toujours** always (**1.3**)
un **tour** tour
une **tour** tower **la tour Eiffel** Eiffel Tower
le **tourisme** tourism, travel
un **touriste, une touriste** tourist
**tous** all **tous les jours** every day
la **Toussaint** All Saints' Day (*November 1*)
**tout** everything, all (**3.2**)

**pas du tout** not at all (**1.2**)
**tout le temps** all the time
un **transistor** transistor radio (**2.2**)
**travailler** to work (**1.4**)
**treize** thirteen (**P.3**)
**trente** thirty (**P.3**)
**très** very (**1.1**)
**triangulaire** triangular
**tricher** to cheat
**trois** three (**P.3**)
**troisième** third (**3.4**)
une **trompette** trumpet
**trop** too, too much (**3.3**)
**trouver** to think; to find (**3.5**)
**trouvés: les objets** *m.* **trouvés** lost and found
**tu** you (**1.3**)
la **Tunisie** Tunisia (*country in North Africa*)
**tunisien (tunisienne)** Tunisian

# u

**un, une** one (**P.3**) a, an (**2.1**)
**uni** united **les États-Unis** *m.* United States (**2.4**) **les Nations Unies** *f.* United Nations
une **unité** unit
**utile** useful
**utiliser** to use

# v

**va: ça va?** how are you? how's everything? (**P.2**) **ça va** everything's fine (going well); fine, I'm OK, everything's all right (**P.2**); good
les **vacances** *f.* vacation (**3.3**) **en vacances** on vacation (**1.5**) **les grandes**

**vacances** summer vacation
une **vache** cow
**vais: je vais** I am going
**vas: comment vas-tu?** how are you? (**P.2**)
un **véhicule** vehicle
un **vélo** bicycle (**2.2**)
un **vélomoteur** motorbike (**2.2**)
**vendre** to sell (**4.5**)
**vendredi** *m.* Friday (**P.5**)
un **verbe** verb
**vert** green (**2.2**)
une **veste** jacket (**4.2**)
les **vêtements** *m.* clothing (**4.2**)
**veux: je veux** I want
la **vie** life **c'est la vie!** that's life!
**vieil** (*see* **vieux**) old (**4.3**)
**vieille** (*see* **vieux**) old (**4.3**)
**vieux (vieil, vieille; vieux)** old (**4.3**) **le Vieux Carré** *the French Quarter in New Orleans*
une **ville** city, town (**3.1**) **en ville** in town, downtown (**1.5**)
**vingt** twenty (**P.3**)
**violet** violet, purple
un **violon** violin (**3.2**)
le **visage** face
une **visite** visit
**visiter** to visit (*a place*) (**1.1**)
**vive…!** hurray for . . . !
le **vocabulaire** vocabulary
**voici** this is, here's, here comes (**P.1**); here you are
**voilà** that is, there's (**P.1**); here (there) are
une **voiture** car (**2.2**)
le **volley, volleyball** volleyball (**3.2**) **jouer au volleyball** to play volleyball (**3.2**)
**vos** your (**3.5**)
**votre** (*pl.* **vos**) your (**3.5**)
**vous** you (**1.3**) (**2.5**); (to) you
un **voyage** trip **bon voyage!** have a good trip! **une agence de voyages** travel agency
**voyager** to travel (**1.4**)
une **voyelle** vowel
**voyons!** come on! come now! (**4.2**)
**vrai** true, right (**2.5**)
**vraiment** really (**P.5**)

## | w |

**un week-end**   weekend **(4.2)**
**ce week-end**   this weekend
**(4.2)**

## | y |

**y: il y a**   there is, there are
**(2.4)**

## | z |

**zéro**   zero **(P.3)**      **il fait zéro**
it's 0° **(P.6)**
**zut (alors)!**   darn (it)! rats! **(P.4)**

# English-French Vocabulary

The English-French Vocabulary contains only active words and expressions.

## a

**a, an** un, une (2.1)    **a little (bit)** un peu (1.3)    **a lot** beaucoup (1.3)

**about** de (1.1)    **about whom** de qui (1.5)

to **adore** adorer (1.4)

**Africa** l'Afrique f. (2.4)

**afternoon** un après-midi (4.2)    **good afternoon** bonjour (P.1)    **in the afternoon** de l'après-midi (P.4)    **this afternoon** cet après-midi (4.2)    **tomorrow afternoon** demain après-midi (4.2)

to **agree** être d'accord (2.1)

**ah!** ah! (2.1)

**album** un album (3.3)

**all** tout (3.2)    **all right** d'accord (2.1)    **all right!** ah bon! (3.4)    **everything's all right** ça va (P.2)    **not at all** pas du tout (1.2)

**also** aussi (1.1)

**always** toujours (1.3)

**am** (see **to be**)

**A.M.** du matin (P.4)

**America** l'Amérique f. (2.4)

**American** américain (2.4)

**amusing** amusant (2.1)

**an** un, une (2.1)

**and** et (P.3)    **and you?** et toi? (P.2)

**animal** un animal (pl. animaux) (3.4)

**annoying** pénible (2.3)

**any** des (2.4)    **not any** pas de (2.2)

**appointment** un rendez-vous (3.1)

**April** avril (P.5)

**are** (see **to be**)    **there are** il y a (2.4)    **these/those/they are** ce sont (2.4)

to **arrive** arriver (1.1)

**as** comme (4.4)    **as . . . as** aussi...que (4.3)

**Asia** l'Asie f. (2.4)

to **ask** demander (à) (3.5)

**at** à (1.1)    **chez** (3.2)    **at . . .'s (house)** chez... (3.2)    **at home** à la maison (1.5) chez (moi, toi...) (3.2)    **at least** au moins (3.2)    **at . . . (o'clock)** à...heure(s) (P.4)    **at (the pharmacist's)** chez (le pharmacien) (4.5)    **at the restaurant** au restaurant (1.5)    **at what time?** à quelle heure? (P.4)

**August** août (P.5)

**aunt** une tante (3.3)

**automobile** une auto, une voiture (2.2)

**autumn: in (the) autumn** en automne (P.6)    **this autumn** cet automne (4.2)

## b

**back: to come back** rentrer (1.2)    **to go back** rentrer (1.2)

**bad** mauvais (2.3)    **I'm/everything's (very) bad** ça va (très) mal (P.2)    **it's bad (weather)** il fait mauvais (P.6)    **not bad** pas mal (3.3)    **that's bad** c'est mal (2.5)    **(that's) too bad!** (c'est) dommage! (1.1)

**badly** mal (1.1)

**bag** un sac (2.2)

**baker** un pâtissier, une pâtissière (4.5)

**bank note** un billet (4.1)

**basketball** le basket(ball) (3.2)

**bathing suit** un maillot de bain (4.2)

to **be** *être (1.5)    **to be . . . (years old)** avoir...ans (3.3)    **to be cold** avoir froid (4.4)    **to be hungry** avoir faim (4.4)    **to be lucky** avoir de la chance (4.4)    **to be right** avoir raison (4.4)    **to be thirsty** avoir soif (4.4)    **to be warm** avoir chaud (4.4)    **to be wrong** avoir tort (4.4)

**beach** une plage (3.1)

**beautiful** beau (bel, belle; beaux) (2.1) (4.3)

**because** parce que (1.3)

**Belgian** belge (2.4)

**Belgium** la Belgique (2.4)

to **belong to** *être à (3.5)    **to whom does/do . . . belong?** à qui est/sont...? (3.5)    **which belongs to** de (3.2)

**below: it's (five) below** il fait moins (cinq) (P.6)

**best: the best . . . (in)** le meilleur...(de) (4.4)    **best friend** un meilleur ami, une meilleure amie (3.3)

**better** meilleur (4.3)

**bicycle** un vélo, une bicyclette (2.2)

**big** grand (2.1)

**bill** (money) un billet (4.1)

**bird** un oiseau (pl. oiseaux) (3.4)

**birthday: (Marc's) birthday is (May 3rd)** l'anniversaire de

(Marc) est le (3 mai) (**P.5**)
**my birthday is (March 2nd)**
mon anniversaire est le
(2 mars) (**P.5**)
**bit: a little bit** un peu (**1.3**)
**black** noir (**2.2**)
**blond** blond (**2.1**)
**blouse** un chemisier (**4.3**)
**blue** bleu (**2.2**)
**book** un livre (**2.2**)
**bookseller** un (une) libraire
(**4.5**)
**bookstore** une librairie (**4.5**)
**bookstore owner** un (une)
libraire (**4.5**)
**boots** des bottes f. (**4.2**)
to **borrow** emprunter (**3.2**)
**boy** un garçon (**2.1**)
**boyfriend** un petit ami (**2.3**)
**brother** un frère (**3.2**)
**brunet(te)** brun (**2.1**)
**but** mais (**1.1**)
to **buy** acheter (**4.2**)

## c

**café** un café (**3.1**)
**cafeteria** une cafétéria (**3.1**)
**cake** un gâteau (*pl.* gâteaux)
(**4.4**)
to **call** téléphoner (**1.1**)
**camera** un appareil-photo
(*pl.* appareils-photo) (**2.2**)
**movie camera** une caméra
(**2.2**)
**Canada** le Canada (**2.4**)
**Canadian** canadien (canadienne) (**2.4**)
**candy** des bonbons m. (**4.5**)
**car** une auto, une voiture (**2.2**)
**cards: (playing) cards** des cartes
(**3.2**)
**cassette** une cassette (**2.2**)
**cassette recorder** une mini-
cassette (**2.2**)

**cat** un chat (**3.4**)
**certainly** mais oui (**1.2**)
**chess** les échecs m.
(**3.2**)
**children** les enfants m.
(**3.3**)
**China** la Chine (**2.4**)
**Chinese** chinois (**2.4**)
to **choose** choisir (**4.1**)
**church** une église (**3.1**)
**city** une ville (**3.1**)
**clarinet** une clarinette
(**3.2**)
**class: in class** en classe (**1.5**)
**to class** en classe (**3.1**)
**classmate** un (une) camarade
(**2.1**)
**close friend** un ami, une amie
(**2.1**)
**clothing** les vêtements m.
(**4.2**)
**coat** un manteau (*pl.* manteaux)
(**4.3**)
**coed** une étudiante (**2.1**)
**coin** une pièce (**4.1**)
**cold: it's cold (weather)** il fait
froid (**P.6**) **to be (feel) cold**
avoir froid (**4.4**)
**college student** un étudiant,
une étudiante (**2.1**)
**color: what color?** de quelle
couleur (**2.2**)
to **come** arriver (**1.1**) **come on!**
**come now!** voyons! (**4.2**)
**here comes** voici (**P.1**) to
**come back** rentrer (**1.2**)
**complicated** compliqué
(**4.5**)
**concert** un concert (**3.1**)
**conservative** conservateur
(conservatrice) (**4.3**)
**contrary: on the contrary** au
contraire (**1.2**)
**cool: it's cool (weather)** il fait
frais (**P.6**)
to **cost** coûter (**4.1**)
**country** un pays (**2.4**)
**country(side)** la campagne (**3.1**)
**course: of course** bien sûr
(**1.2**) évidemment (**4.3**)
**of course not** mais non
(**1.2**)
**cousin** un cousin, une cousine
(**3.2**)

## d

to **dance** danser (**1.2**)
**dark-haired** brun (**2.1**)
**darn (it)!** zut! zut alors! (**P.4**)
**date** (*on the calendar*) la date
(**P.5**) un rendez-vous (**3.1**)
**I have a date with** j'ai
rendez-vous avec (**P.5**)
**daughter** une fille (**3.3**)
**day** un jour (**P.5**) **what day
is it?** quel jour est-ce? (**P.5**)
**dealer** un marchand, une
marchande (**4.5**)
**dear** cher (chère) (**4.4**) **oh
dear!** oh là là! (**P.3**)
**December** décembre (**P.5**)
**degrees: it's . . . degrees** il
fait...degrés (**P.6**)
**department store** un grand
magasin (**4.1**)
**depends: it depends** ça dépend
(**4.1**)
**diet** un régime (**4.1**) **to be
on a diet** être au régime
(**4.1**)
**difficult** difficile (**2.5**)
**dinner: to have (eat) dinner**
dîner (**1.1**)
to **dislike** détester (**1.4**)
**distant family** la famille
éloignée (**3.3**)
**dog** un chien (**3.4**)
**doing: nothing doing!** pas
question! (**3.5**)
**downtown** en ville (**1.5**)
**dress** une robe (**4.3**)
**drugstore** une pharmacie (**4.5**)

## e

**easy** facile (**2.5**)
to **eat: to eat dinner** dîner (**1.1**)
**Egypt** l'égypte f. (**2.4**)

**Egyptian** égyptien (égyptienne) (2.4)

**eight** huit (P.3)

**eighteen** dix-huit (P.3)

**eighth** huitième (3.4)

**eighty** quatre-vingts (4.1) **eighty-one** quatre-vingt-un (4.1)

**elegant** chic (4.2) élégant (4.3)

**eleven** onze (P.3)

**eleventh** onzième (3.4)

**England** l'Angleterre f. (2.4)

**English** anglais (2.4)

**er . . .** euh… (P.6)

**Europe** l'Europe f. (2.4)

**evening** un soir (4.2) **in the evening** du soir (P.4) **this evening** ce soir (4.2) **tomorrow evening** demain soir (4.2)

**everything** tout (3.2) **everything's all right** ça va (P.2) **how's everything?** ça va? (P.2)

**excuse me** pardon (P.3)

**expensive** cher (chère) (4.1)

## f

to **fail** ne réussir pas (4.1)

**fall: in (the) fall** en automne (P.6) **this fall** cet automne (4.2)

**false** faux (fausse) (2.5)

**family** la famille (3.3) **distant family** la famille éloignée (3.3) **immediate family** la famille proche (3.3)

**fashion** la mode (4.3) **to be in fashion (fashionable)** être à la mode (4.3)

**fat** gros (grosse) (4.4) **to get fat** grossir (4.1)

**father** un père (3.3)

**February** février (P.5)

to **feel: to feel like (having)** avoir envie de (4.4)

**fifteen** quinze (P.3) **3:15** trois heures et quart (P.4)

**fifth** cinquième (3.4)

**fifty** cinquante (P.3)

to **find** trouver (3.5)

**fine** ça va (P.2) **fine!** d'accord! (2.1) **it's fine (weather)** il fait beau (P.6) **that's fine** c'est bien (2.5)

to **finish** finir (4.1)

**first** premier (première) (3.4) **(June) first** le premier (juin) (P.5)

**fish** un poisson (3.4)

**five** cinq (P.3)

to **flunk** (a test) ne réussir pas (4.1)

**flute** une flûte (3.2)

**for** pour (1.5) **for whom** pour qui (1.5)

**forty** quarante (P.3)

**four** quatre (P.3)

**fourteen** quatorze (P.3)

**fourth** quatrième (3.4)

**France** la France (2.4)

**French** français (2.4)

**Friday** vendredi m. (P.5)

**friend** un ami, une amie (2.1) **best friend** un meilleur ami, une meilleure amie (3.2) **school friend** un (une) camarade (2.1)

**from** de (1.1)

**funny** drôle (2.3)

## g

to **gain weight** grossir (4.1)

**game** un jeu (pl. jeux) (3.2)

**generous** généreux (généreuse) (4.3)

**gentleman** un monsieur (pl. messieurs) (2.1)

**German** allemand (2.4)

**Germany** l'Allemagne f. (2.4)

to **get: to get fat** grossir (4.1) **to get thin** maigrir (4.1)

**girl** une fille (2.1)

**girlfriend** une petite amie (2.3)

**give me** donne-moi (familiar), donnez-moi (formal) (P.3)

**glasses** des lunettes f. (4.2)

to **go** *aller (3.1) **let's go!** allons! (3.1) **to be going (to do something)** aller + inf. (3.1) **to go back** rentrer (1.2) **to go home** rentrer (1.2)

**goldfish** un poisson rouge (3.4)

**good** bon (bonne) (2.3) **good morning (afternoon)** bonjour (P.1) **that's good** c'est bien (2.5)

**good-by** au revoir (P.1)

**good-looking** beau (bel, belle; beaux) (2.1) (4.3)

**grandfather** un grand-père (3.3)

**grandmother** une grand-mère (3.3)

**grandparents** les grands-parents m. (3.3)

**gray** gris (2.2)

**great** magnifique (1.1) fantastique, formidable, sensationnel (2.2) **that's great** c'est magnifique (1.1)

**green** vert (2.2)

**grocer** un épicier, une épicière (4.5)

**grocery** une épicerie (4.5)

**guitar** une guitare (2.2)

## h

**half past (two)** (deux) heures et demie (P.4)

**handbag** un sac (2.2)

**hard** difficile (2.5)

**hat** un chapeau (pl. chapeaux) (4.3)

to **hate** détester (1.4)

to have  *avoir (2.2)  to have dinner  dîner (1.1)

he  il (1.2)

to hear  entendre (4.5)

hello  bonjour (P.1)

her  elle (2.5)  son, sa, ses (3.4)  what's her name? comment s'appelle-t-elle? (2.1)

here  ici (1.5)  here comes, here's  voici (P.1)  this . . . over here  ce...-ci (4.2)

hey!  tiens! (1.2)  eh! dis (donc)! dites (donc)! (1.4)

hi  salut (P.1)

high school student  un (une) élève (2.1)

him  lui (2.5)

his  son, sa, ses (3.4)  what's his name?  comment s'appelle-t-il? (2.1)

home, at home  à la maison (1.5)  chez (moi, toi...) (3.2)  to go home  rentrer (1.2)

horse  un cheval (pl. chevaux) (3.4)

hospital  un hôpital (pl. hôpitaux) (3.1)

hot  chaud (4.2)  it's hot (weather)  il fait chaud (P.6)

house  une maison (3.1)  at/to . . . 's house  chez... (3.2)

how  comment (1.3)  how are you?  ça va? comment vas-tu? comment allez-vous? (P.2)  how do you say . . . ? comment dit-on...? (4.5)  how many  combien (de) (4.1)  how much  combien (P.3) combien de (4.1)  how much is it?  c'est combien? (P.3)  how old are you? quel âge as-tu (avez-vous)? (3.3)  how's everything?  ça va? (P.2)  how's the weather?  quel temps fait-il? (P.6)

hundred  cent (4.1)

hungry: to be hungry  avoir faim (4.4)

## I i

I  je (1.1)  moi (2.5)  I don't know  je ne sais pas (P.1)  I have a date with  j'ai rendez-vous avec (P.5)  I know  je sais (P.1)  I'm okay  ça va (P.2)  I'm (very well; well; so-so; bad; very bad)  ça va (très bien; bien; comme ci, comme ça; mal; très mal) (P.2)

idea  une idée (4.4)

if  si (3.5)

immediate family  la famille proche (3.3)

in  à (1.1)  dans (3.3)  (a country)  au, aux, en (4.5)  in class  en classe (1.5)  in style  chic (4.2)  in the afternoon  de l'après-midi (P.4)  in the morning (evening)  du matin (soir) (P.4)  in town  en ville (1.5)

inexpensive  bon marché (4.1)

instrument  un instrument (3.2)

intelligent  intelligent (2.1)

interesting  intéressant (2.1)

to invite  inviter (1.1)

is  (see to be)  isn't it (so)? n'est-ce pas? (1.3)  there is  il y a (2.4)

it  il, elle (1.2)  it depends ça dépend (4.1)  it doesn't matter  ça n'a pas d'importance (3.1)  it's  c'est (P.1)  it's . . . francs  c'est ...francs (P.3)  it's . . . (o'clock)  il est...heure(s) (P.4)  it's (fine, nice, hot, cool, cold, bad)  (weather) il fait (beau, bon, chaud, frais, froid, mauvais) (P.6)  it's (September 10th)  c'est le (10 septembre) (P.5)  it's raining (snowing)  il pleut (neige) (P.6)  that's it  c'est ça (2.1)  what time is it? quelle heure est-il? (P.4)  who is it?  qui est-ce? (P.1)

Italian  italien (italienne) (2.4)

Italy  l'Italie f. (2.4)

its  son, sa, ses (3.4)

## J j

jacket  une veste (4.2)  ski (down) jacket  un anorak (4.2)

January  janvier (P.5)

Japan  le Japon (2.4)

Japanese  japonais (2.4)

jeans  un blue-jeans (4.2)

July  juillet (P.5)

June  juin (P.5)

## K k

know: I don't know  je ne sais pas (P.1)  I know  je sais (P.1)

## L l

lady  une dame (2.1)

least: at least  au moins (3.2)  the least . . . (in)  le moins... (de) (4.4)

less  moins (4.3)  less . . . than  moins...que (4.3)

let's go!  allons! (3.1)

library  une bibliothèque (3.1)

like comme (4.4) **what does he/she look like?** comment est-il/elle? (2.1) **what's he/she like?** comment est-il/elle? (2.1)

to like aimer (1.4)

to listen (to) écouter (1.4) **listen!** écoute! écoutez! (2.5)

little petit (2.1) **a little (bit)** un peu (1.3)

to live habiter (1.1)

long long (longue) (4.3)

look! tiens! (1.2) **to look at** regarder (1.4) **what does he/she look like?** comment est-il/elle? (2.1)

to lose perdre (4.5) **to lose weight** maigrir (4.1)

lot: a lot beaucoup (1.3)

to love adorer (1.4)

lucky: to be lucky avoir de la chance (4.4)

month un mois (P.5) **this month** ce mois-ci (4.2)

more plus (4.3) **more . . . than** plus...que (4.3)

morning un matin (4.2) **good morning** bonjour (P.1) **in the morning** du matin (P.4) **this morning** ce matin (4.2) **tomorrow morning** demain matin (4.2)

most: the most . . . (in) le plus...(de) (4.4)

mother une mère (3.3)

motorbike un vélomoteur (2.2)

motorcycle une moto (2.2)

Mr. Monsieur (M.) (P.1)

Mrs. Madame (Mme) (P.1)

much, very much beaucoup (1.3) **how much?** combien? (P.3) **how much is it?** c'est combien? (P.3)

museum un musée (3.1)

my mon, ma, mes (3.3) **my birthday is (March 2nd)** mon anniversaire est le (2 mars) (P.5) **my name is** je m'appelle (P.2)

nice sympathique (2.1) **it's nice (weather)** il fait bon (P.6)

night une nuit (4.2) **tomorrow night** demain soir (4.2)

nine neuf (P.3)

nineteen dix-neuf (P.3)

ninety quatre-vingt-dix (4.1)

ninth neuvième (3.4)

no non (P.3) pas de (2.2) **no?** n'est-ce pas? (1.3) **no way!** pas question! (3.5)

noon midi (P.4)

not ne...pas (1.1) **not a, not any** pas de (2.2) **not at all** pas du tout (1.2) **not bad** pas mal (3.3) **of course not** mais non (1.2)

nothing doing! pas question! (3.5)

November novembre (P.5)

now maintenant (1.3) **come now!** voyons! (4.2)

# m

man un homme, un monsieur (*polite term*) (2.1)

many: how many combien de (4.1)

March mars (P.5)

matter: it doesn't matter ça n'a pas d'importance (3.1)

May mai (P.5)

maybe peut-être (2.4)

me moi (2.5) **excuse me** pardon (P.3) **me too** moi aussi (P.2)

merchant un marchand, une marchande (4.5)

Mexican mexicain (2.4)

Mexico le Mexique (2.4)

midnight minuit (P.4)

million million (4.2)

Miss Mademoiselle (Mlle) (P.1)

Monday lundi *m.* (P.5)

money l'argent *m.* (4.1)

# n

name: my name is je m'appelle (P.2) **what's . . .'s name?** comment s'appelle...? (2.1) **what's his/her name?** comment s'appelle-t-il/elle? (2.1) **what's your name?** comment t'appelles-tu? (P.2)

nationality une nationalité (2.4)

to need avoir besoin de (4.4)

new nouveau (nouvel, nouvelle; nouveaux) (4.3)

newspaper un journal (*pl.* journaux) (4.5)

# o

o'clock heure(s) (P.4) **at . . . o'clock** à...heure(s) (P.4) **it is . . . o'clock** il est...heure(s) (P.4)

October octobre (P.5)

of de (1.1) **of course** bien sûr (1.2) évidemment (4.3) **of course not** mais non (1.2) **of whom** de qui (1.5)

often souvent (1.3)

oh! ah! (2.1) **oh dear!** oh là là! (P.3)

okay d'accord (2.1) **I'm okay** ça va (P.2)

old âgé (3.3) vieux (vieil, vieille; vieux) (4.3) **how old are you?** quel âge as-tu (avez-vous)? (3.3) **to be . . . years old** avoir...ans (3.3)

on sur (3.5)   come on! voyons! (4.2)   on the contrary au contraire (1.2)   on vacation en vacances (1.5)
one un, une (P.3)
one (*you, they, people*) on (4.5)
or ou (1.1)
our notre, nos (3.5)
over: over there là-bas (1.5)   that . . . over there ce...-là (4.2)   this . . . over here ce...-ci (4.2)
to own *avoir (2.2)

piano un piano (3.2)
picture une photo (3.3)
to play jouer (1.1)   to play + *instrument* jouer de (3.2)   to play + *sport* jouer à (3.2)
pleasant sympathique (2.1)   it's pleasant (weather) il fait bon (P.6)
please s'il te plaît (*familiar*), s'il vous plaît (*formal*) (P.3)
P.M. de l'après-midi, du soir (P.4)
pool: swimming pool une piscine (3.1)
poor pauvre (3.1)
poorly mal (1.1)
pretty joli (2.3)
price un prix (4.2)
problem un problème (4.4)
pullover un pull (pull-over) (4.2)

record un disque (2.2)
record player un électrophone (2.2)
recorder: cassette recorder une mini-cassette (2.2)
red rouge (2.2)
relatives les parents *m.* (3.3)
restaurant un restaurant (3.2)   at the restaurant au restaurant (1.5)
rich riche (3.1)
right vrai (2.5)   all right d'accord (2.1)   all right! ah bon! (3.4)   right? n'est-ce pas? (1.3)   that's right c'est ça (2.1)   to be right avoir raison (4.4)

## p

pants un pantalon (4.2)
paper un journal (*pl.* journaux) (4.5)
parents les parents *m.* (3.3)
park un parc (3.1)
parka un anorak (4.2)
party une surprise-partie (2.1)
to pass (*a test*) réussir (4.1)
past: half past (two) (deux) heures et demie (P.4)   quarter past (two) (deux) heures et quart (P.4)
pastry une pâtisserie (4.4)   pastry cook un pâtissier, une pâtissière (4.5)   pastry shop une pâtisserie (4.4)
to pay (for) payer (4.4)
people on (4.5)   young people les jeunes *m.* (4.2)
perfect parfait (4.2)
perhaps peut-être (2.4)
person une personne (2.1)
pharmacist un pharmacien, une pharmacienne (4.5)
pharmacy une pharmacie (4.5)
to phone téléphoner (1.1)
photograph une photo (3.3)

## q

quarter of (two) (deux) heures moins le quart (P.4)   quarter past (two) (deux) heures et quart (P.4)

## r

racket une raquette (2.2)
radio une radio (2.2)   transistor radio un transistor (2.2)
raining: it's raining il pleut (P.6)
rarely rarement (1.3)
rather assez (2.1)
rats! zut! zut alors! (P.4)
really vraiment (P.5)

## s

sandals des sandales *f.* (4.2)
Saturday samedi *m.* (P.5)
saxophone un saxo(phone) (3.2)
say: how do you say . . . ? comment dit-on...? (4.5)   say! dis (donc)! dites (donc)! (1.4)
school une école (3.1)   school friend un (une) camarade (2.1)
second deuxième (3.4)
seldom rarement (1.3)
to sell vendre (4.5)
September septembre (P.5)
seven sept (P.3)
seventeen dix-sept (P.3)
seventh septième (3.4)
seventy soixante-dix (4.1)
she elle (1.2)
shirt une chemise (4.3)
shoes des chaussures *f.* (4.2)
shop un magasin (4.1)
short petit (2.1)   court (4.3)
shorts un short (4.2)
sick malade (3.1)
silly bête (2.3)

**simple**  simple (**4.5**)

**sincere**  sincère (**2.1**)

to **sing**  chanter (**1.4**)

**sister**  une sœur (**3.2**)

**six**  six (**P.3**)

**sixteen**  seize (**P.3**)

**sixth**  sixième (**3.4**)

**sixty**  soixante (**P.3**)

to **ski**  skier (**1.1**)

**ski jacket**  un anorak (**4.2**)

**skirt**  une jupe (**4.3**)

**slender**  mince (**4.4**)

**slim**  mince (**4.4**)

**snowing: it's snowing**  il neige (**P.6**)

**so**  alors (**1.5**)  **so what?**  et alors? (**1.5**)  **so-so**  comme ci, comme ça (**P.2**)

**soccer**  le foot(ball) (**3.2**)

**socks**  des chaussettes *f.* (**4.2**)

**some**  des (**2.4**)

**son**  un fils (**3.3**)

**Spain**  l'Espagne *f.* (**2.4**)

**Spanish**  espagnol (**2.4**)

to **speak**  parler (**1.1**)

to **spend**  dépenser (**4.1**) (*time*) passer (**4.5**)

**sport**  un sport (**3.2**)

**spring: in the spring**  au printemps (**P.6**)  **this spring** ce printemps (**4.2**)

**stadium**  un stade (**3.1**)

**stamp**  un timbre (**3.5**)

to **stay**  rester (**3.1**)

**stockings**  des bas *m.* (**4.3**)

**store**  un magasin (**4.1**)  **department store**  un grand magasin (**4.1**)

**storekeeper**  un marchand, une marchande (**4.1**)

**student**  (*high school*) un (une) élève, (*college*) un étudiant, une étudiante (**2.1**)

to **study**  étudier (**1.2**)

**stupid**  bête (**2.3**)

**style**  le style (**4.3**)  **in style** chic (**4.2**)

to **succeed**  réussir (**4.1**)

**suit**  un costume (**4.3**)

**summer: in (the) summer**  en été (**P.6**)  **this summer**  cet été (**4.2**)

**Sunday**  dimanche *m.* (**P.5**)

**sunglasses**  des lunettes *f.* de soleil (**3.1**)

**sure**  bien sûr (**1.2**)

**sweater**  un pull (pull-over) (**4.2**)

to **swim**  nager (**1.4**)

**swimming pool**  une piscine (**3.1**)

**swimsuit**  un maillot de bain (**4.2**)

**Swiss**  suisse (**2.4**)

**Switzerland**  la Suisse (**2.4**)

## | t |

to **talk**  parler (**1.1**)

**tall**  grand (**2.1**)

**teacher**  un professeur (**2.1**)

**tee shirt**  un tee-shirt (**4.2**)

**television set**  un téléviseur (**2.2**)

**temperature**  la température (**P.6**)  **what's the temperature?**  quelle température fait-il? (**P.6**)

**ten**  dix (**P.3**)

**tenth**  dixième (**3.4**)

**terrific**  fantastique, formidable, sensationnel (**2.2**)

**than**  que (**4.3**)

**thank you**  merci (**P.3**)

**that**  que (**3.5**)  ce, cet, cette (**4.2**)  **that is**  voilà, c'est (**P.1**)  **that's bad**  c'est mal (**2.5**)  **that's good (fine)** c'est bien (**2.5**)

**that's great!**  c'est magnifique! (**1.1**)  **that's it (right)**  c'est ça (**2.1**)  **that's too bad!**  c'est dommage! (**1.1**)

**who is that?**  qui est-ce? (**P.1**)

**the**  le, la, l' (**2.1**)  les (**2.4**)

**theater**  un théâtre (**3.1**)  **movie theater**  un cinéma (**3.1**)

**their**  leur, leurs (**3.4**)

**them**  eux, elles (**2.5**)

**then**  alors (**1.5**)  **well then**

alors (**1.5**)

**there**  là (**1.5**)  **over there** là-bas (**1.5**)  **that . . . over there**  ce...-là (**4.2**)  **there is (are)**  il y a (**2.4**)  **there's**  voilà (**P.1**)

**these**  ces (**4.2**)  **these are** ce sont (**2.4**)

**they**  ils, elles (**1.2**)  on (**4.5**)  **they are**  ce sont (**2.4**)

**thin**  mince (**4.4**)  **to get thin** maigrir (**4.1**)

to **think**  penser (**3.5**)

**third**  troisième (**3.4**)

**thirsty: to be thirsty**  avoir soif (**4.4**)

**thirteen**  treize (**P.3**)

**thirty**  trente (**P.3**)  **3:30** trois heures et demie (**P.4**)

**this**  ce, cet, cette (**4.2**)  **this is**  voici (**P.1**)

**those**  ces (**4.2**)  **those are** ce sont (**2.4**)

**thousand**  mille (**4.2**)

**three**  trois (**P.3**)

**Thursday**  jeudi *m.* (**P.5**)

**tie**  une cravate (**4.3**)

**time: at what time?**  à quelle heure? (**P.4**)  **what time is it?**  quelle heure est-il? (**P.4**)

**tired**  fatigué (**4.4**)

**to**  à (**1.1**)  chez (**3.2**) (*a country*)  au, aux, en (**4.5**)  **to . . . 's (house)**  chez... (**3.2**)  **to class**  en classe (**3.1**)  **to (the pharmacist's)**  chez (le pharmacien) (**4.5**)  **to whom** à qui (**1.5**)

**today**  aujourd'hui (**P.5**)

**tomorrow**  demain (**P.5**)  **tomorrow morning (afternoon, evening/night)**  demain matin (après-midi, soir) (**4.2**)

**tonight**  ce soir, cette nuit (**4.2**)

**too**  aussi (**1.1**)  trop (**3.3**)  **me too**  moi aussi (**P.2**)  **(that's) too bad!**  (c'est) dommage! (**1.1**)  **too much** trop (**3.3**)

**town**  une ville (**3.1**)  **in town** en ville (**1.5**)

**transistor radio**  un transistor (**2.2**)

to **travel**  voyager (**1.4**)

**true**  vrai (**2.5**)

248

**Tuesday** mardi *m.* (**P.5**)
**TV set** un téléviseur (**2.2**)
**twelfth** douzième (**3.4**)
**twelve** douze (**P.3**)
**twenty** vingt (**P.3**)
**two** deux (**P.3**)

# u

**uh . . .** euh... (**P.6**)
**uncle** un oncle (**3.3**)
**United States** les États-Unis *m.*
(**2.4**)
**us** nous (**2.5**)

# v

**vacation** les vacances *f.* (**3.3**)
**on vacation** en vacances
(**1.5**)
**very** très (**1.1**) **very much**
beaucoup (**1.3**)
**violin** un violon (**3.2**)
to **visit** (*a place*) visiter (**1.1**)
**volleyball** le volley(ball) (**3.2**)

# w

to **wait** (**for**) attendre (**4.5**)
to **walk** marcher (**2.2**)
to **want** désirer (**1.4**) avoir envie
de (**4.4**)
**warm** chaud (**4.2**) **to be**
(**feel**) **warm** avoir chaud (**4.4**)
to **waste** perdre (**4.5**)
**watch** une montre (**2.2**)
to **watch** regarder (**1.4**)
**way: no way!** pas question! (**3.5**)

**we** nous (**1.3**) on (**4.5**)
to **wear** porter (**4.2**)
**weather: how** (**what**) **is the**
**weather?** quel temps fait-il?
(**P.6**) **it's . . . weather** il
fait... (**P.6**)
**Wednesday** mercredi *m.* (**P.5**)
**week** une semaine (**P.5**)
**this week** cette semaine (**4.2**)
**weekend** un week-end (**4.2**)
**this weekend** ce week-end
(**4.2**)
**weight: to gain weight** grossir
(**4.1**) **to lose weight**
maigrir (**4.1**)
**well** bien (**1.1**) **I'm/every-**
**thing's** (**very**) **well** ça va (très)
bien (**P.2**) **well!** eh bien!
(**2.3**) **well then** alors (**1.5**)
**what** comment? quoi? (**2.1**)
qu'est-ce que (**4.1**) quel
(quelle) (**4.2**) **at what time?**
à quelle heure? (**P.4**)**so what?**
et alors? (**1.5**)
**what color?** de quelle
couleur? (**2.2**) **what day is**
**it?** quel jour est-ce? (**P.5**)
**what does he/she look like?**
comment est-il/elle? (**2.1**)
**what is it?** qu'est-ce que
c'est? (**4.1**) **what time is**
**it?** quelle heure est-il?
(**P.4**) **what's . . .'s name?**
comment s'appelle...? (**2.1**)
**what's he/she like?** comment est-il/elle? (**2.1**)
**what's his/her name?** comment s'appelle-t-il/elle? (**2.1**)
**what's the temperature?**
quelle température fait-il?
(**P.6**) **what's the weather?**
quel temps fait-il? (**P.6**)
**what's this?** qu'est-ce que
c'est? (**4.1**) **what's your**
**name?** comment t'appelles-
tu? (**P.2**)
**when** quand (**1.3**)
**where** où (**1.3**)
**whew!** oh là là! (**P.3**)
**which** quel (quelle) (**4.2**)
**white** blanc (blanche) (**2.2**)
**who** qui (**1.5**) **who is that**
(**it**)? qui est-ce? (**P.1**)
**whom** qui (**1.5**) **about**
**whom** de qui (**1.5**) **for**

**whom** pour qui (**1.5**) **of**
**whom** pour qui (**1.5**) **to**
**whom** à qui (**1.5**) **with**
**whom** avec qui (**1.5**)
**whose . . . is it/are they?** à qui
est/sont...? (**3.5**)
**why** pourquoi (**1.3**)
**winter: in** (**the**) **winter** en hiver
(**P.6**) **this winter** cet hiver
(**4.2**)
to **wish** désirer (**1.4**)
**with** avec (**1.1**) **with whom**
avec qui (**1.5**)
**woman** une femme, une dame
(*polite term*) (**2.1**)
to **work** travailler (**1.4**) (*function*)
marcher (**2.2**)
**wow!** oh là là! (**P.3**)
**wrong** faux (fausse) (**2.5**) **to**
**be wrong** avoir tort (**4.4**)

# y

**year** l'année *f.* (**P.5**) **this**
**year** cette année (**4.2**)
**to be . . . years old** avoir...
ans (**3.3**)
**yellow** jaune (**2.2**)
**yes** oui (**P.3**)
**you** tu, vous (**1.3**) toi (**2.5**)
on (**4.5**) **and you?** et
toi? (**P.2**)
**young** jeune (**3.3**) **young**
**people** les jeunes *m.* (**4.2**)
**your** ton, ta, tes (**3.3**) votre,
vos (**3.5**) **what's your name?**
comment t'appelles-tu? (**P.2**)

# z

**zero** zéro (**P.3**) **it's 0°** il
fait zéro (**P.6**)

# INDEX

# Index

# Photo Credits